AFRICAN ISSUES

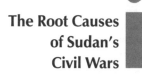

The Root Causes of Sudan's Civil Wars

'Anyone wanting to understand this African tragedy should read Douglas Johnson's "The Root Causes of Sudan's Civil Wars"... Mr Johnson offers a brilliant analysis of the war and its causes written in simple, clear prose.' – The Economist

'Douglas Johnson has written a landmark book that deserves not only to change the nature of Sudan studies but how we think of war, peace and development generally. It is a task for which he is well qualified. As a historian with an anthropologist's eye, his interests span the pre-colonial, colonial and post-colonial conditions. Unique among contemporary writers, Johnson has not only made major contributions to the historiography of Sudan and the interpretation of its rich ethnography, he has also worked for the aid agencies that now populate much of this country. From this wide vantage point Johnson's critical book succeeds in rescuing Sudan from the heart of darkness that continues to be conjured by whistle-stop journalists and self-serving NGOs... an important book.' – Mark Duffield, Professor of Politics and International Relations, University of Leeds, in the *Journal of Refugee Studies*

'This authoritative and detailed study of Sudan's contemporary conflicts aims to discourage "quick fix" thinking by tracing the historical patterns of power and politics that have brought the country to its current impasse... Never just a matter of competition between religions, races, or regions, Sudan's multiple internal conflicts today are as seemingly intractable as ever, despite serious peace efforts. Students and researchers will benefit from the extended bibliographic essay and chronology included in this excellent book.' – Foreign Affairs

'The plural of the title is sadly significant. Johnson's introduction points out that much of the writing on conflict in the Sudan... has recurred to a sterile debate, between those who identify "the war" as the continuation of a long pattern of "northern" oppression and those who attribute the conflict to the baleful consequences of British colonial policies which encouraged racial and ethnic tensions. The real value of this book is that it rises above this, partly by the remarkable breadth and depth of knowledge on which the author calls, but more importantly by its consideration of the multiplicity of the current conflicts.' – Justin Willis, University of Durham, in *Journal of African History*

AFRICAN ISSUES

Published in the US & Canada by Indiana University Press

Undermining Development The Absence of Power among Local NGOS in Africa*
SARAH MICHAEL

'Letting them Die' Why HIV/AIDS Prevention Programmes Fail
CATHERINE CAMPBELL

Somalia: Economy without State Accumulation & Survival in Somalia
PETER D. LITTLE

The Root Causes of Sudan's Civil Wars
DOUGLAS H. JOHNSON

Asbestos Blues Labour, Capital, Physicians & the State in South Africa
JOCK McCULLOCH

Fortress Conservation The Preservation of the Mkomazi Game Reserve, Tanzania
DAN BROCKINGTON

Killing for Conservation Wildlife Policy in Zimbabwe
ROSALEEN DUFFY

Mozambique & the Great Flood of 2000
FRANCES CHRISTIE & JOSEPH HANLON

Angola: Anatomy of an Oil State
TONY HODGES

Congo-Paris Transnational Traders on the Margins of the Law
JANET MACGAFFEY & REMY BAZENGUISSA-GANGA

Africa Works Disorder as Political Instrument
PATRICK CHABAL & JEAN-PASCAL DALOZ

The Criminalization of the State in Africa
JEAN-FRANÇOIS BAYART, STEPHEN ELLIS & BEATRICE HIBOU

Famine Crimes Politics & the Disaster Relief Industry in Africa
ALEX DE WAAL

Published in the US & Canada by Heinemann (N.H.)

Peace without Profit How the IMF Blocks Rebuilding in Mozambique
JOSEPH HANLON

The Lie of the Land Challenging the Received Wisdom on the African Environment
MELISSA LEACH & ROBIN MEARNS (eds)

Fighting for the Rainforest War, Youth & Resources in Sierra Leone
PAUL RICHARDS

*forthcoming

AFRICAN ISSUES

The Root Causes
of Sudan's
Civil Wars
Douglas H. Johnson

The International
African Institute

in association with

JAMES CURREY
Oxford

INDIANA UNIVERSITY PRESS
Bloomington & Indianapolis

FOUNTAIN PUBLISHERS
Kampala

E.A.E.P.
Nairobi

The International African Institute in association with

James Currey
73 Botley Road
Oxford OX2 0BS

Fountain Publishers
PO Box 488
Kampala

Indiana University Press
601 North Morton Street
Bloomington
Indiana 47404
(North America)

East African Educational Publishers
P.O. Box 45314
Nairobi

British Library Cataloguing in Publication Data
Johnson, Douglas H., 1949–
The root causes of Sudan's civil wars
1. Sudan – History 2. Sudan – History – Civil War, 1955–1972
I. Title
962.4'04

ISBN 0-85255-392-7 (James Currey paper)
ISBN 0-85255-391-9 (James Currey cloth)

Library of Congress Cataloging-in-Publication Data
A catalog record for this book is available from the Library of Congress
ISBN 0-253-34213-9 (Indiana University Press cloth)
ISBN 0-253-21584-6 (Indiana University Press paper)

ISBN 9970-02-299-7 (Fountain Publishers paper)

Typeset by
Saxon Graphics Ltd, Derby
in 9/10 Melior with Optima display

Printed and bound in Great Britain
by Woolnough, Irthlingborough

CONTENTS

ABBREVIATIONS & ACRONYMS vii
ACKNOWLEDGEMENTS ix
PREFACE xi
MAPS xxi–xxii

1
The Historical Structure of North–South Relations 1

2
British Overrule 1899–1947 9

3
Nationalism, Independence & the First Civil War 1942–72 22

4
The Addis Ababa Agreement & the Regional Governments 1972–83 39

5
The Beginning of the Second Civil War 1983–85 59

INTERLUDE 75

6
The Momentum of Liberation 1986–91 79

7
The SPLA split Surviving Factionalism 91

8
The Segmentation of SPLA-United & the Nuer Civil War 111

9

Multiple Civil Wars   127

10

The War Economy & the Politics   143
of Relief

11

Ideas of in the Sudan   167
Peace & War

BIBLIOGRAPHIC ESSAY   181

APPENDIX: 195
CHRONOLOGY OF EVENTS

INDEX   222

LIST OF MAPS

1. The Sudan in 1983   xxi
2. The Sudan at the beginning of 2002   xxii

ABBREVIATIONS & ACRONYMS

DUP Democratic Unionist Party
EPLF Eritrean People's Liberation Front
EPRDF Ethiopian People's Revolutionary Democratic Front
FO/FCO Foreign Office/Foreign and Commonwealth Office
GOS Government of the Sudan
GPLF Gambela People's Liberation Front (Ethiopia)
HEC High Executive Council, Southern Regional Government (1972–1983)
ICRC International Committee of the Red Cross
IGADD/IGAD Intergovernmental Authority on Drought and Desertification; Intergovernmental Authority on Development (since 1997)
LRA Lord's Resistance Army (Uganda)
NC National Congress (renamed NIF, 1998–)
NDA National Democratic Alliance (Sudanese opposition since 1989)
NEC National Executive Council (SPLA, post-1994)
NIF National Islamic Front (became National Congress in 1998)

NRA National Resistance Army (army of Uganda)
NSCC New Sudan Council of Churches
OLF Oromo Liberation Front
OLS Operation Lifeline Sudan
ORA Oromo Relief Association
PDF Popular Defence Forces (GOS militias)
PMHC Political-Military High Command (SPLA, 1983–1993)
PNC Popular National Congress (Turabi's party, 2000–)
PRO Public Records Office, Kew
RASS Relief Association of South Sudan (humanitarian wing of SPLA-United, later SSIM/A)
RRC Relief and Rehabilitation Commission (GOS)
SAF Sudanese Allied Forces
SPLM/SPLA Sudan People's Liberation Movement/Army (identified as the 'Torit' faction after August 1991, and as SPLA-Mainstream in 1992–94)
SPLM/A-United Name adopted by the breakaway 'Nasir' faction of the SPLA in 1993; retained by Lam Akol as the name of his Tonga-based outfit following the creation of SSIM/A in 1994

SRRA Sudan Relief and Rehabilitation Association (humanitarian wing of the SPLM/A)

SSDF South Sudan Defence Force (armed wing of UDSF); but also the South Sudan Democratic Forum, a coalition of southern Sudanese political and civic organizations formed in September 2001

SSIM/A South Sudan Independence Movement/Army (name adopted by the main faction of SPLA-United in September 1994)

SSLM/A Southern Sudan Liberation Movement (1970–2); South Sudan Liberation Movement/Army (formed in 2000)

SSU Sudanese Socialist Union (the only legal party in the Sudan under Nimairi, 1970–1984)

TMC Transitional Military Council (1985–1986)

TPLF Tigrayan People's Liberation Front

UDSF United Democratic Salvation Front (Sudan)

UNDP United Nations Development Programme

UNHCR United Nations High Commission for Refugees

UNICEF United Nations International Children and Education Fund

USAID United States Agency for International Development

USAP United Sudan African Parties (coalition of Southern-based political parties)

WFP World Food Programme (UN)

ACKNOWLEDGEMENTS

This book has grown out of a report originally commissioned for use by relief personnel involved with the Sudan ('The Southern Sudan. The Root Causes of a Recurring Civil War', report commissioned by ACORD, 1992). It was warmly received by many persons – both expatriate and Sudanese – who urged that it be circulated to a wider audience. Since that time the clear evidence of the failure of the collective memories of governments, relief agencies and journalists has convinced me that the need for an historical analysis of the war has grown rather than diminished, and this has led to an expanded and updated version of my original report.

This work draws on my own research as an historian as well as my experience working with various agencies in the relief effort in the southern Sudan. While it is too much to claim complete accuracy in recording events in a war where reliable reports are notoriously difficult to obtain, information has been gathered on repeated visits to the southern Sudan and North East Africa, and all reasonable care has been taken to verify accounts and sources, even when those sources cannot, for obvious reasons, be publicly acknowledged. A number of people have shared their special knowledge with me, most particularly Muhammad Mahmud, Yosa Wawa, Arop Madut Arop, Jemera Rone, Deborah Scroggins, Alastair and Patta Scott-Villiers, and fellow members of the 1996 OLS Review team, especially Mark Bradbury and Joanna Macrae. I am grateful to numerous colleagues who have made the growing body of 'gray literature' on the Sudan available to me and who have shared their own specific knowledge. Anyone familiar with the written work of Mark Duffield, John Ryle, David Keen and Alex de Waal will immediately recognize my debt to them. They have not only provided me with 'raw data' and interpretive frameworks from which I have borrowed freely, but in numerous personal discussions and debates have helped me clarify and sharpen my own understanding of events.

Over more than a decade there has been a continuous exchange of information and ideas with participants in the North East Africa research seminar at the Institute of Social and Cultural Anthropology in Oxford: particularly at two workshops on the war in the Sudan held at St Antony's College, Oxford in 1992 and 1993, and at the ESRC-sponsored workshops on 'Women and war in North East Africa', 'Ideologies of race, origins and descent in the history of the Nile Valley and North East Africa' and 'The fate of information in the Disaster Zone', the first two convened at St Antony's in 1994 and the last at St Anne's College, Oxford in 1995 (three papers from the latter were subsequently published in *Disasters*, 20(3) 1996). I am indebted in particular to Wendy James, John Ryle, Philip Winter, Peter Nyot Kok, Gérard Prunier, as well as others who cannot be mentioned, for taking the time to comment on earlier drafts. While not wishing to claim complete originality, the interpretation of events presented here is my responsibility and cannot be taken to represent the opinions of any of the persons or organizations with whom I have worked in the past.

Footnotes have been kept to a minimum: this is an interpretive – not a definitive – history. The chronology in the appendix offers a more detailed list of events than is provided in the main text. Readers who wish to pursue specific questions, or obtain further detail, will find a discussion of some published literature and agency reports in the bibliographic essay at the end of this book. In writing Arabic names I have used a modified form of modern literary Arabic transcription, without diacriticals. There are many competing administrative and political maps of the Sudan today; the one I have used here for the Sudan in 1983 shows its old regions and provinces.

The Sudan entered the twenty-first century mired in not one, but many civil wars. What had been seen in the 1980s as a war between North and South, Muslim against Christian, 'Arab' against 'African', has, after nearly two decades of hostilities, broken the bounds of any North–South conflict. Fighting has spread into theatres outside the southern Sudan and beyond the Sudan's borders. Not only are Muslims fighting Muslims, but 'Africans' are fighting 'Africans'. A war once described as being fought over scarce resources is now being waged for the total control of abundant oil reserves. The fact that the overall civil war, which is composed of these interlocking struggles, has continued for so long, far outlasting the international and regional political configurations which at one time seemed to direct and define it, is testimony to the intractability of the underlying causes of the conflict. There are now any number of declarations by various parties that a lasting peace will be achieved only through addressing the 'root causes' of the war, but there is as yet no general consensus as to what those root causes are.

President Jimmy Carter once famously referred to the 1953 overthrow of Muhammad Musaddiq's elected government (the origin of the Iranian revolutionaries' grievance against the US) as 'ancient history'; something which, by definition, should not motivate current political attitudes. Yet what outsiders have forgotten – or never knew – constitutes the lived experience that motivates the actors in Sudan's wars. This book is directed in part at the institutional amnesia afflicting diplomats, journalists, and development, relief and human rights workers: anyone who has dipped into a current of the war with only a vague apprehension of its source. It is also intended for Africanists as a comparative framework with which they can approach one of the longest, and most academically neglected of the continent's postcolonial struggles. Finally, it is offered to Sudanese who might welcome an outsider's perspective on entrenched positions and attitudes.

This book attempts a broad explanation of the origins of the Sudan's multiple and recurring civil wars, and why these wars have not ended. The Sudan conflict is frequently presented as either the continuation of an age-old confrontation between 'cultures' defined by blood-lines ('Arabs' vs. 'Africans'), or the consequence of an artificial division imposed by colonial powers. Here, rather, I examine some of the economic and political patterns which have affected the development and exercise of state power in the Sudan since at least the nineteenth century in an attempt to explain the process and consequences of regional underdevelopment, and the conjunction between perceptions of religion and race specific to this part of Africa.

One of the peculiarities of this war is that the longer it has lasted the greater has been the deterioration in the quality of reporting. The coverage of Africa in the Western media has in any case suffered from an atavistic return to the 'Heart of Darkness' style of explanation which was so characteristic of journalism in an earlier age. An extreme example, perhaps, is this *Time* report from a relief centre in Ayod:

> Buk Thuch Gir, an elderly woman...believes the U.N. relief aircraft landing here each day are sent by her animist gods. 'When the *reynhial* (flyers from heaven) stop, we will die'. ...These are ancient people with close ties to their traditional way of life. In Ayod men and women practice ritual scarification and continue to go without clothes, coating their dark skin with ash to ward off disease. Even the gun-toting rebels hold fast to tribal ways, consulting a leopard man, or shaman, before going into battle and eating raw meat so as not to dilute the power of the animate beast.[1]

It is peculiar, to say the least, for so theistic a people as the Nuer to be described as animists who consult shamans. That *nhial* means 'sky' (or 'above') rather than 'heaven' gives a more direct meaning to the elderly woman's statement; that dung ash repels mosquitoes gives it a practical, rather than a superstitious value against malaria; that bush shops (and thus the supply of clothing) had been absent from this area since 1984 gives a different reason for why most people 'continue to go without clothes'; that so many distortions can appear in so short a space gives the true value of such reporting.

The growing influence of humanitarian pressure groups has also had an impact on the way the war is reported and understood. It is human rights researchers, rather than journalists, who are documenting the war's most cruel aspects. Imbued as they must be with a commitment to an ideal of justice which is both abstract and absolute, many also seem still in search of the ideal liberation group, and it is against this expectation that Sudanese movements are judged ('it reminded me of Nicaragua!' one human rights worker wrote me enthusiastically after a visit to the Nuba Mountains). Yet mindful of the requirements of objectivity, humanitarians strive to apportion blame equally, their reports frequently ending with a pious even-handedness, calling on 'all parties in the conflict' to respect

---

[1] Andrew Purvis, ' "When the flyers from heaven stop, we will die" ', *Time*, April 12, 1993, pp. 46–7.

human rights, having focused on specific acts of war often at the expense of exploring the structural patterns of injustice.

Academic studies of the Sudan are nearly as deeply affected by the divisions of the country as are Sudanese themselves, and Sudanese historiography is fragmented against itself. Scholars often display a difficulty in recognizing the Sudan as a collection of regions, and general accounts of the history and politics of the country still tend to be written from the vantage point and perspective of its central institutions. The most popular and successful general history of the country, P.M. Holt and M.W. Daly's *A History of the Sudan*, has gone through five editions since 1961. New material appears in its updated chapters on current history and in the select bibliography, but the basic structure and historical outline of the book has been scarcely revised, and the southern Sudan first appears only in the chapters on nineteenth-century imperialism.[2] Specialists on the North often resort to simplistic generalizations when attempting to represent the country as a whole. On such an important topic as religion, for instance, two respected experts on Islam wrote this of the South's 'tribal faith systems' in a general survey published early in the war, when the nation's 'multiculturalism', celebrated in their book, was already in doubt:

> The majority of the people of the southern regions continue to maintain tribal patterns of belief and traditional world views that are related to the special identities of their ethnic or tribal groups. The specific content of these guidance frameworks for behavior and world views varies from group to group and has been studied and described by anthropologists. It seems clear from the conclusions of these studies that in most of these local faith systems, it is not possible to speak of religion as a separate autonomous segment of life. There is no separation of church and state because religion and politics are part of an integrated sociopolitical network of relations, an integral part of the daily life and broader social structure of the tribal peoples. The focus of these religions is the relationship between the forces of nature and humanity, in which 'human' is sometimes defined as being a member of a particular tribe. In the cosmos of these belief systems are great forces and lesser forces that are frequently seen as animating physical objects, such as trees, stones, and animals – a type of faith some observers call 'animism'.[3]

This is, to say the least, a misreading of a very sophisticated ethnographic record, one which documented, in detail, religious questioning, the practical separation between the spiritual and mundane, the high value

---

[2] P.M. Holt & M.W. Daly, *A History of the Sudan: From the Coming of Islam to the Present Day*, fifth edition (Harlow/NY, 2000). The first two editions were written by P.M. Holt and published in 1961 and 1963, the third, fourth and fifth editions, revised with M.W. Daly were published in 1979, 1988 and 2000.

[3] John Obert Voll & Sarah Potts Voll, *The Sudan. Unity and Diversity in a Multicultural State* (Boulder CO/London, 1985), pp. 22–3.

accorded to individualism, and the complexity and fluidity of political
and kinship systems. It is, however, indicative of a general weakness in
Sudan studies as a whole: the institutions of the Muslim North command
respectful attention and receive explanation, while the rest of the country
is relegated to an exotic periphery.

The past of the Sudan's regions is not always well served. The history
of the southern Sudan has been written essentially as a chronicle of a
succession of alien administrations, not as a set of internal histories
linked to broader regional patterns. 'Ethnicity' is taken for granted in
history as in political science, often drawing (as we have seen) from a
simplified understanding of ethnography. But the focus of a good deal of
current (mainly American cultural) anthropology also takes 'ethnicity'
and 'culture' for granted, writing of 'ethnic mobilization' and the 'militarization of ethnicity' as if these were unproblematic concepts. Within
anthropology, however, there is beginning to emerge a more sceptical
treatment of the use of such terms, questioning the central explanatory
value currently given to 'ethnicity' in popular writing.[4]

As problematic as Sudan studies are, there have been significant
contributions that point a way to a more nuanced interpretation of the
country's present and its multiple pasts. Work on economic and political
relations in the nineteenth century, and a new development critique in
the late twentieth century highlight important continuities in the country.
I have tried to integrate these advances in historical and development
studies with my own research to produce the interpretation offered here.

Each war is distinctive, because it arises from a specific set of
historical circumstances. 'Any struggle must be anchored in history',
John Garang publicly reaffirmed in March 2002 in London. Clearly, there
is a need to repeat enough historical data to remind external observers of
the precedents influencing the actions of Sudanese now. It is necessary
to focus on the political realities of the country, because it is these, more
than abstract ideals, which influence political action. Furthermore, as
the southern Sudan has been the subject of many ahistorical misconcep-
tions, some preliminary explanation of terms describing both politics
and religion is necessary.

Popular descriptions of the war in the South frequently make use of the
words 'tribe' and 'clan' interchangeably, usually as units of kinship and
descent. Political affiliation is thus represented as being based on, or
organized along lines of primal blood relationships. Yet, 'tribe', in both

[4] Compare Jok Madut Jok & Sharon Elaine Hutchinson, 'Sudan's prolonged second civil war
and the militarization of Nuer and Dinka ethnic identities', *African Studies Review*, 42/2
(1999) and Sharon Elaine Hutchinson, 'Nuer ethnicity militarized', *Anthropology Today*, 16/3
(2000) with Wendy James, 'War & "ethnic visibility": the Uduk on the Sudan–Ethiopian
border', in Katsuyoshi Fukui & John Markakis (eds), *Ethnicity & Conflict in the Horn of Africa*
(London/Athens OH, 1994).

the administrative and anthropological usage in the Sudan, is a political term. 'Clan', when used at all, represents membership of a birth or descent group, relevant mainly in determining degrees of relationship in matters of marriage. A tribe is the largest unit of political combination of smaller, affiliated, sections. The organizing principles of a tribe vary from people to people, and even within peoples; combinations vary over time; and the people within a tribe do not necessarily claim direct common descent or kinship links with each other.

Among the Nuer, a tribe is an amalgamation of sections claiming varying degrees of common relationship who will accept mediation in feuds between themselves, and who will unite in offence or defence. Among most, but not all, Dinka (especially in the Bahr al-Ghazal) tribes are sections who have attached themselves to a central lineage of spiritual leaders, the Spearmasters. Nuer and Dinka tribes and sections will contain many different clans, and representatives of the same clan will be found throughout the political spectrum of sections and tribes. In neither case are tribes permanent fixtures, even though they were given some rigidity as recognized parts of the administrative structure during the later Condominium period (as were the tribes of the northern Sudan). Among the Nuer, for instance, the primary sections of the Eastern Jikany and the Lou have increasingly acted as autonomous political groups.

One cannot, therefore, speak of *the* Dinka tribe or *the* Nuer tribe: rather of the Dinka people and the Nuer people, each of whom are organized into a number of different tribes at any one time, some of which may be socially and politically closer to tribes of neighbouring peoples than to more distant tribes of the same people. In this sense, too, it is not correct to speak of tribes as universal in the southern Sudan. The Shilluk and Azande were organized into kingdoms, sub-divided into chieftaincies, all of which contained persons of diverse origins – as kingdoms do. It was the organizing principle of the kingdom that made the king's subjects into a people.[5]

The war in the Sudan is also commonly described in terms of competition between world religions, as a struggle between Islam and Christianity. Southern Sudanese are not seen as having coherent religions of their own, but are described with depressing regularity as 'Christian and animist' (or sometimes even 'Christian animist'). 'Animism' is an archaic term with little descriptive value. In its original sense it referred to a theory of the origin of primitive religion. It has since been adapted as a pseudo-scientific replacement for 'pagan', to avoid the latter's pejorative overtones

---

[5] The word 'tribe' has been discarded in much anthropology, except where it translates a local word, and is resented in much of Africa as a pejorative term. Its retention here is justified because of its specific political meaning in the ethnography of the Sudan, and because most Sudanese, both Southern and Northern, recognize the existence of tribes and willingly assert their membership of them. The Arabic word for tribe, *qabila*, is commonly used throughout the Sudan.

acquired from centuries of Christian propaganda. As 'animism' is now generally understood – a belief in a natural world animated by super-natural spirits – there are properly no 'animists' in the southern Sudan, which is the home of many pronounced theistic religions.[6] It is true that the contention of world religions in the Sudan has played an increasingly important role in the internationalization of the civil war; that religion has often been invoked by politicians whose motives may have more to do with patronage and control than with piety; and that the current drive to Islamize the South has produced more Christian converts in the last decade than the entire colonial missionary enterprise did during the first half of the twentieth century. Despite this, the indigenous religions of the southern Sudan continue to inform ideas about ethical behaviour, the moral community and political action.

Some time after the main text of this book was completed, Joseph Hanlon, author of *Peace without Profit* (Oxford, 1996), suggested to me that civil wars in Africa have erupted when the internal tensions of a country are exacerbated by the intervention of external interests. As a general theory this covers the Sudan's case uncomfortably well, and it is my argument here that the Sudan's recurring civil wars are a product of the following historical factors:

1) Patterns of governance which developed in the Sudanic states before the nineteenth century, establishing an exploitive relationship between the centralizing power of the state and its hinterlands or peripheries, mainly through the institutions of slavery and slave raiding, creating groups of peoples with a lastingly ambiguous status in relation to the state;

2) The introduction of a particular brand of militant Islam in the late nineteenth century which further sharpened the divide between persons with and without full legal rights within the state;

3) Inequalities in economic, educational and political development within the colonial state of the twentieth century, which often built upon earlier patterns;

4) Britain's decision, based on political expediency, to grant inde-pendence in 1956 to the whole of the Sudan before disparities in development could be addressed, and without obtaining adequate guarantees for safeguarding the interests and representation of southern Sudanese;

---

[6] Southern Sudanese now attack this widely-held simplification, hoping it 'will be consigned to the dust bin of history' and that those 'who relish ridiculing the southern Sudan will have to invent other abusive words or phrases' (Atem Yaak Atem, 'Inappropriate usages – Part one', *SPLM/SPLA Update*, 3(40), 17 October 1994, pp. 6–7).

5) A narrowly-based nationalist movement among the northern élite in the Sudan which confronted the issues of the Sudan's diversity and unequal development by attempting to build a national identity based on the principles of Arab culture and the religion of Islam, leading to the re-emergence of nineteenth-century ideas of governance in centre–periphery relations;

6) Failure to obtain a national consensus in either the North or the South in the 1970s concerning national unity, regional development, and the balance of power between the central and regional governments;

7) The weakened state of the Sudan's economy in the 1970s, coinciding with a Southern awareness of the extent of their own natural resources, that hastened political instability in the 1980s;

8) The Sudan's involvement in the international politics of the Cold War, which exacerbated its own internal war, especially through the distribution of arms on an unprecedented scale;

9) The re-emergence of militant Islam as a major political and economic force, both nationally and internationally, and the qualifications this has placed on the rights of non-Muslim citizens;

10) The interest of foreign governments and foreign investors in the Sudan's natural and mineral resources, especially water and oil.

The Sudan's future is uncertain, but many problems of development will remain and will have to be addressed, whatever the outcome. This book attempts to identify some of these problems, raising these questions:

1) Is relief ultimately a political rather than an humanitarian issue, in that relief and development policies inevitably have political objectives, and agencies must make conscious choices in support of or opposition to the political goals of guerrilla movements, nation states and donor governments?

2) Do relief programmes shorten or prolong conflict?

3) Can a focus on the technicalities of relief lead to a secure peace?

4) Can a secure peace be achieved without addressing issues of social justice and economic and political rights for the whole of the Sudan; including some kind of recognition of the collective claims of returning displaced populations to the land and resources of their home areas?

5) Can the peoples of the Sudan afford another peace which is merely an interim truce between civil wars?

It has been my intention in writing this book to explain matters rather than just describe them. There are causes and principles involved in the war, however much they are obscured by the conduct of the fighting, and to explain the principles is not to condone the conduct. Civil wars are notorious for their inhumanity. Observing the Sudan's war now, I am often forcibly reminded of my own great-grandmother's tales of survival in the border states during the American Civil War, where the great motivating principles of that horrific conflict were scarcely evident in the behaviour of its local protagonists. My home-state of Missouri (to which my great-grandmother fled in the mistaken hope of finding greater security) was then the battleground of the most vicious internal guerrilla war in American history, where all the cruelties of civil conflict were magnified. The American historian Michael Fellman has characterized it as 'the war of ten thousand nasty incidents [where] justice was impossible', and 'restraint and forbearance had not been the guiding qualities.'[7] As it was then, so it is now. But however impossible justice may seem to be, it has not been forgotten, and it can be restored.

[7] Michael Fellman, *Inside War. The Guerrilla Conflict in Missouri during the American Civil War* (New York, 1989), pp. 251, 266.

PREFACE TO THE UPDATED EDITION

The signing of the final three protocols between the Sudan government and SPLM on 26 May 2004 in Kenya completed the series of framework agreements for peace begun in July 2002 and opened the way to a comprehensive ceasefire and formal peace settlement. The culmination of two years of negotiations, with delays continuing up to the last minute, Sudanese greeted news of the signing with ambivalent relief. An end to fighting in the South, if it truly comes, is welcome. There is scepticism, however, about the ambiguity of the 'pre-interim' period and the technicalities of the six-year 'interim' period leading to a referendum for the South. Underlying this scepticism is the conviction of many Sudanese, Northern and Southern, that neither of the two parties is serious about peace, and that the negotiations have focused more on the power relations between them than on the root causes of the conflicts devastating the country.

The talks were prolonged by adjournments, impasses, consultations and withdrawals. The major stumbling blocks to progress were found less in the detail of the security, wealth-sharing and power-sharing protocols, than in the future status of territories outside the South: the 'Three Areas' (Abyei, the Nuba Mountains, Blue Nile), and the national capital, Khartoum, itself. These were issues that had the potential to take the negotiations beyond the arena of the 'North–South' problem to which they had been confined. The government was particularly keen to avoid compromises that would dilute the Islamist state in the North.

The exclusion of other opposition groups from direct participation in the negotiations constituted one of the greatest weaknesses of the peace process. The 2002 Danforth Report's failure to recognize the multiplicity of Sudan conflicts (p.178 below) was only partly to blame. Neither the government nor the SPLM have been eager to engage with the opposition as a bloc. Both opted to deal with groups and leaders individually, seeking to co-opt rivals rather than address broader grievances. The SPLA strategy of reincorporating the leaders of rival movements, rather than seeking a collective rapprochement with the Southern opposition, back-fired, as the government continued to exploit these rifts and used its Southern militias to violate the cessation of hostilities agreed in 2002 and 2003: most notably in the Shilluk kingdom in the first half of 2004, but also in assaulting SPLA positions in Nuer territory in June, only a few days after the signing of the final protocols.

Overshadowing these violations of both the spirit and the letter of the agreements in the South has been the resurgence of fighting in Darfur. The international conscience has been aroused by Darfur far more quickly than by any other war in the Sudan, and it has responded to reports of an 'humanitarian disaster', 'ethnic cleansing' and 'genocide'. The rapidity with which the Darfur crisis expanded, the revelation of the scale of systematic and co-ordinated assaults on civilian settlements by the Sudanese air force, mounted Arab militias (*janjawid*) and regular Sudan army units, and the internationalization of the crisis through its impact on Chad, forced much of the world to realize that the twin issues of war and peace in the Sudan were far more complex than they had assumed.

Because the Darfur war has been between Muslims, most international reporters have seen it as separate from the war in the South. Some governments, too, most notably the US, were keen to detach it from the other wars, lest the fighting in Darfur unravel the Kenya peace talks. So, notwithstanding his own public expressions of concern about the war in Darfur, and despite what the fighting there revealed about Khartoum's real intentions, President Bush confirmed that the Sudan government was negotiating 'in good faith' when he reported to Congress in April 2004.

But, of course, Darfur is not unrelated to the war in the South, or to the wars in the Nuba Mountains, Blue Nile or eastern Sudan. There has been a steady escalation of fighting since 1998, and an increased polarization of the conflict around ideas of race (see Section **9.2.4** and pp. 212, 214, 217, 221). The decision of the Darfur Liberation Front in March 2003 to rename itself the Sudan Liberation Movement/Army in order to gain a higher national and international profile was probably influenced by the acceleration of the Southern peace talks. The government's reaction was a repetition of its behaviour in the South and Nuba Mountains: it declared the problem to be a 'tribal' conflict, mobilized 'tribal' militias, denied the evidence of the involvement of its air force and regular army units (freed from the Southern fronts by the cessation of hostilities agreements), obstructed international relief agencies, and tried to confine relief to designated 'corridors' of its own choosing. The concomitant effect on the peace talks was that, not only did the government prolong negotiations while it strove to bring Darfur back under its control, it hardened its position on the Nuba Mountains and the Blue Nile as it sought to avoid precedents that could be applied to Darfur.

International participation in the peace process – particularly that of the US, but no less of IGAD, the UK, Norway, and the UN – has done much to bring peace talks on the South to fruition. There can be no doubt that the post-9/11 objectives of the US have done much to keep this attention focused on the Sudan. But it is also true that this new international intervention has ignored the multiplicity of issues which have fed into the country's interlocking civil wars (p.142), and that the focus on securing an accommodation between two warring powers has been, initially, at the expense of a comprehensive peace for the whole country (p.180). At the time of writing (June 2004) it remains to be seen whether the same international determination will be brought to bear successfully on Darfur, and whether the proposed six month 'pre-interim' period set aside for wider constitutional consultations will succeed in engaging all opposition groups. Southern Sudanese, having gained the right of self-determination, still have to decide how they wish to govern themselves, and who is to govern. Northern Sudanese have been denied a similar right to freely choose whether or not they want an Islamist state.

Is this the 'bad peace', about which I warned (p.180)? If the unity of the Sudan is to be preserved through the fair and equal treatment of all citizens, then the current regime has already demonstrated that this cannot be achieved within the framework of its existing constitution and laws. An agreement that merely succeeds in entrenching the current government in power will undermine the very possibility of its own implementation. But a pessimism ingrained by twenty-one years of war must be set against the recognition that peace, like war, can have its own momentum. If the initial phases of the peace agreement are implemented with determination and monitored with vigilance, during which the Sudanese peoples are able to create the space in which they can construct their own peace, then, gradually, the momentum of peace-building may accelerate. The protocols agreed over two years do establish mechanisms whereby old grievances, such as Abyei, can be resolved. The wealth-sharing protocol deals not only with oil, but prescribes land commissions whereby land issues, so important in the Nuba Mountains and Blue Nile, as well as in Darfur, Kordofan, and the East, can be addressed. The principle of self-determination, as it applies in different ways to the South, the Nuba Mountains and Blue Nile, has been recognized. We live in hope; but hope tempered by experience.

Map 1: The Sudan in 1983
(showing oil pipeline opened in 1999)

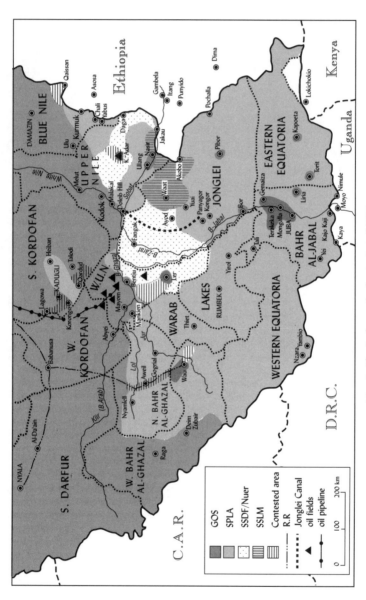

Map 2: The Sudan at the beginning of 2002
(adapted from 'map of areas of control', Rightsmaps.com)

1

The Historical ▮ of North–South
Structure ▮ Relations

1.1 Introduction

The conflict between the northern and southern Sudan has usually been
misunderstood, because the historical roots of the conflict have been
misrepresented. Two opposite explanations are frequently given for the
continuing rift: 1) That the division between the North and South is based
on centuries of exploitation and slave-raiding by the 'Arab' North against
the 'African' South; or 2) That the Sudan was artificially split by imperialist
meddling, since Sudanese Islam, being both 'African' and 'Arab', imposes
no natural or historical division between the two regions. Certainly there is
broad agreement that the Sudan has been undergoing a process of
Arabization and Islamization since the invasion of the Sudan by Arab tribes
from Upper Egypt and across the Red Sea during the Middle Ages. The
'Arab invasion' of the Sudan has been accepted as an historical fact both by
those who think that Arabization is a natural and inevitable process – inter-
rupted in its final stages by British intervention – and by those who see it as
an external threat which should be stopped by the rallying of an indigenous
African opposition. A corollary to the above is that the northern Sudan has
been united by Islam, and therefore confronts the South with a political and
cultural unity which the South itself lacks.

The Sudan is a complex country, with a population of nearly thirty
million, inhabiting an area of about one million square miles. One
language profile which categorized languages according to the number of
speakers, identified Arabic and Dinka as the two major languages,
followed by fourteen minor languages, divided into some 100 dialects. Of
these nearly half are found within the southern Sudan, representing one
third of the country's population, residing within a quarter of its territory;
while more than half are found spread throughout the remaining northern
three quarters of the country.[1] Clearly this diversity makes it difficult to
explain the current North–South conflict in simple cultural, ethnic or
racial terms. It follows that some of the historical 'causes' which have
been offered to explain the conflict must be revised. Religion, local
perceptions of race and social status, economic exploitation, and colonial

---

[1] R. Thelwall, 'Linguistic profile', in R. Thelwall (ed.), *Aspects of Language in the Sudan*
(Coleraine, 1978). The data on which the profile drew were incomplete, the population figures
being especially outdated. Different methods of classification could well increase the number
of languages identified.

1

and post-colonial interventions are all elements in the Sudan's current civil war, but none, by itself, fully explains it. To understand the current situation in the Sudan, one must first understand the role of successive Sudanese states in producing regional underdevelopment and racial and cultural antagonism.

1.2 States, trade & Islam before 1820

The development of states has been the most consistent influence on the definition of economic, political, and ultimately social relations within the Sudan. Early states along the Nile and across the east-west Sudanic belt defined the relationship between their own centres and the outlying regions: from the hinterlands came the manpower, wealth and food surpluses on which the states built their power. As state power in the Muslim era frequently depended in part on standing armies of slave soldiers and involvement in an international as well as domestic slave trade, slave-raiding was originally a state activity, and each state had its own hinterland from which it drew its slaves and other resources.

This process was probably of a greater antiquity than our sources allow us to trace, but some broad historical patterns are discernible. The requirements of the Egyptian Nile valley states may well have been met as much through treaties of trade and exchange as by conquest and raids. The arrangments for a biennial delivery of 'Ethiopian' slaves from Kush to the Persian dynasty in Egypt described by Herodotus[2] bears some similarity to the provisons of the later *baqt* ('pact') treaty between Muslim Egypt and Christian Nubia in AD 652. The latter arrangement may have been more in the nature of a trade agreement than a tribute arrangement imposed by a peace treaty, and provided for the annual exchange of slaves from Nubia for goods from Egypt. The slaves would not have come from the very heart of the kingdom itself (there is no analogy with the Athenian hostages to Crete), but would have been plundered from the outlying regions subject to the state. Those slaves so exchanged with Egypt were not necessarily speakers of today's Nubian languages, but in Egypt they were identified as coming from Nubia; therefore they were Nubian (*Nuba*). The terms 'Nubian' (Nubi), 'Nuba' (Nubawi) and 'Sudanese' (Sudani, i.e., black) entered the colloquial Arabic of the Nile valley as synonymous with 'slave'.

At this early date most of what is now the southern Sudan lay outside the radius of exploitation by the kingdoms of the central Nile, yet each successor state had its own hinterland. Sennar, established along the Blue Nile in the sixteenth century A.D., raided the Ethiopian foothills, the Nuba mountains, and the White Nile plains. The Darfur sultanate, established in the western Sudan in the seventeenth century A.D., raided mainly to the south in Dar Fartit, or what is now western Bahr al-Ghazal. This remained the hunting ground for bands radiating out of Darfur well into the twentieth century. It was only in the nineteenth century that the

---

[2] For the text, translation and commentary on Herodotus 3.97.2–3, see Tormond Eide, Tomas Hägg, Richard Holton Pierce & László Török (eds), *Fontes Historiae Nubiorum*, Vol. I (Bergen, 1994), pp. 312–14.

whole of the southern Sudan was opened up to the exploitation of a state centred at Khartoum. Thus, prior to the establishment of Muslim states from the fourteenth century A.D. onwards, pagan and Christian kingdoms were active in the organized raiding of their peripheries, and part of the impetus of that raiding came from external trade relations. Muslim rulers later continued a tradition already established by their pagan and Christian predecessors.

It was this commercial contact with an increasingly Muslim external world which led to the entrenchment of Islam in the central Nile valley and Sudanic states. There were political as well as commercial reasons which encouraged the leaders of Sennar and Darfur to convert to Islam. The gradual introduction of Islam into the Sudanic states was fostered in part by itinerant merchants plying their trade, and by wandering holy men given land grants by their hosts. With Islam came literacy in Arabic and the introduction of Arabic legal texts. It was through the law books that 'the principles of the Arabs' were introduced, and the governance of the Sudanic kingdoms was brought more in line with Islamic legal principles. The adoption of Arab genealogies (on which most of the evidence of an Arab invasion of the Sudan rests) dates from this period. Arab genealogies helped establish a new political or spiritual legitimacy: Sudanic kings discovered their Abbasid and Ummayid 'origins', while holy men traced their descent from the family of the Prophet Muhammad. The acceptance of Islam by the Sudanic kingdoms helped to sharpen the divide between the states and their hinterlands; between those who could claim the protection of law, and those without legal rights. All the same, many Muslims in the Sudan continued to follow forms of customary law at variance with the *shari'a*, and relations between Muslims and non-Muslims were not characterized by a jihadic fervour. In fact, many Muslim pastoralists, such as the Baqqara in Darfur and the Rufa'a in Sennar, frequently sought protection from the demands of the state by fleeing to or allying with non-Muslim peoples, such as the Dinka, who lived beyond the state's control.

Though Islam eventually became the religion of the Sudanic kings, the kings themselves continued to claim customary rights and powers which were not based on Islamic precepts. The Sudan did not develop an indigenous *ulama*, an official body of experts who defined orthodoxy. Islam in the Sudan was introduced by individual clerics or holy men, and continued to draw its strength from numerous Sufi orders. Thus Sudanese Islam has always been subject to particularistic, sometimes conflicting interpretations by inspired Imams (Muslim leaders). Conflicts within the Muslim community were dramatically brought to the fore during the Mahdiyya at the end of the nineteenth century, and again, in more recent times.

The exercise of state power within the new Muslim context still produced ambiguities. It was only in Islamic times that standing armies of slave soldiers became a central institution of state power. Those peoples living closest to the centres usually gained more benefits from collaboration with the state than those living on the peripheries, but as state power in the eighteenth and nineteenth centuries increasingly rested on standing armies of slave soldiers drawn from the pagan peripheries, free

Muslim peasants and nomads often found themselves coerced by high-ranking military slaves in the name of a Muslim sovereign. The fact that the soldiers frequently became Muslim did not necessarily make them more free. Coming from the peripheries of a state thus defined one's status within the state, and in this respect territorial origin did become a factor in social stratification. It is important to recall however, that even in the nineteenth century terms which now have a specific ethnic or national connotation implied ambiguous or lowly origin or status. 'Nubians' were equivalent to slaves in relation to Egypt; 'Nuba', whatever their geographical origin, were slaves in Sennar; 'Sudanese' were slaves everywhere; and, as far as the riverain peoples (*aulad al-balad*) between Dongola and the Gezira were concerned, 'Arabs' were uncivilized nomads from the west. We cannot read back into the past the ethnic connotations of today. We thus cannot attribute the origins of the current civil war to earlier forms of racial confrontation. We can, however, seek to understand it by reference to analogous patterns of free and servile status within a series of expanding, centralizing Sudanic states. The concentration of state power in the central Nile valley received a new impetus under Egyptian rule.

1.3 The Egyptian conquest

Muhammad Ali, the Albanian soldier who emerged as Egypt's ruler after the Napoleonic Wars, sought to make Egypt an international power in the Near East and Mediterranean in the early part of the nineteenth century. His invasion of the Sudan, begun in 1820, was intended to provide him with the resources to sustain this military build-up through a steady supply of gold and slave soldiers. Neither the gold nor the slaves came in the quantity which he anticipated or needed, but the Turco–Egyptian regime in the Sudan (the Turkiyya) altered the political and economic balance in the country considerably.

The southern Sudan had been largely unaffected by the succession of early states in the North. By the eighteenth century, southward state expansion was effectively halted by the Shilluk kingdom, with its capital at Fashoda on the White Nile, and by the Dinka living along the Kiir (or Bahr al-Arab), White Nile, and Sobat, who even occasionally offered refuge to Muslim pastoralists anxious to escape state power. The Turco–Egyptian conquest of the Sudan upset this regional balance. This new empire had far greater resources at its command than any of the indigenous Sudanese kingdoms. It also made far greater demands on its subjects for slaves and tribute. The northern Sudanese peoples of Nubia, Sennar, Kordofan and the Red Sea were the first to be conquered, and they were the first to be coerced into collaboration with the army in massive slave–raids into the old hinterlands. It was only Egyptian power which was able to penetrate beyond these into the Upper Nile basin, bringing in its wake European, Egyptian and northern Sudanese merchants and adventurers for the commercial exploitation of the South. It was during this period of the nineteenth century that we can identify the beginning of a North–South divide in the Sudan. The two most significant developments contributing to the North–South divide were the impoverishment of some areas of the northern Sudan through new forms of taxation and land ownership, which then contributed to the dramatic expansion of slave-raiding and slave-owning.

Slave-raiding had been the prerogative of the state prior to the Turkiyya, and slave-owning and slave-trading had been confined to the court and aristocracy of the Sudanic kingdoms. The new rulers in the Sudan continued official slave raids on a massive scale, and imposed a tribute in slaves upon their new subjects. Collaboration in slave-raids into non-Muslim territories thus became a virtual duty for some of the Muslim pastoralists in the Sudan. The Shaiqiyya from north of Khartoum, the Rufa'a of the Blue Nile, and the Baqqara along the White Nile and in the west soon were involved in official raids with the army, or were organizing raids of their own. Excess slaves were kept by the raiders for their own use or for sale. Not only did the number of slaves increase during the Turkiyya, but the use of slaves, too, expanded and for the first time domestic slavery became widespread throughout all segments of society in the northern Sudan.

At the same time, Turco–Egyptian reforms in taxation, land ownership and use had a marked impact on the economy of the riverain settlements of Nubia, and especially on the Danaqla and Ja'aliyyin. The need to increase production in order to pay new taxes meant intensifying the use of marginal land. Indebtedness rose as farmers mortgaged their crops in advance of the harvest or transferred common-land rights to private ownership. There was a large outflow of men from Nubia seeking to escape taxation and indebtedness by hiring themselves out to the commercial companies who were exploiting newly opened lands in the South, where the ivory and slave trades became the main avenues for enrichment. Thus hardship created by the government's economic policies in the North contributed to the exploitation and subjugation of the South, and gave certain sections of the Muslim and Arabic-speaking population of the North a personal stake in its subjugation, a pattern which would be repeated in the 1980s and 1990s (Section **6.2.1**).

A religious divide was imposed on the country which was not, in inspiration or intention, religious. Within the structure of the Turco–Egyptian empire Muslims among the indigenous population benefited more than non-Muslims, and Muslim subjects could pass on their losses to non-Muslims on the peripheries.

There was a convergence of military and commercial networks in the exploitation of the South. Both the government and the commercial companies had their own armies drawn from a mixture of free men and slaves. Both made use of overlapping networks of fortified trade centres and caravan routes. Traders and government officials each carved out their own personal fiefdoms, as did some indigenous leaders allied to them, and the maintenance of these fiefdoms through raiding and trading became their own justification (again, establishing a precedent for the conduct of war in the 1990s: see Chapter **8**). When it subsequently attempted to suppress the slave trade in order to meet international obligations in the 1870s, the Egyptian government also incorporated many of the northern and southern Sudanese soldiers from the private armies into its own service. Slaves, both female and male, released from the service of their merchant owners or overlords continued to live around government trade centres as 'voluntary slaves', providing food and labour for government officials and the army.

Slave-raiding reached its peak in the South during the early 1870s. Not all Southern peoples were affected by it, and some benefited from collaboration with the merchant companies or the government. But during the Turkiyya the slave population in the North was drawn very largely from the southern Sudan, and in the popular mind slaves and 'blacks' were synonymous. Even southern Sudanese who became Muslims or exercised some power in the colonial society – as those in the army certainly did – were stigmatized by their slave status or slave origins. The incorporation of the whole of the South as the state's exploitable hinterland, the intensification of racial stratification and the widespread identification of people from the South with low status were thus consequences of the economic and political system of Turco–Egyptian colonialism.

1.4 The Mahdiyya & internal colonialism

The Mahdist state (1883–98), which overthrew the Turco–Egyptian regime, built on this pattern. The Khalifa Abdallahi, who succeeded the charismatic religious figure of Muhammad Ahmad, the expected saviour or 'Mahdi' in 1885, based his autocracy largely on a standing army of slave riflemen (*jihadiyya*), who came mainly from the South and west. In the early stages of the Mahdiyya there may have been some intention to bring southern Sudanese into the Muslim fold, but the Mahdist state lost control of the South at a very early stage. Slave-raiding and slave-trading declined during the Mahdiyya, but this was very largely a result of the contraction of state power during that period. Incursions into the South tended to be almost exclusively for plunder: for food during the great famine of 1888–92, or for more slaves to add to the dwindling supply of domestic labour and military recruitment. This was in part justified by the nature of the *jihad* state, which drew a sharper line between the *Dar al-Islam* (Abode of Peace) and the *Dar al-Harb* (Abode of War) than any of the previous Muslim states in the region.

The Mahdiyya is now often interpreted in Sudanese history as an early form of Sudanese nationalism, and the presence of southern Sudanese in the army (and therefore in some parts of the administration) of the Mahdist state is represented as evidence of the truly nationalist aspirations of the movement. This is to misread the Mahdiyya through modern spectacles. Racial attitudes in the North remained unchanged from the Turkiyya.[3] In many ways the Mahdist state developed its own form of

[3] Hamdan Abu Anja, the Khalifa Abdallahi's most trusted military leader, came from the ex-slave Mandala clients of the Baqqara. Though admired and respected by many Arabs and non-Arabs within the Mahdist army, his servile origins were remembered against him, and he was taunted as 'a slave' by even the Khalifa's own relatives (F. R. Wingate, *Ten Year's Captivity in the Mahdi's Camp* (London, 1892), p. 244). For other expressions of contemporary racial attitudes see *The Memoirs of Babikr Bedri* (Oxford, 1969), pp. 117–18, 240–1.

internal colonialism. The Sudanic kings had ruled through a series of feudal relationships with tribal and hereditary leaders. The Turco–Egyptian administration had also recognized the rights of hereditary rulers. The Mahdist state imposed allegiance through religion and through the personal oath of loyalty to the religious leader of the state as Imam, the Mahdi and later his Khalifa. The country as a whole was divided between the followers of the Mahdi (known as the 'Ansar') and 'unbelievers', whether Muslim or non-Muslim. Administrators, or agents, were appointed to govern the rural areas, and these increasingly did not come from the local areas they governed but replaced or subordinated local rulers and ruling families. This was as true, for a time, of Nubia under the Baqqara autocracy of the Khalifa, as it was for the Sudan–Ethiopian border area, the far west and the South. This is one reason why the Anglo–Egyptian overthrow of the Mahdist state was assisted by specific Sudanese groups who, though often Muslims who had formerly assisted the rise of the Mahdi, were opposed to the latter-day Mahdist government.

The conclusion advanced here, then, is that the origins of the Sudan's current problems predate the unequal legacy of the colonial system in the twentieth century. They can be found in the ideas of legitimate power and governance developed in the Sudanic states of the eighteenth and nineteenth centuries, which were incorporated into the structures of the Turco–Egyptian empire, achieved new force in the *jihad* state of the Mahdiyya, and were never fully replaced, but rather (as we shall see) occasionally adapted by the twentieth century colonial state (Section **2.3**). The exploitative nature of the central state towards its rich, but uncontrolled hinterland, the coercive power of the army in economic as well as political matters, the prerogative of the leader in redistributing revenues to the peripheries, the ambiguous status of persons who are not fully part of the central heritage – all of these have re-emerged with force in the Sudan since independence, especially during the Nimairi period (Section **4.4**). They are receiving a further impetus from the current Islamist reform movement, with its clear distinction between people with and without full legal rights, its move towards personal allegiance to the Imam as national leader, and the intensification of the commercial exploitation of the rural areas through modern Islamic banking and development institutions.

2

British Overrule ▌ 1899–1947

2.1 Patterns of conquest & occupation, North & South

The Anglo-Egyptian Reconquest of the Sudan beginning in the 1890s followed distinctly different patterns in the North and in the South. In the North, Egypt was able to make use of large sections of a disaffected Muslim Sudanese population. Around Suakin and Kassala, Egypt was allied to the religious family of the Mirghanis, founders of the Khatmiyya sect, who had been supported by the Egyptian government before the Mahdiyya, and who subsequently maintained a strong opposition to the Mahdi and his Khalifa as rivals to the Ansar (followers of the Mahdi). In Dongola there were many Nubian dissidents against the Khalifa Abdallahi's Baqqara autocracy, such as the Ja'aliyyin, who became military allies of the Anglo-Egyptian forces. Thus the demise of Mahdism at the Battle of Omdurman on 2 September 1898 was assisted by both old and new allies of Egypt.

The new Anglo-Egyptian Condominium government secured itself from any threat of resurgent Mahdism in the North by reinstating tribal leaders where they had been replaced by Mahdist agents, by supporting orthodoxy against 'fanaticism' in the constitution of a board of *ulama*, and by subsidising the Mahdiyya's religious rivals, such as the Mirghani family and its Khatmiyya order. There was a fairly quick transition from military occupation to civil administration in the North before World War One: civilian British officials replaced all military governors in the northern provinces, and the police took over responsibility for rural security from the army. Northern Sudanese began to be recruited into the police and even some army units, replacing Egyptian and Sudanese (i.e., former slave soldier) troops.

'But not in the South.' The political pattern in the South was different as the Mahdist state had had virtually no control over the region outside its few main garrisons at Fashoda, Bor and Rejaf; therefore there was no need to wean people away from Mahdism by offering them rewards for renewing their loyalty to the government. The small Mahdist garrisons were evacuated and their withdrawal left the land open to Anglo-Egyptian, French, Ethiopian and Belgian imperial competition. The two main problems confronting Britain in the South were to re-assert Egypt's old claims to the territory in the face of this international rivalry by establishing 'effective occupation' at strategic points along the periphery, and to secure the submission of people who had been free from most forms of external control and interference for over a dozen years. International diplomacy quickly settled the competing imperial claims in the region, and the main outlines of the Sudan's borders were set by 1903. The submission of the southern Sudanese was a more complicated matter.

Most peoples of the South actively repudiated the Turco–Egyptian government by rising against it in the early 1880s. Almost all saw the Mahdist government as essentially similar to the Egyptian regime it had replaced. There was, in fact, considerable continuity in the personnel of both in the South: Northern merchants and administrators who had been an integral part of the old colonial administrative and commercial outposts in the South joined in the overthrow of Egypt and resumed their posts; the Sudanese slave soldiers in both the Egyptian garrisons and the private armies of the ivory/slave merchants were incorporated into the Mahdist army. From the Southern point of view, the absence of Egyptians from the government in Omdurman was an unimportant distinction. Similarly, the inclusion of a few British officers in the returning Egyptian army of 1898 – an army which also included Sudanese soldiers who had served in the old Egyptian empire and the overthrown Mahdist state – was a scarcely visible alteration to the fabric of authority. It merely meant that British officials were classed as 'Turks' along with the Egyptians and northern Sudanese by the majority of Southerners.

Britain thus faced a paradox in the South. Its own position in the Sudan was founded on the assertion that Egypt had never renounced its claim to the territories in rebellion. This may have been sound enough in international law, but an appeal to old loyalty due to Egypt and the Egyptian crown found little response in the southern Sudan. In so far as the British officers in the new Anglo-Egyptian administration also believed that the Mahdist rebellion had been provoked in large part by Egyptian misgovernment, they tried to distance themselves from the old authority they were in the process of reasserting. The British officers commanding patrols of Sudanese soldiers in the South frequently declared to the peoples whose submission they sought that the 'new' government was not the same as the 'old' government which had burned Southern villages, stolen Southern cattle, and enslaved Southern people in the past. Appearances were often against them; especially when, in response to local defiance, or even local indifference, the troops of the new government burned villages, seized cattle as 'fines', and carried off war captives and hostages to distant prisons or for conscription in the army, all in the name of establishing government authority.

There was a longer period of 'pacification' in the South than in the North, lasting into the 1920s, for a number of reasons. The Anglo-Egyptian government did not have to negotiate local alliances against a variety of competitors in the region, as it had done prior to and just after the Reconquest in many parts of the North; therefore it faced little inducement to moderate its demands or compromise with powerful local authorities. The re-established Governor-Generalate for the whole of the Sudan, centred at Khartoum, was remote from the South both in physical distance and in its guiding preoccupations. As a whole, the South remained on the periphery of central government thinking throughout the

Condominium period. In the first two decades the South figured in government plans mainly as a reservoir of conscripts for the 'Sudanese' battalions of the Egyptian army, which formed the permanent garrison of the Sudan. These soldiers remained socially separate from the northern Sudanese by virtue of their slave origins. Replenishment of the battalions took place in specific catchment areas which coincided with the old slave-raiding zones of the Nuba Mountains and the southern Sudan, thus continuing (if on a reduced scale) the exploitive pattern of the nineteenth century and entrenching racial attitudes. As southern Sudanese remained reluctant to volunteer for military service, conscription continued to be forced, and prisoners and war captives were regularly funnelled into the army. The South proved an inadequate reservoir, both because of its low population density and the reluctance of its people to be conscripted. Eventually territorial units recruited for local service replaced the old Egyptian army units throughout the country, a process completed only in the 1920s.

Administration thus took the simplest form of maintaining government prestige and authority through the continuation of coercive policies. Among most of the pastoralist societies of the central clay plains and swamp area of Upper Nile and Bahr al-Ghazal, cattle were extracted as tribute, not primarily for their economic value, but as a practical demonstration of government authority and as an obligatory sign of submission by the pastoralist peoples. Government prestige required the seizure of cattle by force whenever the payment of tribute was resisted. The reasons for the South's long period of 'pacification' is thus to be found as much, or perhaps more in government policies than in southern Sudanese 'truculence'. The inadequacies of administration by tribute and punitive patrol were clear to many administrators, but the constraints on government activity during World War One, and the continued demands of the army during that same time, inhibited the development of a more comprehensive administrative system throughout the South up to the 1920s.

2.2 The context of the Southern Policy

The Civil Secretary's now famous statement on 'Southern Policy' in 1930 declared that the administration of the South was to be developed along 'African', rather than 'Arab' lines, and that the future of the southern Sudan might ultimately lie with the countries of British East Africa, rather than with the Middle East. As we have seen, there were already different patterns of administrative development in North and South prior to the enunciation of this policy. The statement put into words what was already administrative practice. This practice has been labelled 'Indirect Rule' in other parts of British Africa, but was more commonly called 'Devolution' or 'Native Administration' in the Sudan. Whatever it was called, its basic principle was that the local administration of colonial peoples should be conducted through indigenous structures of authority, employing indigenous law or custom, as far as this was consistent with British ideas of good government and justice. It followed that in any colonial territory where there was a variety of indigenous power structures, based on different types of customary law, no uniformity could be achieved and in fact was not even desired. Added to this, the Sudan applied a Closed District Ordinance to most districts in southern provinces from the mid-1920s, regulating the movement of non-native persons into the South. Thus the administration of the North and the South, already based on different foundations, continued to diverge in practice.[1]

2.2.1 Native Administration

At the heart of the principles of Native Administration was support for the authority of the chiefs. In the northern Sudan the Anglo-Egyptian government had been keen to re-instate those families who had held authority under Turco–Egyptian rule. In the 1920s this practice was regularized, and such chiefs were given specific judicial and administrative powers, through the enactment of such pieces of legislation as the 'Power of Nomad Sheikhs Ordinance'. Their judicial authority was confined to certain aspects of customary and *shari'a* law, and their administrative work was supervised by British District Commissioners.

There was a much later assimilation of indigenous structures into administration in the South than in the North, mainly because British administrators could not find the same range of executive authorities in the South as they had in their Northern 'sheikhs' and 'omdas'. In only a few kingdoms, such as the Shilluk and the Azande, was an executive hierarchy ready to hand. In the pastoral 'acephalous' societies who constituted the majority of the southern Sudanese (Dinka, Nuer, Murle, Mundari, Toposa, etc.), few such hereditary authorities existed. Committed to working through native structures, British administrators often felt that they had to create suitable structures in the first place. The chiefs' courts which grew up in the southern Sudan after the late 1920s thus owed as much to British innovation as to indigenous custom.[2]

There developed within the South two broadly different patterns of administration: one for the pastoralists, who were found mainly in the central clay plains in Uppper Nile and Bahr al-Ghazal; and another for the sedentary agricultural communities found mainly in what is now Equatoria and on the ironstone plateau of Bahr al-Ghazal. In the clay plains, people and their chiefs were accessible only during the dry season. Courts were mobile and dealt mainly with cattle cases and were empowered to collect fines and taxes. The office of a paramount chief with strong executive authority did not exist. The courts and hierarchies

---

[1] The text of the 1930 'Southern Policy' can be found in Mohamed Omer Beshir, *The Southern Sudan: Background to Conflict* (London, 1968), Appendix 1, and Dunstan Wai (ed.), *The Southern Sudan: The Problem of National Integration* (London, 1973), Appendix 1. There is no evidence that either the Sudan government or the East African governments ever seriously planned, or desired, a wholescale transfer of the southern provinces out of the Condominium to British colonial control, but the Southern Policy did at least keep the option theoretically open until 1946. The Closed District Ordinance was used primarily for economic control (see Section **2.3.1**), regulating the movement of petty merchants. In the East African colonies similar closed district ordinances were usually applied to frontier districts, in an attempt to combat international poaching.

[2] For an example of the different constructions of Native Administration even within one southern province see C. A. Willis, *et al.*, *The Upper Nile Province Handbook: A Report on Peoples and Government in the Southern Sudan, 1931*, Douglas H. Johnson (ed.) (Oxford, 1995).

of the southernmost regions were accessible to administrators most of the year, met regularly in the same centres, had more powerful executives, and developed on much more bureaucratic lines than those in the pastoralist societies. In parts of Equatoria 'lukikos' (local parliaments of hereditary authorities) were introduced, based on models developed in Uganda. When southern Sudanese were recruited into the lower levels of the civil service, in the later years of Anglo-Egyptian administration, they came mainly from those areas with a stronger bureaucratic tradition in Native Administration.

2.2.2 Law & religion

In the northern Sudan law and religion were placed in clearly defined compartments. The main laws governing the Sudan (the Sudan Criminal Code and the Sudan Penal Code) were based on the Indian model. *Shari'a* was preserved mainly as family law for Muslims, regulating marriages, inheritance, and some property rights. In the rural areas different forms of customary law were also allowed. Even in nominally Muslim areas customary law could modify Islamic codes in marriage practices and land rights. Ever mindful of the 'subversive' potential of mystical Islam, the Anglo-Egyptian government attempted to control the activities of Sufi brotherhoods and supported an orthodox interpretation of religion and religious law through the constitution of a board of *ulama*, and the appointment of a network of religious courts under the overall authority of a Grand Qadi (canonical judge). Until 1947 the Grand Qadi was always an Egyptian.

There were no religious orthodoxies in the South. In keeping with the principles of Native Administration, some administrators attempted to define orthodox 'tribal' religions along with the tribal customs and hierarchies which were given form from the late 1920s onwards. Part of the elaboration of different customary laws in the South was the attempt to purge custom of any foreign contaminations – a purging which was part of an attempt to control the movement of peoples between political groups, as practitioners of other rites were often arrested when found outside their home areas. Not only did administrators discourage southern societies from 'borrowing' their neighbours' customs, they also tried to interdict the imitation or adoption of Islamic customs and laws. Native Administration thus encouraged indigenous religious diversity in the South, while in the North religious policy encouraged the tendency towards a greater uniformity of practice among Muslims.

Islam was neither suppressed nor expelled from the South during the Condominium period. It was, however, confined mainly to the towns. The army (and some of the police) remained largely Muslim until the Sudanese battalions were disbanded in the 1920s. Communities of Muslim ex-servicemen and their families continued to live in the *malakiyyas* or civilian quarters of government centres, where they were often involved in commerce and ran religious schools. They, too, were subject to *shari'a* in the regulation of their family affairs. In so far as Native Administration attempted to maintain a clear division between the rural areas and the towns, its influence on rural communities remained limited.

Government policy allowed for the establishment of Christian missions in the South, but in practice local administrators were nearly as suspicious of Christian missionary activities as they were of Muslim proselytizing. Both interfered with the vision of 'custom' on which Native Administration was founded.[3] The missions were tolerated mainly for the schools they provided, but even these received only limited encouragement throughout most of the Anglo-Egyptian period. There were relatively few conversions to Christianity during this time. In principle, education in the Christian missions did not require conversion to Christianity; missions were not supposed to operate a policy of 'no baptism, no schooling'. Since all of the missions required an extended period of religious education before a catechumen was admitted into the church, this principle was respected in practice as many students took what schooling they could without necessarily completing full religious instruction. Yet conversion and baptism usually did follow entry into a school. In order to prevent the sort of violent competition for converts which had characterized late nineteenth-century Buganda, the government established zones within which specific mission organizations were permitted to operate. This succeeded in limiting competition between the Catholic and Protestant churches and it ultimately meant that southern Sudanese internal politics in later years were spared the further complications of sectarian schisms of the kind which emerged in some of the Sudan's immediate neighbours.

The religious and legal pattern of the southern Sudan at the end of the Condominium period was roughly as follows: in the rural areas customary law prevailed, supposedly supported by traditional religion, with only a few individual Muslims or Christians settled outside their home villages. Muslim communities were confined mainly to the towns and administrative centres, where the Sudan Penal and Criminal codes were applied, and *shari'a* arose mainly in family matters. There were small Christian communities centred around the main mission stations, some in the towns, and some in the rural areas. The main influence of Christianity came not in the number of its converts, but in the subsequent strategic influence its converts achieved through their educational qualifications, and their role in administration and politics in the late Condominium and early Independence periods.

2.2.3 *Education in the South*
The British administrators who ruled the Sudan in the early part of the twentieth century had an ambivalent attitude towards education. Looking to both Egypt and India they professed an aversion to creating a class of educated indigenous civil servants: an 'effendi' or (worse) a 'B.A. Bombay (Failed)' class. Education was to be reserved for 'the better class of native'

[3] Given that the majority of missionaries in the South were foreigners (Austrian, Italian and American), they were also suspect for being un-British. Hostility towards Austrian missionaries was marked during World War One. The Italians were more tolerated during World War Two (especially after the liberation of Ethiopia by allied forces) partly because they were seen as politically ineffectual. British administrators always had an ambivalent attitude towards the Americans, whose evangelism, educational standards, accents and obsession with clothing the natives were generally deplored. See for instance the governor of Upper Nile's comments on missionaries in C. A. Willis, *et al*, *The Upper Nile Province Handbook*, pp. 105–11.

(i.e., those merchants and notables with whom the British allied themselves), but it was also to serve limited administrative needs. In the first two decades of Anglo-Egyptian rule a large number of junior administrators were drawn from the Egyptian army (including both Egyptian and Sudanese officers). These were increasingly replaced by educated northern Sudanese (especially from the late-1920s onwards). The educated Sudanese who were employed in government service remained in the lower levels of the administration, technical departments, and the education service, for which nothing higher than a secondary education was considered necessary. In keeping with the religious policy to support orthodoxy, certain religious schools (*khalwas*) also received some assistance from the government.

In the South, educational needs were much more limited. Prior to World War One, the government in Khartoum declared its policy to be that it needed only 'a few educated blacks' to fill minor clerical posts in the South. The first of these came from sons of soldiers rather than the local population. The government invested little in education in the South and before long left it almost entirely in the hands of the religious bodies – the *khalwas* serving the small Muslim urban communities, and the Christian missions which operated fitfully in the rural areas and the far outposts.

The policy of Native Administration adopted in the 1920s tended to discourage, rather than encourage, education in some areas of the southern Sudan, especially among pastoralist people. In so far as clerks literate in the vernacular were needed to keep a record of court cases, some boys were educated in their own languages in the mission stations, but until the late 1940s there was little attempt to educate even the sons of chiefs in pastoralist areas. Mission education was thought to divorce students from the customs of their own tribe, thus reducing their effectiveness as tribal leaders. The longest established school in the pastoralist regions was the CMS school at Malek, in Bor district, founded in 1905. Only one of its students later became a chief within the local Native Administration some forty years later.

Elsewhere, in the more sedentary communities, mission schools and education generally assumed greater importance. This was especially so in Western Bahr al-Ghazal and parts of Equatoria. It was thus far more common for the sons of chiefs in Equatoria to be educated than in any other part of the southern Sudan. The literate products of Equatorian schools also provided recruits for the civil service, the police and the army, many of whom then served outside their home districts and in other provinces.

British educational policy in the Sudan changed less than ten years before independence, when the decision was suddenly taken in London and Khartoum in 1946 to grant independence to the Sudan as a whole. It was only then that Southern chiefs were required to provide a quota of boys for education, especially in the less developed pastoralist districts. Government schools were also established, so that education was no longer the exclusive preserve of the missions. This late awakening had some impact on the training of the first generation of post-independence Southern leaders, but the decades of earlier neglect meant that there were few Southerners experienced in modern forms of administration and commerce when independence came in 1956.

2.3 Development disparities in the Sudan before 1947

There is a paradox in the Sudan, which is that the region which contains most of the nation's natural resources and arable land is also the least developed. This is due to a combination of colonial neglect and older practices of exploitation.

2.3.1 Differences between North & South

During much of the Mahdiyya, Britain and Egypt had successfully managed to limit the Sudan's access to external markets, and very little of the Sudan's standard exports (gum arabic, ivory, tamarind, animal skins) reached the outside world. With the Reconquest, international commerce resumed along with the return of Middle Eastern and European trading companies. Much of that early revival was in the hands of well-financed Greek, Syrian (Lebanese) and Armenian merchants, but northern Sudanese merchants also participated in this revival of both the internal and external trade.

The opening up of the southern Sudan through pacification was of some importance to this commercial revival. Not only did cattle taken in tribute or fines enter the livestock trade, but ivory accounted for some 10% of the Sudan's exports before World War One. Royalties collected on ivory sales and exports went mainly to the central, rather than the provincial governments. Southern Sudanese received little direct benefit from the legal ivory trade. It was only by dealing directly with traders whom the Sudan government considered illegal – Ethiopian and 'Swahili' merchants and poachers – that they derived any profit from ivory hunted in their territory.[4] Thus, from the very foundation of the Condominium the central government not only sanctioned but participated in the exploitation of its southern periphery, in an adaptation of the old Sudanic pattern.

During the first thirty years of the Condominium period not only did various merchants benefit from the increased prospects for trade throughout the country, but religious leaders and tribal notables in the northern Sudan benefited from an administrative system which allowed them to accumulate rights to labour and land, and which by the granting of government contracts gave them a stake in the new political economy of the country. The Mahdi's posthumous son, Sayyid Abd

---

[4] M. W. Daly, 'Economic development in southern Sudan 1899–1940', in *The Role of Southern Sudanese People in the Building of Modern Sudan* (Juba, 1986), p. 79; P. P. Garretson, 'Vicious cycles: ivory, slaves and arms on the new Maji frontier', and D. H. Johnson 'On the Nilotic frontier: Imperial Ethiopia in the southern Sudan, 1898–1936', both in D. Donham & W. James (eds.), *The Southern Marches of Imperial Ethiopia. Essays in History and Social Anthropology* (Cambridge, 1986). An often overlooked aspect of British rule in the South was the extent to which British and Egyptian army officials stationed there financed themselves through big game hunting, and especially the sale of ivory. The famous Sudanese nationalist, Ali Abd al-Latif, supplemented his income though elephant hunting when stationed in the South: see Yoshiko Kurita, *'Ali 'Abd al-Latif wa Thawra 1924* ('Ali Abd al-Latif and the Revolution of 1924') (Cairo, 1997). The granting of hunting licences and ivory concessions by provincial governors was sometimes a controversial matter, leading to allegations of corruption: see Jane Carruthers, *Wildlife & Warfare: The Life of James Stevenson-Hamilton* (Pietermaritzburg, 2001), p.137.

al-Rahman al-Mahdi, for instance, gained considerable wealth through government contracts for wood, fuel and meat, and became a staunch supporter of Britain as a result. The same pattern did not happen in the South, where commerce continued to be in the hands of Greek, Syrian, Armenian and Northern merchants. These were the people who later invested in large-scale production of grain and cash crops such as cotton and tobacco.

The Closed Districts Ordinance, introduced in the 1920s, was designed to facilitate the final abolition of the internal slave trade and to halt the spread of Islam into non-Islamic districts. The Ordinance did not apply to all of the South, nor, as is generally assumed, did it exclude all northern Sudanese or Muslims from the South. The area of Upper Nile Province from Renk to the north was specifically excluded, because of the established economic interests of Northern merchants there. The access of merchants to other districts of the South was controlled through the granting of licences, and while Greek and Syrian Christians were generally favoured in the issuing of these licences, a number of northern Sudanese traders (especially from the well capitalized Omdurman trading houses) also continued to trade, especially in Upper Nile Province, and sometimes through Muslim southern Sudanese agents. The Closed Districts Ordinance did nothing to stimulate a southern Sudanese commercial class to balance the influence of trading companies based in the northern Sudan.

Large-scale economic investment in the Sudan prior to World War Two was concentrated in the northern Sudan, especially in the Gezira scheme which enabled the Sudan to enter the international cotton trade. No similar schemes were attempted in the South until after the war, and then very hurriedly and with unsatisfactory results. By the time the Sudan was set on its path to independence, there were far greater disparities between the development of the northern and southern parts of the country as a whole than there had been at the end of the Mahdiyya. The southern Sudanese lagged far behind many of the northern Sudanese in education, economic development, and involvement in the government and administration of the country. In consequence, they lacked any real or potential voice in the direction of the country's affairs.

2.3.2 Uneven development within the South
There were, of course, disparities of development within the North as well as within the South. In the North those peoples who benefited most during the Condominium were found in the central Nile valley. Their grip on the levers of power within the Sudan continued throughout the post-independence period, so much so that the term *jallaba*, which originally meant a petty merchant, is now applied by Southerners as a general term descriptive of the people of the central Nile valley. Many parts of the North, both Muslim (in the east and far west) and non-Muslim (the Nuba Mountains and southern Blue Nile) suffered from economic neglect. In the South there was also uneven development. We have already noted some differences in the administration of the pastoralist and sedentary communities in the South. This was to be the basis of internal disparities which continue to affect southern Sudanese politics.

The agricultural peoples of the South were among the first to be 'pacified' by virtue of their accessibility and their limited ability to avoid government patrols. They were also among the first to be coopted into the colonial security system when the old Sudanese units were replaced with territorial units. Both the Equatorial Corps (which replaced the Sudanese battalions in the South) and the police were largely recruited from the Zande, Moru, Madi, Lotuko of Equatoria, and the Jur of Bahr al-Ghazal. The final pacification of the Nuer and Dinka of Upper Nile and Bahr al-Ghazal Provinces was accomplished largely by the Equatorial Corps (with substantial assistance from Northern army units in the case of the Nuer). The police who replaced the army in rural outposts throughout the South were also mainly recruited from Equatoria. Very few pastoralists were recruited into either service throughout the Condominium period, so the Southern security forces remained unrepresentative of the whole of the South.

Disparities in the distribution of educational institutions also affected the recruitment of Southerners into the lower echelons of the civil service. All the clerical staff in Bahr al-Ghazal Province by 1947 came from the Catholic schools in Raga and Wau and were all therefore from the minority Fartit and Jur peoples. The Dinka majority were unrepresented. Most of the few Dinka anywhere in the South who had access to education came from Bor District, where the CMS had a school at Malek. As the local economy of Bor has always been precarious, because of its susceptibility to floods, many Bor school children found greater opportunities in government service far earlier than other Dinka or Nuer pastoralists. This helps to explain the appearance of 'Bor Dinka domination' in the 1970s when the products of Malek took their places in administration and politics. Their numbers were still small relative to the growing need for trained Southerners in the clerical and technical services in the 1940s, and many of these posts were filled by Equatorians, even in Upper Nile.

The unequal distribution of educational facilities throughout the South and the uneven incorporation of educated persons within the structures of Native Administration were largely the results of administrative decisions taken by British officials either in Khartoum or in the provinces. Yet the disparities which were the result of these decisions were explained in terms of cultural differences or differences in 'mentality' among Southern peoples. The British in the 1940s commonly characterized the Nilotic Dinka and Nuer as conservative and backward, and the peoples of western Equatoria (particularly the Azande and the peoples of Yei River District) as progressive and advanced. These stereotypes linger today and have resurfaced as part of an Equatorian grievance at the loss of political dominance in southern Sudanese politics.

The educated Southerners in both the civil and security services were the ones who were suddenly called upon to articulate a Southern response to the plans for the Sudan's independence. They were thus the first to form the political leadership of the South, as unrepresentative as they were of the Southern population as a whole. We will return to the implications of this development later (Sections **3.2.3** and **4.5**).

As in the North, there were some places in the South that were more productive and prosperous than others. Because agriculture received priority attention for development, especially in the late 1940s, the agricultural areas benefited most from government intervention. Even though the Zande Scheme (the most ambitious development scheme in the South during the Condominium period) was badly conceived and ill-executed, farmers in Western Equatoria did benefit from the introduction of a variety of new crops over the years. Even if commercial links with the northern Sudan remained tenuous, much of Equatoria was linked with the flourishing formal and informal economies of the Congo and Uganda just across the border. These links only served to emphasize the overall potential of the South and its uneven, arguably misdirected, development.

3

Nationalism,   & the First Civil War
Independence   1942–72

3.1 Sudanese independence

The Sudan was the first African territory administered by Britain to be granted independence after World War Two. The Sudan's civil war, also the first in post-colonial Africa, began, with the Torit Mutiny, a few months before independence was attained on 1 January 1956. Both the timing and the terms of the Sudan's independence were less a product of nationalist mobilization than of international diplomacy, arising out of the Sudan's *de facto* status as a colony of two countries.[1] Britain was forced to take the issue of self-determination for the Sudan seriously when Egypt raised the issue of the Sudan's future status after the war, thus giving the early nationalist parties their opening.

3.1.1 Post-war Anglo-Egyptian competition in the Sudan
Britain's dominant position in the Sudan had been formalized in the Anglo-Egyptian Treaty of 1899, which recognized the Sudan as an Egyptian possession administered by British officials on behalf of the King of Egypt. The Governor-General was appointed by the Egyptian King on the recommendation of the British government. At the time Egypt was under British occupation. From 1898 to 1924 the Governor-General of the Sudan was also Commander-in-Chief (Sirdar) of the Egyptian army. The issue of sovereignty was thus academic, as the Egyptian crown could scarcely be said to be exercising full sovereignty in Egypt itself. During World War One the British further bolstered their position in the Sudan by rehabilitating Sayyid Abd al-Rahman al-Mahdi, the posthumous son of the Mahdi and leader of the Ansar sect, which was ideologically both anti-Turkish and anti-Egyptian. This opportunistic alliance on both sides not only undercut the appeal to Sudanese Muslims of Britain's war-time enemy, the Turkish Sultan, but it also provided a focus for anti-Egyptian sentiment in the years immediately following the war, and helped to further distance the British (through their patronage of 'SAR') from Egypt in Sudanese eyes. After the war,

[1] Veterans of the Sudan Political Service object to the terms 'colony' and 'colonial' being applied to British rule in the Sudan, as the Sudan was the responsibility of the Foreign, rather than the Colonial, Office. This distinction is merely technical, and the Foreign Office itself was in the habit of describing its administration in the Sudan as a 'colonial' or 'quasi-colonial' government.

Egypt achieved formal (though still qualified) independence from Britain, but its share in the administration of the Sudan was progressively limited, until all Egyptian soldiers and administrators were expelled from the country in 1924. From that time until 1946 the internal administration of the Sudan was a British administration, whose main decisions were made without reference to Egypt. Despite the fact that the 1936 Anglo-Egyptian Treaty (which was essentially a treaty of military alliance) allowed the return of a limited number of Egyptian troops to Khartoum, British officials in the Sudan firmly believed they were administering a British territory.

The re-negotiation of the Anglo-Egyptian treaty soon after the end of the Second World War revealed that Britain's international position concerning the Sudan was not as secure as had previously been believed. Although the treaty was mainly about British bases in Egypt and the Suez Canal, the Egyptians insisted on the public recognition of the Egyptian crown's sovereignty over the Sudan. The British government found that it could counter Egypt's strong case in international law only by invoking the principle of self-determination then favoured by the United Nations. Having rejected this principle when it was first raised by northern Sudanese graduates in 1942 (Section **3.1.2**), Britain now accepted the idea of Sudanese independence as a tactic in its confrontation with Egypt, long before a strong nationalist movement in the Sudan had even developed a compelling argument for independence as their right. ←

From 1946 until the overthrow of King Faruq in Egypt in 1952, the British in the Sudan were very conscious of having to keep ahead of the momentum for self-government, leading to independence, in order to keep a large section of the northern nationalist movement on their side against Egypt's claim of continued sovereignty over the Sudan. The Free Officers' coup of 1952 which brought Najib and Nasir to power in Egypt changed the political map, in that the new Egyptian government of its own accord renounced the claims to the Sudan of the monarch it had just deposed, and committed itself to the principle of self-determination for the Sudan, at the same time trying to persuade Sudanese to agree to union with Egypt. This improved Egypt's political standing among the northern Sudanese and meant that Britain had even less room for manoeuvre.[2]

The competition between Egypt and Britain for the hearts and minds of the northern Sudanese nationalists helps to explain why the nationalists themselves felt under no pressure to reach a genuine accommodation with southern Sudanese in order to broaden their political base within the country, or to increase the momentum for independence against imperial recalcitrance. It also helps to explain why British officials in Khartoum and London were disinclined to push for a separate formula for the South, or to insist on qualifications or guarantees for the South in any independence agreement. In the end, what was negotiated for the South was the transfer of the colonial structure intact from Britain to the northern Sudanese nationalists.

---

[2] Documents concerning Britain's advocacy of Sudanese self-determination in opposition to Egypt's claim of sovereignty, and the implication of this for colonial policy generally, can be found in BDEEP series B, vol. 5, D. H. Johnson, ed, *Sudan* (London, 1998), hereinafter referred to as BDEEP, *Sudan*.

3.1.2 *Limitations of the nationalist movement in the northern Sudan*

The Sudanese nationalist movement never achieved a mass following, and in fact was divided within itself about whether to follow a purely Sudanese nationalism, or a broader pan-Arab nationalism. It can be argued that it never fully pursued either.

In the 1920s a pan-Arabist form of nationalism, associated with Egyptian nationalism and proposing the Unity of the Nile Valley, was advocated by a small group of Sudanese intellectuals, mainly associated with the Egyptian army in the Sudan. One irony was that many were not, in fact, 'Arabs', but descendants of Sudanese slave soldiers ('detribalized blacks' in contemporary British terminology). Their most prominent leader, Ali Abd al-Latif, had been born in Egypt, the son of a Nuba soldier and a Dinka slave woman. Joining the Egyptian army as a cadet, he received much of his education in Egypt and Khartoum before being commissioned as an officer in the army. His being assigned to a Sudanese battalion was more a matter of his parents' origins than his own. In some ways, the pro-Egyptian nationalist movement of the early 1920s can be seen as more of an anti-British than a pro-Sudanese movement. The pro-Egyptian mutiny of troops in Khartoum and Omdurman in 1924 was quickly suppressed and the nationalist leaders arrested. Their greatest weakness was that they were divorced from the mainstream of Northern society by virtue of their origins. As the British administration had, by this time, built a firm alliance with tribal notables and leading merchant and religious families, the early nationalist movement had little appeal to those classes who would later take the lead in the independence movement.[3]

The independence leaders received their training in the Graduates' Congress, formed in the late 1930s, over a decade after the collapse of the first 'nationalist' rising. The Congress (open to any graduate with a secondary school education or higher) became a meeting place for northern Sudanese who were employed in the lower levels of the civil service. As early as 1942 it had raised the issue of self-determination for the Sudan after the war in a memo to the Civil Secretary following the publication of the Atlantic Charter. The Congress memo was rebuffed as an impertinence; the British objection that Congress did not represent all of the Sudanese was true enough, yet the brusqueness of the response only hardened attitudes in the Congress and led to the search for powerful political patrons outside of Congress.

Ismail al-Azhari was in the forefront of a movement to forge an alliance with Egypt, advocating union with Egypt. Those within the Congress opposed either to al-Azhari or Egypt sought the patronage of Sayyid Sir Abd al-Rahman al-Mahdi Pasha (to give him his full Sudanese, British and Egyptian honorific titles), and this brought Sayyid Sir Ali al-

---

[3] In recent years Ali Abd al-Latif has become a nationalist hero as an Arabic-speaking Muslim 'Southern' pioneer of Sudanese nationalism. This is more respect than he was accorded in his lifetime. In the late 1940s leading northern Sudanese nationalists still held him in contempt as the son of a slave. In an interview with Sayyid Abd al-Rahman al-Mahdi and the prominent Umma politician, Judge Muhammad Salah Shinqiti in 1946, Lord Stansgate reported, 'Shangetti [*sic*] boasted that the Sudanese had come from Arabia. He spoke very contemptuously of Abdel Latif (now in an insane asylum). He said his mother was a negress, his father was unknown, and that he, Latif, had at one time collected old tins from barracks' (document 116, BDEEP *Sudan*).

Mirghani, head of the Khatmiyya sect, out in support for al-Azhari, and *against* Sayyid Abd al-Rahman. The nationalists were thus divided according to ultimate goals, tactics, and personalities, the real questions being whether it was best (and even possible) to achieve independence for the Sudan on its own, or in formal union with Egypt, and whether total independence would lead to the resurrection of the hereditary leadership of the al-Mahdi family.

By their alliance with the two most influential religious sects of the day, the nationalists attached themselves to organizations which could, when called upon, mobilize an electorate far more efficiently than the rudimentary political network of the Graduates' Congress. But the nation-alists in the Congress were never able to develop a truly national political movement, and reliance on religious patrons and sectarian voting have dominated Sudanese electoral politics up to the present day. Effectively, this curtailed any real nationalist debate and any real attempt to define a broad Sudanese national identity. The politics of the centre were once again dominated by affiliations forged in the nineteenth century. Those who had not been part of those original affiliations were largely denied a voice in national affairs.

Sudanese nationalism was further undermined by the paradoxical dependence of the early political parties on the two colonial powers. Egypt provided the funds for the pro-unionist parties, and in 1952 insisted on their amalgamation into a single National Union Party (NUP), with whom the Egyptian government could negotiate. The Umma Party relied for its funds mainly on the private business of Sayyid Abd al-Rahman al-Mahdi, thus subordinating it not just to the Ansar sect, but to the personal interests of the al-Mahdi family. This did not prevent Sayyid Abd al-Rahman from seeking financial and other support from the Sudan and British governments, and while no money seems to have changed hands, the Umma Party did receive 'practical assistance' from the Sudan government during the 1953 election. The short-lived Socialist Republican Party, designed to attract pro-independence Khatmiyya voters away from the unionist parties, also received active encouragement from the Civil Secretary's office in Khartoum. The suggestion that southern Sudanese should form their own party came from, among others, Selwyn Lloyd, Minister of State for Foreign Affairs, during his visit to Khartoum in 1953.[4]

Al-Azhari became the leading nationalist in this period. He helped to set the agenda for debate with the British administration. He raised the issue of the southern Sudan as early as 1946 in terms which, in retrospect, were indicative of old attitudes. The southern Sudan, he told the Graduates' Congress, was necessary for the economic prosperity of *the North*. When he referred to the contribution of southern Sudanese to past Sudanese states in a memo to the Sudan government, all the examples he cited, though presented in the most positive language, were drawn from the Sudanese slave experience, especially military slavery. Before he raised this issue, the Foreign Office had assumed that there might be different timetables for self-

---

[4] For details of these contacts see BDEEP, *Sudan*, especially documents 226, 305, 311, 312, 314 & 319.

government in the North and in the South. Al-Azhari made it clear that nationalists would insist on taking control of the South.[5]

3.1.3 Implications for the southern Sudan

Up until 1947 Britain, or at least the Foreign Office, had not been fully committed to administering the South as part of the Sudan, entertaining the untested notion that it might eventually be linked to the East African colonies (see Section **2.2**).[6] With Egyptian and northern Sudanese nationalist insistence on a united Sudan, however, this option (never vigorously pursued) was closed. A Legislative Council was established in the North as a preliminary step towards a national parliament. Southern participation in this assembly was secured at the Juba Conference of 1947. The Juba conference highlighted just how unprepared the South was for any form of self-government. The delegates to the conference were chosen by the provincial governments and included a sergeant major of the police, a few chiefs, and some very junior administrators. Not all were educated to the same standard. Coming from different provinces they also lacked a common experience to draw them together, as the Graduates' Congress had initially drawn many northern Sudanese civil servants and intelligentsia together. Only on being reassured that civil service pay scales (then much lower in the South) would be regularized throughout the country did they agree to attend the Legislative Assembly. At no time in the discussions did the Civil Secretary, who convened and chaired the conference, allow the possibility of a separate administrative future for the South to be put forward as a practical alternative. It has since been claimed in the North that the Juba conference settled the question of the unity of the Sudan, but that question was merely deferred. As the Civil Secretary was to write many years later, 'No decisions could be made at the conference, since members had received no mandate from their peoples... The only decision resulting from the conference was taken by myself.'[7]

The policy of separate administration and separate development for the northern and southern Sudan which the government had followed for nearly twenty years meant that there were few Northerners in the new politically active class who had any practical experience of the South; nor were there many southern Sudanese who shared the experiences or outlook of this class. It is not necessarily the case that Northerners and Southerners would have developed a common national understanding had the policy of administrative segregation never been imposed, but the gulf of misunderstanding which separated North and South was all the greater as a result of that segregation.

---

[5] See documents 26 & 38, BDEEP, *Sudan*. Sayyid Abd al-Rahman al-Mahdi was rather more direct when he spoke to the Air Minister, Lord Stansgate: '*S.A.R.*, also, when the South was mentioned indicated that they, the *North*, could deal with it very satisfactorily. The people in the south were called slaves...' (document 116, BDEEP, *Sudan*).

[6] Throughout the early nationalist agitation for self-determination during the war years, and even as late as 1948, some members of the Foreign Office held the view that self-government would come later to the South than in the North, and ultimately the South might attain a separate independence. See documents 6, 11, 38 & 132 in BDEEP, *Sudan*.

[7] J. W. Robertson, *Transition in Africa: From Direct Rule to Independence* (London & Khartoum, 1974 & 1975), p. 107.

One effect of the inclusion of Southerners in the Legislative Assembly was that the most senior and experienced southern Sudanese administrators and teachers now entered national politics, and by virtue of their presence in Khartoum were withdrawn from active participation in the development of civil society and self-governing institutions in the South. This was among the reasons why so few Southerners of requisite seniority were available for the eventual 'Sudanization' of the civil service.

3.1.4 Terms of independence, 1953–6

The Legislative Assembly passed a self-government statute in 1952 which laid down the process by which the Sudan would elect its first self-governing legislature and the conditions which would have to be met for self-determination. The statute was originally an agreement between the pro-independence parties and the Southern and provincial members of the Assembly, in which the Northern members had rejected the creation of the post of minister for the South in the new government, but had accepted specific safeguards for the South enshrined in the Governor-General's reserve powers. As the Khatmiyya and pro-unionist parties had boycotted the Assembly their views were not directly represented, but the Sudan government had secured their participation in a Constitutional Amendment Commission which contributed to the final draft of the statute. Thus, in its final form, the statute did represent a compromise between all the main political groups within the Sudan, as brokered by the British members of the Sudan government.

The abolition of the Egyptian monarchy by the Free Officers' coup in July 1952 was followed by Egypt's renunciation of all claims to sovereignty over the Sudan. This paved the way to agreements between the new Egyptian government and the Northern parties in 1952 and 1953 on the terms for the forthcoming elections to the new parliament and the process by which the Sudan would finally choose its future. No southern Sudanese leaders were included in these agreements, which were made exclusively with leaders of the organized parties, or parties created – as in the case of the NUP – for the express purpose of negotiating with Egypt. At the insistence of the Umma Party delegates, Egypt proposed to remove the Governor-General's reserved administrative powers for the South, and in fact any special reference to the Southern provinces, from the self-government act. Sayyid Abd al-Rahman himself informed the Governor-General that 'the Southerners would have to accept [this agreement] in their best interests'.[8] In effect the Umma Party specifically repudiated the self-government statute it had helped to pass in the Legislative Assembly, where the South had been represented. Thus the issues which most concerned Southerners were once again decided without their participation.

The elections to the first self-governing parliament were held at the end of 1953 and were contested in the South by the newly formed Liberal Party, to which most Southern politicians belonged. Al-Azhari's NUP, which still advocated union with Egypt, also fielded some of its own candidates in the South (including a few Southerners), and campaigned with the assistance

---

[8] Documents 268 & 289 in BDEEP, *Sudan.* For events surrounding the All Parties Agreement and subsequent negotiations leading to the Anglo-Egyptian agreement of 1953 see documents 252, 255–8, 260–1, 263–5, 268–97.

of representatives from the Egyptian government, promising Southerners full representation at all levels of the civil service in the forthcoming Sudanization. The NUP won some seats in the South, but the majority went to the Liberal Party. Throughout the country the NUP was the largest single party elected to parliament, and therefore formed a government. The majority of seats, however, were divided between several parties opposed to union with Egypt and a number of independents, many of whom subsequently aligned themselves with the NUP. Al-Azhari formed a government as Prime Minister, under the Governor-General.

With an anti-unionist majority in parliament, union with Egypt became a dead letter, and Liberal Party representatives tried to raise the issue of a separate administrative status for the South, proposing federalism as a constitutional solution. The results of the Sudanization commission, announced after the election, were a severe disappointment, as Northerners were appointed to all the senior positions in the South. Most politically active Southerners saw this as the beginning of Northern colonization of the South. In October 1954 the southern Sudanese leadership – including members of the Liberal and National Unionist Parties, tribal chiefs from all three provinces, and representatives of the southern Sudanese diaspora in Khartoum – convened their own conference in Juba to discuss the political future of the Sudan as a whole, and the political future of the South within the Sudan. There it was resolved to vote for independence of the Sudan from Egypt, but on the condition that a federal system for the entire country be adopted, with an autonomous state in the South. Failing that, the South reserved its right of self-determination, which included the option of complete independence from the North.[9] But within parliament no consensus emerged on the form of the Sudan's permanent constitution, and the main Northern parties appeared willing to consider federation only as a tactic to secure Southern votes in the parliamentary manoeuvres which preceded independence.

3.1.5 The 1955 Mutiny

There was thus widespread discontent in the South as a result of the outcome of the 1954 elections and the Sudanization process. The rapid increase of Northerners in the South as administrators, senior officers in the army and police, teachers in government schools and as merchants, increased Southern fears of Northern domination and colonization. There was some economic hardship also in Western Equatoria around Yambio with the winding down of economic schemes started in the late 1940s as part of the attempt to help the South 'catch up' with the North. Soldiers of the Equatorial Corps, whose British officers had only recently been replaced by northern Sudanese officers, feared that they would be disarmed and moved to the North. Some Southerners now began to see union with Egypt as the last chance to curb the power of the North, now that the British had been physically removed from almost all positions of influence and authority in the country. The Egyptian government, which still hoped for union between the two countries, encouraged disaffected Southerners in this belief.

[9] Minutes of Juba Conference, 18–21 October 1954, in PRO FO 371/108326, no. 193, and document 369 in BDEEP, *Sudan*.

This general dissatisfaction was most actively expressed in Equatoria, where the main economic activity had been concentrated, and from where most recruits for the army and police were drawn. After several weeks of growing tension in the summer of 1955 (including the shooting of demonstrating textile workers at Nzara, outside Yambio), a mutiny broke out among the garrison at Torit, headquarters of the Equatorial Corps. The mutiny spread to other garrisons of Southern soldiers and police, including those based in Malakal, though not Wau. It was not, however, a well organized or coordinated movement. Soldiers in Torit and elsewhere in Equatoria killed not only some of their Northern officers, but Northern administrators, Northern merchants, and their families. Very few Southerners were killed at this time.

The mutiny had its most disruptive effect in Equatoria, because this was where most mutineers were based and where they came from. In Bahr al-Ghazal and Upper Nile Provinces, the Equatorian police and soldiers were generally not regarded with great sympathy by the Nilotic Dinka and Nuer. Equatorians were not necessarily seen as colonial collaborators and oppressors, but they had been part of the coercive apparatus of the colonial administration. Thus, while the mutiny was an expression of an anxiety which was general throughout the South, the mutineers themselves were unable to mobilize that discontent behind their leadership.

Many missionaries, especially the Italian Catholics at Torit, risked their own lives to protect Northern officials. Some British missionaries of the Church Missionary Society were among those who fled to Uganda and urged Britain to reassert its authority in the South in order to avert a Northern retaliatory 'bloodbath'.

The British government refused. To send its own troops into the Sudan would have invited Egypt, still the other co-dominal power, to do the same, and Britain did not want to do anything to increase Egypt's influence in the Sudan. Instead, British officials assisted al-Azhari's government and the Sudanese army to restore order in Torit and other parts of the South. Most mutineers and their families fled to Uganda, still a British colony, where the government refused to repatriate them, fearing the reaction such forcible repatriation might produce among related peoples along the border. Some mutineers were caught by the Sudanese army, tried and executed. There were also reports of army retaliation against the civilian population. It is still difficult to assess the evidence for this: Southerners believe that more Southerners than Northerners died in the mutiny and its aftermath; Northerners, supported by the lack of any mention of retaliation in the report of the official enquiry, believe the opposite.

The Sudanese drew different conclusions from the mutiny. Egyptian encouragement of Southern disaffection was overlooked (partly because the NUP itself owed much of its political position to Egyptian support), and the foreign missionaries took Egypt's place in northern Sudanese nationalist demonology. Though no evidence was uncovered in the enquiry which followed of any missionary propaganda urging Southerners to rebel, most Northerners continued to believe that if the missionaries did not actually encourage the rebellion, they at least did nothing to discourage it. The Uganda government's refusal to extradite the mutineers also seemed to point to an imperialist conspiracy. Southern Sudanese regard the mutiny as the beginning of the Southern struggle against Northern oppression, but memories of the mutiny still divide Southerners themselves. Equatorians base their claim to having founded and led the Southern 'nationalist' movement on the overwhelmingly Equatorian composition of the mutineers. They have presented the refusal of Dinka and Nuer to be drawn into the sporadic acts of violence which followed the news of the mutiny in Torit as evidence of Nilotic backwardness and even of collaboration with the North. There is little evidence to suggest that later guerrilla and exile leaders sought to draw any conclusions from the disorganized planning of the mutineers and their lack of widespread popular support; these weaknesses continued throughout the early armed struggle of the 1960s.

3.2 Southern disappointment & the beginning of the first civil war

The mutiny only served to hasten, rather than delay, Sudanese independence, as it brought home forcibly to the British government the paradox of its continued vague responsibility in the Sudan without any longer having the power to control or shape events. Britain was thus anxious to grant formal independence, even before the Sudanese parliament had agreed on a permanent constitution, and initiated a circumvention of the legal procedure for self-determination that had already been agreed between the British and Egyptian governments.[10] Southern politicians were persuaded to go along with this after the Sudanese government gave them a general assurance of exercising restraint in restoring order in the South, and a specific promise that a federal constitution would be given serious consideration.[11] Thus, the date of independence was brought forward, and the Sudan became a fully independent nation, with numerous issues of its nationhood still unresolved, on 1 January 1956.

The final paradox of Sudanese independence was that it was thrust upon the Sudan by a colonial power eager to extricate itself from its residual responsibilites. It was not achieved by a national consensus expressed through constitutional means. A precedent was set that has haunted Sudanese politics ever since: the precedent of taking the popular will for granted, and therefore circumventing agreed legal procedures in all major constitutional issues. The first post-independence Constituent Assembly was dissolved in 1958 rather than allow it to take a decision on federalism; the referendum in the South was aborted in 1982 rather than let the people of the South register their opposition to the subdivision of the Southern Region; parliamentary government was overthrown in 1989 rather than let it reach a compromise over the Islamic state. These acts

---

[10] For the circumvention of the self-determination process see documents 410, 413–15, 420–5, 428–32, 435–7, in BDEEP, *Sudan.*

[11] It has also been claimed that a number of Southern parliamentarians were blackmailed into voting for independence because their own alleged involvement in the 1955 disturbances were then under investigation.

were all committed by Sudanese leaders; but they learned from Britain at the very inception of the Sudan's independence the rewards for ignoring democratic and constitutional procedures.

3.2.1 Failure to achieve a federal constitution

The Sudanese gained independence with a temporary constitution drafted for them by a British academic constitutional expert. Two issues arose which were to prevent agreement on a permanent constitution: whether the Sudan should be a federal or a unitary state, and whether it should have a secular or an Islamic constitution. We will deal with the first question here.

Most of the early Southern politicians favoured federalism as a way of protecting the Southern provinces from being completely subordinated to a Northern-dominated central government. The argument most Northerners offered against federalism was that it was the first step towards separation. The political and legislative inexperience of the South's leaders told against them. Few could translate the slogan of federalism into a concrete proposal. Many were distracted by personal rivalries. They also got a reputation in Khartoum for being easily manipulated and corruptible. For form's sake, however, one or two Southerners were given ministries in successive governments, the Minister for Animal Resources becoming the token Southern seat in any cabinet.

The rejection of the idea of federation by the government and the Northern parties shortly after independence galvanized the southern Sudanese political movement into more effective organization. A new party, the Federal Party, was formed to contest the first post-independence elections in 1957, and it succeeded in winning almost all of the South's seats in parliament. Along with some of the South's veteran politicians, it brought in a new generation of leaders, such as the Catholic Priest, Fr. Saturnino Lohure. Learning something from past failures, the Federal politicians sought to establish alliances with politicians from other underdeveloped regions of the Sudan, in both the east and the west. It may be going too far to say that the Federal Party had formed an effective political coalition with these other regions, but the momentum behind federalism was one of the main reasons for the Umma government's handover to the army in 1958. This not only brought an end to civilian rule and electoral politics, it put an end to any public debate concerning Sudanese national identity and the most suitable constitutional arrangement for the country.

3.2.2 The origins of armed struggle in the South

The military government of General Abbud followed a policy of Arabization and Islamization in the South, focusing on education. There was a programme of school building, financed by USAID. Mission schools were transferred to government control, and Arabic was progressively introduced as the medium of instruction (English remained the medium of instruction even in Northern secondary schools until the Arab-Israeli war of 1967). Conversion to Islam was encouraged, especially among students. The activities of Christian missionaries were placed under increasing restriction, until all in the South were expelled in 1964.

Ironically, conversions to Christianity increased dramatically once the churches were subjected to this government assault.[12]

During this time there had been only a desultory military campaign against the few 1955 mutineers who remained hiding in the bush, but the army began to burn villages in the late 1950s. Such repressive activities, especially those aimed at educated southern Sudanese, increased opposition to the government. This was met by further repressive action, including arrest and torture of civilians. In 1960–2 a number of senior political figures (including Fr. Saturnino Lohure, Aggrey Jaden, Joseph Oduho and William Deng), as well as a far greater number of students, left for the bush and neighbouring countries where they joined with the remaining mutineers to form both the exile political movement and the core of a guerrilla army. The exile movement eventually called itself the Sudan African Nationalist Union (SANU) in emulation of the East African nationalist parties. The guerrillas became known colloquially by the vernacular name of a type of poison – Anyanya. It is from this time, rather than the 1955 mutiny, that one can date the true beginning of the Sudan's first civil war.

By modern standards, the first years of the war were very modestly conducted. The guerrillas were knit together very loosely and had no external military support, arming themselves mainly by theft from police outposts, the occasional ambush of army patrols, or through the defection of Southern police or soldiers. Ironically, the Anyanya obtained their first substantial quantity of military hardware only after the 1964 overthrow of Abbud, and then only through the unwitting generosity of the Sudanese government. The transitional government which replaced Abbud adopted a more interventionist foreign policy in the region and, along with other Arab states, supported the Simba movement in neighbouring Congo. Shipments of weapons sent overland through Sudan to the Simbas fell into Anyanya hands. When the Simbas were subsequently driven out of the Congo into the Sudan early in 1965, the Anyanya relieved them of the rest of their arms. Thus for the first (but not the last) time, international political conflicts began to shape the internal conflict in the Sudan.

The public political objective of SANU was 'self-determination', which had been offered to the Sudan as a whole, but not to the South. Behind this lay the conviction that, given a free choice, the South would opt for independence. By taking this position, SANU ran directly counter to the newly-formed Organization of African Unity's pledge to maintain the old colonial borders of the emerging states. It is largely for this reason that SANU's slogan was self-determination rather than secession. Throughout the 1960s, political sympathy and support for southern Sudanese was very limited in Africa. Even when Tanzania supported Biafran secession, it did not extend the principle to the Sudan. Southern Sudanese grievances and reports of the Sudan government's oppression

---

[12] Baptisms into the Catholic church at Isoke and Torit increased dramatically between 1960 and 1964, and the Christian population nearly trebled from around 38,000 to 90,000 (Karl-Johan Lundström, 'The Lotuho and the Verona Fathers. A Case Study of Communication in Development', doctoral dissertation, Uppsala, 1990, p. 191). In the southern Blue Nile conversion to the local evangelical church also rose after the missionaries were expelled (Wendy James, *The Listening Ebony. Moral Knowledge, Religion, and Power among the Uduk of Sudan* (Oxford, 1988), pp. 241–52).

were received with embarrassment by other African nationalists, and the fact that only the Union of South Africa and Malawi gave them publicity to counter anti-apartheid propaganda did little to win the southern Sudan more friends on the continent.

3.2.3 Problems of disunity among Southerners

The leadership of the exile movement in the early 1960s was predominantly Equatorian. Both Fr. Saturnino and Joseph Oduho were Lotuko from Torit, and Aggrey Jaden was a Bari from Juba. William Deng was the first influential Dinka leader, coming from Tonj in Bahr al-Ghazal. Uganda continued to receive most southern Sudanese refugees, and the majority of exiles therefore were Equatorians who had easier access to East Africa than Southerners from Bahr al-Ghazal and Upper Nile. The exile movement achieved a loose-knit unity at this time. The first major split came in the disagreement over how to respond to the downfall of Abbud and the return to civilian rule in Khartoum.

Abbud had no effective economic policies for the Sudan, and the country's economy was badly affected by fluctuations in the international price of cotton, its main export. When political restrictions, which were by now commonplace in the South, began to impinge on other parts of the country, demonstrations were held in Khartoum. Abbud stepped down in October 1964, to be replaced by a caretaker civilian government. With the resumption of civilian rule came the legalization of political parties. The Southern Front was formed in Khartoum. Led by Clement Mboro, a veteran of the 1947 Juba conference, it was composed mainly of a new generation of educated southern Sudanese civil servants. Mboro was made Minister of the Interior in the caretaker government, and the exiles were invited to return to the Sudan to take part in a round-table discussion on the resolution of the Southern problem.

This ultimately caused a split in SANU. The leaders returned for the Round Table Conference in Khartoum early in 1965, but only William Deng abandoned the call for self-determination and stayed on as leader of SANU 'Inside' to campaign for a federal solution. Aggrey Jaden and Joseph Oduho returned to Uganda as leaders of SANU 'Outside', maintaining separation as their goal. Fr. Saturnino Lohure confined himself increasingly to military matters in the guerrilla army, until he was killed by the Ugandan army when recrossing the border in 1967.

The resumption of electoral politics in the Sudan and the departure of William Deng left the exile movement in disarray and prone to internal personal leadership disputes. Jaden and Oduhu fell out, but joined forces again to replace SANU 'Outside' with the Kampala-based Azania Liberation Front in 1965. The guerrillas' two main military commanders, Emilio Tafeng (a former mutineer), and Joseph Lagu (a former lieutenant in the Sudanese Army), were at odds with each other, and in the mid-1960s, exile politicians were periodically arrested by Anyanya guerrillas in the bush. The Azania Liberation Front was replaced by the Southern Sudan Provisional Government in 1967, briefly headed by Jaden and enjoying the support of Tafeng, but also including for the first time a number of younger Dinka leaders such as Gordon Muortat Mayen and Akwot Atem. Jaden left the movement, claiming domination by the

'Dinka Clique'. In 1969 the SSPG renamed itself the Nile Provisional Government, and Joseph Lagu formed his own Anyanya National Organization. Other small groups of guerrillas elsewhere in the South kept themselves to themselves or formed their own 'republics.' Fighting between Anyanya factions was common.

Examples of the conflicting but inflated claims of exile politicians at this time are recorded in the East African newspapers in the six months after Nimairi came to power and issued his June declaration on self-government for the South (Section **3.4.1**). First, two members of the Azania Liberation Front in Kampala announced that they were returning to Khartoum, as 'it was the responsibility of Southerners to fill the posts that would be offered in a self-governing Southern Sudan'. They were denounced by Barri Wanji, 'Foreign Affairs Minister' of the Nile Provisional Government, who claimed that the Azania Liberation Front had been defunct for three years. Two weeks later Eliaba Surur, 'Finance Minister and Acting Information Minister' of the Anyidi Revolutionary Government announced the overthrow of the Nile Provisional Government and its replacement by the new government under General Emilio Tafeng. The council of the new government included Aggrey Jaden (Foreign Minister) and Akwot Atem (Interior Minister). Aggrey Jaden, then living in Nairobi, denounced his inclusion in the council of the Anyidi government as 'ridiculous and meaningless'. Gordon Muortat Mayen, President of the Nile Provisional Government, denied that he had been overthrown. Shortly after this, Colonel Joseph Lagu circulated an open letter to the Pope on behalf of his Anyanya South Sudan freedom fighters. Gordon Muortat and Barri Wanji then called a press conference in Kampala to announce that the Nile Provisional Government was willing to negotiate with Khartoum, but not on the terms of self-government for the South. Then, in November Barri Wanji called another press conference in Kampala to announce that the Nile Provisional Government would shortly launch conventional warfare in the southern Sudan, and that Tafeng would be captured 'dead or alive'.[13]

It is little wonder that a year later when Colonel Lagu and other provincial military leaders formed a united military command under the Southern Sudan Liberation Front, with the political wing subordinated to the military (Section **3.4.2**), many southern Sudanese welcomed that development with relief.

3.3 Constitutional issues

3.3.1 From the Round Table Conference to the Constituent Assembly
The Round Table Conference on the South which was convened in Khartoum in March 1965 revealed the gulf which still separated southern and northern Sudanese political leaders. Both factions of SANU and the Southern Front advocated holding a plebiscite in the South to determine southern Sudanese opinion. They differed on what they hoped the

---

[13] Taken from *The Uganda Argus, The East African Standard*, and *The Daily Nation*, 25 June–23 July, 14 November, 1969.

outcome would be, the Southern Front being rather closer to the exile wing of SANU than to William Deng. But the delegates from the main Northern parties rejected any form of self-determination, federalism, or regional autonomy. No agreement was reached, and no minutes were ever released, so the full scale of that disagreement was not immediately apparent.[14] As at Juba in 1947 and so many other times afterwards, a decision was deferred, this time to a Twelve Man Committee. However, as was also later to be the case in 1985–6, the Northern parties were really only interested in holding elections to decide who would form the next government. The state of insecurity in the South meant that the 1965 elections were held in the North only. The Southern parties were not only ignored at the conference, but were effectively denied a voice in the new parliament.

From 1965 to 1969 the war in the South was fought with growing ferocity, while in Khartoum coalition governments rose and fell with increasing rapidity. The first substantial massacres of Southern civilians took place during the period of the first Umma government in 1965. Both SANU and the Southern Front alternately boycotted and contested the succession of elections held in the South. The Southern Front (led by Clement Mboro and Abel Alier) had the reputation of being more radical than William Deng's SANU, but this was less a matter of the policies the two parties advocated as it was the more uncompromising approach the Southern Front took concerning elections and participating in government. The Southern Front drew its membership from all three Southern provinces. Many of its members were also in touch with the Anyanya and forwarded them supplies. SANU was strongest in Bahr al-Ghazal, William Deng's province. In the 1968 elections William Deng agreed to an electoral alliance with Sadiq al-Mahdi's faction of the Umma Party, but Deng was assassinated by the army shortly after being returned by his own constituency. Deng was respected by many Northerners as a 'moderate' Southern leader, and his murder, after agreeing to an alliance with a Northern party, was convincing proof to many Southerners that no compromise with the North was possible.

After William Deng's death, both SANU and the Southern Front joined forces with other independents (including those representing the Nuba and the Beja) in the Constituent Assembly to argue for devolutionary powers to regional governments and against the adoption of an Islamic constitution. It was not a strong coalition, and when finally voted down on both issues, the representatives of the two Southern parties, led by Abel Alier, walked out of the Assembly. Shortly after this, on 25 May 1969, a combination of Free Officers in the army, Communists and Socialists, with Colonel Jaafar Nimairi as their figurehead, staged a coup.

3.3.2 The religious policy of the Khartoum governments

Until the late 1940s the principle of the separation of religion from the state, under which the British governed the Sudan, seems to have been

---

[14] The secretary of the Round Table Conference was the Northern academic, Mohamed Omer Beshir. Some Southern delegates to the conference later blamed him for failing to produce a final set of public minutes, while presenting his own interpretation of the conference's outcome (with which they disagreed) in his subsequent book, *The Southern Sudan, Background to Conflict* (London, 1968).

widely accepted by Muslim Sudanese leaders. Following the end of World War Two, a new religious element entered Sudanese national politics, and the introduction from Egypt of a Sudanese branch of the Muslim Brothers (later to become the National Islamic Front), with its advocacy of a theocratic society, was indicative of this change. In a revealing comment to British officials, Sayyid Abd al-Rahman al-Mahdi officially deplored this development, saying that the Muslim Brothers' platform of uniting spiritual with temporal rule was bound to appeal even to some of his own 'less sophisticated' followers.[15] It was a perceptive, even prophetic, observation.

The sectarian nature of Northern political parties meant that the mobilization of votes in the North was conducted essentially along lines of religious affiliation. This is one reason why Islamization of the South has been a constant policy of all governments dominated by the sectarian parties (NUP/DUP, Umma, NIF). In the 1950s Islamization and Arabization were presented as necessary policies to create national unity. By the 1960s, however, the positions of the major parties had evolved to advocacy of an Islamic state. As this would have denied full legal and political rights to non-Muslims, it was opposed by Southerners, people from various marginalized areas of the North, and some liberal and radical Northerners.

Parliamentary government in 1965–9 was dominated by a series of coalition governments, with leadership oscillating between the Umma Party and the Democratic Unionist Party (a revived NUP). Splits within both parties (especially the fracturing of the Umma following a breach within the al-Mahdi family) made these coalitions unstable. The party of the Muslim Brothers, the Islamic Charter Front, was much smaller at this time than either of the two main Southern parties, and there were strong challenges to the main parties from independent groups in some parts of eastern and western Sudan. The parties' own internal weaknesses, the insecurity of their hold on power, and the challenges they faced from non-sectarian parties in the remoter regions, made them less willing to compromise on the issue of religion, this being the only appeal which justified their contention for power.

Sadiq al-Mahdi's alliance with William Deng's SANU (above, Section **3.3.1**) seems to have sprung more from the need to secure parliamentary support against his rivals in his own party than from the liberalism for which he was then given credit. His religious policy was uncompromising in its commitment to conversion of the South to Islam. His most liberal statement was a public appeal to the Pope to agree with him to convert all southern Sudanese into 'believers', whether Muslim or Christian. Speaking to Muslim audiences outside of the Sudan, however, he was on record as declaring that the southern Sudan must be converted to Islam. He, too, supported the draft for an Islamic constitution.

Conversion to Christianity accelerated in the South in the 1960s once the foreign missionaries were expelled, and the churches were seen to be under assault from the government, rather than collaborating with it, as in the Condominium days. This pattern was to be repeated in the 1980s and 1990s when new Islamization policies were imposed from Khartoum.

[15] Sudan Political Intelligence Summary No. 55, December 1945, PRO FO 371/53328.

3.4 The road to negotiation, 1969–71

3.4.1 Political developments in Khartoum

The group which took power on 25 May 1969 was itself an unstable coalition of radical factions. It immediately demonstrated a different approach to the war in the South by announcing that the conflict would be solved by political, rather than military means, and by issuing a declaration in June 1969 outlining its plans for regional self-government. A southern Sudanese Communist, Joseph Garang, was appointed as the new Minister for Southern Affairs.[16] Clement Mboro of the Southern Front was imprisoned (on charges of corruption), but Abel Alier (also of the Southern Front) was included in the new cabinet.

There was a confused response by Southern exiles to the June 1969 declaration, as we have already seen above (Section **3.2.3**). Joseph Garang was unable to persuade the most influential Southern leaders to negotiate. There was also a jockeying for position within the Revolutionary Council. The result was that throughout 1970 and much of 1971 there was an intensification of fighting in the southern Sudan. Then, in July 1971 the Communist members of the Council tried to push Nimairi aside in their own coup. This coup failed after three days, Nimairi returned to power, and a massive purge of Communists took place. Joseph Garang was executed along with other leading Communists. He was replaced as Minister for Southern Affairs by Abel Alier.

Nimairi, who was opposed by the traditional parties, now lacked the support of one of the main factions which brought him to power. Unpopular in the North, he needed a new ally to keep him in power. This gave him an added incentive to reach an accommodation with the South. Abel Alier, a lawyer by profession who had been involved throughout the 1960s in drawing up a comprehensive plan for regional autonomy for the South, was better placed than Joseph Garang had been to contact the exiled Southern opposition, given the old contacts between the Southern Front and the guerrillas and the prominence of many former Southern Front members in the exile movement. The new willingness of the government to negotiate was paralleled by a new ability of the Southern guerrilla movement to negotiate with one voice.

3.4.2 Political developments in the South

The position of the southern Sudanese guerrilla movement improved dramatically after 1969. The Sudan government's more militant espousal of Arab causes after the 1967 Arab–Israeli war meant that not only did the Ethiopian government become more sympathetic to the Southern guerrillas (because of the Sudan's support for Eritrean secessionists), but Israel, too, became interested in the Sudan's civil war. With the overthrow of Obote in Uganda in 1970, a much more friendly Idi Amin came to power. He not only came from the ambiguous border region between the Sudan and Uganda, but he had already recruited many southern Sudanese into the Ugandan army, and was also, at that time, a willing

---

[16] Joseph Garang, a Luo from Bahr al-Ghazal, is no relation to John Garang, a Dinka from Upper Nile. 'Garang' is a common name among the Dinka and is also found among many of their neighbours, such as the Luo and Nuer.

client of the Israelis. The guerrillas were thus secured a regular supply of arms, plus access to modern training.

Joseph Lagu was Israel's main beneficiary, and using their supplies he persuaded a number of provincial Anyanya commanders to join him throughout 1970. He thus engineered a series of internal coups which left the old exile politicians without any military constituency. In January 1971 he formed the Southern Sudan Liberation Front (later renamed the Southern Sudan Liberation Movement) under the command of his much expanded Anyanya Armed Forces. The unified command, with a secure supply of weapons, not only subordinated the fractious politicians to the military wing, but also began to show greater military strength and activity in engagements outside Equatoria. Not all of the officers of this rejuvenated Anyanya army were enthusiastic about negotiating with the government, but when the government accepted the SSLM's demands to recognize it as an equal negotiating partner, and to meet in a 'neutral' African country (in this case, Ethiopia), the conditions for negotiation appeared to be far better than they had ever been before.

4

The Addis Ababa ▮ & the
Agreement ▮ Regional Governments
▮ 1972–83

4.1 The Addis Ababa negotiations

The Addis Ababa Agreement, negotiated in February 1972 between the government and the Southern Sudan Liberation Movement (SSLM), not only brought peace to the Sudan, but, as a unique resolution to civil war never before achieved in post-colonial Africa, brought great international acclaim to the nation and its leaders. Within eleven years it was repudiated by two of its principal beneficiaries: Nimairi and Lagu. Before its demise it was seen as a failure by most southern Sudanese. Many outside observers (and many northern Sudanese as well) have misjudged the political climate of the South by thinking that the second civil war can be brought to an end by a return to the 1972 Agreement's provisions for regional autonomy. To understand why this is not possible we must look not only at the failures in the implementation of the Agreement, but the issues the Agreement itself failed to resolve.

Negotiations were proposed with a united Sudan as the one precondition. Many exiled Southerners were unhappy about abandoning the goal of independence, and there was a clear difference of understanding between the government and SSLM delegations about the 'regional autonomy' then proposed for negotiation. To the SSLM 'autonomy' meant federation, and they came armed with a proposal for a full federal structure. In the end they were offered, and finally accepted, something far less in what became the Southern Regional Government.

At the beginning of the negotiations it was proposed that the two delegations form into political, economic and security sub-committees to draft the relevant proposals under each heading for inclusion in the final agreement. The SSLM requested that no economic sub-committee be formed, since its delegation was too small to be sub-divided into three. The result was that the political sub-committee reached rapid agreement on the terms of the establishment of the regional government, and the security sub-committee was able eventually to provide a basis for ending the fighting and absorbing the guerrilla forces into the national army and other security branches. There was no separate discussion of the economic powers of the new regional government, nor of national development policy as it applied to the South.

The SSLM delegation initially proposed that the whole country be divided into a Northern and a Southern region, with a single federal government in which both regions participated. They argued that without a federal system, the central government would in practice be a Northern government, rather than a national one, and they felt it was vitally important 'to define the sort of country they were going to have' by defining the government structure. Mansour Khalid, then a member of the government's delegation, ended any further discussion of federal status for the North by insisting that 'they could not impose Regionalism on the North when they had not asked for it'. The question then became one of defining what powers should be reserved for the central and regional governments. The SSLM was anxious to define clearly and in detail the powers and limitations of the central government, leaving all remaining powers to the regional government. In the end the negotiations centred on defining the qualified autonomy of the regional government.[1]

The regional government created by the Addis Ababa Agreement consisted of a Regional Assembly which was empowered to elect and remove the President of the High Executive Council (HEC), subject to the confirmation of the President of the Republic (Chapter V Article 13.i, Chapter VI Article 19). The Regional Assembly could also vote to request the President of the Republic to exempt the Southern Region from any national legislation it considered detrimental to Regional interests.

The Agreement granted the Southern Regional Government powers to raise revenues from local taxation (including corporation taxes, business profits tax and royalties), and promised additional revenues from the central government. The regional government was specifically denied the right to legislate or exercise any power over economic planning (Chapter IV Article 7.viii). It was able to legislate in matters of mining, but 'without prejudice to the right of the Central Government in the event of the discovery of natural gas and minerals' (Chapter V Article 11.xiv).

The most contentious issue in the negotiations was the question of security for the Southern Region. The SSLM, in proposing to divide the nation into two regions, proposed two regional armies in addition to a third national army, to which the regions would contribute. The government rejected this proposal, and in negotiating an alternative, the SSLM delegates made it clear that Southern soldiers should remain in the South for the protection of Southern civilians from the Northern army. They accepted the retention of an equal number of Northern soldiers to help allay the fears of the central government that a Southern garrison composed entirely of former guerrillas was a potential secessionist threat. The interim provisions for security were set out in a separate protocol (Protocols on Interim Arrangements, Chapter II). The Southern Command was to be composed of equal numbers of Northern and Southern troops.

The semi-autonomous region thus had qualified legislative authority, poorly defined economic powers, and an ambiguous understanding about the nature of the security forces. Most Southerners assumed that integration of the two armed forces would take place *after* a period of five years, that the proportions of Northern and Southern soldiers in the Southern Command would remain equal, and that Southern troops would

---

[1] All quotations are taken from 'Minutes of Conference on the Southern Sudan held in Addis Ababa between Sudan Government and Southern Liberation Movement', 1972.

remain garrisoned in the South. The army insisted that the absorption process would be completed *within* five years. There were no clear provisions in the Agreement for the status of the army after that period.

The Addis Ababa Agreement was ratified and embodied in the Regional Self-Government Act in March 1972, and it was incorporated in the Permanent Constitution of 1973. The constitution recognized a strong executive presidency for the nation as a whole, and appeared to safeguard the Agreement by requiring the holding of a referendum in the South before any amendment to it could be made. This set up a fundamental contradiction within the constitutional structure between the central and regional governments. The powers reserved for the president were a matter of concern for many northern Sudanese, but since at that time southern Sudanese leaders tended to regard Nimairi as their personal protector against Northern opponents of the Addis Ababa Agreement, Southerners in general were not only willing to let Nimairi have the powers he claimed, but were glad that he had them.

4.2 Security

The implementation of the cease-fire and the gradual absorption of the Anyanya guerrillas into various security branches were the most delicate tasks confronting the national and regional governments. There were many guerrillas in the bush who were unwilling to comply with the security provisions in the Addis Ababa Agreement. There were others who complied but were still suspicious of the army and wished to remain in their own units indefinitely. Among those who were absorbed into the army, many were dissatisfied with the low ranks they received, and still others were disappointed at not being absorbed into the army at all. Most of the older, more experienced fighters had low formal educational qualifications and did not receive the consideration which they thought their service in the bush merited. Absorption into the army was directed by a joint commission made up of senior national army and ex-Anyanya officers. The pace and direction of the integration of the two armies remained under central government control. Provisions were also made for absorbing a number of Anyanya into the police, prison service, wildlife and forestry departments, all of which were under the control of the regional government and were all-Southern bodies.

The process of integration was marked by a number of violent incidents. Guerrillas often feared for their own safety in a Northern-dominated army; many were concerned lest they be transferred for duty to the North; and a significant number still disliked Northerners after years of fighting them. A number of Southern leaders felt that the pace of integration was proceeding too quickly and should be slowed down, so that the guerrillas' suspicions could be allayed. As the five year integration period (insisted on by the army) drew to a close, a number of serious incidents took place (see Appendix). There were no full-scale mutinies, and many of the grievances of soldiers were localized and highly personal. There were, however, numbers of ex-Anyanya soldiers who refused to accept integration, and some of these returned to exile, principally in Ethiopia. These soldiers were to play an important role in the revival of guerrilla activity in the 1980s (Section **5.1**).

The integration of the Anyanya into the army was accomplished within the five year period, but many in the region were still dissatisfied. While the full quota of Anyanya (just over 6000) were absorbed into the army, the number of Northern troops in the South was not reduced to 6000; many senior ex-Anyanya officers were retired early or purged from the army; and some ex-Anyanya soldiers were transferred for duty out of the South. This last issue was increasingly resisted in the early 1980s and was one of the factors contributing to the Bor mutiny in May 1983, immediately preceding the presidential abolition of the Southern Region.

4.3 Electoral politics in the regional governments, 1973–81

Throughout the eleven-year period of the Southern Regional Government, Nimairi intervened in every election for president of the High Executive Council. The fact that a good deal of central government interference occurred with the acquiescence or active participation of Southern leaders (both the Alier and Lagu factions sought Nimairi's support to oust each other) did not alter the perception of many Southerners that the constitutional guarantees for Southern autonomy were too weak.

During Alier's presidency of the HEC in 1972–8, there was growing criticism of what was seen as his deference to Nimeiri and the central government over many issues, and his willingness to allow the central government to define by precedent restrictions on the regional government's authority. Throughout the eleven years of regional government, the Southern Region exercised no autonomy in economic planning or education, two highly sensitive issues, and the regional ministries were regarded in Khartoum merely as departments of the central government ministries.

There was considerable dissatisfaction with the failure of the central government to fulfil its financial obligations to the Southern Region. During the lifetime of the first regional government, the region received annually on average only 23.2% of the central government's allocated grant for the special development budget.[2] Few development programmes ever really got under way. In addition, many Southerners felt that veterans of the Anyanya movement and other exiles were not being given their due share of government appointments. This dissatisfaction led to the election of retired Lieutenant General Lagu, the former guerrilla leader, as President of the Southern Region in 1978.

Lagu's two year presidency was plagued by controversies over his own unconstitutional use of power (Appendix). The crisis he created was not resolved through the Supreme Court, where such constitutional issues

---

[2] See Peter Nyot Kok, 'Adding fuel to the conflict: oil, war and peace in the Sudan', in M. Doornbos, L. Cliffe, Abdel Ghaffar M. Ahmad & J. Markakis (eds), *Beyond Conflict in the Horn: The Prospects for Peace, Recovery & Development in Ethiopia, Somalia, Eritrea & Sudan* (London, 1992), p. 106.

could have been heard, but by the personal intervention of President Nimairi. He took advantage of the reorganization of the North into new regions to dissolve both the National and Regional Assemblies in February 1980 and call for new elections. Lagu was replaced by an 'interim president' appointed by Nimairi. Following the new elections, Abel Alier, with Nimairi's support, was elected unopposed by the Regional Assembly to a new term as president of the HEC in June 1980.

In forming his new government Alier had to contend with the existing political and tribal divisions which had assumed daunting proportions in the southern Sudan since 1972. He also had to face the problem of corruption within the civil service, as well as the frustrated aspirations of many southern Sudanese, especially a large number who had returned to the Sudan from Uganda only after the fall of Idi Amin in 1979. The most important issues confronting the regional government, which would eventually lead to its demise, were: 1) conflict with the central government over the Southern Region's borders (as raised in the Addis Ababa Agreement), 2) the role of the Southern Regional Government in developing the region's resources, and more particularly the benefits that were to accrue to it through the exploitation of its oil fields, 3) the growing confrontation in regional politics between the 'Equatorians' and the 'Nilotics' (particularly the Dinka), 4) dissatisfaction within the region over the fate of the Anyanya guerrillas absorbed into the national army.

4.4 Economic confrontations with Khartoum

The economic confrontation between Khartoum and the regional government which arose in the early 1980s has to be seen within the context of the failure of the Sudan's 'bread basket' strategy for the rapid growth of mechanized agriculture in the 1970s, and the country's resultant spiralling indebtedness. The Sudan's agricultural output declined, as did the annual growth rate of exports, down to –5.7% by 1980. The annual balance of payments deficit rose from £S 30.5 million in 1973–4 to £S 310.6 million in 1981–2. The Sudan's outstanding external debt at the end of 1982 was $6.3 billion, one third of which was owed to the Arab countries who had invested in 'bread basket' schemes.

The Sudan's first economic crisis came in 1977–8 when its debts fell due and it was unable to pay them. This was to have far-reaching external and internal political consequences, which in turn accelerated the reorientation of the Sudan's economy. Externally, the Sudan became dependent on the US, not only to negotiate the rescheduling of the Sudan's debt and further loans from the IMF, but for foreign aid through USAID (the Sudan was the largest recipient of US foreign aid in sub-Saharan Africa, receiving more than $1.4 billion in all). Internally, Nimairi brought back his Islamist opponents (the Umma and the Muslim Brothers) through 'national reconciliation' in order to guarantee political stability. The condition the US and IMF imposed for their financial support in the early 1980s was the forced reduction of the state budget and the privatization of nationalized corporations. The condition the Islamists imposed for 'national reconciliation' was the reform of the law on Islamic principles, beginning with financial reforms and the establishment of Islamic banks. They were in a strong position to benefit from privatization and the new investment climate (Section **4.4.4**).[3]

The impact of the Sudan's financial crisis on state-generated development was disastrous. Of the $225 million allocated for development in the Southern Region for the 1977–83 Six Year Plan, only $45 million had been paid by 1982. There was a rising percentage of external aid in the central government annual grant to the South: in 1980–1 it amounted to 56%, but rose to 90% in 1981–2. This desperation helps to account for the sharpening of the confrontation over the Sudan's oil, most of which is to be found in the South (Section **4.4.2**).

4.4.1   The borders
The border issue at first revolved around those areas adjacent to the Southern Region which, by the provisions of the Addis Ababa Agreement, were under consideration for transfer to the region. These included certain areas which had been part of southern provinces before independence in 1956, as well as areas deemed culturally similar to the South. The former were supposed to be automatically retransferred, and the latter were to be allowed to vote on whether they should remain in the North or join the South (Chapter II Article 3.iii). The mineral-bearing areas of Kafia Kingi and Hofrat al-Nahas, ceded to Darfur in the 1960s, should have been returned to Bahr al-Ghazal Province by 1977 but were not. Within that same time period, referenda should have been held in the Dinka district of Abyei in Southern Kordofan, and in the Chali area of Blue Nile Province (which had been part of the South until 1953). No referendums were scheduled.

The border issue was sensitive for a number of reasons. In Kordofan the prolonged drought of the 1970s meant that there was increased hardship for Arab cattle herders who shared with the Dinka of Abyei the dry season pastures of the Kiir (Bahr al-Arab). There was some concern that if the territory were to be transferred to the Southern Region, pastoralist Arabs would be denied access to the river. Throughout the late 1970s, and with increasing ferocity during the early 1980s, gangs of armed Arabs (mainly Misiriyya) began attacking Dinka villages with the intent of driving the Dinka out of Kordofan, into Bahr al-Ghazal. It was widely thought at the time that members of the Umma party were involved in arming and encouraging the nomads: the area had been an Umma stronghold before 1969, and the Umma leadership was initially hostile to the Addis Ababa Agreement. There was certainly evidence of collaboration by local police and army with the Misiriyya.

The border region of Chali in southern Blue Nile excited less emotion in the North but was still contentious. It had been administered by Upper Nile Province until 1953, when it was transferred to Kurmuk district. Because it had been part of a southern province, a mission station of the Sudan Interior Mission, run by Protestants mainly from the southern United States, was set up in Chali in the 1940s and remained active until the missionaries were expelled by government order in 1964. A local

---

[3] See Alex de Waal, *Famine Crimes: Politics & the Disaster Relief Industry in Africa* (Oxford, 1997), Chapter 5.

church continued to function among the Uduk of Chali and survived the first civil war. The end of the war placed the Uduk and the Chali church quite literally on the front line of any new North–South confrontation. Throughout the 1960s Chali had been a very small rural backwater, defended by only a handful of police. By 1983 it boasted an army garrison, a new Islamic school (*mahad*), and a Saudi-financed mosque. The activities of the local church elders were scrutinized just as much as they had been during wartime. When the church leaders petitioned for a referendum to be held on Chali's future, they were harassed by provincial officials, and some were arrested and beaten.

The issue of the Southern Region's borders became entwined with the issue of oil and economic development. In November 1980 the new National Assembly considered a bill to set the boundaries of the new regions in the North. At Hassan al-Turabi's instigation, the bill redrew the Southern Region's boundaries, placing the oilfields of Bentiu and the agriculturally productive areas of Upper Nile Province inside neighbouring northern provinces. This action provoked an immediate confrontation between the Southern Regional Government and the National Assembly, which was resolved by appeal to the President of the Republic. In this issue the opposition of the Southern Region was unanimous, and transcended the political divisions which were already at work within it. This time President Nimairi decided in favour of the Southern Region, reaffirming the central government's commitment to the provisions of the Addis Ababa Agreement concerning the South's boundaries, a commitment which would be repudiated within only a few years.

4.4.2 Oil

The Southern Region's main asset is oil, but this was discovered only after the Addis Ababa Agreement was signed and the regional government established. The regional government was not consulted on the granting of concessions to the Chevron and Total oil companies for prospecting and drilling for oil within the region. Almost all of the Sudan's known oil deposits were located in Upper Nile and Jonglei Provinces. At one time Chevron, who did the initial surveys, estimated the Sudan's total oil reserves at 10 billion barrels. It certainly assumed nearly a billion-barrel oil reserve in its fields in Upper Nile Province. Chevron began to exploit the three 'Unity' fields outside of Bentiu (near the border with Southern Kordofan), and fields of oil and natural gas in the Meban area of northern Upper Nile (near the border of Blue Nile). There is even a substantial oil deposit straddling the Sudan–Ethiopian border between Nasir and Gambela. The Total concession was located outside of Bor, far from any regional or international borders.

It was Chevron's policy to keep most of its Sudan concession in reserve, bringing it into full production only if the international oil supply and prices warranted. Total took a much lower profile than Chevron over the Sudan's oil. Chevron's desire to keep the production of Sudanese oil at a low level contributed to the confrontation which developed between the regional and central governments over this issue.

Abel Alier has subsequently claimed that the issue of oil turned Nimairi against the Addis Ababa Agreement and the provisions it made for the regional government to levy a corporation tax on any non-government owned factory in the region, as well as to tax the profits from the export of products from the region.[4] This would have given it considerable revenues from any refinery sited in the region, and on the export of any refined, or unrefined, petroleum products. The regional government insisted that a proposed oil refinery to be built by Chevron should be placed inside Upper Nile Province, close to the oilfields. The central government was just as adamant that the oil refinery be placed inside the northern Sudan. At the heart of this dispute lay a conflict in development philosophies, with the central government wanting to concentrate development in the industrial and agricultural areas of central Sudan, and the Southern Region arguing that taking business to already developed areas would condemn underdeveloped regions to perpetual underdevelopment. The controversy united the Umma and Muslim Brother members of Nimairi's cabinet in excluding the Southern Region from any decisions in petroleum affairs.[5] President Nimairi, not surprisingly, ordered the construction of the refinery outside the Southern Region. Even that project was deferred in favour of a pipeline direct from the Bentiu oil fields to Port Sudan, via Khartoum, enabling a quick export of crude oil to offset some of the Sudan's deficit. Another pipeline proposal, linking the fields with the Kenyan seaport at Mombasa, was favoured by 'Tiny' Rowland of Lonrho. His support for this project was one reason why he, too, lost Nimairi's favour, and why he was to become one of the SPLA's earliest financial backers.

The Southern leader who is credited with sharpening the confrontation between the regional and central governments on the issue of oil is Bona Malwal, formerly Central Minister of Information and a strong ally of Nimairi's, until Reconciliation in 1977 brought Sadiq al-Mahdi and Hassan al-Turabi into the government. Bona Malwal was appointed Regional Minister of Industry and Mining in Alier's government in 1980. As the nation's spokesman to the international community for a number of years, Malwal used his contacts with the West and the Arab world to negotiate agreements totalling some $9 million for agricultural and industrial development in 1980–1. The bulk of the Sudan's resources needed for the nation's revitalization – oil, water, fertile soil and various minerals – are to be found mainly in the Southern Region; these new initiatives taken by the region for the exploitation of its own resources raised for the first time the prospect of an independently prosperous South which could, in future, take a commanding role in the affairs of the nation. In June–July 1981 President Nimairi insisted that Abel Alier drop Bona Malwal from his cabinet. Alier's response was to

---

[4] Abel Alier, *Southern Sudan. Too Many Agreements Dishonoured* (Exeter, 1990), pp. 219–24.
[5] Peter Nyot Kok, 'Adding fuel to the conflict: oil, war and peace in the Sudan', pp. 104–8. Kok accuses Chevron of siding with the government and failing 'to use its weight and its corporate diplomacy to press the government to act with justice and due consideration to southern legitimate demands and expectations with respect to oil' (p. 104). J. Millard Burr & Robert O. Collins, *Requiem for the Sudan: War, Drought, & Disaster Relief on the Nile* (Boulder CO, 1995) make no mention of the oil controversy as a contributary cause to the war. Chevron's contribution to famine relief is mentioned (pp. 129–30), but not its support to local militias who helped cause famine. This omission is all the more surprising, considering that one of the authors was an adviser to Chevron for much of the 1980s and early 1990s.

transfer Malwal from the Regional Ministry of Industry and Mining to the Augean stables of the Regional Ministry of Finance and Economic Planning, a far more central position from which to direct the development of the Southern Region. Within a few weeks of this move Nimairi once again dissolved both the National and Regional Assemblies, dismissing Alier's government and calling for new elections. This time he appointed a military-led interim government in Juba, and instructed it to carry out a referendum to determine whether the Southern Region should be sub-divided into three smaller regions, a proposal Lagu had been advocating since Alier's return to office.

4.4.3 The Jonglei Canal

The South's other main asset is water. It has higher rainfall than the North, and it is the meeting place of numerous rivers arising in East Africa, Ethiopia and Central Africa. Both the northern Sudan and Egypt make heavy demands on water from the Nile through numerous irrigation schemes, but their share of the water was regulated by the 1959 Nile Waters Agreement. Any major increase in the use of water through the expansion of such schemes and through anticipated population increase thus leads inevitably to plans to increase the total amount of water available. As a great deal of water which flows into the Sudan from East Africa is dispersed through the great central swamps of the South and never reaches the North, this is one of the obvious places to look to increase the volume of water available for use. This was the inspiration for the original idea of a swamp diversion scheme in the South, first proposed in 1901, and it has been the impetus for the scheme's constant revival throughout the twentieth century.

Before invoking the forces of inexorable demand and the historical inevitability of hydropolitics, however, it has to be recognized that there is as yet no adequate measure of a) the amount of water available, b) the demands on that water, and c) the wastage of the water used.[6] It is highly likely that a more efficient use of water in Egypt would fulfil its needs for many years to come, but prior to 1984, both Cairo and Khartoum pressed the perceived needs of the developed downstream areas to the detriment of the needs of those within the Jonglei area, and this was one factor contributing to local discontent.

The proposal to build the canal was presented by the central ministers of Irrigation and Agriculture to the president of the HEC, and then to the HEC itself in 1974. Their argument was that the canal was needed to meet planned agro-industrial expansion in both Egypt and the Sudan (part of the Sudan's 'bread basket' strategy). Some minor benefits to the local area in improved transport, cash crop production schemes, drinking water and drainage were also proposed. With some hesitation, the HEC agreed 'not to oppose the canal'.[7]

From this point onwards, support of the canal project almost became a prerequisite for any Southern politician wishing to maintain an active political career. The importance the government attributed to the

---

[6] P. Howell, M. Lock, S. Cobb (eds), *The Jonglei Canal. Impact and Opportunity* (Cambridge, 1988), chapter 3, especially pp. 65–73.

[7] Alier, *Southern Sudan. Too Many Agreements Dishonoured*, pp. 197–200.

construction of the canal can be gauged by its response to any opposition in the Southern Region. When there were demonstrations against the canal plan in Juba in 1974, and when some Regional Assemblymen publicly opposed the canal, the demonstrations were crushed by police and the assemblymen were arrested or forced to flee the country. They were effectively barred from holding elected office throughout the remaining short life of the Southern Region.

'Consultation' with local people, which was combined with 'socio-economic research' to allay public apprehension, was perfunctory and the publicity surrounding the canal often disingenuous. Over the next few years the central government's commitment to socio-economic development in the Jonglei area was shown to be a sham. The all-weather road which was to be constructed along the canal's eastern bank was made in the cheapest manner possible, so that it was frequently damaged by erosion in the rainy season and needed constant repairs. The proposed crossing-points for cattle were progressively reduced in number. Offtake pipes for local water use were not laid during the canal's construction, as originally promised, and many people began to suspect that they would never be installed. The attitude of some members of the Permanent Joint Technical Commission – the body with the final say in the construction of the canal – was increasingly contemptuous and dismissive of local concerns. A five-year pilot project in mechanized farming concluded that the proposed schemes would be far too expensive to introduce and maintain. A few school buildings and dispensaries and a few rain water reservoirs were constructed, but that was the extent of socio-economic development in the Jonglei area by the time civil war broke out again and put an end to the canal's construction.

The conduct of the central government over the construction of the Jonglei Canal was a crucial test of its intentions. In the end it demonstrated that the development of the southern Sudan was not an equal priority with the expansion of existing irrigation schemes downstream. As with oil, so with water: Khartoum proved itself to be more concerned with the extraction of the South's resources with the minimum return for the region itself, an attitude more in keeping with the old Sudanic states' exploitation of their hinterlands than with modern nation-building.

The regional government demonstrated a curious lack of involvement with what was the largest development project planned in its territory. It did not insist on having a say in the planning and implementation of the project at the highest level. It did not oversee or review the plans and insist on its own development priorities being included. It allowed the future of the peoples of the Jonglei area to be decided by national priorities as defined by the central government.

The outbreak of war in 1983, and the SPLA's early attacks on canal and oil installations brought these two major economic projects to a halt by 1984. Though dormant, they continued to exercise a powerful influence on political events. Egypt's perceived need for increased water lies behind its commitment to the Jonglei Canal scheme and its unwavering opposition to an independent, or even politically powerful southern Sudan. The determination to secure the oil fields for northern needs, first demonstrated by Turabi as Attorney General when he attempted to redraw the Southern Region's boundaries in 1980, had been a consistent policy of the Islamist government he helped to usher into power in 1989. This was one of the motivations for backing the Nuer factions in the SPLA, and one of the main objectives of the 'peace from within' strategy of the 1990s (Section **8.5**). The oil revenues that have accrued since bringing the Bentiu oilfields on stream in the late 1990s are in the process of transforming the government's position in the war. Not only is the government now better able to afford the purchase of war material, but several countries, including many Western governments, are eager to line up to do business in Sudan's oilfields, despite the human rights abuses documented there (Section **10.5**).

4.4.4 Mechanized agriculture & migrant labour

The 1970s were supposed to see the growth of agro-industry in the Sudan through increased investment in mechanized farming and high profile projects such as the Kenana Sugar refinery. In the event, rain-fed agricultural schemes expanded far more than irrigated schemes. The opening up of an international market in the Middle East for Sudanese millet and sorghum brought these crops from the subsistence sector into the cash crop sector. All of this has had a marked effect on the Sudan's economy and on socio-economic relations within the country, and has proved one of the generating causes of its further fragmentation and the extension of the current civil war into the North (Section **9.2**).

Investment in mechanized schemes by civil servants and merchants in the northern Sudan has had a long history, and has been part of the struggle for control of the levers of government by the various nationalist parties.[8] One of the new developments of the 1970s was the activity of Islamic banks and their heavy investment in rain-fed mechanized schemes, especially in the western Sudan. The banks, and the schemes they have financed, contributed to the growing economic power of the National Islamic Front (NIF) (Section **6.1.2**).

The establishment of the schemes has hastened a process of social and economic dislocation. Customary rights in land for either small-holding farmers or pastoralists in Kordofan and elsewhere have been eroded by the legal backing given to the schemes by the Sudanese courts. Those who can no longer work the land on their own have been brought into a large wage-earning agricultural work force. In Kordofan and Darfur herders were doubly hit by the droughts of the 1970s and the interference of large schemes in their access to pastures and water. This dispossession was again a contributory factor to the outbreak of fighting between Northern militias and southern Sudanese in northern Bahr al-Ghazal during the early years of the current war (Section **6.2.1**), and of fighting in the Nuba Mountains (Section **9.2.1**).

The effect of rural development on the southern Sudan before 1983 was more potential than actual. Expansion of mechanized agriculture parallel to the Jonglei Canal was clearly intended, but it was highly problematic. Mechanized pump schemes owned by Northern merchants had already been established in northern Upper Nile Province and were

---

[8] See T. Niblock, *Class and Power in Sudan. The Dynamics of Sudanese Politics, 1898–1985* (London, 1987).

expanding. There was a growing Southern migrant labour force, involving mainly Nuer, but also Dinka and Shilluk from Upper Nile and Bahr al-Ghazal. The labour force grew with the displacement of population during the early years of the civil war, but before 1983 it was largely uncoerced. Throughout the 1980s the combination of an expanding mechanized farming sector with the growth of a displaced Southern population raised serious implications for future economic development in the Sudan. Today, insecurity of land tenure for displaced and war-affected populations throughout the Sudan constitutes one of the most serious challenges confronting relief and development programmes (Sections **9.2** & **10.3**).

4.4.5 Development summary of the Southern Region
It would be misleading to conclude that there was no development in the Southern Region between 1972 and 1983, or that all development projects were exploitative and misdirected. There were several internationally-financed projects of both small and large scale, focusing on the improvement of infrastructure and services, as well as experimenting with improving the overall economic productivity of the South. However, there was very little coherent planning or supervision of development by the Southern Regional Government, nor was there much practical co-ordination of projects undertaken by different agencies. Development, in the end, was uneven.

The least-developed areas of Bahr al-Ghazal and Upper Nile were those where some of the most grandiose schemes were proposed: the White Nile Brewery in Wau and the Aweil Rice Scheme (neither of which ever went into production), and a mixture of oil and water projects in Upper Nile. There was very little effective investment in the infrastructure (especially roads and communication) in either area. There was a far denser concentration of projects in Western and Eastern Equatoria Provinces, especially in districts where some development had already taken place (especially Torit, Yei River and Yambio districts). Here agriculture and marketing were far more advanced than in other parts of the South, and some progress was made in the development of coffee, tea and forestry products. Infrastructure was also better served, with a number of road and rural water projects. The irony of this uneven development was that by and large those living in the better developed areas of Equatoria complained that they were being neglected, and pointed to the expensive mechanized projects in such 'Dinka' areas as Aweil and Jonglei as proof of the diversion of development funds.

In the effort to hasten the revival of infrastructure and social services damaged by the first civil war, the Southern Regional government tended to contract out the provision of such services to foreign NGOs. In some areas NGOs became substitutes for state administration, collecting fees to pay for these services when the regional government no longer bothered to levy its own social service tax. The provision of services, depending as it did on external grants, was not based on the improvement of regional government finances, and could not be sustained. The NGOs, in effect, contributed unintentionally to the further erosion of the authority of a very weak state, undermining not only its accountability, but its legitimacy in the eyes of many of its citizens.[9]

4.5 Regionalization & 'tribal' politics

4.5.1 The issue of 'Dinka domination'
Throughout the late 1970s and early 1980s there were many Southerners who claimed the region was threatened by 'Dinka domination'. The numbers of Dinka in the regional government, in the administration, and in some branches of the security forces appeared to them to be out of proportion to their qualifications. Since many Northern leaders, including Nimairi and Sadiq al-Mahdi, justified a weakened Southern Region by reference to the protection of the 'minority' rights of non-Dinka, these charges require investigation.

The 1983 census placed the population of the southern Sudan at about 6 million, of which the Dinka, taken altogether, numbered about 2 million, or one third of the region. This is roughly the same proportion given in the 1956 census. Both the 1956 and 1983 censuses have been disputed by Southerners as being too low, but the percentage of Dinka-speakers in the region seems to be consistent from 1956 to 1983. Dinka is the second largest language group in the Sudan after Arabic, and there are more Dinka-speakers in the Sudan than for any other indigenous language.

The Dinka do not form a single 'tribe', being divided into more than twenty-five tribal groups, each made up of an aggregate of political units, varying in number and size.[10] They have no political centre, and are found in at least five of the pre-war provinces (Bahr al-Ghazal, Lakes, Upper Nile, Jonglei and Southern Kordofan). They have shown no tendency in the past to unite either politically or militarily. In national and regional politics, Dinka have been found on virtually every side. During the 1960s Dinka were found in the two main, but opposed, Southern parties, SANU and the Southern Front (see above, Section **3.2.3**). In the Regional Assembly some of Abel Alier's strongest critics were Dinka. Dinka assemblymen voted for Equatorian candidates for President of the HEC in 1978 and 1982.

The administrative polices of the Condominium government up to 1947 actively discouraged pastoralists, the Dinka among them, from entering what would now be called the modern sector. Before Independence the majority of government clerks, police and soldiers in the South were drawn from Equatoria and western Bahr al-Ghazal. These were the ones most eligible for promotion during Sudanization, and the most disappointed at its outcome. The earliest Southern leadership (especially in the guerrilla movement) came mainly from Equatoria, which was also the main focus of guerrilla activity until the last few years of the war. After the Addis Ababa Agreement, the Nilotic (Anuak, Dinka, Nuer, Shilluk) representation in the administration and security forces

[9] Terje Tvedt, *Angels of Mercy or Development Diplomats? NGOs and Foreign Aid* (Oxford/Trenton NJ, 1998), pp. 189–201.
[10] See G. Lienhardt, 'The Western Dinka', in J. Middleton & D. Tait (eds.), *Tribes Without Rulers* (London, 1958), esp. pp. 102–4.

increased with the absorption of ex-guerrillas from Upper Nile and Bahr al-Ghazal provinces. Despite this, there was still a preponderance of Equatorians in the clerical services and the police throughout the Southern Region. The majority of those employed in the civil service by the regional government in Juba were also Equatorians.

The number of Dinka in government service increased from 1972 onwards; it had been unrepresentatively low before Independence. The gradual increase in numbers of educated or trained Southerners generally was masked by the civil war and the disruption caused to local educational institutions. Many of those Southerners who did get education or training during that time had to do so outside of the southern Sudan. For those used to the pre-war pattern, the sudden jump in the number of Dinka in government service thus looked unnatural and contrived.

It was alleged that the 'insiders', those who had remained inside the Sudan during the war, usually active in one or other of the legal parties before 1969, obtained the most senior appointments after the war. The rewards they received were greater than their contribution to the struggle merited, it was believed. By contrast the 'outsiders', those who had fought in the bush or had gone into exile, claimed to have received less than they deserved. Abel Alier, a senior Southern Front leader, a cabinet minister, leader of the government delegation to Addis Ababa, a Vice-President of the nation, Nimairi's first choice for president of the High Executive Council, and a Dinka, was seen to represent the 'insiders'. Lieutenant-General Lagu, leader of the guerrillas and an Equatorian, was seen to represent the 'outsiders'.

The insider/outsider disparity was never quantified, partly because it was and still is difficult to say just who belonged to which group. Many active members of political parties maintained contacts with the guerrilla groups in their provinces, forwarding to them guns, ammunition, and other supplies at great risk to their own lives. Some were forced into the bush or exile upon the discovery of their activities by the authorities. Many of those in exile had no active role, and fared rather better in education or jobs in their host countries than many of the 'insiders' in the Sudan.

Lagu's election in 1978 was supposed to redress the balance and bring more rapid development to the South. He failed on both counts. Among his most prominent critics were Dinka, but these included many who had initially voted for him to obtain government reform. Facing opposition within the Assembly, Lagu retreated from a regional to an Equatorian-only constituency. The fall of Amin in 1979 forced a number of southern Sudanese still in Uganda to return home, but it also brought a number of Ugandans (many associated closely with Amin) in to the South as refugees. Lagu publicly welcomed them to 'their second home' in the southern Sudan, thus arousing suspicions that he would seek to incorporate Amin's former supporters in his own constituency in the South. From this time the tribal rivalries already in play in the region were transformed by the emergence of an overt 'anti-Nilotic' form of racism, reminiscent of Amin's 'anti-Nilotic' propaganda.

The dismissal of Lagu by Nimairi, and the return of Alier in the regional elections of 1980 did not end the matter. Alier appeared insensitive to Equatorian complaints when he appointed Dinka to half the ministerial posts in the HEC. Many of these included prominent former SANU opponents to Alier and the Southern Front. Alier's actions could therefore be interpreted as an attempt to win over the largest bloc of his most consistent opponents. It was taken as proof, however, of an active defence of 'Dinka integrity' (the phrase originated with Bona Malwal). From this point Lagu and his supporters began to campaign for a separate Equatoria Region to escape 'Dinka domination'.

4.5.2 Regionalization, 1981–3

Lagu lobbied extensively in Khartoum and elsewhere in the North. He claimed that further decentralization in the South was a logical extension of the decentralization policy then being applied in the North. He further argued, somewhat disingenuously, that following regionalization in the North there was no longer a 'North' for the South to fear. Lagu and his supporters used the language of development to support their arguments. In this they were only repeating the slogan already adopted for the region-alization of the northern Sudan. 'Decentralization for development' was a fashionable slogan then, and had the general approval of a number of aid agencies and donor governments. The United States, in particular, was committed to financing the construction of new regional government offices and other necessary infrastructure throughout the northern Sudan.

It was not too difficult to make a plausible argument that the Southern Region's economic retardation was a product of its unwieldy size and the remoteness of the regional government in Juba from the basic units of government in the rural areas. The question that opponents of further regionalization raised, and that its advocates at no time answered, was whether any of the smaller proposed regions would have sufficient strength on their own to oppose effectively the encroachment of the central government, as the whole Southern Region had done over the border issue (Section **4.4.1**). Under the proposed system, Southerners as a whole would no longer be able to bring to bear the weight of public opinion they had begun to mobilize on issues of development, because in future each of the successor regions would have a say in only those resources actually found within their own borders. While the debate about what became known locally as 'redivision'[11] was conducted in the vocabulary of development, at the heart of the matter was the political future of the southern Sudanese themselves, and whether the creation of smaller regions would increase or decrease the political strength of southern Sudanese in relation to the central government. The fact that among the strongest advocates for the redivision of the South were those northern Sudanese who had opposed the creation of the Southern Region from the very start led many Southerners to doubt Khartoum's assurances that real decentralization was being offered them.

Nimairi was already under pressure from Northern opponents of the Addis Ababa Agreement to dissolve the Southern Region (Section **4.6**). When the new Alier government began to show signs of taking a more active role in economic matters, sometimes questioning his decisions and authority, Nimairi aligned himself with Lagu during the campaign for

---

[11] The proposal to divide the Southern Region was referred to by its opponents as 're-division'. Lagu repudiated that term and spoke only of further regionalization or decentralization.

further 'decentralization', and sought to divide the South into three in order to neutralize it.

Nimairi dismissed Alier's government in October 1981 and called for a referendum on dividing the South. This united Alier with some of his former critics (Equatorian and Dinka). The elections to the National Assembly in January 1982 returned a two-thirds majority of Southern members opposed to regionalization, despite the arrest of some of the most prominent opponents to this policy, and despite some election irregularities in the two Equatorian provinces. The strength of the internal Southern opposition and international pressure (notably from the OAU and neighbouring friendly African countries, who took very seriously the threat of a return to civil war if the South was divided), eventually led Nimairi to withdraw his call for a referendum, and instead to declare new regional elections within the existing framework of a united Southern Region.

With redivision no longer an issue, the former Unity coalition split apart. Those who were dissatisfied with Alier campaigned on a platform of administrative reform. Some eighty percent of those subsequently elected to the Regional Assembly were opposed to formal regionalization, but many were also sympathetic to transferring some of the powers of the regional government from Juba to the provinces. A coalition was formed among the reform politicians, many of whom were Dinka, Nuer, Shilluk and Anuak (all Nilotic) who aligned themselves with the large pro-divisionist Equatorian bloc led by James Joseph Tembura, a Zande from Western Equatoria. It was because the Equatorians had the largest bloc in this coalition that Tembura was subsequently elected president of the HEC.

The official policy of Tembura's government, as worked out by its coalition members, was for devolution of powers to the provinces, not regionalization, but 'decentralization' became a code-word for regionalization in the South. Tembura lobbied for it, spending more time in Khartoum during his one-year presidency than he did in the Southern Region. In addition, President Nimairi himself, his first Vice-President, Umar al-Tayyib, and the Attorney General, Hassan al-Turabi, all spoke out in favour of 'decentralization' (though sometimes in guarded terms) on visits to the Southern Region between December 1982 and April 1983.

During this time, there was a growing feeling of unease among many Southerners about the strengthening ties between the Sudan and various Arab governments. The Sudan's support for Iraq against Iran was demonstrated in a recruitment drive for Southern volunteers to fight in Iraq (see Appendix). The Integration Charter between Egypt and the Sudan in 1982 aroused fears of Egyptian support for the suppression of the South. Even though both the Iraqi and Egyptian regimes were anti-Islamist, these closer international ties convinced many Southerners that the central government was drifting closer to becoming an Arab Islamic state.

During all this time Nimairi prepared the way for regionalization by decree. The most prominent opponents to 'redivision' of the South were arrested. With the civilian opponents silenced, the recalcitrant ex-Anyanya garrison at Bor was attacked (see Appendix). After Bor was retaken, Nimairi announced his intention of dividing the South into three regions, an announcement timed to coincide with the annual May Revolution Day celebrations (though the formal decree followed on 5 June). There was no one left to organize open opposition to this unconstitutional move.

4.5.3 Regionalization, South & North compared

In the end, Equatoria did not get what it wanted. The powers of the three new southern regions (Bahr al-Ghazal, Upper Nile and Equatoria) were no greater than those of the recently created regions in the North, and considerably less than the powers granted to the former Southern Region by the Addis Ababa Agreement. Whereas in the old Southern Region the Assembly was empowered to elect the president of the HEC, subject to the approval of the President of the Republic, in the new regions the President directly appointed the governors, selected from a list of nominees provided by the assemblies.

The financial powers of the new regions were considerably less than those of the old Southern Region, which at least had the power to raise its own taxes. Taxes from the new regions were remitted to Khartoum for redistribution by the President (recalling the older pattern dating back to the Sudanic kings). This provision was a particular blow to Equatorians, who had assumed that the potential wealth of their region would be retained for their own use.

4.6 Internal pressures on Nimairi to repudiate the Agreement

The Addis Ababa Agreement was never popular with the Northern politicians whom Nimairi had displaced in 1969. Those in the DUP and Umma parties thought it granted too many concessions to the South and would only foster separatist tendencies. Those who favoured an Islamic state (including those in the Umma, DUP and Muslim Brothers) also saw the Agreement, and the 1973 Constitution into which it was incorporated, as an obstacle to the creation of such a state. The support Nimairi gained from the South as a result of the Agreement was also seen – rightly – as an obstacle to the eventual overthrow of Nimairi himself.

The leaders of these former parties did not feel bound by the Agreement, since they saw it as being imposed on them by a military dictatorship. Southern leaders throughout the Nimairi years were frequently criticized for having accepted an agreement on such terms, rather than seeking a peace that was broadly backed by the consensus of political opinion in the North. The lack of commitment of Northern parties to the Agreement was later to influence the SPLM's negotiating strategy in the second civil war.

Nimairi certainly achieved immense personal popularity in the South because of his willingness to make peace. He was able to count on considerable political support from Southern leaders, as well as on the personal loyalty of ex-guerrillas absorbed into the army (especially a small body of ex-Anyanya recruited into the Presidential Guard). The support of the region helped him to survive two serious Muslim coup attempts in 1975 and 1976. The 1976 Libyan-backed coup of Sadiq al-Mahdi was contested on the streets of Khartoum during two days of serious fighting, in which the ex-Anyanya stationed in Khartoum played a significant part defending key government and military installations. Southern members of the government also helped co-ordinate opposition to the coup, and broadcasts from Radio Juba let the outside world know that Nimairi still had substantial support in the country.

Despite repulsing two coup attempts in so many years, Nimairi calculated that the threat from his enemies was such that it was better to have them inside the country, where he could watch them, than outside the country planning another attack. In 1977, in a gesture of National Reconciliation, he brought Sadiq al-Mahdi back from exile and released his brother-in-law, Hassan al-Turabi, leader of the Muslim Brothers, from prison. Sadiq al-Mahdi continued to have an uneasy relationship with Nimairi and finally left his government. Hassan al-Turabi was eventually appointed Attorney General and from that position exerted steady pressure for the Islamic reform of the legal system.

Many Southern leaders were highly sceptical of National Reconciliation, fearing that the inclusion of Muslim factions in government would erode the South's autonomy and lead to an Islamic state. The Permanent Constitution of 1973 established the Sudan as a secular state with freedom of worship not only for Christians and Jews, but for followers of traditional religions as well, those usually dismissed by Muslim law as 'unbelievers' (*kuffar*). A secular law governed relations between citizens in civil and criminal matters, and personal or family matters were covered by *shari'a* for Muslims and customary law for a large number of rural people in the North as well as in the South. Any attempt to alter the law for the nation would thus alter the rights of all non-Muslims within the nation.

Nimairi's move towards Islam after some years in power followed the pattern of expediency which had governed his political manoeuvres since his initial alliance with the Communists. It was reinforced by a growing personal mysticism which was a consequence of a combination of factors: poor health, personal isolation and growing paranoia were reputed to be among them. But by championing Islamic reforms he tried to steal a march on the Islamic opponents to his regime, and thus guarantee his own political survival. The imposition of *shari'a* law in September 1983 (now known as the September Laws), followed soon after the dissolutioin of the Southern Regional Government, and took place immediately before a pro-*shari'a* demonstration planned by the Muslim Brothers.

As foreseen by some Southern leaders, the assault on the Southern Region was hastened by this new alignment in Khartoum, and the division of the South into smaller regions could now be seen as a predictable tactic to facilitate the institution of an Islamic state. Under the Addis Ababa Agreement, the Southern Regional Assembly could vote to request the President of the Republic to withdraw any bill before the National Assembly which adversely affected 'the welfare, rights or interests of the citizens of the Southern Region'. It could also request the President to postpone the enactment of any law deemed detrimental to those rights and interests (Chapter III, Articles 14 & 15.i). Thus the Southern Region could have attempted to block any legislation put before the National Assembly. It is significant that Islamic laws were brought into force only after the Southern Region had been abolished. The new regional assemblies had no such defensive powers.

4.7 International factors in the demise of the regional government

Sudanese independence was achieved by repudiating the colonialism of both Egypt and Britain. This placed some distance between Khartoum and Cairo until the Arab-Israeli War of 1967 when the Sudan, too late to take part militarily in the war, drew much closer to the Arab League as a result of the Arab defeat. Breaking diplomatic relations with the United States brought the Sudan no benefit, and in fact was followed by the cancellation of US aid.

Nimairi's coup in 1969 and his promotion of socialism at first brought the Sudan's government ideologically closer to Eastern Europe, but Nimairi's survival of the pro-Communist coup attempt of 1971 and subsequent reprisals precipitated a rupture with the Eastern bloc. 1972 saw the resumption of diplomatic relations with the USA, and from that time on Nimairi strengthened his relations with the West, especially with the US. This alienated him from Libya's Qaddafi, but that was more than offset by the economic and military assistance which now flowed from the US.

Chevron's exploration for oil created a stronger US interest in the Sudanese economy, and after 1980 the US became increasingly involved in development schemes, in funding the infrastructure for regionalization, and in servicing the growing Sudanese national debt. But a succession of international events, beginning with the overthrow of Haile Selassie in 1974, the subsequent alliance between Ethiopia and the Soviet Union, the Camp David Accord brokered by the US, Libya's growing hostility to Egypt, and the election of a Republican government in the US in 1980 all combined to influence the Sudan's role in international politics.

The Sudan became important to the US as a regional counterweight to Soviet-backed Ethiopia. The Reagan administration's high profile hostility towards Libya, which justified a US naval build up in the Mediterranean, drew the US and the Sudan into a closer military alliance. The Sudan became part of the Rapid Deployment Force, allowing US forces to carry out joint manoeuvres with the Sudanese army on Sudanese soil. Alleged Libyan military threats to the Sudan enabled the US to deploy its ships off the Libyan coast in February 1983.

Nimairi exploited US propaganda to his own benefit. He had proposed early in 1982 that the US improve the Sudan's air and naval facilities, but this request was treated very coolly in Washington. From 1983 onwards, Nimairi played the Libyan and Ethiopian cards to secure his military supplies from the US. The US, too, found that the 'defence of Sudan' was a useful propaganda tool against Libya.

Having given Nimairi its support, the US government was reluctant to undermine him in any way, seeing in Nimairi personally a useful ally in the region, and betting on his survival against the possible Sudanese backlash for helping to keep him in power. The US government was concerned about the consequences of abolishing the Southern Region and imposing Islamic Law, and made its concern known to Nimairi before the fact. What the US government did not acknowledge was that it had provided the very weapons which gave Nimairi the confidence to ignore these expressions of concern.

Nimairi had come to power in 1969 on the platform that the war in the South could not be solved militarily. By 1983 he was convinced that he had sufficient hardware from the US to deal with any potential military revolts. He gauged – correctly, as it turned out – that the American government's ideological commitment to opposing Russia's allies in Libya and Ethiopia meant that it would continue to supply him with weapons against this external threat, no matter what he did with them in his own country. In 1983, prior to the abolition of the Southern Region, one of Nimairi's most senior officials warned a group of Southern politicians that Khartoum had built an 'air bridge' from America to the Sudan for the supply of arms, and the first place such arms would be used would be in the South.[12] This turned out to be no idle threat.

---

[12] Alier, *Southern Sudan*, pp. 249–50. The official in question has been identified as Umar al-Tayyib, first Vice-President of the Sudan and Chief of Security.

5

The Beginning of ▮ the Second Civil War
1983–5

5.1 Residual guerrilla warfare, 1975–82

5.1.1 Sudanese dissidents & the Ethiopian connection

Most of the Anyanya guerrillas had accepted the Addis Ababa Agreement
in 1972, even if they retained a suspicion of, or were disappointed by, the
integration process. Only a few remained in Ethiopia in their own camps,
but they were not a significant military or political force, even after they
were joined by various mutineers in 1975–6. The Addis Ababa Agreement
also represented a rapprochement between the Sudan and Ethiopia (the
Sudan had, along with many Arab nations, supported Eritrean separatists),
so Haile Selassie's government imposed some control over border activity.
This did not survive the Emperor's fall in 1974, when his government was
replaced by a pro-socialist military Derg (committee) that subsequently
came under the control of Mengistu Haile-Mariam. The Sudan came under
increased pressure from various Arab states to renew its support for the
Eritreans, and this affected Ethiopia's attitude towards its neighbour.

In 1976 Mading de Garang, a former guerrilla spokesmen and then
regional Minister for Information, led a Sudanese government delegation
to Ethiopia and was told quite explicitly by the Ethiopian Foreign
Minister that unless the Sudan ceased supplying the Eritrean rebels,
Ethiopia would give active support to the Anyanya remnants in Ethiopia
who had refused to accept the Addis Ababa Agreement. Nimairi's support
for the Eritreans, and subsequently for anti-Derg forces, continued despite
this warning. Ethiopia's support for various Sudanese dissidents dates
from 1976. In addition to arming and training Southern guerrillas, colloquially known as Anyanya-2, the Mengistu government enabled Sadiq al-
Mahdi to beam anti-Nimairi radio broadcasts to the Sudan after the failure
of his 1976 coup attempt.[1]

Ethiopian and (briefly) Libyan support for Southern guerrillas, and
later for the SPLM/SPLA, brought internal Sudanese discontent into the
arena of the Cold War. The SPLA's early dependence on Mengistu's

---

[1] It is incorrect to claim that Sudanese support for the TPLF stemmed from Mengistu's greater
support for the SPLA (John Young, 'The Tigray People's Liberation Front', in Christopher
Clapham (ed.), *African Guerrillas* (Oxford/Athens OH/Kampala, 1998), p. 44). Direct
Sudanese support to the TPLF was only part of the spectrum of support given to Eritrean and
Ethiopian opposition groups (including the OLF and the GPLF), beginning before the foun-
dation of the SPLA.

government was used by some officials in Washington to justify continued military support to Khartoum. Given the configuration of international politics in the early 1980s, Southerners had few other options open to them. The Sudan's support for the Camp David Accord meant that Israel would not support Southern guerrillas, as it had done towards the end of the first civil war. Uganda under Obote also would not give sanctuary or support to southern Sudanese, as they were seen to have been a prop to Idi Amin's regime after 1972. Kenya was eager to remain on good terms with the Sudan and in 1982 had arrested (some would say kidnapped) a number of exile Southern leaders then visiting Nairobi and returned them to the Sudan. Pleas by many internal Southern leaders to the United States not to supply Khartoum with arms went unheeded. It was only later, when Sadiq al-Mahdi as Prime Minister had moved the country closer to Libya and Iran and human rights abuses under his government could no longer be ignored, that US military aid was suspended.[2] So for many years Southern guerrillas had no choice but to seek help from regimes unsavoury to the West.

Anyanya-2 was not a unified military organization, and in fact 'Anyanya-2' was more a generic term applied locally to many guerrilla bands operating in the South between 1980–3, not all of whom had direct contacts with Ethiopia. One group which was more closely tied to Ethiopia than many others was the Sudan People's Revolutionary Party (SPRP), which drew its support mainly from Nuer ex-Anyanya and negotiated the supply of some arms and funds from Libya, with Ethiopian help. Aside from a few cattle raids along the Sudan–Ethiopian border, the Anyanya-2 made no significant appearance inside the southern Sudan until 1980. Their military successes were meagre, and by the end of 1981 the Southern Regional government appeared to have contained their activities. But as evidence grew of Khartoum's intention to abrogate the Addis Ababa Agreement, the various Anyanya-2 groups gained more support from Southern soldiers and civilians.

5.1.2 Anyanya-2 & Southern soldiers, 1980–3

The issue which divided the ex-Anyanya from the Anyanya-2 was acceptance of the Addis Ababa Agreement. In 1981 and 1982 former guerrillas in the police and army stationed in Upper Nile, Jonglei and Bahr al-Ghazal were quite clear that they were defending the Addis Ababa Agreement, and they were willing to lead the fight against their recalcitrant former comrades-in-arms. When Nimairi's own commitment to the Agreement began to waver, however, former guerrillas lost their rationale for fighting on the side of the government, and those who had always been sceptical of the Agreement had their scepticism confirmed.

The guerrilla bands which began to proliferate throughout Upper Nile, Jonglei, Bahr al-Ghazal and Lakes provinces often had very local grievances. In 1980 and 1981 local people were often perplexed by the behaviour of the guerrillas and apprehensive about the future. This began to change as confrontations between the regional and central government became more frequent. During the border dispute late in 1980 some Anyanya-2 moved into Bentiu district, announcing they had come to

---

[2] Formal suspension of all military and economic aid did not take place until 1990.

protect the South's oil fields. In 1981 and 1982 the guerrillas in Nasir, Bentiu and Fangak districts began to make direct contact with Southern police and soldiers explaining that their quarrel was not with them, but with the North. The number of northern troops in the South increased during this time, and army harrassment of civilians became common in the towns of Nasir, Bentiu and Malakal, and shooting of civilians was frequent in the rural areas around Nasir, Bentiu and Aweil. Southern soldiers stationed in the rural areas of Upper Nile and Jonglei complained of the army's tactics. Civilians began to talk more favourably about the guerrillas, contrasting their increasingly disciplined and principled behaviour (in not targeting civilians), with the behaviour of the Northern soldiers.

By 1982 there were also more positive contacts developing between some southern army officers and the guerrillas. One of the most influential guerrilla leaders operating out of Ethiopia was Akwot Atem, a Twic Dinka from around Kongor who had been 'interior minister' in one of the previous Anyanya governments, and who had never accepted the Addis Agreement. Three former Anyanya officers who had served together in Upper Nile, Colonel John Garang, retired Major William Abdallah Cuol and Samuel Gai Tut (then a minister in the interim Southern Regional Government) were in contact with Akwot Atem and were involved in efforts to smuggle arms to his forces. Samuel Gai Tut was found out and arrested. Another serving ex-Anyanya officer, Major Kerubino Kuanyin Bol, had been actively engaged fighting the Anyanya-2 in Jonglei province. By 1982 he, too, was in contact with them and was even reported to have visited their camps in the bush some months prior to the events in Bor in May 1983. Throughout April and May 1983 more and more police and soldiers deserted their units for the bush. It needed only an overt action by Khartoum to push all of these groups together into an active alliance.

5.2 Mutinies of 1983 & the foundation of the SPLA

5.2.1 The foundation of the Movement, July 1983
Sudanese army battalion 105, with garrisons at Bor, Pibor and Pochalla, was still commanded in 1983 by officers absorbed from the original Anyanya.[3] When its soldiers refused the order to move North in January 1983 they did so partly on their interpretation of the Addis Ababa Agreement: that they were to serve only in the South. Dhol Acuil, vice president of the HEC, attempted to mediate, but his arrest in Khartoum for opposing the redivision of the South effectively ended that effort. John Garang, then head of the Staff College in Omdurman, also went to Bor, ostensibly to mediate. In fact, Garang was already party to the conspiracy among some officers in the Southern Command who had been planning the defection of battalion 105 to the guerrillas. The original plans called for a rising later in the year, but in fact Kerubino Kuanyin,

---

[3] Ann Lesch refers to the soldiers of battalion 105 in Bor and Pibor as 'Dinka soldiers' (Lesch, *Sudan: Contested National Identities* (Bloomington IN/Oxford, 1998), p. 44). This is a common mistake, as the soldiers in this battalion were drawn from a wide area and included other peoples, such as Nuer.

always unpredictable, precipitated a crisis by coming under suspicion for the misallocation of funds and poaching. This drew attention to his activities in Bor, and fighting broke out in May. Garang was present when the Sudanese army attacked Bor, and were repulsed by the garrison under Kerubino. When the battalion pulled out of Bor, Garang left by another route, and ended up in Ethiopia with them.

The combination of the attack on Bor and the subsequent abolition of the Southern Region prompted further mutinies and desertions from garrisons across the South. By July 1983 about 2,500 soldiers had defected to the new guerrilla base being established in Ethiopia, and another 500 remained in the field in Bahr al-Ghazal. This was in addition to the Anyanya-2 troops already under arms. By July there were also some 15,000 Northern troops in the South, supported by American-made aircraft.

There were some difficulties for the re-aligned dissidents in combining Sudanese army units and Anyanya-2 soldiers in a new army under a unified command, when they had so recently been fighting each other. There were problems of seniority to be sorted out, as well as matters of policy (Sections **5.2.2** & **5.2.3**), but by the end of July a new organization and leadership was established, with Ethiopian backing. Just as Lagu had decided at the end of the first civil war, the political and military wings of the movement were united under one commander, John Garang.

5.2.2 The programme of SPLM/SPLA: unity v. separation

The formation of a large army composed almost entirely of southern Sudanese who had been forced into rebellion by the failure of the Addis Ababa Agreement immediately resurrected the prospect of a second war for southern Sudanese independence. Many of the old Anyanya veterans had never been comfortable with the Addis Ababa Agreement and now rededicated themselves to Southern separatism. There were many reasons why the SPLM did not adopt this policy, some tactical but others based on a different appreciation of the South's dilemma.

The SPLM/SPLA's immediate problem was Nimairi and the support he was receiving from the West (mainly the USA). The overthrow of Nimairi was thus the first practical goal to be achieved, and while the SPLM/SPLA was the largest and most powerful of the anti-Nimairi groups then based in Ethiopia, it was not the only one. Some tactical alliance was needed with the opposition, and a platform of Southern separatism would have precluded such an alliance.

Ethiopian interests, also, would not have been served by Southern separatism. Ethiopia wished to see Nimairi go, but it was also fighting against its own separatists. Clearly it would not support the precedent of dismembering a neighbouring state. It was also still true at this time that African support for separatist movements was virtually non-existent, whereas there were some governments who were likely to be sympathetic to a 'national liberation' movement.

Quite apart from this were the practical problems of implementing separation. The South's boundaries follow no natural geographical barrier. There was no clear dividing line: the border issue of 1980 had already shown that. 'The North' could no more be excluded, physically or economically, from 'the South' than 'the South' could be excluded from 'the North'. The question thus arose, where was the South's most effective first line of defence: in Juba or in Khartoum? The experience of the regional government, with the minimal involvement of the South in the central government, suggested that to draw the front line at Juba was already to have sold the pass.

It was for all of these reasons that 'revolution', rather than separation, became the SPLM/SPLA's announced goal. The rationale for revolution, as presented in the Manifesto, focused on the specific grievances of the South, but the language of underdevelopment, nationality and religion were deliberately broadened in an attempt to appeal to other regions and sectors of Sudanese society who would have been hostile to a Southern independence movement, but who had their own grievances against Nimairi and the central government.

The Manifesto issued in July 1983 presented the aims of the SPLM/SPLA firstly by giving an historical overview of the pattern of underdevelopment in the Sudan, then by giving a critique of the failure of the first Anyanya movement, and finally by listing specific grievances over the failures of the Addis Ababa Agreement. The Manifesto began by redefining 'the so-called "Problem of Southern Sudan" ' as a more general ' "problem of Backward Areas" in the whole country.'[4] The attack on colonialism and neo-colonialism that follows is unspecific and presented in Marxist jargon. The questions of racism, tribalism, and ethnicity are encoded under 'the questions of nationality and religion', terms then part of Ethiopian and Eritrean Marxist discourse (adapted from the internal political discourse of the Soviet Union). However much the language may have been borrowed from the movement's Ethiopian patrons, the analysis of specific events and developments in the Sudan was not, and reflected criticisms which had been made publicly in the southern Sudan throughout the political crisis precipitated by Nimairi's support for redivision. The specific references to socialism which appeared in the Manifesto were also no more radical than contemporary public pronouncements of the Sudanese Socialist Union (the Sudan remained officially a socialist republic until Nimairi's downfall).

Underdevelopment was identified as characterizing most of the Sudan outside of the Central Region, the site of most colonial and post-colonial investment. This pattern of unequal development continued after independence because the majority of post-independence governments, it was claimed, had been in the hands of people from the most developed area. The common grievance the South shared with other areas (especially the west and east) was obscured, it was further alleged, by 'the questions of nationality and religion', by which was meant the attempt by a succession of governments to establish a Sudanese national identity on the foundation of Arabic language, Arab culture and Islam.

Though various groups in the underdeveloped areas of the Sudan reacted against this inequality, the South's response was undermined by the small Southern elite's pre-occupation with government jobs. Southern politicians had distinguished themselves by establishing a range of parties, provisional governments, republics and states, each with a hierarchy of office holders and ministers. The military wings of the exile

[4] *Manifesto. Sudan People's Liberation Movement*, 31 July, 1983, p. 1.

movements were also noted for the over-abundance of officers 'without armies to command'. The lesson the modern movement learned from the past was clear: 'The SPLA will never allow such fake governments and parties to exist.'

The Addis Ababa Agreement was dismissed as an arrangement about jobs reached between elites. None the less, the grievances listed were mainly concerned either with failures to implement the Agreement fully, or the deliberate undermining of its provisions. Specific grievances were: 1) Khartoum's interference in the selection of the leadership of the Southern Region, 2) plans to construct the Jonglei canal, 3) the unconstitutional dissolutions of the Regional Assemblies and governments, 4) attempts to redraw the Southern Region's borders, 5) the decision first to build an oil refinery outside of Bentiu, and then to pipe the Bentiu oil directly to Port Sudan, 6) the deliberate neglect of the South's socioeconomic development, 7) the Integration Charter and Joint Defence Treaty with Egypt, 8) the redivision of the South into three regions, 9) failure to adequately provide for the livelihood of the majority of ex-Anyanya soldiers, 10) the incomplete integration of the ex-Anyanya into the Sudanese army, and 11) plans to transfer the ex-Anyanya battalions to the North.[5]

The SPLM/SPLA's strategy, therefore, was to treat the South's specific grievances within the context of underdevelopment and unequal development throughout the Sudan, and to try to establish a progressive movement which was not 'concerned only with the South, jobs and self interest'. It declared its intention of bringing all current guerrilla units in the southern Sudan under one united, integrated liberation army which was not organized on tribal lines. It identified its potential friends and allies as 'progressives' throughout the Sudan, Africa and the world. Its general enemies were reactionaries and imperialism, but its specific enemies were listed as those in the northern and southern Sudanese elite who were primarily concerned with their own jobs, religious fundamentalists, and local 'warlords' of the Anyanya-2 who resisted incorporation into the SPLA.

The Marxist rhetoric of the Manifesto was used as an excuse by Nimairi, the US government and opponents of Mengistu to dismiss the SPLM/SPLA as a Communist-front organization. But when Garang addressed a wider audience over Radio SPLA, broadcast from Ethiopia, he reiterated the main arguments of the Manifesto without the ideological jargon and spoke directly to the real experiences of many Sudanese. Nimairi's unconstitutional abrogation of the Addis Ababa Agreement was only one theme. Increasingly, Garang cited the general deterioration of the Sudan, the fall in the production of essential foods, mounting unemployment, inflation and the devaluation of the currency, the deterioration of social services throughout the country, and oppression by the State Security Organization. He consistently represented the South's grievances as being simply a more intense form of the general problem of the Sudan, and he specifically repudiated the idea that the South could solve its own problems through separation from the rest of the Sudan. The remedies the SPLM offered, as the foundation of a 'New Sudan', were

[5] *Manifesto*, Chapters 4–6.

genuine autonomous or federal governments for the various regions of the Sudan, a restructuring of the central government, a commitment to fight against racism (exemplified by such policies as *kasha*, or 'urban cleansing', see Appendix), and tribalism.[6]

Nevertheless, Southern independence remained an unspoken or even coded option. Vernacular broadcasts by Radio SPLA tended to dwell more on grievances against the Arabs (*jallaba*) than on visions of a united 'New Sudan'. There were many in the movement who saw talk of unity as merely a tactic and separation as the desired goal. Others were guided by whether northern Sudanese were willing to make real concessions of power to keep the Sudan united before making an equal and irrevocable commitment to unity. If all else failed, at least the SPLA might be militarily strong enough to declare the unilateral independence of the South. There was an implicit threat to northern Sudanese: either support us, or accept de facto separation. But as long as separation remained in the background, there was also potential for internal dissension to arise over the movement's ultimate objective.

5.2.3 Early splits within the Movement

Garang's involvement with two Nuer officers, Samuel Gai Tut and William Abdallah Cuol, in trying to arm Akwot Atem gave him the credentials needed to contend for leadership. Kerubino Kuanyin Bol (a Dinka) and William Nyuon Bany (a Nuer), who had led their own units into rebellion were reported to have felt somewhat uneasy about their reception by their former enemies; therefore they willingly backed Garang's leadership. But the older Anyanya commanders felt that their former seniority over Garang should be retained. They also preferred a separation of the military from the political wings of the movement, as in the pre-Lagu Anyanya days (neither had been an enthusiastic supporter of Lagu), and proposed Gai Tut as the head of the military wing and Akwot Atem as head of the political wing. They offered the post of deputy commander to Garang.

In general, the older Anyanya veterans were in favour of reconstituting the old Anyanya and the platform of independence for the South, despite the structural weaknesses of the Anyanya and their failure to achieve their goal. What tipped the balance against them was Ethiopia's support for Garang on ideological as well as personal grounds. Garang's commitment to fighting for a united Sudan paralleled Ethiopian arguments against separatist movements within Ethiopia. Garang was also the younger, better educated man, with more varied experience than the other contenders. A number of prominent Southern politicians in exile also supported him.

The split in the leadership was thus based on ideological and personal differences, not tribal, since both Garang and Akwot Atem were Twic Dinka from Kongor district, and there were Dinka and Nuer commanders ranged on either side. Gai Tut and Akwot Atem kept their units separate from the main body of the newly formed SPLA at Itang, which soon received supplies and training from the Ethiopians. The SPLA's early denunciation of 'warlords' helps to explain their uncompromising attitude towards these other commanders, but it was the Ethiopian army

---

[6] John Garang, *The Call for Democracy in Sudan* (London, 1987), pp. 19–21, 26–7.

who precipitated the split between Garang and the Anyanya-2 by initi-ating the first attacks against residual Anyanya-2 camps along the border.

Throughout 1984 the SPLA tried to neutralize the Akwot Atem/Gai Tut threat, while at the same time contacting independent Anyanya-2 units further afield and incorporating them into the new military structure (Section **5.3.3**). Gai Tut and Akwot Atem continued to operate independ-ently in their respective home areas of Waat and Kongor. On their own, their forces had little impact on the SPLA and became a threat only when they received military support from the Khartoum government (Section **5.3.2**). There were also deep splits within the leadership of the old Anyanya-2 at this time, and by the end of 1984 both Gai Tut and Akwot Atem were killed and William Abdallah Cuol seized control of their combined forces. The force that William Abdallah Cuol led was almost entirely Nuer. The SPLA forces ranged against him were Nuer as well as Dinka, and the Anyanya-2/SPLA confrontation which developed soon took on aspects of a Nuer civil war.

The early resolution of the leadership contest was to have a significant impact on the Movement's development. Garang brought with him broad experience outside of the Sudan and a highly trained intellect: he had attended school in East Africa before getting a B.A. in the US, and ended the first war as a Captain in the Anyanya, in which he had served for only eight months. His educational qualifications ensured his absorption into the Sudanese army as an officer and further education within the army, first training at a US army base, and subsequently obtaining a Ph.D in agri-cultural economics at Iowa State University. Garang applied his academic training to developing a critique of the Sudanese political economy. His breadth of experience enabled him to see beyond parochial concerns. In his doctoral thesis on the Jonglei Canal he criticised the development planning in the Jonglei area, with reason, as mere 'misery management'. The ideas later found in the SPLA Manifesto were those he had expounded to other southern Sudanese prior to 1983, with an assurance some felt crossed over into intellectual arrogance.

Garang's leadership qualities, however, were untried. Though a full Colonel, his field experience was mainly limited to the few months he had served in the Anyanya after completing his training. This was far less than Gai Tut, or William Nyuon Bany, who ended the war as an Anyanya Major, but because of his lack of formal education was absorbed into the army as a Regimental Sergeant. It was only by proving his loyalty to the new dispen-sation by tracking down ex-Anyanya mutineers that he regained a commis-sioned rank. In the early years of the new insurgency, Garang was to rely on many of the more expeirenced Anyanya veterans, such as Kerubino, William Nyuon, and later Salva Kiir Mayardit, for the actual conduct of the war on the ground. Garang's lack of combat experience was an element of tension in his relations with field commanders, including some of the more senior Sudan army defectors, such as Arok Thon Arok.

5.3 Military response to the SPLA

5.3.1 *The internationalization of the civil war*
US support for Nimairi personally ensured that the civil war would be

seen in Cold War terms by some members of the Defense and State Departments, as well as in the White House. Visits were exchanged between Washington and Khartoum, with Vice-President Bush seeing Nimairi in Khartoum in 1984, accompanied by a bevy of Christian tele-evangelists. Privately and unofficially, some members of the State Department expressed concern about Nimairi's actions and acknowledged that the war had not been instigated by Ethiopia or Libya. Publicly, the US government emphasised Ethiopian and Libyan involvement. Defense Department officials were less ambivalent in their support, claiming that the Sudan was free to use US equipment to 'interdict' the infiltration of guerrillas into the Sudan. Mild objections voiced by members of Congress had no effect on restricting military aid.

In the election year of 1984 the Reagan administration campaigned on its record of supporting friendly countries against subversion. Ambassador Jeane Kirkpatrick cited US support for the Sudan as a foreign policy success.[7] After the election the administration showed an inclination to become actively involved in 'destabilizing' Libya and Ethiopia, and US support for anti-Mengistu forces based in the Sudan was increased. Nimairi was a significant player in this pressure on Ethiopia, and though some US officials speculated on whether a more acceptable soldier might replace him in time, the US gave no encouragement to democratization within the Sudan while Nimairi remained in power.

Following the popular uprising in Khartoum which led to Nimairi's removal and replacement by his defence minister, Suwar al-Dahab, in April 1985 (Section **5.4**), the international context of the war changed. US military aid and the military pact with Egypt both continued, but the Transitional Military Council (TMC) concluded a further defence pact with Libya. The TMC also sought additional support from the Arab states of the Gulf, and early in 1986 appealed for money and arms in the defence of 'Arabism' and Islam. Thus, the old Cold War confrontation receded into the background (though it continued to be part of US calculations in the region), and was replaced by an appeal from Khartoum for cultural, racial and religious solidarity within the Arab world.

5.3.2 Formation of tribal counter-responses to the SPLA

Much of the fighting in the civil war has been reported by external observers in tribal terms, and for years the SPLA was described as a Dinka army. The organization of tribal opposition, not just to the SPLA, but to the Dinka rural areas began in the first months of the civil war. It is important to understand its origins.

Anti–Dinka politics still motivated many in the Equatorian leadership. Some, Lagu and Tembura reportedly among them, had supported the government's 1983 assault on Bor as a means of 'cutting the Dinka down

---

[7] At the Republican National convention she declared, 'They said we could not use America's strength to help others – Sudan, Chad, Central America, the Gulf States, the Caribbean nations – without being drawn into war. But we have helped others resist Soviet, Libyan and Cuban subversion, and we are at peace,' *New York Times*, 21 August 1984, p. 11.

to size'. Harassment of 'Nilotic' civil servants (especially Dinka, but including Nuer) intensified in Juba in the early months after the regional government was abolished. In the immediate aftermath of the fighting at Bor, the Toposa around Kapoeta, hearing that 'the Dinka army' had left, organized a series of long-distance raids into Bor district, where they not only captured cattle, but killed a number of civilians, including women and children. The local Dinka organized their own defence, supported by a few of the remaining Jonglei Province police, and repulsed the raiders. The bodies of uniformed Toposa policemen were found interspersed among the dead Toposa warriors, leading to suspicions that the raids against Bor Dinka civilians had political backing within the new Equatoria Region.

One of the first tribal militias the Equatorian regional government armed was also drawn from pastoralists in conflict with the Bor Dinka. The Kabora Mundari, who straddle the main channel of the Nile between Terekeka and Mongalla, had been in dispute with the Dinka for many years over Dinka encroachments on Mundari grazing land (following the floods of the 1960s which permanently covered many Bor pastures). There was economic competition between Bor Dinka and Mundari in Juba within the meat supply trade, and Mundari were part of the street brawling in Juba which accompanied the regionalization debate (see Appendix). The argument that the Mundari were armed for self-defence against the SPLA is thus only part of the story. Not all Mundari were involved in this militia. Those living on the west bank, who had inter-married with the Dinka of Lakes Province, were not enthusiastic about being drawn into a tribal war.

The national government was directly involved in supplying arms to the Murle around Pibor for raids against the Dinka and Nuer from whom the SPLA then drew their support. This began within months of the Bor mutiny and was reputedly ordered by Nimairi himself. The Murle had a long history of fighting the Bor Dinka and the the Nuer of Ayod and Waat, and had earlier been armed to fight the Anyanya in the first civil war. They had never been effectively disarmed after the peace. Murle raids into Akobo, Waat or Bor districts took place nearly every rainy season throughout the 1970s. With the beginning of the new civil war, they were given effective licence by the government to continue these raids, and the main recipient of government arms was the former army officer and Murle chief, Ismail Konye. His raids were also aimed more at the Dinka and Nuer civilian population than against SPLA units.

The fighting between the SPLA and the Akwot Atem and Gai Tut remnants of the Anyanya-2 soon attracted Nimairi's attention. Under pressure to come to a security arrangement which would enable Chevron to begin to exploit its fields in Upper Nile, Nimairi hoped that he could raise a Nuer army to fight the 'Dinka' SPLA. In late 1984 contacts were arranged through D.K. Matthews, the Gaajak Nuer governor of Upper Nile Region, and William Abdallah Cuol. A new 'Anyanya-2' emerged, with William Abdallah Cuol as its leader, receiving arms, ammunition, uniforms and other supplies from the government. William Abdallah Cuol moderated his platform of separation to federation, but the moti-vation of a government-backed Anyanya-2 had less to do with ideology than with individual ambition.

The new Anyanya-2 drew its support mainly from the Bul Nuer (under Paulino Matip), the Lak Nuer (William Abdallah Cuol), a number of Lou Nuer sections and their neighbours the Jikany Nuer (including the Gaajak on both sides of the Ethiopian border).[8] It did not enjoy the support of the Nuer as a whole, and continued to fight the Nuer in the SPLA; thus contributing to the ferocity of the fighting between the Anyanya-2 and the SPLA. The Anyanya-2 attacked many of the recruits and refugees whom the SPLA tried to escort from Bahr al-Ghazal to Ethiopia. They also effectively cut the SPLA's supply lines from Ethiopia into Bahr al-Ghazal, with very serious consequences for SPLA strategy there (Section **6.2.1**). There was heavy fighting between the SPLA and the Anyanya-2 in Waat and Nasir districts. Anyanya-2 tactics made civilians in SPLA districts particular targets. The SPLA retaliated indiscriminately against the Lou, Gaajak and other Jikany Nuer, who responded by killing individual SPLA soldiers for their weapons.

The government strategy of supplying tribal militias began under Nimairi and was continued under all successive Khartoum governments. Its aims were two-fold: as a propaganda argument that the war in the South was really a product of internal Southern tribalism, and therefore unrelated to national policies; and as a way of waging war through surrogates. It enabled successive Khartoum regimes, and even some of their international backers, to deny that there was a civil war in the Sudan at all.

5.3.3 The war on the ground, 1983–5
During the later part of 1983 the war was characterized by small clashes between the SPLA and the army, mainly along the Sudan–Ethiopian border, following the classic guerrilla pattern with the SPLA trying to inflict damage and capture equipment, but not attempting to hold ground. In early 1984 the SPLA began contacting other guerrilla units in more distant districts, such as Bentiu, Aweil, and Southern Kordofan. Many recruits joined the SPLA at this time not because of a general grievance with the North, but in order to get training and equipment so that they could protect themselves from attacks by government militias raised among such peoples as the Baqqara and the Murle. The SPLA policy of taking new recruits to Ethiopia for training and reorganization was not always popular, and it also left the home areas of the recruits vulnerable. The guerrilla outfit among the Bul Nuer refused to be moved by the SPLA to Ethiopia because it had taken up arms specifically to defend the Nuer against Missiriya incursions. (Later, it accepted arms from the government as part of the new Anyanya-2.) The SPLA were able to gather a number of eager Dinka recruits from northern Bahr al-Ghazal because they, too, wanted to defend their home territory from Baqqara raids which had begun in 1980. They agreed to go to Ethiopia, but when

---

[8] The Gaajak are one of three major divisions of the Eastern Jikany Nuer of Nasir and Akobo districts. They live on both sides of the Sudan–Ethiopian border and form part of the permanent population of Gambela district inside Ethiopia. Fighting in the Sudan during both civil wars accelerated the movement of Gaajak into Ethiopia, where they began to encroach on Anuak settlements around Gambela. Under Mengistu, many Gaajak were brought into influential positions within local Ethiopian administration.

they returned to Bahr al-Ghazal they were later infiltrated around Rumbek and Tonj, leaving northern Bahr al-Ghazal open to increased raiding (Section **6.2.1**).

In Equatoria, the SPLA was still seen as a Dinka army and received substantially less support than elsewhere. In January 1985 the SPLA infiltrated two columns of soldiers into Equatoria, but the troops were ill-disciplined and mistreated civilians in areas already known for their anti-Dinka sentiments. Both columns were repelled by combined forces of the Sudanese army and armed civilians.

By the end of 1985 the SPLA position inside the Sudan was strengthened by its capture of Boma, which became its headquarters in the country, and its occupation of Yirol. The heartland of its recruiting area remained Upper Nile and Bahr al-Ghazal Regions, and its main supply and training bases were Itang, Bonga and Bilpam, inside Ethiopia. It was also active along the northern border of Western Equatoria (especially around Amadi and Mundri). It did have some Equatorian recruits but had yet to make strong inroads into Equatoria. Its repulse from Eastern Equatoria would force it to make its own alliances with local, tribally-organized militias.

5.4 The SPLM/SPLA & other political forces after Nimairi's fall

5.4.1 The SPLM/SPLA's response to the military coup

The war in the South, a collapsing economy, and continuing political repression in Khartoum itself led to a popular rising (*intifada*) of street demonstrations by the citizens of the capital in April 1985. It was spearheaded by the National Alliance for National Salvation, a group of professional and trades unions with contacts with many exile movements. Their Charter of National Salvation, issued at the height of the *intifada*, called for a return to democratic rule under the 1956 constitution. Nimairi was removed by the Sudanese army in Khartoum on 6 April while he was on a state visit to the US. He was replaced by his Defence Minister and Commander-in-Chief, Abd al-Rahman Suwar al-Dahab. The military immediately set up its own Transitional Military Council, and eventually agreed upon an interim council of ministers, drawn mainly from the National Alliance.

The SPLM/SPLA had been in contact with various Sudanese opposition groups before Nimairi's removal, but given the ideological differences between them, there was no close co-operation. Prior to Nimairi's fall some of the northern Sudanese exile opposition leaders complained to Qaddafi about his support for the SPLM/SPLA, because of its commitment to a non-sectarian, secular state, and its opposition to Arab unity. Qaddafi's support for the SPLA began to decline, and was cut off entirely almost immediately after Nimairi fell.

While the northern Sudanese opposition rushed back to the Sudan to take part in the transitional government and to revive old parties or found new ones, the SPLM held aloof. Garang broadcast a speech three days after Nimairi's overthrow, welcoming the popular uprising, but remarking that, 'The ugly shadow of Nimairi looms ominously over the military administration in Khartoum', which, given that the TMC was composed entirely of senior army officers promoted by Nimairi, was almost self-evident. He reiterated the SPLM's platform and vowed that the SPLA would continue its fight against both racism and bigotry.[9]

Garang was vigorously criticized by most northern Sudanese and many southern Sudanese politicians for his intransigence. However, the SPLM's experience in exile had taught them that the northern Sudanese opposition was not yet ready to commit themselves unconditionally to a secular state; many still held to their pre-Nimairi platforms of an Islamic state. Moreover, there was nothing in Suwar al-Dahab's past which indicated a strong break with Nimairi's policies. He repealed the 1973 Constitution, which enshrined a secular state and freedom of religion, yet refused to repeal the 1983 September Laws (other than to suspend the extreme punishments of flogging and amputation). His promulgation of a transitional constitution which recognized *shari'a* as the basis of the country's legal system also indicated his sympathies. When Suwar al-Dahab's Prime Minister, Dr. al-Jizuli Dafallah, invited Garang to return to Khartoum, he offered to rehabilitate the Addis Ababa Agreement (already a dead letter) but gave no commitment to repeal the September Laws. Both Suwar al-Dahab and al-Jizuli showed public sympathy for Islamist programmes during their tenure of office.

The SPLM refused to accept a cease-fire or take part in elections until after a constitutional conference was convened that would include *all* political parties. The opponents of Nimairi had been critical of the South once before for striking a deal with a military dictator, and there was no chance of reaching an agreement with the TMC under the terms offered. Garang explained the SPLM's position in a memo to the OAU summit, dated 18 July 1985, saying, '... the Central Problems in the Sudanese war are the dominance of One Nationality; the Sectarian and Religious Bigotry that dominated the Sudanese political scene since Independence; and the unequal development in the country...unless the Nationality Question is solved correctly, the Religious bigotry is destroyed and a balanced development for all the regions of the Sudan is struck, war is the only invited option in the Sudan'. He hoped that the National Alliance for the Salvation of the Nation could take a more prominent role in constitutional discussions without interference from the army, before the sectarian parties had a chance to regain power. He was to be disappointed.

5.4.2 Northern parties & Koka Dam

Contacts between the SPLM and the National Alliance bore fruit in the Koka Dam meeting in Ethiopia on 20–24 March 1986, a bare month before the first post-Nimairi elections were held. The National Alliance delegation included representatives from the Umma Party, various secular, pan-Arabist, revolutionary, progressive and regional parties, as well as all of the Southern parties. It was significant, however, that neither the Democratic Unionist Party (DUP) nor the National Islamic Front (the Muslim Brothers) chose to attend.

[9] Garang, *The Call for Democracy in Sudan*, pp. 40, 43–6.

The Koka Dam Declaration which resulted from this meeting proposed a constitutional convention to be attended by the government and all political forces, 'to discuss the *Basic Problems of Sudan* and not the so-called problem of Southern Sudan'. The agenda of the convention would include (but would not be confined to) discussion of the 'nationalities question', the 'religious question', basic human rights, the system of rule, development and uneven development, natural resources, the regular forces and security arrangements, the 'cultural question', education and the mass media, and foreign policy. In the meantime the state of emergency would be lifted, the September Laws and other restrictive laws repealed, and the 1956 constitution – amended to incorporate regional government – would be adopted as an interim constitution. In addition, all military pacts concluded between the Sudan and other countries would be abrogated, and both the government and the SPLA would endeavour to effect a ceasefire. The date of the constitutional convention was set for June that year.

The elections were concluded in the North before the convention was to meet. The Umma and DUP parties emerged with the most votes, concentrated geographically in their traditional strongholds. The NIF emerged as the third largest party, their representation artificially enlarged through the manipulation of voting for the graduates' seats. Sadiq al-Mahdi became Prime Minister, leading a coalition of the Umma and DUP – the two parties that had alternated in power in the previous parliamentary periods. Though the Umma were included in the delegation at Koka Dam, the DUP had refused to attend and thus was not a party to any decisions made in the Koka Dam Declaration. On 31 July 1986, Sadiq al-Mahdi met with Garang in Addis Ababa to 'clarify' the SPLM's position. Garang insisted on the main provisions of the Koka Dam, but agreed to link the lifting of the state of emergency with the establishment of a ceasefire. The talks foundered, however, on Sadiq al-Mahdi's refusal to commit himself to a straightforward repeal of the September Laws – those same laws that he had denounced when he was in opposition. Throughout Sadiq al-Mahdi's premiership the Koka Dam Declaration remained on the table, but as a dead letter rather than a working document.

A constitutional convention would still have remained problematic, even if all the major Northern parties had agreed to it and to the preconditions for its convening. The question of representation at the convention remained. The elections of 1986 showed that the sectarian parties would have outnumbered the non-sectarian parties and, if the formula of the 1960s were to be adopted again, could have out-voted the South on crucial measures. There was always the possibility that in 1986 the convention would not produce a solution, given that the main Northern parties had only just re-entered the political arena with their old platforms intact. Nevertheless, it was an option which remained untried.

5.4.3 Southern parties & the SPLA
A number of Southern parties briefly flourished between the fall of Nimairi and the 1986 elections. SANU was revived, but failed to establish a significant constituency at the polls. The Southern Sudan Political

Association (SSPA) was composed mainly of politicians who had held ministerial office in various regional governments, including former opponents as well as former allies. It was considered by many to be tainted by the collective failure of its leaders. There were two other parties active in Equatoria: the People's Progressive Party (PPP), and the Sudan African People's Congress (SAPCO). Both wished to retain devolutionary powers within Equatoria Region but were not opposed to some reformulation of the Southern Region. Both tended to be suspicious of 'Dinka-domination' and were initially suspicious of the SPLA. They divided along the lines of provincial and generational cleavages which had developed in Equatoria under Tembura's governorship. The Sudan African Congress (SAC) and the Sudan People's Federal Party (SPFP) were both mainly confined to Upper Nile Region; the SPFP was restricted to the Nuer. Both advocated some form of federal system rather than reversion to the old Southern Region, while the SPFP was also openly anti-SPLA.

All the parties received funds from the Umma Party, the DUP or the NIF. Some even received funds from Iraq. No true picture of their electoral strength can be gained because the continuation of war prevented the holding of elections in all of the South's constituencies, with 'partial' elections held in only a few of them. The SSPA was often denounced by younger Southerners as 'those exiles in Khartoum', but it was also the only party that managed to return candidates from all three Southern regions. SAC and the SPFP each made a very dismal electoral showing. As in the North, many of the same faces returned to the Southern parliamentary scene.

In relation to the SPLM/SPLA, all the Southern parties had agreed to the Koka Dam Declaration. All, including the Equatorian parties, agreed that the SPLM must be included in any future negotiations. The SSPA maintained a political line closest to that of the SPLM while the two Equatorian parties were politically the most distant. The SPFP formed a loose, and not very happy alliance with the Anyanya-2. Whatever the policies of the parties, old political and personal antagonisms, nurtured during the period of the regional government, served to keep them apart.

Having given an account of the causes leading to the first civil war, and the failure of the peace that brought it to an end, what are some of the patterns that emerge from the first half of this study that will persist through the description of the current war?

The structural divide between Muslim and pagan peoples established in the Sudan by the end of the nineteenth century was not solely religious. It was a divide that encompassed participation in or exclusion from state activities and the degree of access to economic activities, fostered or protected by the state. To the extent that the divide was territorial, identifying those who lived within state boundaries and those who lay beyond them, it also came to be perceived as racial. Those fully participating within the state increasingly identified themselves with Arab lineages, while at the same time identifying those who lived outside the state not only as unbelievers, but as slaves, or as enslavable. This social divide was formalized territorially in the administrative structures and policies of the Condominium period. Investment in the economy, infrastructure and social services was greatest in the central heartlands of the former Sudanic states, and least in the old pagan hinterlands. This had a marked effect on the economic and political integration of the developing and undeveloped regions of the country, and on the social and political integration of the peoples from the undeveloped regions, following independence (Chapters 1, 2 & 3).

The pattern established during the Turkiyya, whereby religion and racial origin influenced access to political power and economic opportunities, has intensified since independence in the mid-twentieth century. It lay behind the failure of the Addis Ababa peace, in so far as the South's most important natural resources, oil and water, could not be allowed to remain under the control of the Southerners themselves (Chapter 4); and it underlies the economic policies of the current Islamist state. While international church groups focus on the religious issue as exclusively defined by the freedom to worship, and Western politicians see religious affiliation in terms of 'minority rights', the economic aspects of religious, and racial oppression in the Sudan are largely ignored, masked as they are by the language of development (Chapter 10). It has been one of the major ironies of the war that the actual and potential wealth of southern societies, and the southern Sudan as a whole – be it in land, livestock, water, oil or minerals – has been the source of their vulnerability. We shall see in the following chapters (especially Chapters 8 & 10) that the control of exploitable resources is one of the features which distinguishes the second civil war from the first. It has intensified the spiral of violence in the South beyond anything experienced before and has also led to the fracturing of the Muslim consensus in the North (Chapter **9**).

The conduct of the war has both ancient and modern patterns. The militia strategy adopted by successive governments to subdue the South (Chapters **5, 6 & 8**), and the use of slave-abductions to terrorize and destabilize civilian populations (Chapter **10**), have distinct 19th-century roots, even if they serve 21st-century objectives in the control of the economy. So, too, does the refinement of the definition of Islam in the exclusion of individuals or groups from participation in political power at the centre (Chapter **9**). For the SPLA, on the other hand, the conduct of the war presented them with thoroughly 20th-century dilemmas.

The guerrilla struggle in the first civil war was hampered by factional and tribal divisions, as well as by confusion over political objectives (Chapters **4 & 5**). The SPLA leadership learned the lessons of the first war extremely well and made the suppression of internal factions one of their initial political objectives – something they had in common with other more successful African liberation movements. Their cohesion was one of the factors in their military successes up to 1991 (Chapter **6**). But having learned the lessons of the previous war, their learning curve flattened out, and they have not met many of the challenges thrown up by their early military success.

Part of this has to do with the objectives of the war. Recruitment into the Movement has been based on the mobilization of grievances against the central government, as an institution, not just against its occupants. These grievances are not confined to the South, a fact that has enabled the SPLA to expand beyond the South's old borders, with a policy of creating a New Sudan in a united country. But having placed the unity of the Sudan at the centre of their political analysis (Chapter **5**), the SPLA failed to make it the centre of their political programme. Not only were they unable to persuade the majority of northern political parties that unity on the SPLA's terms was worth having, but they have similarly failed to convince the majority of their own constituency that unity within a New Sudan will be infinitely preferable to independence for the South alone (Chapter **7**). The SPLA has lost the clarity of its objectives with which it began the war, and this has not only encouraged factionalism, but has enabled the current government to exploit differences within the SPLA, and within the broader national opposition. The party's lack of direction is a major factor in the continuation of the war.

The constellation of international actors has shifted throughout the war. The fall of Nimairi and the realignment of Khartoum in Middle Eastern politics, the collapse of Mengistu and the end of the Cold War, have not brought about in their wake the end of the Sudan's civil war, as many external observers once thought likely. The military and economic interventions of superstates, distant nations, regional powers and neighbouring countries have at different times supported or weakened the government or the opposition, variously affecting the direction and duration of the war. Much of this has been detrimental to the prospects of peace.

However, there is a positive role for international actors to play, as was shown in the initial phases of the IGAD peace process (Chapter **7**), and as may become clear in future mediations. However such discussions are conducted, peace will have to be based on Sudanese ideas of peace, at different levels. These are currently in conflict, and some way will have to be found to build an internal consensus, moving beyond traditional round-table negotiations (Chapter **11**). The temptation for a quick fix is always a danger when new players arrive on the scene, and in this respect any international peace-brokering will be successful only if it returns to the root causes of war, and fully confronts the failures of past peace.

6

The Momentum ▮ of Liberation
1986–91

6.1 Political issues

6.1.1 The commitment of Northern parties to an Islamic state

Sadiq al-Mahdi, the leader of the Umma Party, once had a reputation in the West as a liberal Muslim politician but was fully committed to the establishment of an Islamic state in the Sudan long before the fall of Nimairi. His articulation of this position was in direct opposition to the secular state Nimairi presided over up to 1983. Before Nimairi's fall in 1985 Sadiq advocated the inevitable Islamization and Arabization of the southern Sudan through the manipulation of differences between Southern leaders, and through the activities of Islamic scholars and merchants. In public statements made in Saudi Arabia shortly after Nimairi's fall, and in Iran shortly after he became Prime Minister, he aligned himself with an international expansionary Islamic policy.

In public statements after becoming Prime Minister in 1986 Sadiq offered no real compromise on the issue. He criticised Nimairi's September Laws for being an affront to Muslims needing to be replaced by laws based on sound Islamic principles. He announced himself in favour of 'the full citizen, human, and religious rights' of non-Muslims, but he also declared 'non-Muslims can ask us to protect their rights – and we will do that – but that's all they can ask. We wish to establish Islam as the source of law in Sudan because Sudan has a Muslim majority.'[1]

His coalition partner, the Khatimiyya-backed DUP, adopted an even harder position: any concession to regional autonomy or federalism in the South undermined a future Islamic state. The National Islamic Front (the party of the Muslim Brothers under Sadiq's brother-in-law, Hassan al-Turabi) was committed not just to an Islamic state, but to a particular interpretation of Islamic law that included the death penalty for apostasy. The NIF did accept that in a regional or federal system individual regions could choose whether or not to be governed by *shari'a*, but this concession was qualified in two ways. Firstly, *shari'a* would apply (as in fact it did then apply) to non-Muslims living in the North. Secondly, the

---

[1] Open Letter in *The Guiding Star* (Khartoum), 24 April, pp. 2–3; interview in *Newsweek*, 19 May 1986.

NIF was by no means willing to see the old Southern Region reconstituted. Rather, it preferred to see the maintenance of the three separate regions of Upper Nile, Bahr al-Ghazal and Equatoria, and calculated that Muslim governments could be established in the first two regions within a relatively short time.

Both the DUP and the NIF had refused to attend the Koka Dam conference and were thus not committed to its declaration. Sadiq al-Mahdi's governments were all formed as coalitions with one or the other of these parties. He presented their non-acceptance of Koka Dam as the reason why his Umma Party was no longer bound by the declaration. His vacillation on the issue of *shari'a* and an Islamic constitution was the main obstacle to negotiating an end to the war.

6.1.2 The influence of Islamic banks

The political strength of the sectarian parties was increasingly underwritten by Islamic banking, introduced in the late 1970s as part of Turabi's reform of the financial laws. The NIF was the first to benefit from this new form of finance capital, which gave it a political influence far exceeding its electoral support. The other two parties soon established their own banks. Offering partnership rather than interest to their depositors, Islamic banks encourage speculation in schemes promising quick profits rather than long term investment for future returns. As 'Islamic' institutions the banks have also been favoured by tax exemptions and government contracts and licences. NIF supporters especially profited from investments in privatized state corporations, real estate and large-scale mechanized agriculture for export production. The result has been a convergence of interests between the Islamic banks and the supporters of political parties (the NIF especially) in economic and political policies which favour investors and maintain a supply of cheap wage labour. The labour force came from increasingly marginalized areas in the North and from Southerners displaced by the war. Immediately following the 1984–5 famine there was an expansion of Islamic bank-financed mechanized farming schemes into the Nuba Mountains and the southern Blue Nile, ultimately drawing new regions into the civil war (Chapter **8**).

6.1.3 Common ground within the South

Southern opposition to an Islamic state is founded on more than religious loyalty. Since the main religious parties also drew their support from those Northern merchant and capitalist groups which Southerners perceived as having controlled the central government since independence, the religious and 'nationalities' questions were interconnected with the issue of the economic future of the country. The failure of the regional governments between 1972–83 to assert control over the South's economic development was one of the main Southern disappointments with the Addis Ababa Agreement. The renewed support that the Islamic banks gave to the supporters of the main sectarian parties in the North deepened the economic divide between the centre of the country and the undeveloped peripheral areas. Islamic banking had yet to make major inroads into the economy of the South, but certain productive areas of Upper Nile (especially between Renk and Jabalain) were already under the economic control of heavily capitalized farmers from the North. Sadiq al-Mahdi's public comment on a BBC Radio phone-in programme in 1987, that displaced Southerners in Khartoum should be given 'disciplined' labour on farming schemes, was indicative of his attitude towards the South's economic future.

The Southern parties in the National assembly soon found themselves in permanent opposition. The renewal of the war, the atrocities committed against civilians (Section **6.2.1**), Sadiq al-Mahdi's obvious reluctance to give serious consideration to Southern proposals, and the utter contempt for Southern leaders he showed by including in his government only those Southern leaders who lacked a political constituency of their own, all combined to draw the Southern leaders closer together. They overcame their personal differences enough to begin to speak with one voice in the National Assembly and to send united delegations abroad to meet with Garang and the SPLM.

Given the fact that the 1986 elections in the South were incomplete, and that many rural constituencies went unrepresented, the Southern presence in the Assembly was much less than it might have been. Southern leaders were aware that they would be overlooked altogether, were it not for the SPLA's continuing (and growing) strength on the ground in the South. This was a powerful incentive for them to reach some sort of understanding with the SPLM/SPLA. The SPLM, for its part, sought to reassure the Equatorian leaders, especially, of its willingness to see some form of devolved power within a new Southern Region. Thus one positive effect of the restoration of democracy in the Sudan was that it required the SPLM/SPLA to make its own accommodation with leaders of proven constituencies. It would go through the same process with leaders of Northern constituencies.

6.2 The war on the ground, 1986–9

When Sadiq al-Mahdi became Prime Minister in 1986, Khartoum appeared to be in a much stronger position than the SPLA for any protracted conflict. Libya was now on the side of the Sudanese government, US military assistance was still coming in, and Suwar al-Dahab had rallied the Gulf states to the defence of Islam and Arabism. These factors may have increased Sadiq's unwillingness to deal seriously with the SPLA. Yet Sadiq's political support in the army was weak, especially in the officer corps where the Khatmiyya sect was traditionally strong and where the Muslim Brothers had recently made inroads. This was one reason why Sadiq tried to circumvent the army in his own war strategy, by channelling supplies to surrogate forces and pro-Ansar militias. This strategy not only failed militarily, but also encouraged gross human rights violations against the civilian population.

6.2.1 *Tribal militias, famine & human rights*
The use of tribal militias to fight the SPLA began, as we have already seen (Section **5.3.2**), before 1985, but they became a more significant factor in the war after the fall of Nimairi. The Misiriyya and Rizaiqat Baqqara

Murahalin (militia) of Kordofan and Darfur, especially, received support from western Sudanese members of the TMC, and large well-armed raiding parties of 500 to 1000 men began chasing the Ngok Dinka of Abyei (Southern Kordofan) into northern Bahr al-Ghazal, where the Abiem, Malual and Twic Dinka also came under attack. The main incentive to join the Murahalin in the early 1980s was economic. Many pastoralists had not only lost stock in the drought but had been dispossessed of land-use rights by the mechanized agricultural schemes. Thus in the late twentieth, as in the mid-nineteenth century, some Northerners were impelled towards the exploitation of the southern Sudan in part by their own dispossession and loss of entitlements.

Increased support came from Sadiq al-Mahdi's government in 1986, as the Misiriyya and Rizaiqat were generally members of the Ansar sect and supporters of the Umma Party. As the Murahalin raids also supplied a lucrative cattle trade in the hands of pro-Umma merchants, commercial, political and military needs all seemed neatly met in one policy.[2]

Murahalin raids were at their peak in 1986 and 1987. Their impact in creating famine and spreading human rights abuses have been well documented. Not only were cattle taken, but Dinka villages were attacked and burned, civilians (including women and children) were killed or abducted and taken back to the North where they were traded or kept in slavery. Families split in order to survive: women, children and the elderly tried to follow the rail line from Aweil into Kordofan, and from there made their way to the displaced settlements around Khartoum. As young men were usually killed by the army or the Murahalin if they were caught in northern Bahr al-Ghazal or Southern Kordofan, they tended either to go with the cattle as far south as they could, or head east for Ethiopia, to settle in the refugee camp at Itang or to join the SPLA (or, in sequence, both).

The SPLA began to combat these raids only in 1987, defeating both the Murahalin and the army in a series of clashes (one such defeat led to retaliation against the Dinka refugees in Al-Da'ain in Southern Darfur). Early in 1988 the Murahalin appealed to the army for protection from the SPLA, but by now elements within the army had become worried about supporting what to all intents and purposes was an Umma militia, and refused. Some Murahalin groups expanded their activities into Darfur and the Nuba Mountains, where the threat of SPLA retaliation was less. By 1989 the SPLA was able to secure most of the border from Murahalin attack, and were even able to deny the Misiriyya and Rizaiqat the use of essential dry-season pastures and water along the Kiir (Bahr al-Arab).

Compared to the Murahalin, many of the other tribal militias were far less devastating. They all, however, preyed on the civilian population: the Rufa'a in southern Blue Nile, the Fartit militia in western Bahr al-Ghazal, the Toposa, Lotuko, Mundari and Acholi militias in Equatoria, the Murle militia in Jonglei, and the Anyanya-2 (or 'Friendly Forces') in Upper Nile and Jonglei. For their part, the SPLA struck particularly hard at civilian populations they deemed to be supporting the militias. Thus civilians on all sides became targets as a result of the militia policy.

[2] See David Keen, *The Benefits of Famine. A Political Economy of Famine and Relief in Southwestern Sudan, 1983–1989* (Princeton, 1994) for a detailed analysis of state-generated famine in this area of the Sudan.

Sadiq tried to regularize the militias through his proposal for 'Popular Defence Forces' early in 1989. Most of the senior officers in the army opposed this. One of the few officers who had been involved in supporting the militias in the field was Brigadier Umar al-Bashir. So the policy remained and was expanded, even after Bashir deposed al-Mahdi in June 1989.

The use of armed militias, or 'friendlies', to harass the civilian population during pacification patrols or raids had its precedents not only in the first civil war, but in the Condominium period and even in the nineteenth century. Raiding in the nineteenth century contributed to commercial activity, just as it did in the 1980s. What was distinctive about militia activity in the second civil war was the scale of its military and financial support, not only from the government, but from economic and political allies of the government.[3] The importance of the militia strategy to subdue the South was yet another indication of how closely political attitudes among some factions in the North resembled those of the nineteenth century.

6.2.2 SPLA advances

In 1985 and 1986 the SPLA focused many of its attacks on civilian populations deemed 'hostile' in Jonglei, Equatoria and Bahr al-Ghazal: the Murle, Toposa, Mundari and Fartit especially suffered. The ferocity of SPLA attacks (in part induced by revenge, but also in part induced by desperation to replace supplies lost in Anyanya-2 attacks) served to inhibit the formation of militias elsewhere, especially in Western Equatoria.

In 1987 the SPLA began to adopt a different approach to the militias. It was not always consistently applied, but it helped to win over some militia groups, and laid the foundation for later SPLA military successes in the South and their expansion of the war into the North. In Equatoria the SPLA adopted a more mobile strategy of keeping their units on the move in order to keep the army out of an area, but not to impinge too much on the civilian population. In Bahr al-Ghazal and Jonglei it tried to regularize its search for supplies by imposing a food tax which, once paid, generally freed the civilian population from arbitrary seizures. At a time when the SPLA was trying to improve its relations with the rural population, the army, conversely, continued to alienate civilians by attacking their homes once the SPLA vacated their areas. The SPLA's popularity increased, relative to the army, throughout 1987 and 1988. In 1988 and 1989 it won over a series of local militias to its side, the most significant defection being the bulk of the Anyanya-2 in Upper Nile and Jonglei in 1988. As recruits from areas throughout the South increased, the SPLA gradually began to lose its image as a Dinka army.

Unlike the guerrillas of the first civil war, the SPLA were able to move the war out of the South into Blue Nile, Southern Kordofan (including the Nuba Mountains) and Darfur. The way was often prepared for them by

[3] Even Chevron Oil Company financed a Misiriyya militia, ostensibly to protect its camp at Muglad in Southern Kordofan. Though based nearly a hundred miles away from the border, this militia also tried to raid into Bahr al-Ghazal in 1990, and was decisively defeated by the SPLA.

Arab militias such as the Murahalin and the Rufa'a, who victimised the non-Muslim (and even some Muslim) black populations of those areas, and thus produced ready sympathisers for the SPLA. The SPLA even succeeded in crossing from Ethiopia to take the Northern border towns of Kurmuk and Qaissan with Ethiopian help in November 1987. While the government concentrated on retaking these two towns (readily abandoned by the SPLA), the SPLA was able to take Kapoeta near the Kenyan border, a much more useful prize.

The rapprochement between the Anyanya-2 and the SPLA meant that SPLA supply lines were now secure. By 1988 the SPLA was able to move through much of the southern Sudan without major hindrance and to concentrate its forces around the main government garrisons. 1989 marked a turning point, beginning with the capture of Nasir, and proceeding with a string of victories through May (see Appendix). The SPLA thus secured the entire Ethiopian border from Jokau to Kapoeta and controlled a continuous stretch of territory from the border to northern Bahr al-Ghazal. The Sudanese army now had considerable problems supplying its troops. The old Anyanya had never held a town of any significance; by June 1989 the SPLA held three former provincial capitals (Torit, Bor and Nasir).

6.3 Pressure in the North for a solution

By 1988 dissatisfaction in the North with Sadiq al-Mahdi's parliamentary manoeuverings and his failure to address the major issues facing the country was widespread. The fractious Southern parties had formed themselves into a loose coalition called the United Sudan African Parties (USAP), and had sent several delegations to meet with the SPLM in Ethiopia and East Africa (see Appendix). The DUP, looking forward to the approaching elections, experienced a change of heart in relation to the SPLM. Between May 1987 and November 1988 the DUP held a series of meetings with the SPLM in Addis Ababa, culminating in a direct meeting between Muhammad Uthman al-Mirghani and Garang. Together they signed a declaration which was a modified Koka Dam, with the SPLM dropping its demand that the government dissolve itself, and agreeing merely to a suspension of *shari'a* while a constitutional conference settled the future of the country. The enthusiastic public welcome al-Mirghani received on returning to Khartoum was an illustration of how desperately the Northern public wanted an end to the war. When the Council of Ministers refused to endorse the DUP–SPLM accord, the DUP withdrew from the coalition, leaving the Umma to try to run a government with the NIF.

Early in 1989 the army issued Sadiq with an ultimatum, criticising his war strategy and insisting that he take serious measures to make peace. Sadiq al-Mahdi was forced, reluctantly, to form a new coalition with the DUP and to come closer to negotiating a peace settlement with Garang himself. The NIF refused to accept any terms which qualified their goal of an Islamic state and left the coalition. With a peace settlement now very close, a group of committed Muslim officers in the army, supported by the

NIF, staged a pre-emptive coup on 30 June, 1989, shortly before Sadiq was scheduled to meet Garang in Addis Ababa. The peace process, so long in the making, but so close to a real breakthrough, was thus brought to a complete halt.

6.4 SPLA advances, 1989–90

The new military government in Khartoum hoped to regain the military initiative in the South in 1990, but singularly failed to do so. The Gulf crisis of 1990–1 cost the Sudan some of its backers in the Arab world, as its support for Iraq alienated Saudi Arabia and other Gulf states. Iraq, a consistent supporter of the Sudanese army, was no longer in a position to supply the Sudan with arms.[4] The SPLA, on the other hand, enjoyed a temporary diplomatic respectability and secured new sources of arms and supplies in 1990 (mainly from Namibia and some of the former Front Line States of southern Africa, mediated by 'Tiny' Rowland of Lonrho). Government strategy at the end of 1990 reverted to fighting through militias, especially Anyanya-2 stationed at Mayom and New Fangak, and Toposa infiltrated out of Juba behind SPLA lines.

The territorial gains of the first half of 1989 presented the SPLA with new challenges and opportunities. Militarily, it was tempted to alter its strategy from guerrilla to conventional warfare. It retook, and briefly held, the town of Kurmuk at the end of 1989. With new supply routes of its own through East Africa, it launched an attack in the area west of Juba and took Kajo-Kaji and Kaya in February 1990. Later in the same year, again making use of its new supply routes as well as its old bases in Ethiopia, the SPLA shifted significant numbers of soldiers from the Blue Nile and Upper Nile to the new southwestern theatre. The Nuer soldiers who figured so prominently in the siege and fall of Nasir were part of the spearhead which took the whole of Western Equatoria in November 1990 and closed in around Yei and Juba. In western Bahr el-Ghazal some of the Fartit militia also began making their peace with the SPLA. Even the Murahalin in Southern Kordofan and Southern Darfur found it in their interest to negotiate their return to the dry season pastures denied them by the SPLA. The local SPLA commander encouraged them to do so, but insisted that they use Dinka chiefs as intermediaries. By early 1991 the military initiative seemed to lie securely with the SPLA.

6.5 The SPLA & Equatoria

The reception of the SPLM/SPLA in Equatoria has long been ambivalent. Equatorian chauvinism in the early 1980s was satisfied by the expulsion of the Dinka and other 'Nilotics' from Equatoria. The overwhelmingly 'Nilotic' character of the early SPLA was thus enough to alienate many Equatorians. The inclusion of Joseph Oduho in the SPLM did little to alter

---

[4] There have been numerous reliable reports of the transfer of Iraqi weapons, especially missiles and airplanes, to the Sudan, as well as Iraqi assistance in the development of Sudanese chemical weapons plants.

this perception, as Oduho had already lost support among many of his own people through his alliance with Alier in 1980. Equatorian particularism was not satisfied, however, with the terms of regionalisation in 1983. The SPLM's advocacy of greater strength to the regions throughout the Sudan thus had some appeal. Paradoxically, the SPLM's public insistence on a united Sudan may have undercut its potential support in Equatoria, where there was strong separatist sympathy.

The behaviour of successive Khartoum governments and the Sudanese army did much to move public opinion in Equatoria closer to the SPLM/SPLA. The obviously conciliatory behaviour of Garang towards delegations of Equatorian politicians (especially when the USAP delegation helped the SPLA establish a working relationship with Museveni's newly installed government in Uganda), and the attempt to tighten discipline among SPLA soldiers in Equatoria after 1984 also encouraged this move. Continued attacks on some rural communities, as well as the intermittent shelling of Juba, however, reinforced doubts about the SPLA's commitment to the 'liberation' of the civilian population. Two contrasting patterns developed in the SPLA's approach to Eastern and Western Equatoria, one based on a network of local alliances, and the other initially showing more restraint in dealings with civilians.

In Eastern Equatoria the SPLA sought to establish itself through military alliances with various militias. This inevitably involved them in fighting against the rivals of their allies. Thus by allying with the Boya against the Toposa the SPLA were also brought into conflict with the Longarim. By allying with the Sudanese Acholi they were brought into a further alliance with the Ugandan Acholi against Ugandan Madi refugees in the Sudan. The SPLA tried to broaden its support by recruiting a few soldiers from local communities, and then sending those early volunteers back to their home areas to recruit more soldiers. Thus their base slowly expanded and by 1988 they counted Mundari and Toposa among their ranks.

Yet much of their support in Eastern Equatoria was still based on alliances of expediency, where loyalties could change. Those communities, such as the Toposa and the Mundari, which were internally split over alliances with the SPLA, were particularly susceptible to strains on their allegiance. Mundari soldiers in the SPLA were unhappy with the behaviour of other SPLA troops in the Terekeka and Tali areas in 1990, and showed signs of dissatisfaction. The Toposa adopted a more materialistic approach, appearing to side with whoever offered them the most in weapons and food. Because the SPLA alternated between harsh repression and reconciliation with both the Toposa and Mundari, they never achieved the firm alliances with either that they needed. Renewed government support for a Toposa militia based in Juba seriously destabilised the SPLA position around Kapoeta in 1990–1 and led to its recapture by the government in 1992.

In Western Equatoria (which for military purposes includes Kajo-Kaji and Yei), the civilian population had been wary of the SPLA, but the local commanders at first showed greater restraint in their approach to local peoples than was evident on the east bank in 1983–6. There was considerable fighting around Maridi and Mundri before 1986, but because locals did not form themselves into pro-government militias the SPLA did not attack them. Government repression of people inside the towns did much to increase local sympathy for the SPLA. In the Yei area the appointment of James Wani Igga as SPLA Zonal Commander helped to engage public sympathy, if not win popular support. James Wani is reported to have had some disagreements with Garang over the disciplining of SPLA soldiers, and most of his subordinate commanders were not Equatorian, but he himself commanded great respect among civilians. The fall of Western Equatoria in 1990 was accompanied by the flight of many civilians to the Central African Republic, Zaïre and Uganda, and their evident reluctance to return home in 1991, even after all threat of fighting had receded, spoke of a continuing suspicion of the SPLA. It may be for this reason that the civil/military administration initially set up in Western Equatoria was designed to increase confidence and was originally far less centralised and authoritarian than other administrations elsewhere in the South. Local markets and commercial activity flourished (though much reduced from pre-war levels), and relief was handled through relief committees which included local representatives, rather than being subordinated entirely to the SPLA's Sudan Relief and Rehabilitation Association (SRRA).

By the end of 1991 the SPLA in Equatoria was tolerated. A growing number of Equatorians were to be found in the SPLA, in the civil administration, and in relief operations. The commitment of the Khartoum government to the National Islamic Front's brand of militant Islam had done much to alienate Equatorians, especially those living in Juba. In 1990–1 the SPLA was improving its treatment of people escaping from Juba. All the same, those who lost members of their family to SPLA landmines or shelling were among those whose opposition to the SPLA hardened. In general, the majority of Equatorians appeared to prefer the SPLA, as a Southern movement, to Khartoum, but they were still wary of the movement's leadership.

6.6 The parallel war in Ethiopia

6.6.1 SPLA involvement in internal warfare in Ethiopia
The Mengistu government already faced armed resistance from some local groups in southwestern Ethiopia before the Sudanese civil war began. Anuak fleeing conscription into peasant militias in the late 1970s were formed into a 'Gambela People's Liberation Front' (GPLF) under Sudanese patronage in 1980. The Oromo Liberation Front (OLF) was founded in eastern Ethiopia in 1975 and opened a front in Wallega Province in 1980 with the assistance of the EPLF and the Sudanese army. Throughout the early 1980s the OLF worked closely with the Sudanese army and were often garrisoned alongside them inside Sudan. The attitude of the OLF towards the non-Oromo peoples of Wallega, was far from benign. The GPLF for their part often targeted Ethiopian Nuer whose numbers in Gambela grew as more and more crossed the border to escape the war in the Sudan. These Nuer were increasingly incorporated into the local administration by the Mengistu government, and this was another grievance for the Anuak, who felt themselves doubly displaced from their homes: first by highland resettlement schemes, and then by the Nuer. The

Anuak were by no means united: the Ethiopian government armed both Nuer and Anuak as local home guards, but Anuak who resented the Nuer intrusion under SPLA auspices joined the GPLF.

As the SPLA presence in southwestern Ethiopia grew, it was brought increasingly into Ethiopia's internal war, partly as the price for Ethiopia's substantial military and logistical support, and partly as an extension of the war against Khartoum's militias. Some of the earliest military activity inside Ethiopia was aimed at the Gaajak Nuer supporters of the Anyanya-2. Knowing the close relationship between the Sudan army and the OLF and GPLF, the SPLA willingly (and, according to some reports, enthusiastically) attacked OLF and GPLF camps, both inside Ethiopia and in the Sudan, and victimised civilians associated with the two organizations. The SPLA's successes against the OLF as early as 1985 brought it nearly unlimited military support from Ethiopia and cemented the personal alliance between Mengistu and Garang. Further south, it is alleged the SPLA also raided local peoples for cattle, but their forces cannot be held responsible for all atrocities laid at their feet. Many of the raids were carried out by other groups living on either side of the border who had received arms from the Sudanese army or its militia allies (the Nyangatom used weapons they got from the Toposa to attack the Mursi).[5] In either case, the Sudanese civil war only added to the political instability and insecurity of life in southern and southwestern Ethiopia.

6.6.2 The impact of the fall of Mengistu on the SPLA

The collapse of the Mengistu government in Ethiopia in May 1991 seriously reversed the SPLA's military momentum. The SPLA refused to enter into any talks with the Ethiopian rebel groups who were poised to take power in early 1991, as a result of which there was a very hasty evacuation of SPLA camps and personnel from Ethiopia (including over 200,000 Sudanese refugees who had been living in SPLA-protected centres near the Upper Nile border). The most immediate effect on the SPLA was its loss of protected bases, secure supply lines, a source of supply for non-military as well as military goods, and its highly effective radio station. The new Provisional Government of Ethiopia was not only hostile to the SPLA but had close links with the Sudanese army. It handed over all of the old Ethiopian government's security files on the SPLA. There was a very real possibility that Ethiopia would allow the Sudan army to launch attacks on the SPLA from their territory. The GPLF took control of Gambela town on 25 May. Fighting broke out between Ethiopian Nuer and Anuak militias, as the Anuak sought to re-establish their control over Gambela reigon, where most of the SPLA bases were located. Groups of armed men, under nobody's direct control, became a very real threat to the Sudanese refugees inside Ethiopia.

6.6.3 The crisis of the Sudanese returnees

The Sudanese refugee population around the three camps of Itang, Fungyido and Dimma was officially tallied at just over 400,000 in

---

[5] David Turton, 'Mursi political identity & warfare: the survival of an idea', and Serge A. Tornay, 'More chances on the fringe of the State? The growing power of the Nyangatom: a border people of the Lower Omo Valley, Ethiopia (1970–1992)', both in Fukui & Markakis (eds), *Ethnicity & Conflict in the Horn of Africa* (London/Athens OH, 1994).

February 1991, but unofficially the estimate was much lower, around 222,000 to 262,000. The population at Itang represented virtually every area affected by the Sudan conflict, with refugees from the Blue Nile and Southern Kordofan as well as all three southern regions. There had been movements between the refugee camps and the southern Sudan throughout 1989–90, with some refugees going home, but more taking their places. There was no large-scale return of refugees from Ethiopia reported by any relief agency for any part of the southern Sudan before 1990. Relief personnel did, however, observe new movements of displaced persons from Southern Kordofan, western and central Upper Nile, and Malakal going to Ethiopia during the rainy season of 1990, when it was impossible for relief agencies to supply them with emergency food in the districts along the Sobat river through which they passed. As late as February 1991, when the fall of the Mengistu government was already anticipated, the donor community supplying the Sudanese refugee camps was contemplating the eventual repatriation of the refugees through increased relief efforts in the southern Sudan. The Multi-Donor Technical Mission report on the Sudanese refugee camps recommended: 'Eventual repatriation should always be kept in mind. It is interesting that many of the refugee representatives suggest that international relief efforts should henceforth be concentrated in Sudan itself to prevent further substantial influxes.'[6]

The Sobat, Nasir, Waat, Akobo and Pibor areas had all suffered serious food shortfalls in 1988–90. They had been at the farthest end of the Operation Lifeline Sudan supply line from East Africa and had received very little in the way of food, seeds, tools or fishing equipment, relative to the affected population (Chapter **10**). WFP's OLS Nairobi office did plan to position buffer stocks of food in those areas during the dry season of 1991, but this was forbidden by the WFP Khartoum office, responding to the government of Sudan's ban on relief convoys in this area. The local population of these areas therefore had no reserve margin of their own, and the agencies had not been able to establish a relief network. Thus both the local populace and the international relief community were unprepared to meet the sudden return of refugees which began in May 1991.

The SPLA administration of the camps had anticipated the fall of Mengistu, and when fighting broke out in the Gambela region they organized a mass evacuation of the Itang, Funygido and Dimma camps. No accurate figure can be given of the number of returnees, because not all who came through Nasir, Pochalla and Pakok (near Boma) were registered; nor were the registers accurate. Available figures suggest that at least 132,000 came through Nasir, between 75,000 and 100,000 (from Itang and Fungyido) settled around Pochalla, and some 20,000 went from Dimma to Pakok. The returnees were highly mobile, despite it being the rainy season, and many moved back and forth along the Sobat and Pibor rivers in response to reports of the arrival of relief aid. Subsequent visits along the Sobat and to Ayod and Bor revealed that substantial numbers had either circumvented Nasir or had passed quickly through it in order to get to their home areas before the heavy rains set in. By July as many as

---

[6] Multi-Donor Technical Mission on Refugees and Returnees, *Report on Mission to Western Region Sudanese Refugee Camps*, February 1991.

96,000 returnees had probably settled in and around the food and medical distribution centres established near Nasir. Of these, some 40,000 (including about 25,000 from Blue Nile Province) had no ties with the local population and were completely dependent on relief supplies.

The international relief effort was both ill-coordinated and inadequate and was incapable of confronting the government strategy of splitting the SPLA through manipulating relief. The UN failed to reach an agreement with Khartoum that would guarantee an unbroken delivery of supplies of all types in quantities adequate for the needs of the largest group of returnees on the Sobat. The US government obstructed the relief effort, disputing the UN's figures and proposing to divert relief aid to help stabilize the new Ethiopian government's control over its provinces. The US even floated a proposal that relief to the Sudanese returnees be cut off and all those who could not return to their homes should be required to return to Ethiopia as refugees. The returnees thus became a political football, and the relief effort was seriously undermined.[7] This opened the way for further intervention from Khartoum, which ultimately split the SPLA.

[7] D. H. Johnson, 'Increasing the trauma of return: an assessment of the UN's emergency response to the evacuation of the Sudanese refugee camps in Ethiopia, 1991', in Tim Allen (ed.), *In Search of Cool Ground: Displacement and Homecoming in Northeast Africa* (London, 1996). A. Scott-Villiers, P. Scott-Villiers & Cole P. Dodge, 'Repatriation of 150,000 Sudanese refugees from Ethiopia: the manipulation of civilians in a situation of civil conflict', *Disasters*, 17 (1993), emphasizes SPLA manipulation of civilians but makes no admission of US and UN (including UNICEF) acquiescence in the Sudan government's more sustained and systematic manipulation of civilians and relief supplies both before and throughout OLS.

The SPLA Split | 7 Surviving Factionalism

7.1 Internal differences within the SPLA

The South's first civil war had been plagued by factional fighting between guerrilla movements, and the SPLA's policy of preventing military factionalism was a direct attempt to apply lessons learnt from this past. In its suppression of internal dissent and its attack on military rivals, the SPLA followed a pattern similar to that of many other contemporary African liberation movements.[1] The SPLA's military organization was the foundation of its success on the ground. It achieved far greater centralization and cohesion than the old Anyanya and maintained an expanding ability to take and hold territory far beyond that of any of the Southern guerrilla movements of the 1960s.

The political price of the policy was that the leadership relied on force rather than persuasion to maintain cohesion. Dissenters were removed while the causes of dissent were not, and the civil base of the Movement was neglected in favour of the military organization. Civil administration was most advanced in those areas providing the strongest popular support (Bahr al-Ghazal, Upper Nile and much of Lakes and Jonglei), and where political mobilization was easiest. In the remoter regions of the southern Blue Nile and Nuba Mountains, SPLA presence before 1989 was seasonal, at best. In the territories formerly opposed to the SPLA (Eastern Equatoria and Pibor) administration was more military occupation than popular liberation.

As long as Garang had Mengistu's support he was able to exert considerable control over the Movement's hierarchy. After its founding meeting in 1983 the SPLM held no national convention until 1994, and civilian figures, such as the respected judge Martin Majier or the veteran politician Joseph Oduho, had scarcely any role in the formulation or implementation of policy. The central organizing body of the Movement, the Political-Military High Command, whose members were appointed by Garang, was not convened in full between 1986 and 1991. In 1987 it became a double-tiered structure of full (or permanent) members and alternate commanders

---

[1] For the suppression of dissent within SWAPO in Namibia, see Colin Leys & John Saul, *Namibia's Liberation Struggle. The Two-Edged Sword* (London/Athens OH/Cape Town, 1995). For attacks on rival liberation movements by the EPLF in Eritrea and the TPLF in Ethiopia, see the chapters by David Pool and John Young in Clapham (ed.), *African Guerrillas* (Oxford/Bloomington IN/Kampala, 1998).

with limited voting rights and duties.[2] Garang was often aloof or unapproachable, frequently on the move between the Movement's headquarters in Addis Ababa and Boma, its bases around Itang or in the Sudan, or visiting the capitals of friendly countries. Thus, even at the highest level of the Movement, there was no regular forum where questions of accountability could be raised on political matters, financial affairs, internal discipline, military strategy, external alliances and peace negotiations.

The SPLA, the military wing, was modelled on the Sudanese army, complete with an internal security branch. The escalation of the war with the Anyanya-2 after 1984 was accompanied by internal purges of suspected government agents. There were confrontations with various commanders, including members of the PMHC, which ended in their arrest and detention. These culminated in a succession of confrontations in 1987–8. Kerubino Kuanyin tried to enlist Mengistu's help in overthrowing Garang, but instead, Mengistu assisted in Kerubino's arrest and detention by the SPLA. Arok Thon Arok, who was senior to Garang in the Sudanese army, was openly insubordinate, challenging Garang's leadership of the SPLA and establishing personal contacts with the Sudanese government before his own arrest. Some of those charged with offences against military discipline were executed, but most prisoners were never formally charged and were kept alive in harsh conditions.[3]

There was centralized control over the formulation of policy and strategy, but there were limits to this control. Members of the PMHC fulfilled their specific duties in their own ways, rather than out of collective responsibility. The very terrain of the southern Sudan, which had defeated all other past forms of centralized administration, limited the degree of centralization which could be imposed by a guerrilla movement. The use of two-way radios (and even the broadcasts of Radio SPLA from Ethiopia) improved contact between the high command and the field units, but in practical matters local commanders had a great degree of autonomy, especially in administration, taxation and recruitment. Frequently voiced criticisms of Garang were that he gave far too much leeway to commanders in the field and did not hold them to account for the behaviour of their troops. In theory, for instance, all sentences of death imposed by the SPLA-supervised courts were supposed to be referred back to the high command for confirmation. In practice sentences were imposed and carried out by local commanders, with or without the benefit of courts. Kerubino Kuanyin Bol, Arok Thon Arok and Lam Akol – who all subsequently denounced Garang for dictatorial behaviour – are reported to have carried out

[2] The difficulties of recalling commanders from distant postings in order to convene a meeting should not be underestimated. When the SPLM finally did convene a National Convention in 1994, it took some delegates from the remoter areas of SPLA-held territory (such as the Nuba Mountains) a hundred days of travelling by foot to reach the SPLA headquarters in New Cush, near Chukudum.

[3] The origin of Garang's most influential opponents and detainees makes it difficult to substantiate the charge that Garang's actions were tribally motivated. Joseph Oduho was a Lotuko from Eastern Equatoria, but Arok Thon Arok was a Twic Dinka, like Garang himself, Martin Majier was a Bor Dinka, and Kerubino Kuanyin Bol and Faustino Atem Gualdit were both Dinka from Bahr al-Ghazal.

summary executions of their own troops, acts for which they were never held accountable.[4] The 'New Sudan' administration being set up in the SPLA-controlled areas was thus very uneven.

Towards the end of the 1980s there was some recognition that an alteration in this policy was needed, even if for no other reason than that military considerations required it. The approaches made to individual units of the Anyanya-2 in Jonglei and Upper Nile in 1986–8 were a demonstration of the practical advantages of resolving differences through negotiation (Section **6.2.2**).[5] The local peace negotiated with many Arab militias along the Bahr al-Ghazal border with Kordofan and Darfur in 1990 was a further demonstration of the benefits of reconciliation (Section **6.4**), as was the truce negotiated between the Nuer, Anuak and Murle at Akobo during the late dry season that year. In spite of these examples, the concerns of civil administration throughout much of the SPLA-controlled territory remained subordinated to the military command and to military goals.

As the war moved into its seventh year, many people in the Movement began to question its overall strategy, and some suspected that Garang was allowing Mengistu to drag out the war purely as a political ploy to undermine Khartoum's support for anti-Derg forces in Ethiopia. There were many in Bahr al-Ghazal and Upper Nile who objected to the concentration of troops and equipment in the Equatoria fronts, under the direct command of Garang and his kinsman, Kuol Manyang Juk. These were all serious and legitimate questions, but aside from taking them up personally with Garang, there seemed no institutionalized way in which they could be raised, openly debated or resolved.

Two commanders who did raise the issue of accountability and the need for a more democratic procedure with Garang in 1990 and 1991 were the two senior commanders of Upper Nile: Riek Machar and Lam Akol. Both had been promoted by Garang over the heads of longer-serving SPLA officers and had been appointed alternate (i.e. non-voting) members of the PMHC. Both had been actively involved with Garang in international missions on behalf of the SPLA in 1988–9. Lam Akol, as Director of the External Relations Department, had been influential in the negotiations which led to the creation of the UN Operation Lifeline Sudan (OLS) in 1989. By the end of 1990 both had been reassigned to field positions in Upper Nile and appeared to be politically and militarily marginalized.[6] The shift in focus of the SPLA's military strategy from the northern part of

---

[4] Peter Adwok Nyaba, *The Politics of Liberation in South Sudan: An Insider's View* (Kampala, 1997), pp. 68–9.

[5] One impetus for this reconciliation with the main Nuer opposition may have come from the threat posed by Kerubino Kuanyin and other Dinka officers in their unsuccessful attempt to remove Garang that same year.

[6] A complaint Riek Machar voiced in 1991 was that Garang had excluded him and other commanders from diplomatic missions. This complaint now seems difficult to credit. At the time Riek had been back in the field for scarcely more than a year, after involvement in missions to Europe and East Africa in 1989–90. Despite having removed Lam from the position of Director of External Affairs in early 1990, Garang sent him to represent the SPLA at a meeting of the NDA in Cairo in December 1990. It should be recognized, also, that as alternate commanders, they had neither the automatic right to attend or to demand meetings. See Nyaba, *The Politics of Liberation in South Sudan*, pp. 45, 78–82.

the southern Sudan to Juba and Equatoria left Riek Machar, Zonal Commander of northern Upper Nile, feeling neglected and exposed.

The initiative for removing Garang came from Lam Akol. Since his university days in the 1970s he had shown a genius for antagonizing colleagues and subordinates. He had exhibited a marked lack of tact when in command of SPLA forces in the Shilluk area in 1987–8, alienating even the Shilluk *reth* (king). Some of the individuals he approached initially suggested that any movement for internal reform should include Riek Machar, who had proved himself a popular field commander with substantial backing among the Nuer. The proximity of Riek's headquarters at Nasir to the refugee camps and training bases in Gambela region in neighbouring Ethiopia gave him access to the SPLA's rear base. It was here that Lam and Riek could lay the political groundwork, and by early 1991 there was strong support among Nuer in the Gambela camp adminis-tration, including, even, the Ethiopian Nuer authorities of the region, for a change of leadership within the SPLA.[7] Aside from the Nuer, most of those within the SPLA who gave a sympathetic hearing to the two commanders' complaints were those who responded most positively to the idea of insti-tutional and structural reform rather than a change of leadership.

By late 1990, at the SPLA's military high point, the end of Mengistu's regime in Ethiopia was clearly on the horizon. Garang seems to have calculated that an all-out military push to capture Juba could be achieved before Mengistu's demise would have an appreciable effect on the SPLA's military effort. He displayed a personal faith in the political survival skills of Mengistu, even when urged by Mansour Khalid to open contacts with the anti-Derg coalition, the Ethiopian People's Revolutionary Democratic Front (EPRDF). The deployment of SPLA units in support of the Ethiopian army against the OLF and GPLF in Assosa ended in a serious defeat and rout of both the Ethiopian army and the SPLA. To those opposed to Garang the timing of military events was crucial: Garang would be weakened by Mengistu's fall, but Garang in control of Juba would be almost impossible to remove.

7.2 Vulnerability of the Nasir command

The fall of Mengistu in May 1991 had a more immediate impact on the security of northern Upper Nile than on any other SPLA command. New factors were added to the existing concerns of the commanders, affecting their situation.

7.2.1 Military vulnerability
Having been denuded of many of its troops for the Western Equatoria offensive, and having lost Melut the previous year, the northern Upper Nile SPLA command was in a precarious position. With the onset of the rains the SPLA was unable to shift reinforcements to the area. Following an initiative by Garang at the beginning of the year, some of the remaining Anyanya-2 camps at Doleib Hill (near Malakal) and New Fangak joined

---

[7] Nyaba, *The Politics of Liberation in South Sudan*, pp. 78–85.

the SPLA, but they brought few supplies with them. In the meantime government forces were resupplied with heavy equipment in Malakal, and there were rumours of the Sudan army units taking up positions inside Ethiopia. Because of their earlier confrontation with Garang, the two commanders had reason to doubt that Garang would resupply them prior to the government's expected dry-season offensive. They may have feared that Upper Nile was to be sacrificed to an all-out offensive against Juba. Though the SPLA had lost their major supplier in nearby Ethiopia, Garang had secured SWAPO's surplus supplies from Namibia, but this was all being concentrated far away in Equatoria.

7.2.2 The burden of the returnees and the influence of relief agencies

The Nasir command faced the immediate task of dealing with the sudden return of most of the refugees evacuated from Itang (Section **6.6.3**). The Sobat and Pibor river areas had never received much relief assistance from Operation Lifeline Sudan, and had no relief network or adminis-tration in place to cope with the new problem. The problem of relief was not confined to the 100,000-plus returnees who settled along the Sobat and Pibor rivers during the rains of 1991; the existing population of this area had suffered several years of bad harvests and shortages and had little reserve to share with the newcomers. Their needs had to be added to the needs of the returnees, but the international relief effort was unable to cope with either. Khartoum refused to allow sufficient supply of food or shelter materials to Nasir by air; the overland route from Ethiopia was both uncertain and insecure; and the provision of food by barge under UN control from Kosti was subject to manipulation by government authorities in Khartoum and Malakal. The returnees who were temporarily settled around Nasir in order to receive relief supplies were also vulnerable to air attack. This only added to the commanders' anxiety that they could be faced by simultaneous overland assaults from Malakal, Blue Nile, and even Ethiopia.

The returnee emergency brought an unprecedented number of repre-sentatives of various agencies, donors and governments to Nasir to assess the situation for themselves and to talk to the two commanders. Riek Machar and Lam Akol, who had earlier expressed resentment at being excluded from the SPLM/SPLA's diplomatic activity, were now in a position to negotiate directly with relief agencies, and to speak directly to representatives of the UN and various governments. Though specific international agencies (and even persons) were later accused of complicity in the Nasir coup at the end of August 1991, their influence was less direct. Nonetheless, the two commanders' assessment of their likely chances was based, in part, on their assessment of international opinion as represented by their visitors.

In international eyes, the SPLA was tarred by its association with Mengistu, and it was soon clear that this was influencing the relief policy of the USA. The tone of US comments was highly critical of the SPLA, and ultimately obstructive of the UN relief effort for the returnees (Section **6.6.3**). In particular the US began to raise various 'humanitarian' issues, especially concerning the thousands of young boys (the 'unaccom-panied minors') who came out of the Itang and Funygido camps, and were alleged to be recruits for the SPLA. Since Garang was seen as the principal ally and beneficiary of Mengistu, it appeared to the two commanders that a change in SPLA leadership would lead to a change of heart by the US. Certainly there were contacts from US government agencies who encouraged them in this belief.

Whatever may have been said, or hinted, by representatives of different US organizations, the two commanders took up issues which were then favoured in US circles. In line with their support for the 'ethnic federalism' then being imposed by the EPRDF in Ethiopia, the US government was the only one to respond favourably to the Nasir commanders' call for a separate South, and the Nasir faction certainly interpreted that as a sign of intrinsic support.

7.2.3 Contacts with the government

In addition to the presence of various Western relief agencies, Khartoum manipulated the relief emergency to put further pressure on the Nasir commanders. They limited the UN airdrop to providing 500 MT of grain for over 100,000 persons at the height of the returnee crisis, and insisted that additional food be delivered by barge from Kosti, making deliveries to government-held areas (with no known food needs) on the way. Thus, not only did Khartoum restrict the amount of food coming in, it was able to manipulate the timing of deliveries as well, creating recurring mini-crises and food shortages. But of greater importance was the barge-link established between the government in Malakal and the Nasir command. Eventually it was Riek Machar's brother-in-law, Taban Deng Gai (former camp administrator of Itang and newly appointed head of the SRRA, the SPLA's relief wing, in Nasir), who became the main contact between the government and Nasir.

Direct contact between the Nasir commanders and the Khartoum-appointed Governor of Upper Nile State in Malakal (Lt. Colonel Gatluak Deng, also a Nuer) had already begun by July 1991. By August there was an agreement for military support from the government for the Nasir commanders against Garang, and even for the transfer of the remaining Anyanya-2 units in Doleib Hill, New Fangak and Mayom to the Nasir command. This was of some importance because, by August, support for a change of leadership within the SPLA was on the wane.

Initially, the Nasir commanders had tried to prepare the way for Garang's removal by circulating their arguments for a change of leadership and a change of policy to as many SPLA commanders as they could reach through Nairobi. They also contacted Nuer and Shilluk security officers based in Equatoria. The loss of the SPLA's Ethiopian bases in May 1991 altered the equation. Many who earlier had been receptive to Lam and Riek's arguments now felt that a change in leadership – especially a violent change in leadership – before the SPLA could recover from these losses, would further weaken it. Others whom the Nasir commanders sought to bring to their side simply failed to respond. The Nasir commanders had now committed themselves to ousting Garang, not to a process of reform. The only allies they were certain of at the time of the coup announcement were the government authorities in Malakal.

7.3 Declared aims of the Nasir coup

The 'overthrow' of John Garang was first announced by the Nasir commanders to SPLA units via the SPLA two-way radio network on 28 August 1991, then repeated in a BBC radio interview. They denounced Garang as a dictator, called for greater democracy in the SPLM/SPLA command structure, and pledged themselves to a greater respect for human rights, especially in regard to the release of political prisoners, and a halt to the recruitment of 'child soldiers'. They also announced that the SPLM/SPLA's new objective was to obtain the independence of the southern Sudan (the ambiguities of that position, in relation to their alliance with the government, will be examined in Section **8.1**). Riek and Lam were supported in their coup announcement by Gordon Kong Cuol, the Nuer commander of the former Anyanya-2, an organization previously favouring secession of the South and previously allied with the government.

The three commanders hoped that dissatisfaction with Garang would be widespread in Equatoria, where both separatist and anti-Dinka feeling was strong, and in Bahr al-Ghazal, which felt neglected both in terms of the overall military strategy of the movement and in securing of relief supplies. But there had been no systematic domestic preparation for the coup; both commanders had concentrated more on securing external support. In the end the only areas to rally immediately to the Nasir faction were the Nuer districts already under the Upper Nile Command. The Bul Nuer and Lou Nuer Anyanya-2 units at Mayom and Doleib Hill declared for the coup as previously agreed with the government.

7.4 Events of September–December 1991

7.4.1 Garang's response

There were some skirmishes between soldiers who declared for Riek and those who remained loyal to Garang along the Sobat and in Waat and Ayod districts. There was a more serious split among the Shilluk SPLA along the White Nile, where many soldiers refused to join Lam Akol. Even an appeal from the *reth* of the Shilluk failed to avert a bloody confrontation. The Meban under Lam's direct command also disobeyed his orders and withdrew to join other loyal SPLA units.

Though Garang had assured various exile Southerners that he had no intention of attacking the Nasir faction, he gave orders to one of his Nuer commanders, William Nyuon Bany, to advance along the Jonglei Canal line towards Ayod in September–October. Whether he was responding to attacks on Garang loyalists or had always intended to advance on them is still a subject of debate.[8] The fighting between the two factions included attacks on civilians on both sides of the border. The Nasir faction troops based in Ayod beat back this attack and, reinforced by the Anyanya-2 from New Fangak and Doleib Hill, counter-attacked deep into the Dinka territory around Kongor. The Anyanya-2 were under no proper control

---

[8] After breaking from Garang in 1992, Nyuon is reported to have said that he had been acting on Garang's direct orders.

and targeted the Dinka civilian population. The violence of the attack was probably inspired by the knowledge that John Garang himself came from Aborom, just south of Kongor.

Garang's SPLA (now being called the Torit faction)[9] countered on two fronts: the first to move troops from Bor to Kongor, to push the Ayod troops of the Nasir faction back, and the second to send a contingent of troops by barge to attack Adok and Ler, Riek Machar's home area. The reasons for this assault were more strategic than personal, as the Mayom Anyanya-2 had just declared for Riek. Garang's troops destroyed fuel and other supplies stored near Adok and tried to seize the Ler landing-strips to prevent further supplies being flown by Khartoum to Riek's supporters (see Section **7.4.2**). The troops were repulsed, and Riek launched another more serious attack against Garang's forces at Kongor and Bor in November. On this occasion, the invading force consisted of Nasir SPLA, Anyanya-2, and armed Nuer civilians.

The talk in Nasir suggested that most of Riek's supporters hoped that by defeating Garang in his home territory, the other SPLA commanders would come off the fence and join them, but not all of Riek's commanders advocated taking the war to Garang's home. Several have claimed that they warned Riek of the dangers of unleashing Nuer soldiers on the Dinka districts, but that he ignored these warnings. When the first reports of the slaughter of civilians in Kongor and Bor districts arrived in Nasir, Riek was again urged by at least one of his Nuer officers either to order the immediate withdrawal of the troops, or to send a senior commander to the area who could impose some discipline and order on the fighters. Displaying that inability to arrive at fast, decisive action which subsequently plagued his leadership, Riek issued no orders until his forces around Bor had already begun to disperse in the face of the SPLA-Torit advance on the town.

The reaction of the rest of the SPLA, other Southerners and even the international community, was not what the Nasir group anticipated. The main targets were civilians, and their casualties during the fighting were significant. This indicated a continuation of strategy from the Anyanya-2, who were in the forefront of the fighting. This raised serious doubts about the Nasir commanders' commitment to human rights. During the fighting, it became clear that the Nasir faction was receiving weapons and ammunition from Khartoum (Section **7.4.2**). Many Southerners came to the conclusion that Riek and Lam were in the process of allying themselves with Khartoum, as the pro-secessionist Anyanya-2 had done. The rest of the SPLA did not rally behind Nasir, while Southern exile opinion was seriously divided, and the international community began distancing itself from the Nasir group. The Torit faction diverted troops from around Juba to retake Bor, and the Nasir faction troops withdrew to the Ayod-Duk area.

---

[9] The SPLA never officially changed their name but were referred to in various documents as 'SPLA-Torit' or 'SPLA–Mainstream'. The Nasir faction had a more serious identity crisis, calling itself first SPLA-Nasir, SPLA-United in March 1993, the South Sudan Independence Movement/Army (SSIM/A) in September 1994, and finally the United Democratic Salvation Front and South Sudan Defence Force (UDSF/SSDF) in 1997 when it joined the government. I apply the terms chronologically, but references to SPLA alone should be taken to mean SPLA-Mainstream.

7.4.2 *Military contacts between Nasir & Khartoum*

Contacts between the government and the Nasir commanders began prior to the coup, and military support from Khartoum increased as the conflict between the factions of the SPLA intensified (Section **8.1**).[10] Lam Akol was flown to Nairobi in September 1991 to lead the Nasir faction delegation in reconciliation talks with Garang's group. During that time he was assisted by Tiny Rowland of Lonrho (an early supporter of the SPLA) and met the government's representative, Ali al-Hajj Muhammad. As a result of these contacts, money from the government was channelled into the Nasir faction's Nairobi operation through Lonrho, and Taban Deng Gai was sent to Khartoum where he established a liaison office and met personally with Umar al-Bashir, Hassan al-Turabi and senior army commanders. He was given the use of an Antonov transport plane and personally supervised the airdrops of supplies to Duar, Ler, and elsewhere in Upper Nile and Jonglei.

As far as Garang's SPLA was concerned, such activity (monitored over the radio airwaves) was proof that the split had been manufactured by Khartoum from the start and had nothing to do with the internal reform of the Movement. Testimony from within the Nasir faction presents a rather more complex picture. At least as far as Riek Machar was concerned, the alliance with the government was originally tactical, designed as much to secure immunity from attack (in the absence of protection from Ethiopia) as support against Garang. With the failure of the rest of the SPLA to rally behind the coup, the support of the Sudanese army became essential for survival. From that point on the Nasir faction's military strategy was increasingly directed by Khartoum.

7.5 Government advances, 1992–4

The split in the SPLA, and the material support that Khartoum offered the Nasir faction, enabled the government to regain the military initiative in many parts of the South. In the 1992 offensive, Sudanese troops moved without hindrance through SPLA-Nasir territory and also through Ethiopia, regaining considerable territory in Jonglei and Eastern Equatoria by July 1992. In response, SPLA-Torit attempted a major assault on Juba in June and July, assisted by Southern soldiers within the government garrison, an action that briefly succeeded in taking large sections of the

---

[10] By December 1991 when Nasir troops withdrew from Bor, leaving large amounts of government supplies behind, there was clear evidence of collaboration with Khartoum. Many of Riek Machar's well-wishers, especially journalists influenced by his British wife, Emma McCune, refused to believe this evidence for many years. *Africa Confidential*, for instance, failed to publish evidence of Riek's collusion with the government, long after the evidence against him was overwhelming. The account given here is based on captured documents released by the SPLA, personal testimony by former members of the Nasir faction and written accounts by Nasir faction insiders, e.g.: Richard K. Mulla, Department of Information, General Headquarters, South Sudan Freedom Front (SSFF), 'The truth of what is happening in Eastern Equatoria', 30 March 1995; letter from Richard K. Mulla to Riek Machar Teny Dhurgon, Nairobi, 5 May 1995; Dhol Acuil Aleu, Amon Mon Wantok, Chol Deng Alak and Isaac Cuir Riak, 'Why we resigned from SPLM/SPLA United', 6 August 1994; Nyaba, *The Politics of Liberation in South Sudan*.

town and disrupting the government's strategy. It was, however, decisively repulsed, with heavy losses to the SPLA in supplies and equipment that it could ill afford. This assault was followed by government retaliation against their own Southern soldiers and Southern civilians resident in the city.

William Nyuon's defection to the Nasir faction and his link up with the Sudanese army followed the attack on Juba (Section **8.1**). There was no major government offensive in the dry season of 1992–3, partly because the American intervention in Somalia raised the prospect of a US-enforced 'no-fly zone' over the southern Sudan, and the government held back until it could gauge the outcome in Somalia. There was considerable fighting of a more 'low-tech' nature, no less brutal for all that, throughout much of 1993 (see Appendix). Government troops and government-backed militias radiated out from regained bases to attack civilian settlements in territory held by Garang's forces.

The government resumed its offensive in the dry season of 1994, with the objective of reaching and sealing off the Sudan-Uganda border. It failed to retake Western Equatoria, but it succeeded in opening a number of 'rumbling' fronts in other areas which kept SPLA troops occupied over a wide region and prevented them from reinforcing the main front at Nimule. By July 1994 the government had concentrated most of its troops in the Juba–Nimule area. The SPLA's defence was hampered by lack of supplies. Arms still got through from Uganda, but Sudan government support for the LRA helped to disrupt both the SPLA's supply-line and relief convoys headed for refugee camps in the southern Sudan and northern Uganda.

The SPLA's strategy was to contain the government thrusts while at the same time trying to deal with Nasir faction forces operating in its rear. Troops were diverted to deal with Nyuon's forces in Eastern Equatoria, to break the supply-line between him and Riek by securing Kongor, and to counter attacks emanating from the western Upper Nile and Kerubino's bases in Abyei and Gogrial. These actions sharpened fighting along civilian fault lines (Section **8.2**). On the military front with the Sudanese army, however, the SPLA succeeded in halting the government's momentum by the end of 1994 and was beginning to position itself so that it could seize the initiative itself.

7.6 The revival of the SPLA

By 1994–5 the SPLA's diplomatic and political position improved, enabling it to recover from recent setbacks with greater internal unity and increased international support. A series of external mediations, beginning with the Abuja talks in 1992 and culminating in the IGAD process, created a diplomatic climate more sympathetic to SPLA aims, at the same time that Khartoum's support for Islamic revolution abroad made it into a pariah state. In addition, Khartoum was experiencing numerous other problems. The armed forces were split against themselves with field commanders of the professional army openly contemptuous of the PDF. Public dissent in the capital was put down with a ruthlessness not attempted by previous military regimes. The economy was clearly unable to meet the daily cost of the war in the South, a cost compounded by Khartoum's growing diplomatic isolation. All these factors had an effect on Northern exile parties, and the SPLA soon emerged with a leading role at the centre of a new national opposition.

7.6.1. The role of peace talks in the SPLA's revival

Serious peace talks with Khartoum had been precluded ever since the NIF take-over in 1989, especially while the SPLA had been militarily on the ascendant. The split within the SPLA served to put peace talks back on the international agenda, but now the priorities were different. The government was eager to bind the Nasir faction to a separate agreement, which would protect the central role of the Islamist state and dilute any conditions for the Southern exercise of self-determination. International mediators exerted nearly as much energy in finding common ground between the Southern factions as seeking peace between the North and South. The contents of this succession of negotiations will be discussed later (Sections **8.1**, **8.4** & Chapter **11**). Here we will analyze their role in the political revival of the SPLA.

Early attempts by external mediators (the churches, the Kenyan government) to bring the two factions back together failed (Section **8.4**). With the SPLA convinced that the Nasir faction was a puppet of the Sudanese government, and SPLA-Nasir convinced that Garang's faction was in imminent collapse, neither side had an incentive to negotiate seriously with each other. But in internationally brokered negotiations with the government, each faction strove to demonstrate what it could achieve on behalf of the South, and in this way some common ground began to emerge.

Prior to the SPLA split, Nigerian President Ibrahim Babangida had been charged by the OAU to mediate peace between the government and the SPLA. By the time the peace conference convened in Abuja in 1992, there were two SPLA delegations, not one. Largely at the urging of the Nigerians, the SPLA merged their delegations, though the two factions still submitted separate proposals. The Torit faction preferred a secular, decentralized, united Sudan as its first option, while the Nasir faction publicly declared itself in favour of complete independence. Together they agreed to the principle of self-determination for the South. In the second round of talks in 1993, the government dealt separately with SPLA-Mainstream in Abuja and SPLA-United (formerly Nasir) in Nairobi. Talks with the Mainstream broke down over the issues of religion and decentralization before self-determination could even be raised. Following the failure of the Abuja talks, the leaders of the two SPLA factions met in Washington at a Congressionally-sponsored meeting, and again accepted the common language of self-determination.

As inconclusive as the Abjua talks and the Washington Declaration were (and in the latter case, irrelevant to any political solution), they demonstrated that the main parties to the conflict were willing to engage in mediated talks. They also indicated where there were areas of agreement within the fragmented Southern movements. This was subsequently confirmed in the regional initiative of the IGAD governments, begun at the end of 1993 and carried through to July 1994. The IGAD sponsoring governments and the two Southern movements agreed to a draft Declaration of Principles (DOP) which endorsed both the right of self-determination and the importance of establishing a secular demo-cratic state in the Sudan as a precondition for unity. The Sudan government refused to accept this draft and broke off negotiations; when they finally accepted the DOP as one of the bases for negotiation in 1997, they did so with reservations and qualifications. But the very existence of this widely-agreed set of principles on which peace could be based was to have a significant impact on the international community and, ultimately, on the Sudanese opposition.

Part of the reason why the Sudan government had been intransigent at Abuja but willing to accept the IGAD mediation was that it was convinced its forces would soon win on the battlefield. In their war with the SPLA the government believed it could rely on the support of both the Eritrean and Ethiopian governments, whom the Sudan had supported in their war against Mengistu. But by 1993 the international context was changing, as the Sudan was about to find out to its cost.

The new governments in Eritrea and Ethiopia did indeed owe the Sudan a political debt, but the NIF squandered this advantage by its continued support of Islamic revolution, including its support for Islamist groups in both Eritrea and Ethiopia. By the end of 1993 Eritrea declared itself under attack by 'foreign Muslim extremists' (see Appendix), and the assassination attempt on Egyptian President Hosni Mubarak while in Addis Ababa in 1995 did much to convince Ethiopia of the danger that the Sudan posed. For much of the rest of the 1990s (until the Eritrean–Ethiopian war put an effective end to IGAD cooperation) Eritrea, Ethiopia and Uganda in particular gave the SPLA and its NDA partners both political and military assistance.

Collectively, the IGAD countries were also able to rally the support of Western governments, mobilized through the 'Friends of IGAD', which included Australia, Canada, Britain, Italy, Norway and the US. This was to have an impact on the development of the foreign policy of the new US administration.

Initially, the Clinton administration had no policy on the Sudan, but its inauguration in January 1993 meant the departure of those figures in the Republican administrations who had defined the region in the context of the Cold War. The new administration had inherited from the old a commitment to the new governments in Eritrea and Ethiopia, and as this developed into support for an 'African Renaissance' (embracing Uganda's Museveni), Khartoum's hostility to its neighbours became a factor in defining the US's attitude towards its former ally. Association with other militant Islamists such as Hamas and Usama bin Ladin, and continuing military ties with Iraq and Iran were further reasons for the US condem-nation of the Sudan as a terrorist state, and for its decision to support regional defence schemes for the Sudan's most exposed neighbours.[11] By the turn of the twenty-first century, the African-American anti-slavery

---

[11] It is not just politicians and soldiers who keep on fighting the last war. The veteran *Guardian* columnist Jonathan Steele had no hesitation in naming the real villain of the piece in 1998, at

lobby and Christian activists added powerful domestic voices in Congress to keep the Sudan high on the US foreign policy agenda.

7.6.2 The NDA

The SPLA offensive of 1995–6 was its first in four years. By March 1996 it had rolled back the government's 1992 advances in Eastern Equatoria, leaving the remaining garrisons precariously exposed (see Appendix). A new cordon was drawn around Juba. This was facilitated by a provisional resolution to the SPLA split: SSIM/A forces operating in the SPLA's rear in Eastern Equatoria had made their peace with Garang, and the remainder of SSIM/A was embroiled in its own civil war, fought far from the main battle front (Sections **8.2** & **8.3**). While locally destructive, Kerubino's activity in northern Bahr al-Ghazal had no immediate impact on the overall strength and strategy of the SPLA.

Many of the SPLA's gains were made possible by a growing political and military cohesion between the Northern and Southern opposition groups, beneath the umbrella of the National Democratic Alliance (NDA), a cohesion fostered by the Sudan's neighbours.

Exile opposition was formed within months of the 1989 coup, with the creation of the NDA coalition of political parties and the foundation of a Legitimate Command of Armed Forces. The SPLA signed accords with both groups and gave them airtime on Radio SPLA, but these agreements were little more than tokens at first, because neither the NDA nor the Legitimate Command had an active strategy for opposition. Both placed their hopes on risings inside the Sudan – another *intifada* in the streets of Khartoum, or a counter-coup within the army – to topple the regime and bring the old forces back to power. Many Umma and DUP politicians also assumed that Bashir would 'do a Nimairi' and eventually call back the old parties in another move towards national reconciliation.

There was thus little urgency in developing a common platform with the SPLA, who had until recently been the enemy. Satisfied with Garang's commitment to a united Sudan, neither the Umma nor DUP were willing to commit themselves, in exile, to any detailed outline of the country's future constitution, and the issue of the role of religion in the state was resolutely evaded.

The split in the SPLA in 1991, which brought forward the issue of self-determination and Southern independence, came as a rude shock for many in the NDA, especially as Garang was forced to respond by publicly adopting confederation and self-determination as legitimate options for the South (Section **7.6.1** & Chapter **11**). Some in the NDA realized that equivocation over the question of an Islamic state could precipitate the South's secession. This strengthened the momentum within the ranks of

(cont) the height of the government-induced Bahr al-Ghazal famine. 'Welcome to the 1980s. Long live Ronald Reagan', he announced. 'Remember the scenario – a rebel group being trained and armed by the CIA to topple a sovereign government...', and accused US Secretary of State Madeline Albright of sabotaging Khartoum's peace proposals (based on the Islamist federal constitution) during her December 1997 visit to Uganda to meet with SPLA leaders. (Jonathan Steele, 'Stop this war now', *The Guardian*, 1 May 1998, p. 20). John Esposito has taken a similar line, laying more stress on US policy than Khartoum's ideology and intransigence for the failure of negotiations (John L. Esposito, *The Islamic Threat: Myth or Reality?*, 3rd ed. (NY/Oxford, 1999), p. 92).

the opposition towards a more critical appraisal of the Islamic state, a momentum which was hindered throughout 1991 and 1992 by the obvious reluctance of the Umma and DUP to commit themselves to overt opposition to the principle of a theocratic state.

But the NDA had less and less room to manoeuvre. Inside the Sudan, it was becoming clearer that Turabi and the NIF held real power, and that Bashir was not going to 'do a Nimairi'. Any moves Bashir made to coopt the old parties were sabotaged by Turabi, who did not want the strength of the NIF in the government diluted. Government oppression of not just the old Northern parties, but the sects they were allied to, also brought home to many exile politicians that the power of Islam and *jihad* could also be turned against them (Section **9.1**). Despite the fact that the Southern guerrillas continued a brutal war against each other on the ground, their political platforms were drawing nearer, and international acceptance of the right of self-determination and the importance of a secular democratic state was secured through support for the IGAD principles in 1994.

This made many in the NDA nervous – particularly the DUP. But, with international recognition of these principles, Garang was able to argue within the NDA that self-determination was inherent within those basic principles of democracy and human rights to which the alliance was already committed.

By this time, the Umma party was working its way towards a qualified acceptance of the right of self-determination, coupled with the realization that offering the South the clear option of a democratic, decentralized government was the only likely alternative to secession. The Umma party endorsed most of the IGAD principles in an agreement signed with the SPLA at the end of 1994. This was a considerable step forward for any Northern sectarian party, and the NDA as a whole soon adopted the main points of the Chukudum Accord in Asmara in June 1995. The Asmara Declaration still trod warily around the issue of religion, affirming the 'non-use of religion in politics' rather than proclaiming the goal of a secular state. It was still vague on details, especially with respect to the rights of the Ngok Dinka, the Nuba and the peoples of southern Blue Nile. But in its acceptance of self-determination, and the structure of the interim arrangements, the Declaration followed very closely the proposals the SPLA had presented at the Abuja meetings in 1992 and 1993 (Section **7.6.1**).

Acceptance of the Asmara Declaration was due in no small measure to the influence of the conference's host, the Eritrean government. The Eritreans had strongly supported the twin principles of self-determination and a non-religious state in the IGAD discussions, and had helped to ensure that the language of the DOP was forthright on these matters. Eritrea had also pushed for the expansion of the NDA to include the revived Beja Congress and the newly formed Sudanese Allied Forces (SAF), against the objections of the DUP and the Legitimate Command, both of whom saw these two organizations as rivals in what they regarded their natural constituencies. The Beja Congress and SAF set up training bases in Eritrea and were committed – unlike the Legitimate Command – to waging armed resistance in the North, in co-ordination with the SPLA (Section **9.2.3**).

The Asmara Declaration was not to be the final word on either self-determination or the non-religious state (Chapter **11**). It was certainly not accepted by all within the NDA. Many in the DUP, including Muhammad Uthman al-Mirghani, continued to voice their reservations. But it marked a new departure in the war: bringing the Sudanese opposition closer to a consensus on the ultimate causes of the war, and therefore the solution to it, and providing a firmer political and military foundation on which to prosecute the war on old fronts and open up new.

7.7 Reconstructing civil administration in the South

From the start of the war the SPLA saw itself as a movement to bring about a change in the government of the Sudan as a whole, and not as a provisional government for a future southern Sudanese state. It refused to divert its energies into setting up a shadow government with shadow ministries but based the administration of its liberated areas almost entirely on the old structures of Native Administration and the provincial governments of the old Southern Region.

Old chieftaincies continued to be recognized, new ones were created, and elections to chiefs' courts were regularly conducted. Chiefs' courts met to hear cases under customary law and to organize public projects (such as tax gathering and road building), and inter-tribal gatherings of chiefs were arranged periodically to settle inter-community issues. This work was supervised by SPLA officers, the Civil/Military Administrators and Area or Zonal Commanders. In some counties the SPLA officers in charge adopted roles as neutral mediators assigned to provincial administrators in the old system of government. In other places, military considerations overrode all other administrative concerns, and there was little local participation or representation in the structures of administration above the chiefs' courts. With the upper level of administration so weak, there was potential for local SPLA commanders to carve out their own fiefdoms, even where support for the SPLA was strong.

Civil administration has never been strong in the southern Sudan, even at its most intrusive during the late colonial period. The continued erosion of infrastructure (roads, communications, government offices and services) was one of the failures of the Southern Regional government. By 1983 many services that were ostensibly the responsibility of the Regional government had either ceased to function or, in some provinces, had been contracted out to NGOs.[12] The war accelerated this decline. The criticism that the SPLA has failed to provide services therefore lacks historical perspective.[13] The SPLA has certainly found it difficult to replace in war what previous peacetime governments were unable to maintain. What the SPLA did provide, and with increasing success before the split, was the regulation of disputes and the administration of law through the courts.

[12] Terje Tvedt, 'The collapse of the state in southern Sudan after the Addis Ababa Agreement', in Sharif Harir & Terje Tvedt (eds), *Short-Cut to Decay: The Case of the Sudan*, (Uppsala, 1994); and *Angels of Mercy or Development Diplomats? NGOs and Foreign Aid*, (Oxford, 1998), pp. 186–202.
[13] Alex de Waal, *Famine Crimes* (Oxford, 1997), p. 96.

Something of the broad success of the pre-1991 administration in controlling inter-community violence can be seen in the explosion of that violence after 1991, and the failure of the Nasir administration even in regulating inter-Nuer disputes. The procedures which Riek was able to implement as Area Commander of western Upper Nile to forestall raiding along the border were possible because neighbouring commanders in Bahr al-Ghazal were doing the same and could be counted on to cooperate. The Nuer and Dinka border chiefs knew what to do because they knew they would be backed up by local security forces. The SPLA had made considerable strides in expanding the role of chiefs' courts in settling inter-tribal disputes throughout the areas they controlled until 1991 (Section **6.4**).

One effect of the establishment of administration under a direct military chain of command was to militarize chiefly structures. Chiefs were still elected and prominent chiefs still co-opted, but as the supervising authority for elections SPLA commanders often influenced the selection process in order to secure positions for their supporters and allies (even if from the same families who filled those offices in the past). Despite this elective process chiefs were subordinated within the military chain of command and inevitably lost some of their previous autonomy.

The lack of firm institutionalized civil structures was one of the complaints voiced against Garang and his PMHC by the Nasir commanders. Partly to refute this, and partly as a response to continuing pressure from donor governments, the SPLA inaugurated a process of administrative restructuring, beginning with the Torit Declaration issued by the PMHC in 1991, and culminating in the National Convention of 1994. This was the first national convention held by the Movement, some eleven years after its foundation. The convention ratified the setting up of a National Executive Council, ostensibly separate from the military command, with authority over a new hierarchy of rural civil administration.

The reforms in civil administration have been criticized as a paper structure of the sort SPLA condemned in the past. At the higher level the NEC still has no real executive power: on the contrary former SPLA commanders who might have rivaled Garang have found themselves stripped of effective power upon their appointment to the NEC. Another continuing complaint has been Garang's persistent habit of elevating subordinates at will and discarding them before they can establish their own power bases.[14] If the NEC is the SPLA's own version of a 'paper cabinet', then their contempt for such institutions in the past might explain why they have not tried harder to make it work.

But at the lower levels there are signs of greater devolution in local administration. The conflict of jurisdiction between the SRRA and regional administrations is being resolved with the SRRA mainly confining itself to organizing or supervising relief, and leaving social services and development projects to other bodies. The National Convention also opened up other means for Southerners to become

---

[14] One of Garang's critics inside the SPLM remarked to me how exactly Garang's behaviour illustrated the use of disorder to retain power outlined in Patrick Chabal & Jean-Pascal Daloz, *Africa Works: Disorder as Political Instrument* (Oxford/Bloomington IN, 1999).

active in the 'New Sudan'. It helped to inaugurate new working agreements with Operation Lifeline Sudan (Section **10.4**), and the SPLM ceased to have an exclusive hold on all aspects of relief and development. Independent Southern bodies were able to come into existence. The result has been that, today, many Southerners already outside of the SPLM, and many of those discarded by Garang, continue to exercise their own influence, working through new Southern NGOs and civil society groups.

7.8 The crisis of confidence in Southern leadership

Despite many advances during the late 1990s, both on the battlefield and in civilian life, there is a crisis in confidence specifically in SPLA leadership which has led to intense pessimism about the South's future. There is a feeling that the Movement has missed making the most of opportunities that have come its way, and that its ultimate goals are confused. This is evident in the stalled peace process and disarray in the NDA. The leadership is perceived by many to be personally detached, preoccupied with their own positions and uncommitted to civil reform.

At the end of the 1990s the SPLA prospered as much from the difficulties of its enemies as through its own successes. Khartoum's formal alliance with the anti-Garang factions in 1997 at first temporarily improved the SPLA's military position as dissensions within the ranks of Khartoum's Southern allies led to serious fighting in the Western Nuer oilfields and further defections to the SPLA (Section **8.5**). Kerubino's brief realignment with the SPLA in 1998 threw Bahr al-Ghazal into turmoil. The unexpected (and to a large extent unplanned) SPLA assault on Wau was, like the more sustained assault on Juba in 1992, a grand gesture which was beyond the skill or discipline of the SPLA soldiers to pull off. In the international furore over the famine which followed, a local truce for the distribution of relief supplies allowed the government to shift its forces to the Nuba Mountains front, where SPLA supply lines were precarious to non-existent.

Khartoum has been more skilful in turning international events to its favour. The Eritrean–Ethiopian war of 1998–2000 severely curtailed effective political and military support for the NDA and the SPLA. This has had serious consequences for their fielding troops along the Sudan's eastern borders. The government's ability to open up the oilfields for exploitation during the window of opportunity given them by their 'peace from within' policy (Sections **8.5** & **10.5**) led to a marked change in the attitude of many Western governments, especially in the European Union, who have since become eager to do business with Khartoum, whatever its human rights record or association with terrorism. The government's eager cooperation with the United States in the 'war against terrorism' after September 11, 2001 won it, if not new allies, at least some leeway in Washington.

A struggle between Bashir and Turabi for political control of the ruling National Congress in the Sudan in 1999–2000 saw the SPLA and the NDA undecided on how to benefit from their enemies' dissension. Both Turabi and Bashir sought to strengthen their own positions against each other by wooing Sadiq al-Mahdi back from exile, and he signed separate agreements first with his brother-in-law, and then with Bashir. Garang's plea that this was the time to put pressure on the government failed to rally the NDA. After an acrimonious exchange of letters Sadiq withdrew from the NDA and returned to Khartoum in November 2000, claiming that he would orchestrate a positive change from inside the country. Turabi, having come off the worse in the struggle with Bashir, authorised his own memorandum of understanding against his government's authoritarian methods with the SPLA in February 2001.

The political fallout of this confusing turn of events was that Bashir imprisoned Turabi and was able to appear to international observers as a moderating, pragmatic force in Sudanese politics, though the commitment of his government to its Islamist policies has remained unchanged. The SPLA's sudden willingness to do a deal with Turabi, the architect of the South's devastation, was seen by many Southerners as merely opportunistic and unprincipled. Garang justified it on the grounds that the SPLA would seek to work with *all* opponents of the regime. In order to prepare a base for Turabi's followers, the SPLA captured Raga. No pro-Turabi force materialized, and the government regained its lost territory in western Bahr al-Ghazal before the end of 2001. Garang's flirtation with Turabi not only hurt the SPLA militarily, but it cost Garang political support among Southern exiles.

One of the areas where the National Convention's reforms had an initial beneficial impact was in the recruitment of local defence units. In Yei and Torit, for instance, independent observers reported that the devolution of administration and recruitment of such units for local deployment began to give people the feeling that the Movement was their movement, and the struggle was their struggle. But the raising of local defence forces has not necessarily bound the SPLA closer to its civilian constituency. Recent developments in Bahr al-Ghazal and Eastern Equatoria have shown that local mobilization has the potential to increase civilian participation but also to set up tensions between the Movement and local institutions.

The peoples of Bahr al-Ghazal have long felt that their real needs have been subordinated to a strategy decided by Garang and his closest allies. There was a slight improvement in security throughout Bahr al-Ghazal in 1997, following SPLA advances. But the widespread militia raiding and famine which followed the SPLA's failed attempt to take Wau in 1998 only highlighted local grievances against the SPLA throughout northern Bahr al-Ghazal. Not only did the SPLA fail to protect civilians from renewed and intensified PDF raids (which continued to take place despite a formal ceasefire between the army and SPLA), but its administrative structures were unable to cope with the scale of the relief effort needed.

Prior to 1998, and even more since then, Dinka in Bahr al-Ghazal have been putting their own resources into local 'Cattle Guard' (*Tit Weng* or *Gel Weng*) militias.[15] This development has not been entirely welcomed by the SPLA high command, as the Cattle Guards are outside SPLA control. General dissatisfaction with the SPLA's response to insecurity of

---

[15] It is reported that some Dinka have collected money from the 'slave redemption' programmes, presenting local people as 'slaves' to be redeemed, and using the money paid for their 'redemption' to purchase vehicles and weapons for the Cattle Guards (see Section **10.3.3**).

various kinds was a contributory cause to the very public breach in 2000 between Garang and Bona Malwal, former minister, regional minister, and influential editor of *The Sudan Democratic Gazette*. Further, Bona Malwal is a Twic Dinka from Gogrial, one of the areas most devastated by raiding and famine.[16]

In Equatoria, the SPLA moved their headquarters to the Didinga hills after being ousted from Torit in 1992. The heavy and oppressive presence of SPLA units around Chukudum led to fighting between the SPLA and the surrounding Didinga, following the introduction of a local mobilization programme. As the military fortunes of the SPLA improved, its presence around Chukudum did not diminish. Rather, many SPLA officers and soldiers used the area's proximity to the Ugandan and Kenyan borders to become involved in trade. Clashes between SPLA soldiers and locals became frequent, with fighting breaking out between SPLA units in 1999.

An ad hoc committee of SPLA commanders, civil administrators and church leaders was appointed to investigate the causes of the fighting. Their recommendations on dispersing the garrison, bolstering the civil authority, and deploying the newly-trained civil police force were not implemented. The area became so insecure that the SPLA finally transferred its headquarters to Yei. Reluctance to implement agreed administrative reforms has already hampered the SPLA in its efforts to bring about political mobilization throughout those areas currently in active opposition to the government. The example of Chukudum and the Didinga illustrates that the SPLM as a movement has the personnel with the requisite administrative experience to identify the source of problems, and to rectify them. The Movement as a whole knows how to do the right thing, but at its highest level it does not have the will to do it.

A similar criticism can be made about the SPLA's reactions to the grassroots truces negotiated between groups of Nuer and Dinka since 1999. The negotiations could not have taken place without the active support of local SPLA commanders. The NEC welcomed and endorsed them. But Garang was reported to be ambivalent, and some of his subordinate commanders were suspected of trying to undermine the implementation of the peace agreements. The reconciliation finally announced between Garang and Riek in January 2002 (which could have been made on exactly the same terms at any time since 1993) might be a demonstration of the final acceptance of local peace initiatives. It could also be an attempt to build up political support in new areas to counterbalance the loss of support in Bahr al-Ghazal.

There has been increased discussion within the SPLA internally and among the broader southern Sudanese community about the crisis in confidence in Southern leadership. The devastation suffered in the South in the aftermath of the Nasir split has made people wary of violent changes of leadership and further factionalism, but there is a strong desire for at least a change in direction from the leadership. By the beginning of 2002, with new international pressure on the Sudanese combatants, there were signs that Garang was responding to these criticisms. The end of the

---

[16] Following intensive mediation from several quarters Garang and Malwal announced a personal reconciliation on 4 April 2002.

feud between Garang and Riek was followed by the announcement of new initiatives for a broad-based NDA army and public commitment to the expansion of civil authority in the SPLA-controlled areas. If these declarations are translated into activity on the ground, then they are a recognition that the SPLA has been most successful in those areas where popular participation has been greatest, and most vulnerable where its army is seen – and acts – as an army of occupation.

8

The Segmentation of SPLA-United | & the Nuer Civil War

Between 1992 and 1995 the split in the SPLA was entrenched by further defections of dissatisfied commanders to the Nasir faction, and through it to the government. Government support kept the new factions supplied in the field. These defections were not matched by the changing of allegiance of entire military units, or by substantial sections of the civilian population. Rather, as fighting between the SPLA factions intensified, both sides faced continuous desertions as demoralized soldiers refused to fight other Southerners and left their units to return home. Inter-factional fighting was superimposed over the fault-lines of the civilian population, as each side attempted to mobilize civilian opposition against the other.

8.1 Collaboration & defections

The central paradox of the Nasir faction was its military alliance with the government in pursuit of the goal of total independence of the South. It was a paradox that ultimately cost its leaders their political credibility and destroyed their movement.

Throughout the remaining months of 1989 the new military government categorically and publicly refused to compromise on *shari'a* or the Islamic state, closing off any room for compromise on that issue. As the government failed to make any military headway in 1990 they hinted to several quarters that the war could be resolved by granting the South its independence, which was not then a stated objective of the SPLA. But a peace proposal based on this understanding, crafted by US Assistant Secretary of State Herman Cohen, was rejected outright by the government in March 1990.[1] What the government had in mind by 'the South' was, however, considerably less than the old Southern Region. A government official casually revealed to a visiting American journalist at this time the acceptable boundaries of an independent South, which excluded all of its northern oil fields: a proposal reproducing Turabi's 1980 map submitted to the National Assembly (Section **4.4.1**).[2]

In their contacts with the Nasir commanders prior to the coup, it is very likely that the government offered a general prospect of inde-

---

[1] Stephen Wöndu & Ann Lesch, *Battle for Peace in Sudan: An Analysis of the Abuja Conferences, 1992–1993* (Lanham MD, 2000), pp. 15–18.
[2] Deborah Scroggins, *Emma's War: Love, Betrayal and Death in the Sudan* (New York, 2002).

pendence for an undefined South. As subsequent events were to reveal, what the Nasir commanders thought they were going to get was always much less than the government was willing to concede. Negotiations between the two sides shadowed political developments in the Sudan. The NIF strengthened its hold on the economy and proceeded with the adoption of its Islamist project for the whole country which, once in place, effectively precluded the type of arrangement the Nasir faction publicly espoused.

Inside the movement, there seemed to be two parallel approaches. Riek Machar may have genuinely believed in the strategy once espoused by the politburo of the old Anyanya-2: that the adoption of an unambiguous independence platform would ultimately lead to the defection of the entire SPLA to their side, giving them the military clout to break with the government and declare independence. Lam Akol, who took charge of direct negotiations with the government, seems to have had more limited and pragmatic aims. Judging his movement's military capabilities more accurately, he seems to have adopted the strategy of holding out for independence in the hope of obtaining a more secure autonomy in a future federal Sudan.

The dilemma of the Nasir commanders was that by entering into separate negotiations with the government and weakening the SPLA, their own programme became unobtainable. They served the NIF's long-term objectives – to entrench the Islamic state in the North – but they did not have the power to extract further concessions for themselves. As they soon became tied to the government for their own survival, they were tugged back into line each time they attempted any independent move on their own. This was demonstrated early in 1992 with the Frankfurt Agreement and the first Abuja talks.

Collaboration between the Nasir faction and Khartoum was publicly formalized with the agreement between Lam Akol and Ali al-Hajj Muhammad at Frankfurt in January 1992. This two-page public document, which was released, made no mention of independence, containing only a vague reference to deciding the 'special political and constitutional status' for the South in a future referendum. Nevertheless, the Nasir faction presented the agreement as a commitment to self-determination. That the government did not intend this referendum to go so far was later made clear by Ali al-Hajj at Abuja when he declared that the Frankfurt Agreement provided only for a referendum on the degree of decentralization in the South and did not compromise the unity of the country. His offer to table the full text of the agreement, which had not been previously released, and which detailed the extent of collaboration between SPLA-Nasir and the government, was declined by Lam Akol.[3]

The obvious deficiencies of the Frankfurt Agreement led to the first defections from the Nasir faction, as two Dinka members of the delegation resigned in disgust. But the Nasir faction abided by the unpublicised terms of the agreement, allowing the Sudanese army safe passage through their territory to attack the SPLA (Section **7.5**) and dispatching a force of their own to Equatoria in June. During this time, both the Nasir faction and Khartoum attempted to encourage defections of other dissatisfied

[3] Wöndu & Lesch, *Battle for Peace in Sudan*, pp. 50–60.

SPLA officers, and at Abuja they focused their attention on William Nyuon Bany.

Nyuon was then a key figure in Garang's strategy of combating the Nasir split, since he was not only a popular and successful commander, but a Nuer. Garang employed Nyuon in salient and visible positions, appointing him Chief of Staff and choosing him to lead the SPLA-Torit delegation to the first Abuja peace talks in May 1992. These were political decisions which had unsettling consequences. Nyuon had been an aggressive field commander but was only semi-literate and did not command respect as Chief of Staff among many other subordinate commanders in the SPLA. At Abuja, Nyuon was offered financial inducements by the leaders of the government and Nasir delegations to leave the SPLA.[4] After his return to the SPLA's headquarters in the South, Nyuon and his bodyguard withdrew from the SPLA, in September 1992. (He also released a number of political prisoners, including Joseph Oduho, Kerubino Kuanyin and Arok Thon Arok.) Nyuon's force was ambushed and harried by the SPLA before linking up with Riek's men in Eastern Equatoria.

The diversion of troops to the Equatorian front had not been popular among the Nuer of the Sobat. Riek had employed the services of a Nuer prophet, Wut Nyang, to raise this force, and he was among those most vocal in criticism of the Equatorian strategy, especially as he had been led to believe the force was intended to take Malakal. Wut Nyang subsequently launched his own, unsuccessful, assault on the town, little knowing that the Nasir commanders had never seriously meant to attack it.[5] Revealingly, the attack was hailed by Garang's SPLA as a positive contribution to the liberation of the South, and hastily repudiated by the Nasir commanders, who then relapsed into an embarrassed silence.

The ostensible reason for the Nasir faction establishing a presence in Eastern Equatoria was to open a supply route to the Ugandan border. Many within the Nasir faction questioned this reasoning, since there was no indication that the Ugandan government was willing to supply them. Prevented by the SPLA from reaching the border, Nyuon contacted the Sudanese army in January 1993, and he and other commanders moved in and out of government garrisons (including Juba), establishing links with the Ugandan opposition Lord's Resistance Army and facilitating its incursions into Uganda. For the next two years Nyuon worked in close collaboration with the government with the full knowledge of Riek Machar, who continued to send him Nuer reinforcements. Many of Nyuon's attacks on the SPLA were coordinated with government offensives, and Nyuon's base at Jabal Lafon secured a route for government convoys through Eastern Equatoria.

Equatorian disillusionment with SPLA-United only deepened with time. Independence was brought no closer; inter-factional fighting increased and, what was worse, was being fought out in Eastern Equatoria. Despite the movement's rhetoric, Nyuon's troops were guilty of many atrocities against civilians.

---

[4] Nyuon had a large and impoverished family in Nairobi. On his return from Abuja he bought a house for them in Nakuru and invested in a *matatu* mini-bus.

[5] Douglas H. Johnson, *Nuer Prophets* (Oxford, 1994), pp. 348–51; Sharon Hutchinson, *Nuer Dilemmas* (Berkeley, 1996), pp. 338–9.

Parallel to the Eastern Equatorian strategy was the use of Kerubino Kuanyin to destabilize northern Bahr al-Ghazal in 1994–7. Kerubino advanced into northern Bahr al-Ghazal with his own army from western Upper Nile in July 1994 but was defeated by the SPLA and forced to retreat to Abyei, in government territory, where the government subsequently announced his reinstatement to the army. He returned to Bahr al-Ghazal with a newly outfitted force re-styled 'SPLA-Bahr al-Ghazal' (recruited largely from his home area but subsquently reinforced by Paulino Matip's Bul Nuer militia). Operating in conjunction with units of the PDF and the army garrison in Gogrial, Kerubino disrupted the relief effort in northern Bahr al-Ghazal, contributing greatly to the further displacement of the Dinka there (Section **10.3**). Kerubino's targets were entirely civilian; he did not seek out and attack SPLA units.

8.2 Civilian fault lines

The split in the SPLA reintroduced fighting into areas which had been relatively free from violence for some time. Not only did the two factions of the SPLA fight each other, they encouraged civilian involvement. Nuer civilians from Ayod and Akobo joined the attack on Bor; Nuer and Dinka civilians from western Upper Nile and Lakes began raiding each other; and the Torit-faction garrison at Pibor encouraged the Murle to begin raiding into the Nuer districts of Akobo and Waat.

Even civilian areas not directly touched by the factional fighting were affected. Supplied by the army in Juba, the Toposa around Kapoeta became more active against the SPLA. The SPLA had never adequately addressed the problem of Toposa hostility, which was based in part on Toposa particularism, but also on the SPLA's seizing control of the Toposa gold fields. The SPLA alternated between subjugating the Toposa militarily, and wooing them with promises of deliveries of relief supplies. They had only just recently abandoned one attempt at forceful pacification for a more conciliatory approach, but the new vulnerability of the Torit faction persuaded many Toposa that they had nothing to gain by making their peace with the SPLA.

The Nasir commanders were not necessarily personally motivated by anti-Dinka sentiment, but their appeal inevitably attempted to play on anti-Garang and, by extension, anti-Dinka feeling. To everybody's cost, they found that they had overestimated the former and succeeded only in inflaming the latter. As the Nasir faction began to lose southern Sudanese sympathy both inside and outside the Sudan, their internal support was progressively confined to the Nuer, and they began to take on the appearance of a tribalist movement. The wholesale attack on Dinka civilians in Kongor and Bor in 1991–2 helped to rally support for Garang among the Dinka of Bahr al-Ghazal, who were otherwise disappointed in the SPLA leadership for having neglected them, especially in the establishment of relief priorities. Attacks by Nuer on Dinka cattle camps in the eastern Bahr al-Ghazal near the border with Upper Nile only confirmed early suspicions that the real motives of the Nasir faction were tribal, whatever their public professions. So, as in the final years of the Southern

Regional Government, the political debate, this time centred on widely-held grievances against Garang, was diverted and obscured by the resurrection of a tribal idiom.

8.2.1 The 'hunger triangle'

The fracture line between the Nasir and Torit factions of the SPLA (as they were styled throughout 1992 and early 1993) became the Nuer–Dinka frontier within Jonglei Province. The Kongor area had been virtually abandoned by its civilian population as a result of the 1991 attacks, and was consequently thinly defended by an SPLA which was concentrating its forces around Juba and confronting a resurgent Sudanese army in Eastern Equatoria. With people displaced away from the immediate border, the area contained between the points of Kongor, Ayod and Waat was soon to become the focus of what one UN field worker later styled a 'resource war'.

The largest concentration of persons receiving food aid in 1992 was in Waat. Only a small portion were displaced Dinka, though more were reported to be coming in by the end of the year. Most of the rest were Lou Nuer, suffering from continued food shortages, and an increasing number were refugees from fighting around Malakal. Most deaths were reported among the Dinka. Riek's English wife, Emma McCune, actively lobbied for the opening of new relief centres in Ayod and Kongor.

The causes for distress among the displaced and local population in Ayod in December 1992 were clearly attributable to the reintroduction of fighting into the area in 1991–2. Grain stocks were already low because of the 1991 floods, and there had been losses of cattle to the 1991 outbreak of trypanosomiasis and retaliatory cattle raids from the Dinka in 1992. But the main burden local people faced was the influx of soldiers in the Nasir faction garrison, who fed exclusively off local livestock. As a result, many of those displaced by the fighting to the south were not staying around Ayod, but were moving further north, *away* from the frontline. A UN assessment team found no concentration of distress in Ayod in December, but reported, all too prophetically, 'There remains a belief among local authorities that UN teams need to see thousands of starving people clustered together in horrible conditions in order to recommend assistance – perhaps they have assessed us correctly.'[6]

The reasons behind the Nasir faction's occupation of Kongor at this time were political and logistical: a move out of the Nuer districts would demonstrate that the SPLA-Nasir was not solely a Nuer army. Further, the control of Garang's home ground would be a considerable propaganda victory, for it was a land link with government forces in Eastern Equatoria, and it would open up a new source of increased relief supplies. SPLA-Nasir occupied Kongor and neighbouring Panyagor in force early in 1993, called for relief agencies to establish programmes for the 'displaced', and then herded them into the area for the UN to see.

The movements into the Kongor area at this time were mainly military. The Nasir faction force at Kongor linked up with William Nyuon and received supplies from the government through him. The government also sent reinforcements to Bor by river, passing by this sector of SPLA-

[6] PSV to DP/PO'B, Ayod Assessment, 16 December 1992, OLS document.

Nasir territory unmolested. A new headquarters was established at the former UNDP compound at Panyagor, which was also selected as the site of a conference in March 1993 to forge a new 'SPLA-United' out of the Nasir faction and various Equatorian and Dinka leaders, including those prisoners freed in September. The meeting was disrupted by a commando group sent by Garang, but SPLA-United soon reoccupied Kongor, again calling for relief agencies to feed the 'displaced' in the 'hunger triangle' camps at Kongor, Ayod and Yuai, on the Lou Nuer border.

The establishment of a new feeding centre at Yuai puzzled UN relief workers. It was not a population centre; they were aware that Riek was moving people deliberately in that direction; and the majority of beneficiaries were identified to be 'daytrippers', overwhelmingly male, from Waat. The SPLA, who launched a new offensive in April to break this supply link between SPLA-United's main force and Nyuon's in Eastern Equatoria, always regarded Yuai as essentially a military base, especially so after expelling SPLA-United from Kongor and capturing government vehicles and other equipment at Yuai. Riek simultaneously requested the government to airlift resupplies and ammunition to Ayod and Waat and the UN to send relief to the same places.

A ceasefire between the factions was brokered by the US Ambassador to the Sudan, Donald Petterson, in May 1993, but it was never implemented. SPLA-United troops moved back into the area, and SPLA troops fanned out from Kongor towards Duk Faiwil and Bor. Fighting continued throughout June and July and relief camps (with their concentration of supplies) became particular targets. SPLA troops advanced as far as Waat. SPLA-United faced near-annihilation, were it not for the timely intervention of Khartoum, who launched an unexpected rainy season offensive against the bulk of SPLA forces in Eastern Equatoria in June (Section **7.5**), and resupplied SPLA-United with new weapons and stores from Malakal. Fighting shifted out of the hunger triangle area only when factions of SPLA-United in the Waat, Fangak and Sobat areas began fighting each other, and the SPLA shifted its attention to interdicting William Nyuon's convoys moving between Waat and Lafon.

8.2.2 The Nuer civil war

Nuer–Dinka hostility is an accepted fact in scholarly discourse on the Sudan. Anthropologists who might know nothing else about the civil war in the South will recognize in the tribal explanations of the SPLA split the familiar dogma of Nuer–Dinka opposition which has been repeated and elaborated on in endless re-workings of Evans-Pritchard's classic ethnography.[7] In reality the attempt to rally the Nuer in support of the split through escalating Nuer–Dinka fighting only widened fissures within Nuer society, resulting in the renewal of a Nuer civil war. The end to that civil war was finally made possible only by linking it to the end of Nuer–Dinka raiding (Section **8.5**).

---

[7] This is not the place for a critique of the secondary literature on segmentary opposition and the ahistorical and essentialized image of the two peoples presented in the old Nuer–Dinka debate, exemplified in Raymond Kelly, *The Nuer Conquest* (Ann Arbor, 1985). That debate informs some of the ideas in a recent analysis of Abyei, David C. Cole & Richard Huntington, *Between a Swamp and a Hard Place* (Boston, 1997).

The war between the SPLA and the Anyanya-2 in the early 1980s hampered the SPLA's military progress and was extremely destructive to Nuer civilian populations (Section **5.3.2**). The truces which led to the amalgamation of many Anyanya-2 groups into the SPLA (Section **6.2.2**) had been expanded by 1990 to include a series of local truces between other groups of peoples throughout Upper Nile and Jonglei. Whatever progress the SPLA was making towards re-establishing mechanisms for local mediation was halted by the split in the SPLA in 1991.

Many Nuer who rallied to the Nasir commanders did so because they thought that now the Nuer would rule as the Dinka were accused of ruling before. The old antagonism against the Bor Dinka (extending to the Dinka of Kongor district, where Garang and many of his commanders came from) was revived, especially among those group of ex-Anyanya-2 Nuer who lived at some distance from Kongor and Bor districts. The devastation of Kongor and Bor in 1991–2, which resulted in the displacement of virtually the entire population of both districts, appears to have been initiated by the Fangak Anyanya-2 and the Mor Lou from Akobo. The Gaawar and Lou Nuer living directly on the border with the Dinka had many ties of kinship and affiliation which inhibited their participation in attacks on civilians. The Lou Nuer of Waat district had especially depended on their Dinka neighbours for food throughout the previous three years.

In the counterattacks of 1992–3 which followed, many of the reinforcements Garang sent to Kongor came from Bor and Bahr al-Ghazal. These, too, were not inhibited by any local ties of community or kinship and were convinced that the Nuer attack on Kongor and Bor was part of a wider assault on the Dinka. In the devastation visited on Yuai, Waat and Ayod a number of displaced Nuer-speaking Dinka civilians were killed by the Bahr al-Ghazal troops, who accused them of having thrown in their lot with the Nuer.

War along the Nuer-Dinka frontier had a direct impact on security among the Nuer themselves. The serious inter-community fighting which broke out between the Lou and Gaawar in 1992 and the Lou and Jikany in 1993 was a direct consequence of the removal of a single SPLA administration. Prior to the split, the whole of the area south of the Sobat had been placed under the jurisdiction of Bor. In the difficult years following 1988 the Lou Nuer of Waat district had benefited from access to their Dinka neighbours in Kongor and Bor, and from regulated access to the Sobat dry-season grazing grounds and fishing pools, which they shared with the Jikany. Following the split, the Jikany reasserted their exclusive claims to the Sobat, and Riek, dependant on their goodwill as he was, recognized their claims. At the same time the UN relief effort focused on the Sobat around Nasir. The split in the SPLA cut the overland relief route from Bor to Ayod and Waat. Though that had been little used in the past, it meant that the Lou were now cut off from their main source of relief in Kongor and Bor, just when severe late rains virtually destroyed the 1991 harvest. In 1992 some Lou raiding parties attacked the Gaawar for cattle, as it was the only source of food now available to them.

By the end of 1992 the Lou Nuer had numerous grievances: they felt they had not been given sufficient attention in the relief effort, and that they were being excluded from necessary riverain pastures and fishing grounds. These grievances were presented to Riek personally at the end of 1992, but he took no action. The Jikany, for their part, no longer had easy access to the Gambela region, following recent clashes between Sudanese Nuer, Anuak and Ethiopian forces. Fighting between the Lou and Jikany broke out in the dry-season pastures in 1993, just at the same time that heavy fighting broke out between the two SPLA factions along the Lou–Dinka border. Subsequent to this fighting the Lou also complained that they had received very little support from forces in neighbouring Ayod and Nasir areas when Garang's forces counter-attacked as far as Waat in 1993. In the immediate aftermath of the SPLA attack on Waat, various units of Nuer SPLA-United began fighting each other.

SPLA-United commanders from both the Jikany and Lou now approached the government in Malakal seeking arms ostensibly with which to fight Garang. These were given freely, and with them the commanders armed groups of their fellow citizens. Throughout the early part of 1994 there were clashes between the Lou of Waat and the Jikany of Nasir, leading to the destruction of Ulang and Nasir itself and the death of some 1200 persons. Growing concern among educated Nuer exiles led to the convening of a large inter-Nuer peace conference at Akobo during the 1994 rainy season, as an attempt to sort out inter-Nuer problems and improve relations with the Anuak in Ethiopia.

The peace conference achieved one goal, which was to set out the terms by which the main antagonists would agree to stop fighting and the compromise that each was willing to accept. It also revealed the extent to which individual commanders within SPLA-United had collaborated with the government. This reinforced the momentum for repudiating that collaboration and reaffirming the stated goals of the movement. Yet the conference failed to achieve its aims because, in the end, Riek failed to institute those measures necessary to implement the agreement. Troops were not sent into the disputed pastures to keep the peace, and commanders previously involved in the fighting were not convinced that they would be free from retaliation. The fighting that broke out again between armed units contributed to the final disintegration and demise of the movement.

8.3   Disintegration

The main problem the Nasir faction had in establishing its political credibility was its collaboration with the government. The movement's reliance on the government for military hardware at crucial times throughout 1993–4 had a subsequent obvious effect on the course of later inter-factional fighting. Throughout this time the leadership's public insistence that it was fighting for an African identity and independence of the South looked increasingly unconvincing. This accelerated disillusionment and disintegration as more and more of the rank-and-file of the movement began to realize the extent of their leaders' dependence on government support.

In presenting itself as a pan-Southern movement the Nasir SPLA tried to overcome its image as a Nuer break-away faction by including persons from other parts of the southern Sudan in prominent positions. These attempts were, on the whole, unsuccessful. The defection of William Nyuon from the mainstream SPLA in September 1992, and the escape of some prominent SPLM/SPLA detainees at the same time, appeared to offer the possibility of producing a broad coalition, including Dinka from Bahr al-Ghazal (Kerubino) and Upper Nile (Arok Thon), and the most respected of veteran Southern nationalist leaders from Equatoria (Joseph Oduho). The re-formulation of 'SPLA-United' early in 1993 did not have the desired effect. Numerous lower level officials had quit the movement over the issue of Lam Akol's contacts with the government. Joseph Oduho was as consistent in his opposition to the domination of the military commanders in the SPLA-United as he had been in the SPLA and caused Lam Akol considerable consternation when he insisted that no military personnel should be included in the executive of the new movement. His death during an attack by Garang's troops on the SPLA-United at Panyagor in March 1993 left both factions tainted, and many Equatorians left SPLA-United as a result.[8]

The movement's attempt to create a Dinka base of operations was no more successful than its attempt to establish an Equatorian base. It failed to secure Kongor for Arok Thon Arok's scheduled return in 1993, and he resigned from the movement following Riek's dismissal of Lam Akol in 1994. Kerubino's return to northern Bahr al-Ghazal had devastating consequences for the civilian population there. In 1994 the group of Bahr al-Ghazal civilian leaders refused to return to their home districts at the head of armies composed mainly of Nuer soldiers and resigned en masse. All cited serious shortcomings in the movement in their reasons for leaving: the concentration of power in the hands of Riek, the lack of democratic institutions, and the rising level of violence against civilians.

By mid-1994 SPLA-United had failed to live up to its earlier humanitarian and democratic rhetoric. It had been responsible for human rights abuses and had allowed the perpetrators of abuses to go unpunished. It had not introduced greater democracy in its own organization, and it had made little advance in the creation of administrative institutions, beyond the appointment of a short-lived 'cabinet' of ministers. Attempts by some commanders to create their own power bases within the faction had led to fighting between the two largest Nuer groups.

It was the Nuer civil war which exposed SPLA-United's greatest weaknesses. The conference convened to end that civil war in 1994 was hastily converted into a National Convention, whereby SPLA-United renamed itself the South Sudan Independence Movement/Army (SSIM/A), rededicated itself to the cause of Southern independence, and formally 'dismissed' those commanders who were accused of collaborating with the government – Nyuon, Kuanyin and Lam – maintaining the public pretence that this collaboration had been done without Riek's knowledge. This appeared to pave the way towards at least a truce, if not reconciliation, with the SPLA, but the gulf that separated the two movements still ran deep.

---

[8] Each faction accused the other for Oduho's death. It is now clear that he was killed by 'SPLA-Mainstream' troops. Before the Panyagor meeting Oduho was already embarrassing the SPLA-United commanders by his own objections to their authoritarian behaviour. It is the unproven conviction of some Equatorians that Lam Akol deliberately abandoned Oduho to his fate in order to rid the movement of a contentious rival for leadership.

8.4 Attempts at reconciliation between the Southern factions

External mediators tried to get the two factions to resolve their differences almost as soon as the Nasir coup was announced, and there was a succession of talks in Nairobi from late 1991 to early 1992. During this time the Nasir faction attempted to draw other members of the Torit faction into discussions concerning the removal of Garang. With the leadership at issue, there was no reason to expect these negotiations would result in any real agreement, especially as the Nasir faction continued to cooperate with the Sudanese army in fighting the main SPLA. It was during these talks that Khartoum began channelling money to the Nasir faction via Lonrho. This was the real obstacle on which such talks foundered.

The common platform the two SPLA delegations offered at Abuja in May 1992 appeared a more hopeful basis for reconciliation. How serious the Nasir delegation was is difficult to tell, for it was also at Abuja that the wooing of William Nyuon began, and it was ultimately with money provided by the government that Nyuon was persuaded to leave the SPLA. Garang, who was unavailable for prior consultation about the joint declaration, saw it as a smoke-screen and repudiated it.

The government also kept a close watch on US attempts at mediation between the two factions in 1993. It is possible that neither group intended to implement the truce brokered by Ambassador Petterson, but two days after the government denounced the truce, Riek himself announced that he would not be withdrawing his troops from the hunger triangle after all, and fighting resumed some two weeks later. The ending of Tiny Rowland's financial support to SPLA-United in August, coinciding as it did with Garang receiving a new shipment of weapons from Zimbabwe, kept SPLA-United tied even more closely to the government.[9] The government countered Petterson's intervention with its own additional security agreements with Lam at Fashoda in August and Faustino Atem at Bentiu in October. It was the government that announced the fact of the Fashoda meeting shortly before Riek and Lam were due to travel to Washington to participate in a US Congressional-sponsored reconciliation with Garang in October. Lam's presence at the meeting was widely seen as Khartoum's guarantee that no breakthrough would be made, but it seems that Riek himself had assured the government that the meeting would fail.[10] A document was produced, but Riek avoided signing it.

Reconciliation through top-down mediation having failed, a grass-roots rapprochement had more success. By January 1995 Riek had publicly repudiated Lam Akol, William Nyuon and Kerubino for their collaboration with the government. Civil war among the Nuer continued unabated in former Jonglei Province and along the Sobat. Government troops advanced towards Riek's northernmost garrisons. Under pressure from the leaders of Kenya, Uganda, Eritrea and Ethiopia, Riek declared a cease-fire with the SPLA on 10 February. The

---

[9] It was reported that the weapons were intended for pro-Mengistu forces still operating in Ethiopia, but Garang diverted the entire shipment to his forces in Eastern Equatoria.
[10] Scroggins, *Emma's War*.

government reoccupied Nasir on 26 March. The Nuer stationed in Equatoria were increasingly disenchanted. Some just deserted their positions and walked home. Others made contact with the SPLA and on 31 March the garrison at Lafon under its junior officers captured a government convoy passing through their area and subsequently persuaded their commander, William Nyuon, to rejoin the SPLA. On 27 April the local SSIA and SPLA commanders signed the Lafon declaration, approved by Nyuon and Garang, announcing the re-unification of the movement.

The reunification was only partial. Riek wanted to maintain what he called 'parallel' movements. Finally, Nyuon announced Riek's 'dismissal' and the formation of a new provisional executive council, just as earlier Riek had 'dismissed' Nyuon at the founding of SSIM. This action was an echo of the Nasir coup: an announcement that hoped to bring about the effect it proclaimed. It was also reminiscent of the announcement of provisional governments in the 1960s, as a number of those appointed to the new council repudiated it and reaffirmed their support for Riek. The Nuer civil war continued. The anti-Riek commanders moved in with SPLA support. Their initial success enabled the SPLA to launch a highly successful offensive against the government in Eastern Equatoria, but local resistance against the new SSIA culminated in the ambush and death of William Nyuon in January 1996.

8.5 Disunity & the 'peace from within'

By the end of 1995 Riek was the leader of a virtual movement, lacking any real substance or coherence. Publicly he still hoped for external backing which could provide the movement with some credibility, and early in 1996 he travelled to Ethiopia in an attempt to join the NDA. His previous military collaboration with the government undermined his claim to head an anti-Khartoum, pro-independence Southern movement. Added to this was the Northern parties' reluctance either to antagonize Garang or to see a re-unified SPLA.[11] Riek failed in his bid and was ordered out of the country by the Ethiopian government. Crossing the border at Jokau, he returned to his own territory for the first time since the Akobo convention in 1994 and signed a ceasefire with the First Vice-President Major-General Al-Zubair Muhammad Salih at Nasir. Subsequently he and Kerubino, who had been operating independently of SSIM since 1994, formally signed a Peace Charter with President Bashir in Khartoum. This was the culmination of the government's 'peace from within' strategy, towards which they had been working for some time.

The Charter reaffirmed the unity of the Sudan within its known boundaries, the federal system of the NIF (with its twenty-six states),

---

[11] Persons sympathetic to Riek claim that he was genuine in his desire to disentangle himself from Khartoum and saw acceptance by the NDA as his last chance to obtain alternative sources of arms, which alone would free him from dependence on Khartoum. If this is true, it is consistent with the confused, almost schizophrenic attitude towards liberation and collaboration which he displayed from the beginning of the Nasir coup in August 1991 to his resignation from the government in February 2000.

and *shari'a* as the source of legislation. Against this was a promise at the end of an unspecified period for a referendum for Southerners to 'determine their political aspirations'. Riek proclaimed that this agreement would give the South its independence. His representatives in East Africa gave it a more restricted interpretation. SSIM considered itself in a state of ceasefire with the government and at war with the SPLM, as one member explained to an OLS official. 'This is justified by the expla-nation that SSIM finds it impossible to be at war with two parties at once and sees John Garang as a greater threat to the survival of the Nuer people than is the Government. ... One thing is clear: the SSIM and the Nuer people feel a strong sense of persecution. They insist that the international community (USA, Ethiopia, Uganda, etc) as well as the SPLM is seeking to wipe out the Nuer as a political force.'[12] Far from affirming the movement's commitment to independence of the whole South, this agreement was a tactic to ensure the movement's dominance among the Nuer.

The Charter also imposed upon the signatories the duty of imple-menting security arrangements. As Kerubino's SPLA-Bahr al-Ghazal group was already a militia of the government, this involved no change in his activities. Riek's hold on his forces was more tenuous. Paulino Matip, who held the rank of Major-General in the Sudanese army but was theo-retically part of SSIA, was unhappy about Riek's elevation through the Charter and was reported to have refused orders to redeploy his troops from the Bentiu oilfields to Riek's command in Ler. Partly in response to the April Peace Charter, the units of SSIM/A who were co-operating with the SPLA against Riek were formally reabsorbed into the SPLA.

In the year following the signing of the Peace Charter Riek's inability to bring all of SSIM or even all of the Nuer over to the government became evident. The SPLA made little progress in encouraging more Nuer to rejoin them, but elsewhere it and the NDA forces opened new fronts and took more territory. By the end of 1996 the SPLA was on the offensive in the Nuba Mountains and the NDA and SPLA were active in the eastern Sudan. In January 1997 the SPLA retook the Ethiopian border towns of Kurmuk and Qaissan. In March and April the SPLA made substantial gains in its advance on Juba, and repelled government columns in Equatoria, the Nuba Mountains and Blue Nile. The Peace Charter had not only not brought peace, it had failed to halt the SPLA's political and military resurgence. Neither Riek nor the government had much to show for their collaboration.

The government's internal peace agreement signed on 21 April 1997 was intended to give the appearance of a momentum in the opposite direction. More individuals were brought in as signatories, ostensibly representing more political groups, all to operate under the umbrella of a new United Democratic Salvation Front (UDSF), with their armies to be merged into a South Sudan Defence Force (SSDF). The agreement incor-porated the general principles of the Peace Charter (including the unity of the Sudan), and defined the federal structure, with its new Coordinating Council for the Southern States, and promised a referendum on unity or

---

[12] Iain Levine, 'Note for the Record, 13.4.96, Meeting with Dr. Timothy Tutlam of RASS', OLS document. Dr. Tutlam later became Riek's governor of Upper Nile and died in a plane crash at Nasir in February 1998.

secession for the southern Sudan (defined according to its 1956 bound-aries) after an interim period of four years. Control of the armed forces, national security and mining was reserved for the federal government, the states being allowed some control over economic development, but only in accordance with federal planning. The President of the Republic was to appoint the President of the Coordinating Council of Southern States, who would nominate his cabinet and the governors of the Southern States for final appointment by the President of the Republic.[13]

Though this was the agreement the Southern leaders signed, it was not the agreement that was implemented. The version passed by the National Assembly in July gave the President of the Southern States Coordinating Council's right to nominate state governors to an Islamic Consultative Council, controlled by the Speaker of the Assembly (Turabi), and the President of the Republic. The governors so elected by the state assem-blies were to be confirmed in their offices by the President of the Republic. They were thus answerable to their assemblies and the central government, rather than to the Coordinating Council, of which they became members.[14] The Assembly further reduced the number of council members to be appointed on the nomination of the Council President. Riek, who was appointed president of the Council in August, thus found the powers of his office restricted.

The disputes which developed within the Southern organizations signatory to the peace focused on the distribution of offices. Paulino Matip and Riek backed rival candidates for governor of Unity State (western Upper Nile, formerly Liech State under SSIM), and fighting broke out in Bentiu when Taban Deng Gai, Riek's brother-in-law and former quartermaster, was elected. Fighting between the two forces continued throughout 1998 and 1999, propelling Matip out of the SSDF. Kerubino complained of his subordination to Riek and staged a spec-tacular (if temporary) redefection to the SPLA in January 1998 with an assault on government-held Wau, subsequently justifying his actions by complaining of the imposition of ministers and governors on the South by Turabi's National Congress (the revamped NIF).

Nothing demonstrated the falsity of the 'peace from within' more than the continuation and expansion of the Nuer civil war. It was, in fact, the 'peace from within' which added fuel to that civil war. Prior to 1996 it had been confined mainly to factional fighting within Riek's command in Upper Nile and Jonglei. After 1997 its focus shifted to the Western Nuer in Unity State. Here, the power play between two Western Nuer rivals, Riek Machar and Paulino Matip, was fostered by the very government to which they were both allied, in that both were armed and supplied by the Sudanese army. The fostering of the civil war among the Western Nuer, while intensifying insecurity in what was supposed to be a government-held area, served the government's purpose in neutralizing the Southern guerrilla factions best positioned to interfere with the exploitation of the Bentiu oilfields. Matip, who had always worked closely with Bashir since their days in Mayom together, could be counted on to do the government's bidding in the field.

[13] The Sudan Peace Agreement, 21 April 1997.
[14] *Sudan Democratic Gazette*, no. 88, September 1997, pp. 2, 5.

Matip had maintained an autonomous military and economic base in his Bul Nuer territory near Bentiu, building up a small trading empire dealing in sorghum and cattle. As a Major-General in the Sudanese army, he had direct access to military supplies. In reality, Riek had more need of Paulino than Paulino of Riek, and Riek's subsequent attempt to put his own man in the governorship of western Upper Nile after returning to Khartoum led to an open breach, with Paulino's troops taking and sacking Ler, Riek's old headquarters and the centre of his relief operations.

Riek's protests at the government's support for Paulino had no lasting effect. The intensification of oil exploitation in the Bentiu oilfields in 1998–9 brought with it, into the region, an increase of the Sudan army and other armed personnel as well as foreign oil workers (most of them Chinese) contributing directly to another outbreak of fighting between a profusion of Nuer factions beginning in April 1999.

Faced with the demonstration of his powerlessness, Riek complained that while the 1997 peace agreement placed the oilfields under his control, the government's support of Matip undermined his position and the entire agreement. Privately he explained to his supporters both inside and outside the country, and to foreign observers, that he would stick to the letter of the agreement to show all concerned that when it collapsed, the fault was due to the government's own bad faith. Proving the government's untrustworthiness soon became the main justification of his own collaboration.

His position was scarcely credible. Riek's critics, Sudanese and non-Sudanese alike, had predicted the demise of his agreement with the government from the start. Like the Frankfurt Agreement, the wording of the 1997 agreement was subject entirely to the interpretation imposed on it by the government. It shared many of the same weaknesses as the Addis Ababa Agreement, in that its provisions were worded in such a way as to be open to many interpretations, and the powers devolved to the Southern states were highly qualified by Federal control. In matters of economic development the Southern states were to operate 'in accordance with Federal Planning'. The Federal government had jurisdiction over mining, while the states had jurisdiction over quarrying, which left the real control of mineral resources to the central government. The states were entrusted with powers over their own security and public order, but the Federal government exercised power over the armed forces, defence affairs and national security. Thus all government armed forces in the South were subordinated to the central government, and it could be argued that a region contested by civil war was a matter of national, rather than state, security.

Paulino's earlier refusal to place his troops under Riek's command in Ler certainly had the army's full approval, and it kept a loyal militia intact for operations in the oilfields. Large areas in and around the oilfields were depopulated as Nuer civilians fled to Bahr al-Ghazal seeking SPLA protection. At least two groups of Nuer militia began gravitating towards the SPLA. Whatever his interest in the oilfields, Paulino continued amassing cattle at a tremendous rate. Riek blamed the government for the breakdown of the ceasefire, but by late 1999 those of his troops who still retained some loyalty to him were steadily abandoning the state, leaving Paulino, supported by PDF troops and Arab militias from Kordofan, to contest control with the remaining break-away groups. Kerubino added to the confusion by breaking with Garang and flying back to Unity State, where he joined his brother-in-law Matip as an official 'guest', until he was killed in factional fighting in September 1999.

With chaos ramifying throughout the Western Nuer heartland, the SPLA found itself in the unusual position of providing protection for refugee Nuer. This was the context in which an intertribal conference, sponsored by the NSCC and guaranteed by the SPLA, was held at Wunlit between groups of Western Nuer and Dinka from Tonj, Rumbek and Yirol, leading to a peace settlement between them in March 1999, and an agreement by the SPLA not to sanction cross-border raiding. Local truces between SPLA and SSDF forces in Jonglei had held throughout much of 1998 and 1999, with some Nuer forces defecting to the SPLA outright. Some of the same groups and persons who had participated in the Nuer–Dinka reconciliation meeting subsequently organized a large meeting of Nuer in Waat, drawing on people from both the SPLM/A and UDSF/SSDF factions. In December 1999 they announced the formal break of the majority of the Nuer with the government, and in 2000 revived the old name of South Sudan Liberation Movement, an organization formally allied with no one.

The HEC of the SPLM welcomed these moves, but the SPLA military leadership was less forthcoming. Riek's UDSF in Khartoum had had no part in the Wunlit conference and was left stranded by the decision in Waat. Without an army, without followers, Riek was now without a movement. He tried to regain the initiative by leaving Khartoum in December 1999 and resigning from the government two months later. But lacking any real support in his home area he moved to Nairobi, where he tried to maintain the appearance of a leader of a viable political movement, before returning to the field and establishing a base at Maiwut, between Nasir and the Ethiopian border.

Whatever the cosmetic or purely theoretical aspects of SPLA adminis-tration, it can be contrasted with SPLA-United/SSIM, where there were no similar civil administrative structures, and where much of what was announced in the form of internal organization existed on paper only. The excuse Riek offered at the founding SSIM conference was that the movement lacked trained personnel. One reason why they lacked such personnel is that in 1991 they had chased away many of the SPLA admin-istrators, or had them executed.

In the end a movement which proclaims as its goals the achievement of greater democracy and the respect of human rights will be judged by the seriousness with which it has approached those goals. There was a lack of seriousness in SPLA-United constitution-making. It all came out of Riek's headquarters, and even his laptop computer.[15] The behaviour of SPLM/A-United/SSIM/A was precisely what 1960s leaders identified in the SPLM

---

[15] Emma McCune, Riek's English wife who later died in Nairobi, claimed authorship of at least some of these documents. According to one of her friends, 'She said once that it was "an incredible high" to get up from lovemaking to draft constitutions for an independent southern Sudan' (Deborah Scroggins, 'Emma', *Granta 60* (Winter 1997), p. 125).

manifesto as the condition which the unified command structure was designed to avoid: paper cabinets manoeuvring for paper positions. In a sequence of events reminiscent of 1969 (Section **3.2.3**), each time a group of leaders left SPLA-United, a new organization was formed. The Equatorians who left in 1993 re-named themselves the Patriotic Resistance Movement of South Sudan. Others who left in 1994 called themselves the South Sudan Freedom Front. The Bahr al-Ghazal defectors organized themselves as an Independent Group. Kerubino continued to operate independently under the name of SPLA–Bahr al-Ghazal Group. When SPLA-United changed its name to SSIM, Lam Akol announced from his home in Tonga that he remained the leader of the true SPLA-United.

The government's internal peace of 1997 encouraged the proliferation of named groups, in order to give the appearance of embracing the plurality of Southern political opinion. To SSIM and the SPLA-Bahr al-Ghazal Group were added the Independent Bor Group, the Independent Bahr al-Ghazal Group, the Equatoria Defence Force and the SPLA Independent Group from the Nuba Mountains. Each of the these groups had political personnel resident in Khartoum (just as the old Southern factions had offices in Kampala), but none, other than SSIM, had a permanent presence in the South outside of government garrisons. The proliferation of initials did not stop there. Paulino Matip renamed his force the South Sudan United Army (SSUA) when he broke away from Riek's SSDF in 1998, but Riek's initials were replicated in other breakaway factions: an SSDF-2 in Juba, an SSDF-United and an SSDF-Friendly-to-the-SPLA among the Western Nuer. The motivations behind the formation of these small armies is less ideological than personal. For men such as Paulino Matip and Gordon Kong Cuol, what matters is that they have an army to command, and they will ally themselves with whomever is able to supply their troops. It is this reversion to an earlier period of ineffectual political disunity and debilitating internecine feuding that only reconfirmed the SPLA in its suspicion of civil structures and its continued reliance on military administration.

The impact of the long-delayed reconciliation between Riek and Garang in January 2002 was muted by the fact that Riek had very few troops to bring with him: he had alienated many of his former subordinates who were either already ranged between the government and the SPLA, or had chosen neither and were trying to maintain a precarious neutrality. Riek's lasting legacy is the fomenting of civil war among the Nuer, and handing the oilfields over to the government. The Nuer civil war has yet to come to an end, and the government is expanding its control over the oilfields. Nuer unity is needed to contain or reverse the damage done by these twinned events. It remains to be seen if Riek, with Garang, is capable of repairing that unity.

9
Multiple ▌ Civil Wars

The current civil war has intensified in complexity the longer it has been fought. Multiple local grievances have created numerous motives for armed confrontation, and shifting alliances within the wider conflict have produced a pattern of interlocking civil wars, now being fought on different levels.

By 1991 the war in the Sudan could already be described as a network of internal wars, whether within sub-regions or among specific peoples. Some Nuer tribes provided recruits simultaneously to the Anyanya-2 and the SPLA, and other Southern peoples such as the Mundari and Toposa were similarly divided between the government and the guerrillas. Misiriyya groups sought military patrons in the political parties, the army and Chevron oil company. One thing which clearly distinguishes the current war from the civil war of the 1960s is that it has not been confined to the South: fighting has taken place in Darfur, Southern Kordofan, Blue Nile and, most recently, Qallabat, Kassala and Red Sea – all parts of the 'Muslim' North. In each regional case internal tensions have been exacerbated by the intervention of external interests. With the introduction of violent sectarian politics at the national centre, this war has also served to fracture, perhaps irreparably, the Northern Muslim consensus.

Since 1991 the number of internal civil wars has multiplied, paralleled by a deepening involvement of the Sudan government in the internal politics of neighbouring countries, whether in pursuit of its policy of Islamic expansion or for reasons of military expediency. These multiple civil wars have each fed into and intensified the fighting of the overall 'North–South' war. The longer the war has been fought without hope of resolution, and the more entrenched the North–South cleavage has become, so other fractures within the Muslim North have proliferated.

9.1 The civil war within Islam:
redefining the community of Believers

The Sudan has a longer history of territorial integrity than most post-colonial nations in Africa. Territories combined together within the Egyptian empire go back over a century and a quarter, at least to the time of the first conquest of Darfur in 1876. The Mahdist state attempted (unsuccessfully) to maintain this integrity; the Anglo-Egyptian

Condominium re-established it, except where the edges had been nibbled away by other empires; Egypt and Britain bequeathed it to the independent Sudan. That territorial integrity has not been matched by internal coherence, and modern nationalists not only failed to create a sense of nationhood, they did not really attempt to create one. The result of post-war Anglo-Egyptian competition in the Sudan (1945–55) was that the administering codominus, Britain, adopted early the policy of self-government and self-determination. The 'nationalists' based in the urban centres thus did not have to fight for independence, and did not seek to identify common interests and forge alliances with other groups throughout the country to achieve this end, as other African nationalists had to do throughout Africa in the 1940s and 1950s.

The issue of self-determination quickly revolved around who was to inherit the instruments of state, and the internal battle was joined on those grounds. This became a struggle between the two main religious sects of the northern Sudan, the Ansar and the Khatmiyya, who were the only organizations then capable of mobilizing electoral support. Muslims outside those two sects, secular Muslims who preferred non-theocratic forms of government, and non-Muslims from the regions, were thus excluded from the nationalist mainstream, and could enter only through tactical electoral alliances.

The move towards an Islamic state, with the attendant issue of the head of state as Imam to whom an oath of allegiance is owed, intensified competition between the sectarian parties, as each sought to define legitimacy around their own brand of Islam. Ultimately the main challenge to these sects for control in the centre came through a new sect, the Muslim Brothers. A civil war within Sudanese Islam, revisiting the schisms of the Mahdiyya, had always been a possibility.[1] It is inherent in the project of the Islamic state, and as momentum towards that project accelerated it became a reality.

The political project of an Islamic state is both inclusive and exclusive in its intention. Inclusive, because it has been advocated as a way of hastening the conversion of non-Muslims; exclusive because even within the broad category of Muslims it has sought to exclude political secularists. Sadiq al-Mahdi argued in the 1980s for the legal exclusion of secularists such as the Communists and Ba'athists. The Criminal Bill drafted by his brother-in-law Hassan al-Turabi and presented to parliament in 1988 included a provision for outlawing apostasy (*al-ridda*). This provision of the bill came into effect only with the promulgation of the Sudanese Penal Code of 1991, after the NIF-backed coup. Apostasy is covered in Article 126, which states:[2]

> Section (1) Any Muslim who promotes the forsaking of the creed of Islam or who declares openly having forsaken it by a clear statement or an unequivocal act shall be deemed a perpetrator of the offence of apostasy.

---

[1] Britain at one point was more concerned that the move to Sudanese independence would result in a civil war between Muslim sects than war between the North and South. See document 300 in BDEEP, *Sudan*.

[2] I am grateful to Dr Muhammad Mahmud for providing me with both Arabic and English texts of Article 126.

Section (2) He who commits the offence of apostasy shall be called upon to repent and shall be given a grace period that shall be fixed by the court. If he insists on his apostasy and in case that he is not a recent convert to Islam he shall be executed.

Section (3) The punishment for apostasy shall be rescinded as soon as the apostate turns away from his apostasy before the implementation of the punishment.

The law is explicitly aimed at Muslims who, as an act of individual conscience, choose to convert to another religion. But the definition of what constitutes apostasy – by statement or 'unequivocal act' – is vague and can be politically determined, as Nimairi's 1984 execution of the founder of the Republican Brothers, Mahmud Muhammad Taha, has already shown. The threat of the application of the law of apostasy has been used by the current regime not only against secular Muslims and other political opponents, but in the harrassment of other Islamic sects, such as the Khatmiyya, Ansar and Ansar-Sunna. Opposition to an Islamic government can be, and has been, defined as an act of apostasy.

Other laws have had a more direct impact on the daily life of people living in the Muslim heartland of the Sudan. The Public Order Act of 1991 virtually prohibits mixed social gatherings and has been the basis for the almost complete exclusion of women from public life. Women have been subjected to official harrassment in the enforcement of dress codes and public association. Urban women, increasingly confined to the home, have had their economic activities severely restricted. Women who are by custom brewers of beer, have also been particularly hit by the prohibition on alcohol. Even in some rural areas where the seclusion of women is more commonly practised, the switch from subsistence to mechanized farming has reduced women's role in agricultural production.

The arrest, imprisonment and torture of women for contravening the more trivial provisions of the Public Order Act demonstrates how yet another segment of Muslim society in the Sudan is being stripped of its rights by the application of a particular brand of Islam. Recourse to the courts is of limited value, given that under the current interpretation of *shari'a* a woman's testimony is given less weight than that of a man (just as a non-Muslim's testimony is given less weight than that of a Muslim). For all of these reasons it is significant that women have increasingly taken the lead in organizing public protests against the regime's more restrictive policies, especially opposition to forced conscription of students into the PDF.

These developments within the Muslim centre of the Sudanese state set the context for the ultimate extension of *jihad* to Muslim opponents of the state, which was first applied to Muslims in the war along the margins of the North (Section **9.2**). This has now created a profound division within Sudanese Muslim society and gives the legal justification for continued civil war. The targets of the NIF regime's oppression in the capital since 1989 have been overwhelmingly Muslim. This new phase in political repression is the outcome of a history of the progressive exclusion of non-Muslims from full rights as citizens. Northern Sudanese, on the whole, have tolerated violence not only against non-Muslims by

Muslim Sudanese, but the victimization of Muslims in the South and the Nuba Mountains as early as the Juba massacre of 1965. Torture, extra-judicial murder and abduction were common methods of political repression in the war zones during the late 1980s. The transplanting of that violence from the peripheries into the very centre of the state can come as no real surprise. The 'ghost houses' of the Three Towns where the regime tortures its opponents are an NIF innovation, but they have their roots in the policies of previous governments and the acquiesence and silence of the vast majority of Muslim citizens. It is, to paraphrase Malcolm X, a case of 'chickens coming home to roost'.

9.2 Civil war along the margins

The fault lines within the North began to widen during the 1970s with the passage of laws which undermined the control of local authorities and local peoples over the resources of the land, reorienting the national economy towards heavily-capitalized export agriculture. This trend, begun under Nimairi, was accelerated during the coalition governments of Sadiq al-Mahdi and has been pushed to a logical extreme under the current Islamist government.

In the early 1970s Native Administration in the northern provinces was abolished and replaced by province councils where merchants, bureaucrats and persons originally from, or with strong connections to, the central Nile region tended to predominate. In the 1980s very weak regional governments were set up which lacked full administrative or economic autonomy but still relied on grants from the central government for basic budgetary support. The number of regional states has been increased by the current government, but their powers remain limited. In 1970 the Unregistered Land Act abolished customary rights of land use and access to land and set the foundation for the central state leasing of land for large-scale farming schemes. In 1974 the Law of Criminal Trespass strengthened the rights of leaseholders to their lands, further restricting the right of access by nomads and smallholding farmers. The current government amended the Civil Transactions Act in 1990 to prohibit the recognition of customary land rights in the courts throughout the country. The cumulative effect of these legal and administrative reforms was that not only did political power continue to be concentrated in the central government, but control of the very land on which people lived and depended was transferred to those with access to that power.

Before the 1970s people in the remoter rural areas attempted to overcome regional underdevelopment by establishing ties with those who controlled the central government. In the parliamentary periods, electoral alliances with the two main parties were mediated through the religious sects: Khatmiyya/DUP in the East, and Ansar/Umma in the West. By the late 1960s there was disillusionment with the sectarian parties and a brief upsurge in regionally-based parties, such as the Beja Congress, the Darfur Developmont Front and the General Union of the Nuba Mountains. In the parliamentary period of the 1980s the failure of the state to provide basic services, combined with the capture of the economy by merchant capitalists from the centre, hastened regional disillusionment. As the main parties (now joined by the NIF) increasingly failed to come up with national policies which satisfied regional grievances, so they relied more on linking Arab nationalism with religion to mobilize support. This only sharpened internal divides and hastened disillusionment among non-Arab Muslims.

9.2.1 The holy war in the Nuba Mountains
The war currently being fought in the Nuba Mountains combines the new conflict over land with older forms of racial oppression. It is the starkest example of the new land war which has become so much a feature of the civil wars in the North. Whereas in the South, land ownership and the threat of the appropriation of land was not a major factor in the outbreak of war, in the Nuba Mountains it has become one of *the* main issues. Areas of the Nuba Mountains have been subjected to Islamicization programmes since independence, with acts of cultural suppression in the use of Arabic names and prohibitions against local languages or religious observances. Yet it has only been relatively recently that the Nuba have been subjected to the same sort of active targeting of local leaders and forced dislocation of populations which has been typical of the conduct of war in the South. Ironically, it is because of the relatively large Muslim population among the Nuba that there has also been an explicit extension of *jihad* against other Muslims.

There are between 1.3 and 1.6 million Nuba, divided into some 50 languages and dialect clusters, many unrelated to each other and reflecting their diverse origins. Most external supporters of the Nuba, and in fact many exile Nuba, refer to them as 'a people', more as an act of political faith than as an historical, cultural, social or political reality. It would be more accurate to speak of the Nuba *peoples*, and examine the historical reasons why they have not yet achieved anything like the political coherence of the southern Sudan, segmented though that can be.

The hilly region of the Nuba Mountains has often provided refuge for people fleeing the power of expanding and predatory states, but it also lies within the rainfed agricultural belt, and the broad plains of its lowland areas have attracted both farmers and pastoralists from neighbouring areas. In the early twentieth century, British administration sought to bring the Nuba down from the hills to the plains, and relations between groups of Nuba and immigrant Arab pastoralists were regulated through the chiefly structures of Native Administration. For a brief while the Nuba Mountains formed a separate province, and it was intended at one time to attach it to the southern Sudan. The presence and objections of Baqqara pastoralists and merchants from the central Nile valley prevented that, and the Nuba Mountains were reabsorbed into Kordofan.

There was little solidarity between the Nuba Mountains and the southern Sudan during the first civil war. There was little political consciousness or internal solidarity among the Nuba to begin with, and because of their geographical position those who were politically active were anti-secessionist. The periods of democracy were too brief for any meaningful parliamentary alliances to be forged. There was active

Muslim proselytization, and the small Christian population often felt sympathy for Southern Christians, but Nuba soldiers were also recruited into the army and fought in the South. A remote area, the Nuba Mountains suffered from the same lack of services as other remote areas. But it was not until the 1970s, with the abolition of Native Administration and the new land legislation that the peoples of the Nuba Mountains faced the pressure of dispossession, a pressure most Southerners were protected from by the existence of the Southern Region.

Increasing amounts of land were alienated throughout the 1970s and 1980s, and heavy capitalized farming expanded under the Mechanized Farming Corporation. Misiriyya politicians, with strong links to Khartoum, became involved in the expropriation of smallholdings. Nuba villages began to be surrounded by the mechanized schemes, and village farmers were frequently fined (or even imprisoned) for trespass. The mechanized schemes also lay across the grazing routes of Baqqara cattle herders, and to avoid prosecution for trespass they frequently re-routed their herds through Nuba farmland. In the absence of the old Native Administration to arbitrate the disputes which arose, government courts generally took the side of the Baqqara against the Nuba. Dispossessed farmers joined the ranks of migrant wage-labourers seeking work on the schemes or in the main cities. The lack of educational opportunities for non-Muslims was a further deprivation felt by the younger generation. Thus by 1983, there were large numbers of disaffected Nuba whose grievances, while different from those in the South, made them potentially sympathetic to the SPLA, especially when the SPLA made it clear that, whatever the composition of its movement, it was not espousing a separatist political agenda.

In 1983 the Nuba Mountains had neither been part of the Southern Region nor formed a separate administrative unit of its own. It thus lacked the experience of shared political mobilization, activity and internal debate which had been common in the southern Sudan for eleven years. The Nuba did not become involved in the new civil war in any substantial numbers until the war came to them. In 1985, following the arming of local militias by the government, the SPLA attacked a Baqqara camp at Qardud on the border between Southern Kordofan and Upper Nile. In response, the government increased its support to local Baqqara militias, and together the army and militias began a crackdown on Nuba villages, despite the fact that the SPLA had only a fleeting and seasonal presence.

Systematic recruitment into the SPLA began in 1986. It followed a pattern then being repeated throughout the South and even in the Blue Nile. Recruitment task forces were sent in during the rains, and left with their recruits for training bases in Ethiopia. The army and Murahalin then retaliated against Nuba civilians, whether or not they had had any direct contact with the SPLA. In 1988 the government began a policy of systematic elimination of educated Nuba and village leaders, thus producing more recruits for the SPLA. In 1989 Yusif Kuwa, a veteran Nuba politician and a Muslim, returned with a large force of the SPLA New Kush Division and established a permanent SPLA presence. Political mobilization and the reorganization of civil administration began from that point. As in other parts of the South already under SPLA control, the SPLA in the Nuba Mountains used the structures, and often the personnel, of the chiefs' courts of the old Native Administration. The SPLA began to make significant gains against the government, especially in the south and west of the area.

In 1991 the loss of the Ethiopian bases and the split in the SPLA left the SPLA isolated in the Nuba Mountains and their contacts with the SPLA in the South became tenuous. In the 1991–2 dry season the government launched an offensive in the southwest and declared a *jihad* in the Nuba Mountains (*jihad* had long been declared in the South). As a number of the Nuba recruits in the SPLA were Muslim, and as many civilians in the SPLA areas were also Muslim, the declaration of *jihad* necessitated a justification for fighting and killing other Muslims. This was forthcoming in a *fatwa* issued by six shaikhs in El Obeid in April 1992 extending the definition of apostasy, declaring, 'An insurgent who was previously a Moslem is now an apostate; and a non-Moslem is a non-believer standing as a bulwark against the spread of Islam, and Islam has granted the freedom of killing both of them.'[3]

The *jihad* in the Nuba Mountains starkly reveals the extreme logic of the NIF branch of reformist Islam. In providing a religious justification for its policies, it defines its opponents as anti-Islam; by this definition its Muslim opponents become non-Muslims. A clear territorial distinction has been imposed distinguishing the *Dar al-Islam* (Abode of Peace) from the *Dar al-Harb* (Abode of War). Mosques found outside government control have been destroyed and defaced, and Muslims enjoined to relocate themselves to the *Dar al-Islam* of government garrisons. It is another of the war's ironies that while the government has denounced the SPLA for desecrating mosques in the South (which have been left physically intact), it is the government itself which has been actively, and systematically, destroying mosques in non-government-held areas of the North.

The renewal of the government offensive in December 1992 that led to the targeting of the civilian population was not just a military strategy but was part of the government's wider economic strategy as well. In March 1993 the Minister of Planning announced the sale of new parcels of land in the Nuba Mountains and received 40,000 bids from Arab entrepreneurs. This action became an integral part of the 'peace from within' strategy initiated at the end of 1993. Since that time large areas of the plains have been cleared of their original population and sold off to the regime's supporters. The dispossessed population has been relocated to resettlement camps near other agricultural schemes where they work as low-paid or unpaid labourers (similar to the use of displaced Dinka from Bahr al-Ghazal on agricultural schemes in Darfur). This has been advertised by the government as a twin-pronged policy leading simultaneously to development and peace, and as such has had a sympathetic reception from a number of development agency personnel in Khartoum, including, at one time, the UNDP head of OLS.

The pattern of fighting established in 1993–4 was reminiscent of the pattern of fighting in the South in the 1980s. Convoys of army and militia

---

[3] Quoted in African Rights, *Facing Genocide: The Nuba of Sudan*, p. 289, and in *Sudan Catholic Bishop's Conference News Bulletin* No. 4, July/August 1993.

moved out of government strongholds in the dry season, 'combing' through civilian areas, then returned to their garrisons during the rains. In 1995 Yusif Kuwa returned after a two-year absence with new supplies and began retaking garrisons lost to the government since 1992. SPLA training camps were established inside the Nuba Mountains, pre-emptive dry season offensives of their own were launched in 1996 and 1997, and by the end of 1997 the SPLA was reported to have regained all territory previously lost to the government. For all that, the SPLA presence was still confined mainly to the southeast, south and west of the region. Some two thirds of the civilian population were estimated to live under government control (many in resettlement camps) and only one third in SPLA territory. In 1998 the government took advantage of the ceasefire called in the South in the wake of the Bahr al-Ghazal famine and concentrated its troops in the Nuba Mountains (still excluded from relief agreements). In November it renewed its offensive on four fronts, with orders to crush the insurgency in three months. Part of the objective was to keep the issue of self-determination for the Nuba off the agenda of the renewed IGAD talks. The offensive was finally repulsed in February 1999.

The war in the Nuba Mountains has begun to receive considerable international publicity, overshadowing events elsewhere in the Sudan, including the South. The Nuba are often presented as a picturesque people threatened with extinction, deserving of protection like many other photogenic endangered species. In the late Yusif Kuwa (who died of cancer early in 2001) sympathetic outsiders found the charismatic and humane leadership lacking in John Garang. In his project of political mobilization they saw the beginnings of grass roots democracy absent in SPLA territory elsewhere. Admiring descriptions of the Nuba liberation struggle often lose sight of the fact that Nuba achievements in their own defence were based on their inclusion in the SPLA. If political mobilization was given more prominence by the Nuba SPLA leadership than is currently undertaken elsewhere, it is partly because more political mobilization was needed to begin with. In 1989 the Nuba peoples still lacked the widespread level of political consensus in favour of liberation that existed in the South in 1983. They also had weaker and less democratic chiefly structures than in most parts of the South; only under the SPLA are they becoming more like the representative systems which the Nilotic pastoralists have been used to for decades.

These similarities and connections acknowledged, the Nuba Mountains, like other areas outside the South, exercise more autonomy as a theatre of war. There are points of signficant difference and debate between the Nuba SPLM/A and the SPLM/A of the South, focusing on questions of land and self-determination. The SPLM/A as a body has yet to formulate a clear and coherent policy on land rights for the whole of the country, despite the fact that the issue of the appropriation of land has provided them with most of their recruits outside the South, and also despite the fact that the wholesale appropriation of land has been one of the government's underlying economic objectives in the war. The government is attempting, with some success, to get international support for its land appropriation policy in the name of 'development' and 'peace'. International investment in large-scale mechanized schemes based on appropriated land, whether through financial institutions such as the Islamic banks, or through relief and development agencies such as UNDP, will enable the government to make permanent what is now highly contested. The *de facto* transfer of land has yet to be addressed in any of the peace proposals presented in any of the forums of negotiation.

The fate of the dispossessed Nuba has been kept off the agenda of negotiations because self-determination for the Nuba has itself been kept off the agenda. This is potentially a more divisive issue for the SPLA. The inclusion of the Nuba in the SPLA was made possible by the SPLA's original proposition of making a 'New Sudan' out of the old united Sudan. Politically-active Nuba remain anti-secessionist: self-determination to them means self-government rather than independence. The revival of the idea of Southern separation confronts the Nuba with the question, 'Where are the borders going to be?' The late Yusif Kuwa frequently explained that the Nuba are 'prisoners of geography' along the Sudan's 'Arab-African fault line'. It is not just the current government, but the SPLM's partners in the NDA who have objected to extending the right of self-determination to the Nuba, the Ingessana of the southern Blue Nile, or any other people residing outside the South's administrative boundaries. The SPLM's reaffirmation of its commitment to self-determination for the Nuba in October 1997 was greeted with some relief, but anxiety about the strength of that commitment remains.

That anxiety has been reinforced by recent events. The death of Yusif Kuwa has deprived the Nuba of a popular, politically skilful, experienced and committed leader. Some Southern leaders, noting the near-unanimous opposition of the North to inclusion of the Nuba Mountains in any peace agreement, have become more vocal against tying their own future to a structure satisfying Nuba aspirations. The international focus on the Nuba Mountains as a *separate* issue from the South, is leading to momentum for a separate deal for the Nuba (Section **9.3**).

9.2.2 Southern Blue Nile

The area south of Damazin, bordering Ethiopia and Upper Nile Region, is in many ways an anomaly in the northern Sudan. Its indigenous population is mainly non-Arab and mixed Muslim and non-Muslim. The Ingessana hills, inhabited by the Gâmk people, have long been self-contained, and the Ethiopian foothills to the south have, like the Nuba Mountains, given refuge to peoples of diverse origins living on the margins of expansive larger groups and local states. The British contemplated drawing a 'racial boundary' to include all African pagan peoples of the region within the Upper Nile Province, but in fact only the areas of Chali and Yabus were so incorporated, to be reattached to Blue Nile immediately prior to independence.

Southern Blue Nile thus trembled on the verge of the first civil war but was not engulfed by it. The American missionaries at Chali were expelled along with the last of the missionaries in the South in 1964, but Southern guerrillas were never active this far north. It was only after the war that the area became a political front line with the expansion of Islamic proselytization and the opening of the territory to investment through the application of the 1970 Unregistered Land Act. Gulf investors financed loans to the Mechanized Farming Corporation, which began setting up agricultural schemes throughout the lowland areas. The Ingessana hills were opened up to timber and mineral extraction.

For historical and cultural reasons, Chali was designated in the Addis Ababa Agreement as entitled to choose by referendum whether it would join the Southern Region, but no referendum took place, and those who asked for it were harassed (Section **4.4.1**). Harassment, especially of church leaders of the Koman-speaking Uduk people, increased after the outbreak of war and the foundation of the SPLA in 1983. By the end of 1985 the SPLA established its presence in the hills south of Kurmuk just inside Ethiopia.

The 1985 famine provided the opportunity for further religious prose-lytization and confrontation. Dawa al-Islamiyya established its own projects in the area, but declared that relief was available only to prac-tising Muslims. During the same time church NGOs such as World Vision began to distribute famine relief to various local communities via the Uduk church leaders. The 1986 election campaign saw a growth of the Muslim Brothers movement in Kurmuk, who elected an NIF represen-tative. This new representative became active in security and the control of aid distributions in the region. As a result, Uduk church leaders found themselves on a political frontline over the issue of relief.

In 1986 Uduk workers were incorporated into the agricultural labour force on mechanized schemes in central Blue Nile run by merchant entre-preneurs. Others were also recruited by passing SPLA units. Following clashes between the army and SPLA, all Uduk were branded as rebels by the government. The Sudanese army and Rufa'a militia began the systematic burning of Uduk villages and churches around Chali in 1987. The Rufa'a were also active in killing suspected SPLA sympathizers among the agricultural labourers on the mechanized schemes. It was at this point that Uduk SPLA soldiers came to evacuate their people across the border to Ethiopia.

The SPLA captured Kurmuk twice, in 1987 and again in 1989. After the first capture of Kurmuk, the government of Sadiq al-Mahdi attempted to mobilize pan-Arab sentiment both inside and outside the Sudan to retake this 'Northern' city. There were reprisals against civilians in Damazin, with the police and army seizing 'southerners' and 'SPLA sympathizers' on the strength of racial appearance or religious affiliation alone, whether those arrested came from Blue Nile or the South.

In addition to the religious and racial faultlines running through the southern Blue Nile, the area was affected by a third, international faultline as a result of civil war in Ethiopia. The OLF were cooperating with the Sudanese army inside Blue Nile as far south as Yabus at this time, and helped keep the roads open for the Sudanese army based at Kurmuk. The SPLA attacked and dispersed an OLF/ORA camp in Yabus in 1989, and the TPLF and OLF (supported by the Sudanese army) attacked Assosa in 1990, dispersing the Blue Nile refugees at Tsore camp in the process.

With the fall of Mengistu and the evacuation of the SPLA from Ethiopia in 1991, the region continued to be affected by the spill-over of political conflicts in Ethiopia. War- and famine-displaced people were settled on Ingessana land and elsewhere to become labourers on mechanized schemes. A number of these were located outside Damazin and were owned and operated by Usama bin Ladin, supplying the training camps for Ethiopian and Eritrean Islamist groups (see Section **9.2.3**). These camps were attacked by SPLA and SAF forces of the NDA, along with Ethiopian troops, when Malik Agar, a Muslim Gâmk SPLA commander, reopened the Blue Nile front in March 1996, taking Kurmuk and Qaissan in January 1997, and advancing near Roseires and Damazin. By early 1999 the SPLA had seized control of a Chinese-run gold mine in Blue Nile near the Ethiopian border, and were in shelling distance of the Khor Adar oilfields in northern Upper Nile.

9.2.3 The eastern Sudan

The Beja peoples of the Red Sea and Kassala areas (Hadendowa, Amarar, Bishariyin, Bani Amer) number around half a million, and are Muslim but non-Arab in origin and language. They have been predominantly camel herders and small-stock breeders, but increasingly, as a result of their impoverishment during the 1980s, they have worked as labourers in agricultural schemes and dock workers in Port Sudan.

In the 1980s drought the Beja lost up to 80% of their livestock. At the same time the area actively used for stock-rearing retracted because of the decline in livestock numbers. Large parts were occupied by newcomers, many displaced from elsewhere, in a process of resettlement which began before the 1980s: West African migrants, Nubians resettled from the flooding of Lake Nasser, and Eritrean refugees. But there were other economic interests expanding during this time of Beja contraction. Rashaida Arab pastoralists who prospered in cross-border cattle-smuggling during the anti-Mengistu wars in Eritrea and Ethiopia expanded into Beja territory. Other former stock-rearing areas were given over to cotton plantation schemes and mechanized farming in the southern part of the region, following a pattern seen in other parts of the country such as the southern Blue Nile and Southern Kordofan (Sections **9.2.1** & **9.2.2**).

These new economic developments in the region were put to the aid of the government's international Islamist policy in the wake of Mengistu's overthrow. Islamist groups infiltrated Eritrea from the Sudan throughout 1993 and 1994, eventually leading Eritrea to break off diplomatic relations with Khartoum in December 1994. More Beja land was alienated to provide training camps for foreign Islamic organizations and farming schemes to both finance and feed the training camps. One of the most active persons in the area was the Saudi Islamist, Usama bin Ladin, who had a number of construction and other projects in the Sudan. He played a key role in financing and brokering an arms deal with Russia, whereby the Sudan's entire sesame seed crop was put up for sale in exchange for arms. Bin Ladin was rewarded with land in the Port Sudan area for training camps for Hizbullah and Hamas, as well as land elsewhere in the Red Sea area, along the Ethiopian border and in the southern Blue Nile. These areas were used for agricultural schemes and as training camps for the Eritrean Islamic Jihad and the Oromo Islamic Jihad.

There was a progressive neglect of local interests and concerns. The Beja did not fare particularly well from Khatmiyya patronage during the

DUP's partnership with Sadiq al-Mahdi in the 1980s. Sadiq's own Islamist government attempted to suppress local practices among the Beja which they felt did not conform with orthodox Islam, such as *zar* spirit possession rites among women. The people fared even worse under the military/NIF government who executed a number of Beja officers in 1990. The NIF's advocacy of a single Arab culture, along with its own restrictive brand of Islam, the continued alienation of land, the conscription of Beja into the PDF, and reported abductions of children and women by the armed forces all combined to create a resurgence of Beja resistance.

There was a revival of the Beja Congress under the umbrella of the NDA, based in Asmara. In 1994 former Brigadier Abd al-Aziz Khalid formed the Sudanese Allied Forces (SAF), which drew its first recruits from Southern and Nuba defectors from the army, and subsequently recruited from former DUP strongholds in Blue Nile and the eastern Sudan. SAF subsequently became one of the most active military groups in these areas, posing a new political rivalry to the DUP, a fellow member of the NDA (Section **7.6**). With Eritrea's urging, a unified NDA command under John Garang was formed in 1996. Military activity in the eastern Sudan became more co-ordinated, but the Umma and DUP contributions to the NDA forces remained small. Most operations were carried out by SAF, the Beja Congress, and the SPLA's specially formed New Sudan Brigade. The military operations have been on a far smaller scale than in the South, the Nuba Mountains or the southern Blue Nile, where large tracts of territory are under SPLA control. Rather, it has consisted of a series of guerrilla strikes against military installations around Qallabat, Kassala, and along the Kassala–Port Sudan and Port Sudan–Khartoum roads. The new oil pipeline and mechanized farming schemes have been among the targets.

There have been calls for self-determination within the eastern Sudan, but a new separatist movement has not come into existence. The Beja's marginalization from the politics of the centre has accelerated a disengagement from old alliances. In addition, a new international situation was posed by Eritrea's fight for independence. In many ways Beja benefited from the presence of the EPLF in the eastern Sudan during the war, with the EPLF often providing services to local Beja which the Sudan government had ceased to provide. The Sudan's policy of supporting Islamic revival in Eritrea after the fall of Mengistu (as in parts of Ethiopia) placed Eritrea's military ability at the disposal of dissident Beja, an access they had never enjoyed before. This facilitated a direct military link between opposition Beja and the SPLA, something unthinkable under the separatist and racially exclusive policy of the old Anyanya.

The outbreak of the Eritrean–Ethiopian war in 1998, and the defeat of the Eritrean army in May 2000, especially in western Eritrea near the Sudan border, meant that the Sudanese opposition could no longer rely on Eritrean bases and material support. In fact, the position of the opposition forces inside the eastern Sudan became distinctly precarious, and some SPLA units found themselves stranded. But any military advantage that the Sudan government might have gained from disarray in Eritrea could not by itself bring the eastern Sudanese insurgency to an end. Contrary to government claims, the insurgency was not created solely by external forces hostile to the Sudan, however much it benefited from the international hostility provoked by the Sudan's own meddling in its neighbours' politics. The causes are closely tied into the same patterns of dispossession and repression which fuel opposition in other parts of the country.

9.2.4 Darfur

Darfur, an area with a population of between three and half to four million persons, has always had an uneasy relationship with the Khartoum-centred state. The site of independent sultanates until the Turco-Egyptian conquest of the late 1870s, it rallied early to the Mahdiyya in the 1880s, and subsequently fostered a counter-Mahdiyya opposition when control from Omdurman became too oppressive. The sultanate briefly revived itself after the overthrow of the Mahdist state by Anglo-Egyptian forces, and maintained an independent existence until its final conquest and incorporation into the Sudan in 1916. Many of the institutions of the old sultanates were retained under Native Administration, and a history of indigenous administration contributed to the ability of successive administrations to mediate the conflicting interests of sedentary agriculturalist groups (of which the Fur were the most prominent) and the Baqqara and other semi-nomadic pastoralists. Overwhelmingly Muslim, Darfur is not predominantly Arab. There are many non-Arab groups among the pastoralists located mainly in the southern and northern parts of the territory, of which the Zaghawa are the largest, straddling the border with Chad.

Changes in administrative structures, including the abolition of Native Administration, coincided in the 1970s with a sharp decline in rainfall, localized famines, and a rise in political violence across the international border in Chad. As a result of extended drought from the mid-1970s through the early 1980s, there were large population movements of pastoralists from Northern Darfur and Chad into the central farming belt, just at a time when the agricultural use of the land was expanding and intensifying with Fur and other agriculturalists selling to the internal market of the urban centres of Darfur and elsewhere in the Sudan. Those administrative structures which used to mediate inter-tribal relations were no longer in place, and as temporary movement merged into permanent settlement by pastoralists who had lost their livestock, conflicts developed between the immigrants and the settled population. With the upper levels of the regional government being occupied by Fur, the broader structural changes of regionalization from 1981 onwards led to a sharpening of partisan politics in the approach to pastoralist/non-pastoralist confrontations. At the same time the regional government was denied the finances and the means with which to address the cumulative effects of drought. With the central government unwilling to admit there was a drought in the country, external relief assistance was blocked. The Governor of Darfur resigned in protest in 1983.

If the central government under Nimairi was unwilling to deliver food, it was more than willing to ship weapons to the region. In the early 1980s the Chadian civil war was internationalized as a battleground for the indirect confrontation between Libya and the West. The Sudan government, then allied to the US, conveyed arms to Chad via Darfur, benefiting Hissene Habré's non-Arab constituency, including the Zaghawa pastoralists. Libya countered by arming Arab groups, many of them pastoralists who also straddled the Chad–Sudan border. With the fall of Nimairi, closer relations developed between the Sudan and Libya, not least because Libya contributed financially to Sadiq al-Mahdi's 1986 election campaign. The outbreak of the Chad–Libyan war of 1986–7 increased Libyan activities in Darfur, not only with troop movements through Sudanese territory, but also with arms and funds distributed to Arab para-military units organized around a pan-Arab ideology.

The Fur had flirted with the Umma during the 1960s in an attempt to gain access to the politics of the centre, but with Sadiq's return to power in the 1980s the Umma armed both the southern Baqqara and northern Arab tribes. This met not only the religious and political interests of the Umma, as both Darfur groups were Ansar, but also the commercial interests of the riverain merchants involved in the livestock trade, many of whom were also Umma. The army-NIF takeover further enhanced the power of these militias when the Popular Defence Forces Act officially recognized them as paramilitary groups at the end of 1989. As the war in Chad spilled over into Darfur, it sharpened the divide between 'Arabs' and 'Blacks' (*Zuruq*), with the Sudanese Islamist parties now equating Islam with Arabism.

This racial salience led to a realignment of the non-Arab groups in Darfur, the Zaghawa and Fur in particular, toward Habré in Chad and away from the Islamist parties in the Sudan. Warfare in Darfur now focused on land, with migrant and nomad pastoralists trying to carve out 'home territories' from land previously leased from the Fur. As in northern Bahr al-Ghazal, so in Darfur, modes of livelihood were targeted, and orchards, farms, fields and villages were destroyed to make Fur occupation in newly 'liberated territories' untenable. By 1989, 5000 Fur had been killed and 40,000 of their homes destroyed, as against 400 Arabs killed and 700 tents burned. Habré's support ceased after his defeat in December 1990. With twenty-seven Arab tribes now ranged in an alliance against the 'Zuruq', some Fur allied with the SPLA, and in November 1991 Daud Bolad, formerly a Fur activist in the Muslim Brotherhood and National Islamic Front, led SPLA forces into Darfur itself.

The timing was against him. It is difficult to know whether the SPLA regarded their Darfur campaign as anything more than a diversionary tactic to open a schism in the North to counter that in the South. But with supplies from Ethiopia no longer forthcoming, and the main force of the SPLA preoccupied with the Nasir split, Bolad was left on his own. His forces were defeated, and he himself was captured and executed in January 1992.

At present, the government's reassertion of its authority in Darfur has focused on strengthening the military and establishing direct control, with governors being appointed from outside the region. The land issue remains unaddressed and unresolved. Fighting is still going on, though the government has refused to admit that it is fighting anyone other than 'bandits' and 'outlaws'. The Fur who had formed the Sudan Federal Democratic Alliance also joined the NDA and began military training in

Eritrea in 1997. Rising insecurity engulfed the Masalit in 1998–9 when disputes with the Rizaiqat resulted in over 100,000 internally displaced, and anywhere from 20,000 to 40,000 refugees in Chad. The government has insisted that these are only 'tribal' clashes, but the appearance of uniformed men suggests otherwise.

Successive governments have tried to dismiss the fighting that has broken out in the North and along its frontier with the South as merely 'tribal' clashes which have got out of hand. They have claimed this even as they have fuelled such fighting with official and semi-official support to so-called tribal militias. It is a mistake to attribute these new wars entirely to the old oppositional fractures in the northern Sudan. Such fractures exist, and they can be used for the mobilization of political and military support, but that mobilization has persisted for wider goals than disputes over grazing and water rights.

Appeals to Islam and pan-Arabism have been used by parties of the centre to overcome the discontent of marginality elsewhere in the North. The appeal is not only to an internal commonality, but increasingly about access to powerful external allies. The power of pan-Arabist ideology, however fictitious its actual base, can connect local groups to a wider international community and offers them an opportunity to mobilize that support for internal conflicts – the alliance of 'Arab' tribes in Darfur appealing to Libya outside the Sudan and the Umma and NIF parties inside the Sudan; Sadiq al-Mahdi rallying the 'Arab' North to retake Kurmuk; successive governments appealing to wealthy Muslim states for military hardware in the face of an 'anti-Arab' insurgency in the South. If the price of that wider support has been to conform to the international agenda of such Islamists as Usama bin Ladin, then it has been, at least for some (Turabi in particular), not so much a price well worth paying as an additional dividend.

9.3 Many wars: one peace?

At the reopening of the IGAD negotiations in 1997, the SPLM insisted that the unity of the country could be based only on the exclusion of religion from politics. Khartoum rejected this and put its faith in its 'peace from within', providing a new constitution which all other Sudanese would have to accept as a *fait accompli*. Many of the members of the NDA continued to worry about their exclusion from IGAD, fearing that any agreement between the government and the SPLA would inevitably lead to the secession of the South, with the North firmly in the hands of the NIF.

When cracks began to appear in the government's coalition in 1999, with the collapse of the UDSF and a breach between Bashir and Turabi, leading to Turabi's expulsion from government, the NDA also began to fragment (Section **7.6.3**). Some thought they saw the chance of Bashir now 'doing a Nimairi' and making compromises with the old parties. (He had already called Nimairi back from exile and given him a pension.) Sadiq al-Mahdi withdrew from the NDA and returned to the Sudan. This was not a popular move even within the Umma Party, but Egyptian pressure has forced the NDA to acquiesce in Sadiq's move.

Throughout the late 1990s the US government put increasing economic and political pressure on the Sudan, motivated in part by Sudan's open support for Islamist terrorist organizations, but also in response to strong domestic Christian and anti-slavery lobbies. The development of the Sudan's oil brought about a change in international opinion by 2000 (Section **10.5**), with the EU (France and Germany particularly, but with the UK following) increasingly critical of US hostility as their own interest in the Sudan's oil grew. The SPLM/A found itself under renewed pressure to negotiate with Khartoum. With Ethiopia and Eritrea at war with each other the IGAD process was effectively dead. A number of Western donor governments used the opportunity of the SPLM's argument with NGOs, over a memorandum of understanding about their authority as a quasi-government, to cut back relief aid to OLS and the southern Sudan (Section **10.4**). As Garang repeatedly reassured the NDA and Egypt of his personal commitment to a united Sudan, other Sudanese began discussing the prospect of self-determination more seriously. Bona Malwal announced a spectacular break with Garang in the pages of the *Sudan Democratic Gazette* in 2000, and there were reports of a deal being worked out between Sadiq al-Mahdi, Abel Alier and Bona Malwal on terms whereby a government with the Umma Party in it would hold a referendum on Southern independence after an interim period of four years.

As the war continues relentlessly, the question arises, what are people fighting for? There are now many more – and more diverse – combatants than there were in 1983, and they are fighting for different immediate objectives. Ultimately what Southerners have in common with the Nuba, the peoples of the southern Blue Nile and the non-Arab Muslims of Darfur and the eastern Sudan is a desire for a more just country. To a certain extent, this is what they also now have in common with the mainstream opposition groups of the North still in the NDA. But perceptions of that justice vary, and a justice which addresses one set of grievances might do so at the expense of the grievances of others. Fewer and fewer Southerners now are willing to stand by the SPLM's original vision of a united 'New Sudan'. Yet an independent South will not, by itself, solve the problems confronting the other regions which are still part of the conflict. As new international mediators enter the stage in the wake of September 11, 2001 and the West's war against terrorism, there is a danger that the overriding concerns of a new international political agenda will lead these negotiators to ignore the multiplicity of issues which have fed into the country's interlocking civil wars.

10

The War Economy ▌ & the Politics
of Relief

The human cost of the war has been immense, though no reliable figures
exist to tabulate that cost.[1] After nearly two decades of fighting issues of
relief and rehabilitation have become entangled with the related issues of
war aims and the peace process. The relief effort in the Sudan has become
a contested example in current debates concerning the efficacy of humanitarian interventions.[2] In this chapter we return to the questions posed in
the preface: Is relief a political rather than an humanitarian issue? Do
relief programmes shorten or prolong conflict? Can a focus on the technicalities of relief lead to a secure peace?

As has been described in earlier chapters (**4, 8** & **9**), the way the war is
being fought is directly linked to the pursuit of long-term economic objectives in the country. The war economy of both the government and the
guerrillas involves, in different degrees, the capture of labour, as much as

---

[1] Millard Burr, 'Quantifying genocide in the southern Sudan 1983–1993' (Washington DC, U.S.
Committee for Refugees, October 1993), was the first to attempt to make a systematic estimate
of war-related deaths and came up with a figure of 1.3 million in 1993. At the release of this
report the U.S. Committee for Refugees pre-empted criticism by suggesting that anyone questioning that figure was denying the scale of the human devastation. Herein lies the real value of
the exercise: it is designed to attract attention. As David Henige so aptly writes, 'Numbers
wielded for the immediate benefit of others – whether statistics collected on crowd sizes or
numbers of homeless estimated – need have no relation to reality, since it is only the
impression that matters'. (David Henige, *Numbers from Nowhere. The American Indian
Contact Population Debate* (Norman, OK, 1998) p. 20). The first difficulty in accepting Burr's
figure is the unreliability of demographic data coming out of the Sudan, whether the national
censuses, from which percentages of population growth are calculated, or documented and
undocumented reports of deaths. The multipliers then applied to extrapolate a total figure
from these data present yet another problem. Since the publication of Burr's report, the figure
of war-related deaths has grown with each citation, and now figures of 2.5 and even 3 million
are commonly cited and accepted. Adding this to other frequently noted numbers for displaced
and enslaved persons gives a total which equals or even exceeds the recorded population of the
Southern Region in 1983. See also Mark Duffield, *Global Governance and the New Wars*
(London/NY, 2001), pp. 211–12 on the wildly varying figures current within relief circles on
either side of the conflict.

[2] See, for example, Alex de Waal, *Famine Crimes* (Oxford/Bloomington 1997); John
Prendergast, *Crisis Response: Humanitarian Band-Aids in Sudan and Somalia*
(London/Chicago, 1997); Joanna Mcrae & Anthony Zwi (eds), *War & Hunger: Rethinking
International Responses to Complex Emergencies* (London, 1994); Joanna Macrae, *Aiding
Recovery? The Crisis of Aid in Chronic Political Emergencies* (London/NY, 2001); Duffield,
Global Governance and the New Wars.

the capture of territory. On the government's side, relief has become part of their development strategy, and population displacement, slavery and the exploitation of oil, often seen as separate issues by external observers, are inextricably linked in the war effort. In a reinforcing cycle, the economic strategy for the development of the country has produced the war as much as it has been a product of war.

10.1 War & economics

After the end to the first civil war a number of governments and international agencies became directly involved in the economic development of the Sudan. The repeated intervention of the US in rescheduling the repayment of the Sudan's debts enabled a succession of Sudanese governments to survive the economic crises of the 1980s. Dependence on the political backing of the US and the IMF, and increased reliance on the liquidity provided by international Islamist financial institutions, redirected the government's accountability away from its domestic constituency and towards its external backers.[3] The direct involvement of UN agencies and other NGOs in the support of development projects and provision of services formerly the responsibility of the civil administration further distanced government from its citizenry, markedly so in the South, where the regional government was forced by lack of funds to contract out services to NGOs.[4] An unusual constellation was created of foreign donors (including the USA, Saudi Arabia and Iraq), international institutions (the IMF, the UN, Islamic banks) and NGOs of varying denominations and political orientation who were tied to the Sudan's national development strategy and committed to the government's survival.

The demands of relief overtook the needs of development as first famine and then war commanded the attention and resources of donors and international agencies. The transfer of assets, which began before the war, has accelerated throughout the war, especially after the 1989 NIF coup. The NIF has been more systematic and determined than previous governments in the transfer of resources, whether those of rural peoples in land, labour and livestock, or national assets, such as oil, but the development strategy is essentially the same as that prior to 1983. Since 1989 the government has manipulated the international relief effort to further both its economic and strategic goals in the war, but it has also tried to harness the active collaboration of relief agencies through the ideology of development itself, which has been presented as both politically neutral and a strategy for peace. This policy has been propagated by the Peace and Development Foundation created in 1992, now reconstituted as the National Development Foundation. The measure of its success can be gauged to the extent that donors and agencies have accepted its premises about development and have acquiesced in its restrictions on relief.

[3] De Waal, *Famine Crimes*, pp. 88–91; see also Africa Watch, *Food and Power in the Sudan* (London, 1997).
[4] Terje Tvedt, *Angels of Mercy or Development Diplomats?*, (Oxford/Trenton NJ, 1998) pp. 186–202.

The current war is being fought in the context of the massive economic reorientation and dislocation which began in the 1970s. The 'bread basket' strategy of the Nimairi period, which did so much to bankrupt the Sudan (Section **4.4**), set in motion major economic and social disruptions in the rain-fed North. The shift from subsistence agriculture to export-oriented, highly capitalized, mechanized agricultural schemes had its greatest impact in the so-called 'Transition Zone' along Southern Kordofan, Southern Darfur, southern Blue Nile and the Sudan-Ethiopian border region, resulting in the dispossession of small-holding farmers from their customary rights to land, the erosion of land-use rights by pastoralists, and the creation of a large force of agricultural wage-labourers, whose numbers were increased through displacement by drought and war in the 1980s and 1990s (Section **9.2**).

'Development' in the Sudan is not politically neutral. The conflict over what type of 'development' is to be implemented, and who will control and benefit from the country's resources, is not confined just to the assets of the South. This is why the war has moved out of the South into those areas where asset transfer – especially in land – has been most marked. Following a pattern first begun during the Turco-Egyptian transformation of the Sudan's economy in the nineteenth century, religion and race are increasingly determining who has access to the greatest economic opportunities through financing, government leases and concessions, and use and control of the work force.

Within the relief effort itself, the international agencies participating in the UN's umbrella Operation Lifeline Sudan (OLS) are confronted by a central dilemma: they are called upon to alleviate the effects of the disaster-producing activities of their major counterparts: the government of the Sudan and the Southern movements. In the war zones affected by direct fighting, civilian populations have been repeatedly targeted by the Sudanese army, the PDF, the Southern factions and allied militias. In the early period of the war (1984–8) such raids were mainly intended to deny the opposing side supplies or civilian support, and the subsistence economy of the rural populace became the primary target of organized forces as livestock was captured, houses were burned, and wells destroyed. Since 1991 interfactional fighting within the SPLA has intensified the asset-stripping nature of such attacks, where food stores and standing crops have been seized or put to the torch, relief inputs have been captured and relief centres have invited attack. All of these activities have produced widespread displacement, as specific populations have been denied the opportunity or the means to feed themselves, and as groups of people have fled areas of conflict seeking refuge elsewhere. Both the government and the Southern movements have organized forcible relocations of displaced populations at different times in the war.

The pattern of the war indicates that resource depletion and economic subjugation are the objectives of war, not just its incidental consequences. Populations stripped of their assets are deprived of economic independence. Demolitions of displaced settlements around Khartoum, and forcible relocations of displaced persons to schemes and 'peace villages' around Wau and Juba, or in Upper Nile, the Nuba Mountains and along the Ethiopian borderlands have produced a dependent and portable labour reserve who serve a double purpose: 1) to implement the government's 'pacification' programme through resettling and reclaiming territory formerly contested by the SPLA, and 2) to extend political and economic control over the resources of these areas through agricultural schemes owned and operated by interest groups currently represented in the army and government, in a way which the central government and Northern merchants were unable to do in the days of the former Southern regional government before 1983.

The economic strategy of the SPLA is far less clearly defined or focused. In the past, concentrations of displaced civilians have been used to attract relief resources, especially in the refugee camps in Ethiopia before 1991. This tactic cannot be implemented so effectively now, since the SPLA does not exert the same kind of administrative and political control over the new refugee camps in Kenya and Uganda, and displaced populations settled inside SPLA-controlled territory in the Sudan have demonstrated an ability to get up and settle elsewhere. Relief thinking within the SPLA since 1991 has increasingly favoured the rehabilitation of the rural subsistence economy in areas under its control, rather than the creation of more displaced settlements and relief camps. Thus two different 'relief' strategies reflect the opposing political goals in the civil war. In the name of 'development' the government seeks to control the movements and productive capacity of a population displaced by war. The SPLA supports the return of that population to its home areas and the revival of the subsistence economy through the supply of relief inputs. In so far as the Northern and Southern Sectors of OLS have adopted the relief strategies of their respective counterparts in the war, the international relief effort has become divided against itself.

10.2 The international relief effort, neutrality & access

If development is political, so, too, is relief. The international political climate at the beginning of the war had a direct bearing on relief policies of donors, the government and the SPLA.

10.2.1 International obstacles to internal relief
Throughout the early years of the war, the Reagan administration in the US maintained crucial financial support for the succession of Khartoum regimes, as well as hostility towards the Derg in Ethiopia and its associates, including the SPLA. As far as actual relief operations in the Sudan went, there was active complicity between some international agencies and the government, especially in the Bahr al-Ghazal famine.[5] The US cooperated in obstructing the expansion of relief to non-government-held areas. In accepting Khartoum's incredible claim that only 3% of Southern civilians lived outside government control, the US National Security Council asserted that no relief was needed outside government-held towns. The UN followed suit, and in 1986 the General Secretary forbade UNHCR and WFP from cooperating with the SPLA. During this time,

[5] David Keen, *The Benefits of Famine* (Princeton, 1994).

diversions by merchants and the army of relief supplies intended for the civilian populations in southern Sudanese cities and towns, and for Ethiopian refugees in camps along the border, continued without provoking any public complaint, sanctions or suspension of relief either by donors or the UN. In contrasting relief programmes operated by the TPLF and EPLF across the border into Tigray and Eritrea, relief supplies provided by the US and European countries (assisted by the Sudan government) boosted the political credibility of the two liberation movements among their civilian constituency, at the same time that relief supplies were obtained for their military wings.[6]

The collusion between a major donor and the UN in denying relief to civilians outside the government's immediate control, and their failure to respond to the government's relief abuses, had a direct impact on the formulation of the SPLA's own attitude towards relief. They were unimpressed by assertions of neutrality by UN agencies and NGOs, seeing their activities as directly supporting the government's strategy and supplying garrisons in the South. They saw that their own infractions, such as the 1986 downing of a civilian airliner in Malakal, drew far more international condemnation than the government's extensive and systematic abuses. The suspicion engendered by what appeared to be UN and NGO duplicity and hypocrisy lasted well into the early years of OLS, and has never been fully dispelled.

The stark reality for the SPLA was that it was operating in a vast territory where overland transport and communication was only seasonal. The physical infrastructure of civil administration in many rural areas was already in decline prior to the outbreak of war, and the regional government had progressively removed itself from the provision of services by devolving that responsibility to international agencies. The pattern of fighting in the early years of the war meant that there was an immediate retraction of rural services and commercial networks to government-held towns. The military strategy of government troops and their militia allies was to despoil and depopulate the rural areas and to interdict SPLA supplies from Ethiopia. Those wells, schools, dispensary buildings and medical supplies which could not be retained by government troops were destroyed rather than be left in guerrilla hands. The ability of militias such as the Anyanya-2 to infiltrate behind SPLA lines meant that the Movement's supply lines were frequently cut, with often dire consequences for SPLA units operating far from the border in Bahr al-Ghazal and the Nuba Mountains. Attacks on civilian settlements and livelihoods produced a growing displaced population. The scale of destruction was immense and severely limited the SPLA's relief options.[7] As long as government forces could move through the rural areas and target rural services and the subsistence economy, the replacement of the civil infrastructure was not a realistic option.

The military response adopted by the SPLA to confront these threats in the mid-1980s directly shaped their relief policies. First, given the

[6] Tvedt, *Angels of Mercy or Development Diplomats?*, p. 115.

[7] Douglas H. Johnson, 'Destruction and reconstruction in the economy of the Southern Sudan', in Sharif Harir and Terje Tvedt (eds), *Short-Cut to Decay: The Case of the Sudan*, (Uppsala, 1994), pp. 126–43.

chronic insecurity in the rural areas, the SPLA encouraged and organized the movement of people into the Ethiopian refugee camps where at least some services were provided, food and medical supplies were available, and recruits could be sent to the surrounding SPLA training camps and bases. Second, the SPLA attempted to restrict government military activity in the rural areas by besieging administrative centres, garrison towns and major cities, interdicting food and medical supplies to the towns (often brought in by foreign aid agencies), and attacking militia organizations and the civilian populations from which they were drawn. Third, the SPLA's civil administration concentrated on coopting the native courts and reimposing a system of law and order. Chiefs' courts and the use of customary law to settle disputes were incorporated into the SPLA's own legal structures, and SPLA troops were used as police to prevent inter-tribal raiding within areas under their control and to ensure compliance with the decisions of the courts (Section **7.7**). To maintain the SPLA's ground forces, as well as the rudimentary structures of civil administration, the rural population was taxed in kind, providing the SPLA with grain and livestock. By 1988 this combination of strategies was having a marked effect on improving the security of the civilian population under SPLA control.

It was by this time, too, that dissatisfaction with the UN had led a few agencies to make their own contacts with the SPLA and begin limited relief operations in parts of SPLA territory. Inspired by these NGO activities, UNICEF set up an NGO-liaison office in Nairobi and became involved in an extra-legal extension of health projects to SPLA areas. These contacts were part of the momentum which eventually led to the formation of OLS. With the floods of 1988, which attracted many journalists to Khartoum, international attention was finally directed to the large numbers of war-displaced fleeing Bahr al-Ghazal. UNICEF was positioned to negotiate with both the government and the SPLA for an umbrella operation which would allow participating agencies to work on both sides of the battleline.

The agreement was helped by the momentum which was then building up in the Sudan in favour of a negotiated, constitutional settlement to the civil war. The government of Sadiq al-Mahdi was under considerable pressure from public opinion in the North to reach an agreement with John Garang. Garang, for his part, was conscious of the need to conciliate Southern opponents to the SPLA who had formed political parties and were represented in the National Assembly. By 1988 these opponents were speaking with one voice on major issues through the USAP coalition. There was a possibility that the relief effort would coincide at least with an extended truce, if not the beginning of a new period of peace.

10.2.2 The evolution of food aid
The original goal of OLS was to avert an anticipated famine in the South, and the main strategies employed to achieve this nutritional goal in its first two years were distributions of grain and the establishment of feeding centres for specific vulnerable populations. The operation was divided into a Northern Sector, accessing government towns from a head-quarters in Khartoum, and a Southern Sector, accessing SPLA-held

territory from East Africa. Khartoum retained full control over relief operations in the Northern Sector, while accessibility, rather than reported
needs, determined initial food distribution by OLS agencies in the
Southern Sector. The South's food allocation in 1989 was set by UNICEF
in negotiations with the government in Khartoum, before undertaking any
field reports.[8] Food convoys and air lifts delivered mainly to locations in
Eastern Equatoria (a region which had not suffered as much as Jonglei),
western Upper Nile or northern Bahr al-Ghazal.

The official claim that OLS averted famine and saved people from star-
vation in 1989 was not substantiated in the first general survey of the
South carried out in 1990, which documented the degradation and
contraction of the subsistence economy during the first five years of the
war.[9] This had left large parts of the country particularly vulnerable to the
disruptions brought about by natural causes in 1988. OLS came into operation only in the following year and had not reached those territories
experiencing the worst food shortages. The report concluded:

> In 1990 we found that most people were still recovering from the devastation
> experienced in 1988, and they were relying on their own networks of kinship
> and exchange. Food produced is distributed mainly through these networks,
> but lack of transportation restricts their range.[10]

In light of this finding, the 1990 report recommended a shift from food
aid to more sustained support for local production and distribution. The
implementation of the 1990 recommendations was obstructed from the
start by Khartoum's non-cooperation. During the early part of 1991 the
growing famine crisis in the North diverted attention from OLS. The
WFP Khartoum office compared the impending crisis with the 1943
Bengal famine and saw an opportunity for taking charge of one of the
largest relief operations in recent history. While it negotiated with the
Sudan government and donor representatives in Khartoum for overall
logistical control of relief throughout the country, it confirmed the ban
on WFP convoys into the southern Sudan and even the distribution of
WFP food stocks already in the South. OLS food, stockpiled in the North
and earmarked for delivery to the South, was diverted to Kordofan.
Protests from the Nairobi office had no appreciable effect, and clearance
for new convoys came only as the rains began. The result of this delay
was that OLS Southern Sector (especially WFP) was unprepared for the
crisis that came with the evacuation of the Ethiopian refugee camps in
May 1991.

With the fall of Mengistu in May, Itang, Punyido and Dimma camps
emptied their full population of refugees into the Sudan within a period
of less than two months. OLS and ICRC found that they had to try to
airdrop or airlift food and other emergency items for some 200,000
returnees confined to remote areas along the Sudan-Ethiopian border.
Because of the restrictions imposed by the government on the relief effort

---

[8] Ataul Karim, *et al*, *Operation Lifeline Sudan. A Review* (Geneva, 1996), p. 110.
[9] See Vincent O'Reilly, quoted in Larry Minear, *Humanitarianism under Siege* (Trenton NJ,
1991), p. 63.
[10] UN/OLS, *An Investigation into Production Capacity in the Rural Southern Sudan. A Report
on Food Sources and Needs* (Nairobi, June 1990), p. 5.

in the Sobat basin (Sections **7.2.2** & **7.2.3**), OLS found itself unable to serve the returnees adequately.

The split in the SPLA in August 1991, which drew an internal battle line across Jonglei, further inhibited OLS's ability to meet the needs of the majority of southern Sudanese. At this point Khartoum signalled a shift in its access policy, permitting relief deliveries in the SPLA-Nasir areas while restricting access to the much larger SPLA-Torit territory. The WFP Khartoum office, which had enforced Khartoum's earlier restrictions, was in no doubt that Khartoum's shift in strategy was entirely political. 'The GOS [government of Sudan] is trying to capitalize on the split in the SPLA/M and drive a wedge between the two factions. Divide and Rule', reported the WFP country representative. Commenting on the increase of food delivered to Nasir-held areas, he noted, 'It is possible that the GOS either wants or has already worked out an alliance with the Riak/Lamakol [sic] faction.'[11]

Inter-factional fighting within the SPLA and government advances on the ground after 1992 further complicated the planning and implementation of relief, and left it increasingly open to political and military manipulation. The frequent displacement of large sections of the civilian population disrupted many attempts at the rehabilitation of the subsistence economy and local services. The presence of concentrations of displaced persons renewed the demand for the delivery of large quantities of relief supplies, while the intensification of the war meant the diversion of such supplies for military use on a far greater scale than before. Khartoum's approval of relief deliveries to SPLA-held areas (as it had been throughout the history of OLS), was contingent on delivering far greater quantities to often unassessed populations in government-held towns. Relief supplies and the support of relief agencies became objects to be won, especially in the fighting between the factions of the SPLA. SPLA-United's herding of displaced Dinka into camps in the 'hunger triangle' of Ayod-Yuai-Kongor in 1993 (Section **8.2.1**) was perhaps the most blatant manipulation of relief needs in order to supply soldiers, matched only by its 1994 request for a food air-drop to 'displaced' persons at Mankien on the Upper Nile/Bahr al-Ghazal border, while Kerubino Kuanyin was in the same area organizing his troops for an invasion of Bahr al-Ghazal.

Development aid to the Sudan came under an international embargo with the overthrow of the democratic government in 1989 (Section **10.4**). Khartoum's response was to redefine the character of relief in its own territory, giving it developmental goals. The ultimate objective of relief, like development, was to wean war-affected populations off 'relief dependency', towards self-sufficiency. The 1996–7 'peace from within' agreements between Khartoum and some Southern commanders (Section **8.3**) were presented in support of official claims that the majority of the southern Sudan was under government control, and that OLS Southern Sector operations should be transferred to government territory. These claims received a sympathetic hearing from UN officials in Khartoum, but were treated with incredulity by UN and NGO agencies working in the Southern Sector.

[11] Trevor Page, 'Brief for UN Under Secretary General James Jonah', 18 October 1991, OLS document.

Whereas the Northern Sector tended to ignore the war in its advocacy of a move away from relief to development, the Southern Sector was confronted with the stark realities of war almost on a daily basis. Those in the Northern Sector who saw 'development' as a means of transforming the economy appeared to be comfortable with proposals ostensibly aimed at reducing 'relief dependency' among the dispossessed and displaced population produced by the war, but which in effect intensified pressures on the people to became part of a large labour reserve as workers on government or private agricultural schemes. The Southern Sector's increased emphasis on combining food assistance with agricultural and veterinary support, health, water and education projects redefined its goal away from alleviating famine and towards maintaining the independent labour force of rural subsistence economies. The two approaches were, in effect, opposed, especially in such areas as northern Bahr al-Ghazal and the Nuba Mountains where the tactics of war on the government side were squeezing labour from non-government to government-controlled areas.

10.3 War & the targeting of resources

Whatever the broader political and military objectives of the parties to the current conflict, the civil war has been fought on the ground as a resource war. Battles between organized armed groups, with the intention of seizing or holding territory, are only one aspect of the fighting. Civilians have been systematically targeted in 'asset stripping' raids since the outset. The intention has been not only to seize whatever resources they possess, but to deny these resources to the opposing side; in fact civilian populations themselves have often been treated as resources to control.

The targeting of resources has changed as the pattern of war has altered. In the early years of the war (1984–8), the government relied heavily on surrogate forces raised from 'tribal' militias (subsequently incorporated into the PDF), the most prominent being the Murahalin (Misiriyya and Rizaiqat of Southern Kordofan and Southern Darfur), the Rufa'a of southern Blue Nile, the Anyanya-2 (Nuer) and Murle of Upper Nile and Jonglei, and the Mundari and Toposa militias of Eastern Equatoria. These forces adopted tactics which were aimed at denying the SPLA a civilian base of support; thus civilian settlements were attacked at least as often, if not more often, than units of SPLA troops. In Abyei (Southern Kordofan) and northern Bahr al-Ghazal, the attacks had begun before the war and were aimed at driving people away from their settlements: houses were burned, crops destroyed, cattle seized and people abducted and enslaved. The enlargement of Arab cattle herds was not the primary motive: Dinka cattle taken in these raids were often sold on the Omdurman market, frequently for the export meat trade. The Murle, Mundari, Nuer and Toposa militias attacked rural districts known to have provided the SPLA with recruits, though not exclusively so; the cycle of cattle raiding expanded into Ethiopia, affecting groups with no connection with the SPLA or the Sudan conflict. In southern Blue Nile, militia attacks were prompted to forestall potential support for the SPLA (Section **9.2.2**). The SPLA, too, attacked civilian settlements of those groups from which militias were recruited, but on a far smaller scale than government forces.

The net effect of these activities was massive population displacement. In some cases individual families as well as groups of people moved into more secure areas near their original homes, but distant from the scene of fighting. In other cases large groups of people moved out of the war zone altogether, such as the Dinka of Abyei and northern Bahr al-Ghazal moving to sites in Kordofan, Darfur, or Khartoum; the movement of refugees out of Equatoria into Kenya, Uganda, Zaïre/Congo and CAR; or the SPLA-organized movement of people into refugee camps in Ethiopia prior to 1991. Others sought refuge in government-held towns in the South, whether as people connected with pro-government militias, or other groups of civilians forced to move because of attacks by SPLA and government troops alike.

Attacks on civilians were declining by 1988 as the SPLA gained control of more territory and began wooing government-militias to its side, but the eruption of inter-factional fighting between Southern movements from 1991 intensified such attacks at the same time that it focused them more narrowly on certain regions. As in the earlier period of the war, concentrations of civilians became significant targets, especially in the areas of Jonglei, Lakes and northern Bahr al-Ghazal.

The objectives of raiding altered slightly. Asset-stripping was still a method of asset transfer. Livestock looted by PDF units continued to enter the national and international economy through trade to Omdurman, but now also became a currency between the government and its southern guerrilla allies. SPLA-United/SSIA troops exchanged cattle with regular army garrisons for resupplies of weapons and ammunition, and allied southern commanders used their access to looted cattle and cattle markets to build up their own independent economic bases. Relief items continued to be secured for armed forces, either through the oversupply of relief to unassessed populations in government garrisons or through a rough twenty percent 'tax' the SPLA surreptitiously extracted on items supplied for civilian use. But in addition, the *destruction* of relief items and relief centres became on objective of raiding (especially by Kerubino and the PDF), as a tactic to accelerate labour flight.

10.3.1 *Asset stripping & labour flight*

The case of northern Bahr al-Ghazal highlights the issue of access and illustrates the complexity of food aid in relation to food security.[12] It also reveals differences in relief perceptions and strategies, continuing from the pre-OLS emergency. Agencies acting in the relief operations for people displaced from northern Bahr al-Ghazal prior to 1989 approached the emergency as a natural catastrophe which could be alleviated by the provision of food and the establishment of relief and feeding centres. The relief solution was measured in the metric tonnes of inputs. The displaced Dinka viewed the nature of their problem, and therefore its solution, differently. To them the purpose of relief was to enable them to return to their homes and reinvest in their subsistence economy.[13] The

---

[12] This section is based on Ataul Karim, *et al*, *Operation Lifeline Sudan*, chapter 6.
[13] Keen, *Benefits of Famine*, chapter 5.

same resolution was forcefully stated by Dinka who remained in northern Bahr al-Ghazal and were interviewed after the first year of OLS.[14] Despite the recommendations made at that time, OLS failed to provide agricultural support to northern Bahr al-Ghazal, very largely because of the flight ban on the area imposed by Khartoum from early 1990 to December 1992. When OLS did gain access to the area in 1992–3, it gave initial priority to food inputs, and only gradually came round to the Dinka way of thinking. In the displaced centres accessed by OLS Northern Sector, however, the size of the food ration continued to be a major preoccupation and a matter of debate.

Despite the fact that the discovery of the conditions in northern Bahr al-Ghazal in 1987–8 was one of the factors which led to the creation of OLS, OLS has never accessed that area properly. Overland routes are problematic and the railroad from Kordofan to Wau, which is supposed to be used to supply government towns and SPLA villages equally, has been used mostly to resupply government garrisons. Moreover, the PDF units who accompany government trains regularly raid villages and cattle camps on both the outward and return journeys. Air access to the remoter areas of northern Bahr al-Ghazal has remained irregular, due to repeated flight bans imposed by Khartoum. The cumulative effect of these constraining factors has been that the people of rural northern Bahr al-Ghazal, though seriously affected by the war, have not received the relief food that even OLS assessments suggest they need.

The result is that the population of the region has continued to circulate both north into Kordofan and Darfur, and south into other parts of Bahr al-Ghazal and Lakes, seeking the alternatives of wage labour, relief distributions and the subsistence economy, as circumstances allow. The combination of these strategies has allowed for a modest recovery of the subsistence economy at different times, recoveries which have prompted further government intervention, either through direct raiding or indirect restrictions on relief operations.

The truce between the SPLA and Misiriyya and Rizaiqat groups along the border which began in 1990 and continued intermittently into 1996 allowed for freer movement between northern Bahr al-Ghazal and neighbouring regions, thus allowing people to circulate between their homes, relief centres and agricultural schemes in government-held areas. A government ban on relief flights between 1990 and 1992 certainly helped to accelerate labour exodus at that time. With the resumption of relief deliveries late in 1992, people began returning from places in Darfur, Kordofan and Khartoum, and there were even some Misiriyya migrants who came to receive relief food. With a further decentralization of relief distribution centres and a continued return of labour there was a modest recovery in agricultural output throughout 1994 and 1995. As small as OLS food and food production interventions were, their real effect was to keep the household labour force intact, reduce the amount of time spent on gathering alternative sources of food, and reinforce networks of kinship exchange and exchange between nearby communities. Of course, it did all this at the expense of labour-intensive schemes in the North.

[14] UN/OLS, *An Investigation into Production Capacity*, p. 58.

Despite the war, there have also been commercial exchanges, centred on a few markets. The northern Bahr al-Ghazal markets are important cattle auction centres, but people have also bought grain from Misiriyya herders and traders. Commerce between northern Bahr al-Ghazal and Kordofan has contributed to local household economy in a number of ways: in the buying and selling of cattle and grain, in the sale of handicrafts such as grass mats, in the hiring out of labour. A similar pattern of trade between Wau and neighbouring SPLA held areas, with sugar, medicine, clothes and soap going out in return for livestock, grain, honey, charcoal and firewood existed before 1998. The networks of Bahr al-Ghazal linked up with a further SPLA-protected livestock export market to Uganda. It is these cross-border informal markets in livestock and other tradeable items, along with more orthodox exports like timber and coffee which form the foundation of the economy in the SPLA areas.

In 1994 Kerubino made his way back to Bahr al-Ghazal, and was expelled to Abyei in his initial confrontations with SPLA troops. He soon returned, often in concert with Arab PDF units or Paulino Matip's Nuer, seeking out, not SPLA forces, but civilian targets. It was clear from their timing and targets that these raids were aimed at the recovery of the rural economy. Increased PDF activity along the railway line to Wau in 1994–5 was timed to cause the maximum disruption to dry-season cattle movements and late dry-season/early wet-season clearing and planting cycles. Raids out of western Upper Nile into the northeastern and eastern grazing grounds disturbed seasonal cattle movements, forcing cattle owners to send their livestock farther away to more secure pastures, thereby decreasing their family members' access to milk during the dry season. Standing crops were torched and markets were attacked. Relief supplies were attacked and destroyed shortly after delivery.

This pattern of disruption intensified following the 1996 Peace Charter and the 1997 internal peace agreement between the government, SSIM and Kerubino's SPLA-Bahr al-Ghazal group. This strategy appeared to be paying dividends when it was reported early in 1998 that thousands of SPLA soldiers and their families were defecting to the government. In fact, this was only a prelude to the battlefield rapprochement between Kerubino and the SPLA, brought about by Kerubino's dissatisfaction with his rewards from the 'peace from within'. Following simultaneous attacks on Wau and Gogrial and SPLA advances throughout Bahr al-Ghazal in February 1998, the government again introduced a ban on relief flights to the area. With a new influx of people out of government towns into the rural areas a new famine crisis was announced by the international media in April 1998.

Inaccuracy in earlier reporting of food shortages was one reason why OLS's first appeals for emergency relief were dismissed as exaggerations. But the prevailing natural disaster model of famine relief among donors was another reason why many governments and government officials – Britain's Minister for Overseas Development, Clare Short prominent among them – at first failed to appreciate that the immediate causes of widespread hunger in Bahr al-Ghazal were man-made. Many were slow to recognize the link between the explosion of fighting around Wau, the expanded retaliatory raids by PDF units along the railway (the 'relief' artery) which followed, the massive exodus of people released from Wau and its surrounding 'peace villages' into SPLA-controlled territory, and the spread of famine and food shortages throughout much of rural Bahr al-Ghazal. The reflex-calls for 'all sides' to stop fighting implied an even blame for the events of 1998, ignoring, once again, the meshing of the government's military and economic strategies and the intended consequences of years of access denial and resource targeting by government forces.

As in the early 1980s, so now the people of northern Bahr al-Ghazal have become vulnerable not because of their poverty, but because of their economic resources. Government military activity, coordinated as it has been with increasing restrictions on relief access, is designed to undermine, if not halt, OLS support to the rural economy of northern Bahr al-Ghazal. There has been renewed labour outmigration and displacement.[15]

10.3.2 Displaced persons and captured labour
Population displacement on a large scale has become a major feature of the war. It is not an incidental outcome of the fighting but is one of its objectives; it involves not just the removal of whole groups and individuals from their home areas, but the incorporation of those populations either into competing armies, or into a captive labour force. The renewal of slave-raiding has been one aspect of that captive labour force which has received widespread international publicity and will be dealt with in Section **10.3.3**. We deal here with another, less well-publicized form of captured labour, one which has featured in the relief and development policies of the government.

The fate of the war-displaced in the northern Sudan is one of the most important relief issues in the Sudan, but it is one that has been ignored by the UN and international agencies. This is largely so because the scope of OLS Northern Sector's coverage is determined by agreements negotiated with the government, defining the areas OLS can access; it is not based on overall needs. War-displaced populations in Khartoum were excluded from OLS assessments until 1994, and even after that date populations living in unofficial settlements continued to be excluded. The Nuba Mountains were excluded from formal assessment until 1996, when UNICEF and WFP began using OLS resources only in those government-controlled areas that they were allowed to enter. Elsewhere international NGO staff have found their access to displaced people in camps restricted. Agricultural labourers in schemes from the southern border-lands of the northern Sudan through to the eastern Sudan do not even figure on the relief horizon, though many are in fact part of the war-displaced population.[16]

There are common issues affecting the displaced populations right throughout the government-held areas, whether in the 'Transition Zone',

---

[15] For an account of the 1998 famine, see Human Rights Watch, *Famine in Sudan, 1998: The Human Rights Causes* (Washington, DC, 1999). For continued Dinka displacement, see Duffield, *Global Governance and the New Wars*, chapter 9.

[16] For a fuller discussion of relief issues concerning war displaced in the northern Sudan, on which this section is based, see Ataul Karim, *et al*, chapters 4 & 7, and Duffield, *Global Governance and the New Wars*, chapters 8 & 9.

the 'peace villages' of the South, or surrounding the Three Towns. There is a lack of secure land tenure, legal protection and political entitlements, at the same time as there has been a reduction of relief entitlements through externally-imposed 'self-sufficiency' programmes.

Around the Three Towns, the war-displaced are physically separated from the city population. Legislation introduced in 1987 distinguished between 'squatters' (who arrived before 1984) and 'displaced'. Displaced have no right of residence in Khartoum, no right to own land, and no right to construct permanent shelters. In May 1990 a government decree redefined 'displaced' as those who had arrived in Khartoum after 1990. These were the ones to be forcibly resettled into displaced camps. By 1994 there were an estimated 800,000 displaced around Khartoum. The government periodically demolished informal settlements and forcibly relocated inhabitants to temporary camps on the outskirts. By May 1992, according to the Ministry of Housing report, some 105,569 families (over 600,000 persons) had had their houses demolished and were moved to 'peace cities'. Demolitions continue.

UNDP, the lead agency in OLS Northern Sector, accepted the government's programme for the displaced around Khartoum as a programme of development and urban renewal. In 1989 it committed itself to helping the government to integrate large numbers of displaced into the mainstream development process of the country. This effectively defined OLS Northern Sector as a government programme. In the second year of OLS, UNDP further committed the UN to helping the government find 'durable solutions' for the displaced, and finding funding for large scale programmes. Since 1989 government policy has been to resettle war-displaced on 'production' sites, using them as an expanded labour pool in the North. Resolution 56 issued by the Council of Ministers in 1990 aimed at the repatriation of over 800,000 displaced to 'areas of origin' and to 'areas of production' in Upper Nile, Bahr el-Ghazal, Darfur, Kordofan and Central State, where they were expected to work on production projects. Organized relocations took place in 1990, 1991 and 1994.

The development agenda of the Sudan government with regard to war-affected populations is directly linked to its military strategy. In 1990 it explicitly stated that the return of displaced to agricultural production sites would safeguard the armed forces. Since then it has created displaced camps in the Nuba Mountains and around Wau, which has enabled the government to secure its military position in those areas. UNDP, UNICEF and WFP have supported rehabilitation and development programmes in these militarized areas.

UN OLS agencies have seen displacement and food insecurity as transitory problems, and there has been much concern expressed about relief aid creating 'aid dependence'. There has been a systematic compromise of relief entitlements for the displaced. The Dinka in the Wau peace camps before 1998, already made destitute by war, were kept on short rations and had no secure tenure over the land on which they were settled, thus becoming a pool of low-paid wage labourers for the commercial development of mechanized agricultural schemes in the area. This pattern was repeated further north. A number of means have been used to ensure ready labour on commercial projects around Al-Da'ain: the diversion of up to fifty percent of relief food to the host communities, local merchants and government officials; the bonding of sharecroppers to farm owners through indebtedness; and the reduction of food aid itself during labour intensive periods of the agricultural year. The executive manager of the Islamic NGO Muwafaq, for instance, requested that no food aid be distributed during the periods of land preparation and harvesting as a solution to his difficulty in getting displaced Dinka to work on the commercial farms run by his NGO.[17]

By the end of the century, Dinka displacement in the Sudan was a direct result of 'their being Dinka', just as the displacement of Nuba has been because they are Nuba. Those camped in the 'Transition Zone' found themselves caught in a complex web of clientage and indebtedness, with a diminishing entitlement to relief. The displaced have now achieved a 'double utility': as cheap labour to be exploited, and as subordinate clients to be 'managed and manipulated' to attract outside resources. The practical result of nearly two decades of international aid has been to reinforce the subordination of displaced Southerners in the political economy of the Sudan, at the same time that it has reinforced the control exerted by dominant commercial and political groups.[18]

10.3.3 Slavery

The resurgence of slave raiding, and of slave trading, was first revealed in the late 1980s through the publications of Southern and Northern Sudanese investigators, but it was denied vehemently by the parliamentary government and the Arabic press. The current Sudan government also refuses to admit that slave-raiding exists; they will admit only that there have been 'abductions', a euphemism they were able to get the UN General Assembly to accept. It is not only the existence of slavery in the Sudan which is controversial, but the proliferation of slave redemption programmes, backed by Western agencies, as well.

Slavery is specific to the border area between Bahr al-Ghazal, Darfur and Kordofan, one of the old slaving frontiers of previous centuries. Its revival serves several purposes in the war.[19] It was part of the incentive to Baqqara groups to pass on to their southern neighbours their own losses from drought and the creation of agricultural schemes, for by taking mainly Dinka women and children captive they add labour to their own households and increase their incomes through the trade and exchange of slaves. But slavery is also a policy of terror, aimed directly at non-combatants, designed to make them flee their territory. This is one aspect, which clearly distinguishes current slave raids from 'traditional' Baqqara–Dinka clashes over cattle. As the main targets of slavery abductions are women and children, it is specifically destructive of Dinka

---

[17] Ataul Karim, *et al, Operation Lifeline Sudan*, p. 204.

[18] Duffield, *Global Governance and the New Wars*, pp. 205, 209, 230.

[19] For an outline of slavery in the region, and evidence of its revival during the war, see Jok Madut Jok, *War & Slavery in Sudan* (Philadelphia, 2001). The continuity between the past and the present has been revealed by the resurrection of older organizational structures in large-scale slave-raiding. See R.S. O'Fahey, 'The past in the present: the issue of sharia in Sudan', in Holger Bernt Hansen & Michael Twaddle (eds), *Religion & Politics in East Africa* (London/Athens OH/Nairobi/Kampala, 1995), p. 43 n. 4.

families. This, too, is in keeping with the assimilationist project also reported in the Nuba Mountains: Dinka children reared as Muslims and given Arab names, cease to be Dinka; Dinka women raped by their captors give birth to children claimed by Arab lineages.[20]

There is no question that slavery exists in the Sudan today and that it is fed by slave raiding deployed as a tactic of war.[21] There are slaves working alongside displaced labourers in the commercial and private farms of Darfur and Kordofan. What is in dispute are the numbers. There is a large discrepancy between recorded slave abductions (in the hundreds and thousands) and reported slave redemptions (in the hundreds of thousands). Groups such as the Swiss-based Christian Solidarity International, British-based Christian Solidarity Worldwide and the American Anti-Slavery Group each claim to have redeemed tens of thousands of slaves in regular visits to Bahr al-Ghazal. To voice scepticism of these figures, as with the figures of war-related deaths, is to invite the charge of denying the existence of the problem.

Slave buy-back programmes, initially organized by Dinka from the victimized communities, have been in operation since slave raids began in the 1980s. It was only in the mid-1990s, with the involvement of international agencies, that large amounts of hard currency began to be involved. Arguments against slave redemption have included fears that the injection of this cash will either increase slave-taking or drive the price of slaves up. Slave redeemers have countered that the price for a redeemed slave has remained constant for several years at about $50 a head. A more serious and verifiable criticism of slave-redemptions is that they are subject to fraud, and that a significant proportion of those 'redeemed' are not slaves at all, and that the money changing hands is going to the organizers of these false redemptions.[22]

With international agencies now basing their fund-raising campaigns on figures of slaves successfully redeemed, there is an inevitable pressure to inflate numbers, as there is with any agency whose fund-raising success is linked to producing satisfying body-counts (so many children immunized, so many refugees clothed and fed, etc.). The issue of slavery, like no other issue related to the war, has created strong bonds of solidarity between Western constituencies and the southern Sudan. American school children collect money for slave redemptions, African-Americans raise more money for slave redemption than for other relief projects in the Sudan, and it is understandable that southern Sudanese are reluctant to give up the issue, or subject it to sceptical scrutiny. But exaggerated figures of slave numbers enables Khartoum to give plausible rebuttals to the existence of slavery, and

---

[20] For documentation of rape as a weapon of war in the Nuba Mountains see African Rights, *Facing Genocide: The Nuba of Sudan* (London, 1995), pp. 221–42.

[21] In 1990, when I was in northern Bahr al-Ghazal, I interviewed a number of Dinka children who had once been taken as slaves, but who had been able to return home, as well as a number of Dinka parents whose children had been taken from them.

[22] Richard Miniter, 'The false promise of slave redemption', *Atlantic Monthly*, July 1999; Human Rights Watch, 'Background paper on slavery and slave redemption in the Sudan', March 12, 1999; Declan Walsh, 'The great slave scam', *Irish Times*, 23 February 2002; Karl Vick, 'Ripping Off Slave "Redeemers"', *Washington Post*, 26 February 2002. Money raised through false slave redemptions is reported to have been used to purchase weapons with which to arm local communities against raids by PDF units (Section **7.7**).

in 1999 the UN general assembly was persuaded to censure the anti-slavery agencies, rather than the Sudan government. What, then, is really happening in slave redemption?

There is enough evidence to cast doubt on the totals claimed by slave-redeemers, and the very stability of the buy-back price suggests a controlled, rather than a free market subject to fluctuations in supply and demand or competition between suppliers of redeemable slaves. Slave-redeemers base their claims in part on the personal testimonies of reclaimed slaves, recorded through local interpreters. If, as seems likely, there have been fraudulent exchanges, where do these persons come from? One connection to investigate is the circular and seasonal movement of persons between the commercial agricultural schemes of the North and Bahr al-Ghazal. The displaced populations of Darfur and Kordofan have harrowing tales of their own to tell, and their displacement is part of the same process that has revived slavery. They each occupy space on the twin tracks of cultural suppression and captured labour.

10.4 Issues of accountability

Khartoum was acutely aware that the international embargo on development aid had substantially reduced the Sudan's receipts of official development assistance – down from $1907 million in 1985 to $127 million in 1993/4. It was keen to resume development aid relations, not only for financial reasons, but to re-establish its legitimacy within the international community. In 1992 the Peace and Development Foundation was established to address rehabilitation and development needs in areas retaken in the South. The Relief and Rehabilitation Commission (RRC) also signalled new government priorities: the revival and expansion of agricultural economy as part of a comprehensive social programme which included relocating the displaced and promoting Islamic NGOs. The RRC characterized traditional subsistence agriculture and pastoralism as inefficient, wasteful and harmful to the environment. It proposed instead an expansion of mechanized agriculture to increase productive potential of the whole population. A new and expanded social welfare policy (with new ministries of social welfare created in the federal states) was geared to the expansion of mechanized agriculture.

This initiative spoke directly to then current aid thinking, particularly represented by the UNDP in Khartoum, which viewed conflict as arising from poverty and underdevelopment. The UN agencies willingly embraced the strategy of linking rehabilitation, development and peace. There followed a considerable blurring of humanitarian relief and development programmes in the Northern Sector, with a general failure to recognize that relief for conflict-affected populations arises from the impact of war, not from structural food deficits. Programmes for self-sufficiency were aimed at taking the war-displaced 'out of the beggar mentality'.[23]

Khartoum's restrictions on relief activity through a manipulation of development ideology were given force of law through a succession of

---

[23] Karim, *et al, Operation Lifeline Sudan*, p. 100.

acts. The 1992 Relief Act stipulated that once relief enters the country, it belongs to the state. Relief aid therefore cannot be considered to have been misappropriated by the government, since it already belongs to the government. The OLS principle of neutrality was violated both by government insistence on ownership of OLS, and by the failure of the UN to challenge this ownership. In 1993 the government established a new Code of Conduct for international NGOs (INGOs), which relegated humanitarian work to a purely technical activity, excluding INGOs from gathering information on the context or causes of need for humanitarian assistance. They were specifically barred from involvement in land issues. This code, which was accepted by the INGOs, conflicted directly with the international profile many had developed as campaigners on issues of rights and justice, and made them, in effect, little more than extensions of the state, bound by a code of conduct which defined humanitarian aid in purely technical terms.

The only signed agreements by all parties in OLS came out of the IGAD mediation in March 1994, which committed all participants in OLS to ensuring 'delivery of relief assistance to all needy populations regardless of their locations.' This commitment was qualified, however, by the title of the agreement, which relates to 'War Affected Areas'. The government unilaterally abrogated this agreement in November 1995. In December 1995 it reached a new agreement with the UN Resident Representative, who agreed that OLS would not operate in 'war zones'. This allowed the government to define areas as either 'war zones' or 'areas affected by war' and exclude OLS from war zones. Between December 1995 and March 1996 the government imposed a no-go area on Western Equatoria by defining it as a war zone. Since 1992, therefore, OLS has confined its operations to those non-government areas the government was willing to concede were beyond its control. One UN official justified this by stating, 'There is a balance to be struck. To allow the Southern Sector to carry on means that we meet their (the Government of Sudan's) needs in the North.'[24] The political separation of OLS into distinct sectors enabled it to operate in parts of the South by not challenging government restrictive practices in the North. Operations in the South expanded, but the UN Department of Humanitarian Affairs' 'quiet diplomacy' in the North 'achieved little beyond providing an impetus for the GOS to expand its mechanisms of control and regulation', and 'failed to increase international access in the face of government opposition.'[25]

Since the quality of access, and therefore quality of information, continued to be poor in the Northern Sector, changes in food aid policy were taken in the absence of sound data and flowed more from changing fashions in the aid world than from a real knowledge of conditions in the Sudan. The report on OLS commissioned by the UN Department of Humanitarian Affairs in 1996 concluded:

> The failure of the UN to assert humanitarian principles in the Northern Sector is a failure at the level of both analysis and management. It is an analytical failure in the sense that the UN has not properly addressed the nature of the underlying

---

[24] Ibid, pp. 48–9, 27–8, 57, 60, 90.
[25] Ibid, p. 33–4.

political crisis, which constitutes the fundamental threat to the physical and socio-economic security of war-affected populations. Rather, it has concentrated on the more visible crisis of material supply. It is a managerial failure in that neither the contractual relationships the UN undertakes, nor the human resource strategies it follows, have been sufficient to address the challenge to neutrality that OLS faces. This has contributed to the overall failure of the UN to provide an adequate framework for the rights of beneficiaries and material support in the Northern Sector.[26]

Since 1996, Khartoum has continued to place further restrictions on ground operations in OLS. It is not surprising that the supine attitude of the UN and many NGOs has had its effect on the SPLA.

Following the 1991 split, the UN and other agencies in OLS Southern Sector entered into a dialogue with the Southern movements which specified and refined the humanitarian principles underlying relief. Not only did Letters of Understanding define the relationship between UNICEF, as the lead OLS agency, and NGOs, committing both to neutrality and support for civilians only, but also a set of Ground Rules was negotiated between OLS and the Southern movements in 1993–4 which explicitly recognized the humanitarian principles on which OLS was supposed to be based. The fact that the relief wings of the two main movements – the SRRA of the SPLA and RASS of SSIM – were in competition with each other for recognition and practical assistance from the international relief industry, was a major incentive for them to prove their humanitarian credentials. But the establishment of the Ground Rules was followed by a further loosening of the regulatory regime in the SPLA territories, with the creation of southern Sudanese NGOs (SINGOs) independent of the SPLA and SRRA. A number of these SINGOs continue to play a significant role in relief operations in the southern Sudan.

In 1998 the SPLA decided to introduce its own regulations for relief activity in the areas under their control and submitted a draft Memorandum of Understanding (MOU) to participating NGOs. The MOU did not supersede the tripartite agreement with the UN on which OLS was based. It did introduce regulations similar to those common between governments (such as Kenya) and NGOs. It proposed, however, that signatories would implement their obligations 'in accordance with SRRA objectives and international humanitarian principles', while defining those SRRA objectives as 'to render humanitarian relief, rehabilitation and reconstruction in SPLM administered areas without discrimination on the basis of nationality, gender, belief, political affiliation or opinion'.[27]

A number of NGOs objected to signing up to support for SRRA objectives on the grounds that this compromised their neutrality. They also claimed to be concerned about the security of their personnel and their property. In the end, eleven NGOs refused to sign by the March 2000 deadline and withdrew.

The NGOs and the SPLA were both being somewhat disingenuous. Many of the NGOs had accepted far greater restrictions imposed by

---

[26] Ibid, p. 109.
[27] Consolidated text of the Agreement between the Sudan Relief and Rehabilitation Association and Non-Governmental Organizations (19/08/99).

Khartoum. Though the SRRA's regulations were still far looser than those imposed by other governments in the region, the agencies refused to deal with the SPLA as a 'government'. The SPLA, for its part, did want to secure greater cooperation from the NGOs, more like the solidarity support many had given to ERA and REST (the relief wings of the EPLF and TPLF) in the war against Mengistu. In this their tactics failed, and they were roundly criticized, not least by the European Union, who had remained silent about Khartoum's grip on humanitarian relief in the Northern Sector, but were then involved in 'constructive engagement' with Khartoum. The government of Sudan immediately invited all NGOs who wanted to work in the South to operate from Khartoum. A year later they insisted that no Southern Sector foreign relief personnel should enter SPLA-held territories without first receiving a visa issued by the government.

10.5 The oil of development

The development language deployed by the government in relief matters has been echoed chillingly in the exploitation of its oil reserves.

There was an economic impact from the Sudan's international isolation. In 1990 the IMF issued a declaration of non-cooperation against the Sudan for unpaid debts and debt servicing. In 1992 Chevron sold its oil interests in the Sudan. In 1993 the US State Department declared the Sudan a country believed to be sponsoring terrorism and in 1997 US individuals and companies were prohibited by law from doing business with any entity connected with the Sudan government. Khartoum needed to bring in investors who were unaffected by legal prohibitions, or uninfluenced by public condemnations. Its earliest investors in oil exploitation came from Canada (then in the process of creating its own oil industry, independent from US-based firms), China and Muslim Malaysia, but as momentum gathered towards oil production in the late 1990s, European firms became involved.

The Canadian company Arakis first entered the Sudan oilfields in 1995, backed by $750 million funding from the Arab Group International. In 1996 it formed the Greater Nile Petroleum Operating Company (GNPOC) with the Chinese National Petroleum Company (CNPC), the Malaysian Petronus Carigali Overseas Sdn Bhd and the Sudanese state oil company, Sudapet. Their area of operations were the Unity and Heglig fields north of Bentiu, straddling the Upper Nile–Southern Kordofan border. In 1997 the Qatari Gulf Petroleum Corporation began operating in the Adar Yal fields of northern Upper Nile, and the International Petroleum Company (IPC), owned by the Swedish Lundin company also began a partnership in the Adok–Ler area with Petronus Carigali, the Austrian OMV (Sudan) Exploration GmbH and Sudapet.

Arakis was unable to raise more finance to carry out oil operations on the ground, and in 1998 Talisman Energy Inc, Canada's largest independent gas and oil company, bought up Arakis's share and became the operating partner of GNPOC. It built a pipeline from Unity field to Port Sudan in 1999 and began pumping oil in August that year. The Sudan government's share of these first export revenues was $2.2 million.

Once oil production actually began, estimates of the Sudan's oil reserves were revised upward: GNPOC's holdings were put at 800 million barrels, and Lundin's (from a much smaller area) at 300 million. The Sudan government's total future revenues from the Unity and Heglig fields alone were placed at between three and five billion dollars.

With US companies out of the competition for this new bonanza, other countries were soon competing for a share. China, Malaysia and Qatar all expanded their holdings and activities. The British Embassy in Khartoum circulated a report in 1998 stating, 'The oil sector in Sudan is one of tremendous opportunity. There is great potential for investment and the Government of Sudan is taking an extremely flexible approach to those willing to invest in this sector. The spin-off business from the development of the sector is also considerable...The Ministry of Energy and Mining would welcome an approach by British companies...and bemoan the absence of the British.'[28] In 1999 the Netherlands-based Trafigura Beheer BV was the first company to obtain a contract to sell and market the Sudan's oil internationally. By February 2001 even Russian companies were given exploration licences by the Sudan government, signing new deals early in 2002.

Oil exploitation had been made possible by clearing the oilfields of their civilian population through the activities of the Sudanese armed forces and Baqqara militias from Southern Kordofan, and then securing the areas through the alliance with the Nuer break-away factions of the SPLA (Section **8.5**). Once installed, the Sudanese military has used the oil company roads and airfields to attack civilian settlements within a widening security radius.[29]

The war in the oilfields has received wide publicity, partly because it disrupted relief operations, and partly because it helped to bring about the collapse of the Sudan government's 'peace from within'. Protests about human rights violations from Canadian church groups were one reason for Arakis's withdrawal. Since 1999 there have been a succession of reports into human rights violations in the oilfields, including reports issued by the UN Commission on Human Rights and the Canadian government, as well as independent agencies such as Amnesty International, Christian Aid and Human Rights Watch.[30] All document in considerable detail the violent escalation of fighting in the oilfields areas, as well as the contribution of oil revenues to the Sudan government's war effort.

---

[28] 'Sudan oil sector report July 1998'. Foreign Office officials first denied the existence of this report but subsequently claimed that the non-existent report had been withdrawn. The faxed copy cited here bears the British Embassy Khartoum fax ID.

[29] John Harker, *Human Security in Sudan: The Report of a Canadian Assessment Mission* (Ottawa, 2000), pp. 11, 48–9.

[30] See Leonardo Franco, Special Rapporteur of the UN Commission of Human Rights, 'Situation of human rights in the Sudan' (UN Commission on Human Rights, A/54/467, 14 October 1999), the Harker report (ibid.), Peter Verney, *Raising the Stakes: Oil and Conflict in Sudan* (Hebden Bridge, 2000); Amnesty International, *Sudan: The Human Price of Oil* (London, 2000); Christian Aid, *The Scorched Earth: Oil and War in Sudan* (London, 2001); Human Rights Watch, *Sudan, Oil, and Human Rights Abuses* (Washington DC, forthcoming).

The reaction of companies and governments to this evidence is instructive in its repetition of the relief and development debate: the formulation of policy is divorced from any evidence coming from the field, and the policy of 'constructive engagement' is employed as a shield against criticism. The only two companies to respond publicly to evidence of human rights abuses were Lundin in Sweden and Talisman in Canada, both countries where church and human rights groups have kept the issue alive in the press and have lobbied their governments.

In Sweden it was discovered that the former prime minister, Carl Bildt, had joined Lundin's board of directors on the day after Amnesty International released its report in March 2000. He later claimed that he had joined 'to ensure that the firm adopts the U.N.'s and Amnesty International's code of conduct.'[31] Yet, fully a year later Lundin still had not adopted any code of corporate responsibility, had consistently denied that displacements were taking place in its concession area, and were celebrating the confirmation of significant oil fields in its block. Its public policy, as displayed on its website, echoed the underdevelopment mantra, that 'economic gains, when used to improve the socio-economic and humanitarian condition of the Sudanese people, will enhance the prospects of peace in the country.'

The Canadian government, having previously threatened sanctions against Talisman following its own investigations into the war in the oilfields, in the end did not follow through on the logic (or even the specific recommendations) of the Harker report. Instead of any practical action (such as halting the pumping of oil, or diverting the Sudan government's revenues into a trust fund to be used for local development only after the war was over), the Canadian government was content merely to have Talisman sign an 'ethical code of conduct'.[32]

Talisman persistently claimed in its letters to shareholders and public statements that there had been no civilian displacements in its concession areas, despite incontrovertible evidence to the contrary.[33] Not surprisingly it talked up the development spin-offs of its work, emphasizing the bore-hole wells and clinics it had financed for local 'nomads', which turned out to be the Baqqara militias who had displaced local Dinka and Nuer. Talisman embodied its commitment to 'constructive engagement' in a 'community development strategy'.[34] It repeated the line previously employed by some relief and development agencies operating out of Khartoum that underdevelopment is the root cause of the war, and that development will bring peace, hinting that it would even be immoral for the company to withdraw from the Sudan. In 2001, when Talisman share-trading came under increasing pressure from the US Congress, Talisman briefly considered selling its Sudan stake. It was reassured, however, by the fact that 'oil men' were returned to the White House, and

---

[31] 'Swede accused of conflict of interest over Sudan', Zenit.org, 25 March 2001 (ZE01032501).

[32] Taken from www.lundinoil.com/eng/SudanPolicy.shtr (7 March 2001).

[33] In reaction to the Christian Aid report in May 2001 Talisman's CEO Jim Buckee wrote to *The Economist* denying that any fighting or displacements had taken place in his concession area, only to be refuted by John Ryle, who had recently returned from the area as part of a second Canadian government-sponsored investigation team (Letters, *The Economist*, 19 May & 9 June 2001).

[34] Talisman (Greater Nile) B.V., 'Community Development strategy – 2001'.

by the US State Department's own opposition to sanctions against the company or the Sudan, and its sympathy for 'constructive engagement'. And despite a drop in world oil prices in 2001, Talisman increased its cash flow by $0.1 billion, to a record $2.4 billion that year.

Talisman resisted all calls for a public denunciation of attacks on civilians until it could no longer credibly deny such attacks were taking place. The cease-fire in the Nuba Mountains established by the Danforth peace initiative led to increased fighting in the oilfields early in 2002 and public verification of helicopter gunship attacks on civilian targets. Following one such attack, the US government temporarily withdrew from the peace process. Both the US and Canadian governments condemned the attack outright (Britain merely expressed 'concern'), and a class action suit was filed against both Talisman and the Sudan government in New York. It was only then that Talisman produced a public letter of condemnation. 'Constructive engagement' may work well for the oil companies and the Sudan government, but it has not for the people in the war zone.

Peace through development?

Like the government, the SPLA has adopted the slogan 'peace through development', but it sees this as an elaboration of its civil administration, making the SPLA-controlled areas, if not self-sufficient, at least sustainable in their own economy. This does encompass the encouragement of private entrepreneurs and the redistribution of local surpluses to areas of deficit through commerce. But beyond the rehabilitation of local economies the SPLA, unlike the government, has no radical blueprint for the future.

The war effort requires financing, and like other civil wars, this one offers a number of opportunities for the 'informal economy' to flourish, even if on semi-formal terms. The Sudanese war is not like Angola's, where government and rebels each have access to their own valuable exportable mineral resources.[35] The South's underlying wealth in oil and water is realized only when exploited through government agreements. Nor is the war like Sierra Leone's, where government, rebels, and individuals can survive through equal access to a highly exportable resource like diamonds.[36] But like these, and other civil wars, the unregulated trade of a 'collapsed state' (in this case, the collapsed state of the southern Sudan) clearly provides income for movements as well as individuals.

The southern Sudan borders on other areas in Africa where the 'informal economy' not only flourishes, but is often virtually the only economy. Gold is the only precious metal that the SPLA has to export, but there are other raw materials which have been exported through SPLA-protected or controlled trade. Livestock (especially cattle to Uganda) is a major source of income. Coffee and timber have also gone out, while manufactured

[35] Tony Hodges, *Angola from Afro-Stalinism to Petro-Diamond Capitalism* (Oxford/Bloomington IN, 2001).
[36] Paul Richards, *Fighting for the Rain Forest: War, Youth & Resources in Sierra Leone* (Oxford/Portsmouth NH, 1996).

commodities of various sorts have come in. The SPLA can behave almost as if it is a government in setting up bilateral relations, as it did when it ceded the Ilemi Triangle in the far southeastern corner of the Sudan to Kenya. In negotiating on behalf of the Movement, its leaders are also able to strike deals of their own. The South's war economy is now based on a variety of exports into the informal economies of its neighbours, the income of which is divided between the Movement, its leaders and local people in a dispro-portionate percentage. Part of the crisis of confidence in SPLA leadership is the perception that the leaders spend too much time outside the South taking care of their personal business ventures.

This is a highly individualized economic policy with which to confront the regime's more sophisticated and thorough control of the North's economy. If the SPLA is unable to protect and maintain the rural civilian population in their home territories, to provide education and training for future generations, or to shut down the oilfields, it presents no real threat to the Northern development plan.

The answers to the questions posed at the beginning of this chapter are by no means simple. Neither relief nor development are neutral: both are enmeshed in politics, whether or not international humanitarian agencies recognize the political complexity confronting them. There is no evidence that any relief operation has helped to shorten the conflict, but competition for relief resources has certainly directed it into new arenas. The control Khartoum has exerted over both development and relief agendas has meant that international agencies operating in the government sector have assisted in the creation of what Mark Duffield calls 'cheap and desocialised labour'. He sees no prospect for change in the Sudan's violent political economy and predicts that 'peace will probably accelerate the commercial exploitation of the South by the North', ending in the South's 'incorporation as an annex of cheap labour and resources for Northern-controlled projects and enterprises.'[37]

This is a sobering prospect, not only for humanitarian agencies, but for anyone seeking to bring about a negotiated end to the war. On being appointed President Bush's special envoy on the Sudan in September 2001, US Senator John Danforth immediately focused on the technical-ities of relief in the 'confidence-building' measures he set out to lead to peace negotiations. Equating humanitarian relief with a peace process is problematic, as the US ought to have learned in Somalia, but more so in the Sudan where the government has successfully restricted relief agencies to purely technical activity, divorcing them from the broader issues of rights and justice. These must figure in any peace process (Section **10.4**). Having captured the relief effort, Khartoum will continue to work for the subjugation of Southern labour and Southern resources. It has already co-opted oil companies and many development agencies in this endeavour and has scored an early success in co-opting the peace mediators. If Duffield's pessimistic prediction is to be avoided, then the Sudan's future development will depend on the type of peace it achieves. Ideas of peace are the subject of the next chapter.

---

[37] Duffield, *Global Governance and the New Wars*, pp. 208, 255.

11
Ideas of ▮ in the Sudan
Peace & War

After nearly two decades of fighting, the Sudan's civil war is Africa's second-longest continuous conflict, coming just behind Angola for intractability.[1] It is its very duration which makes it so baffling. The contention of the preceding chapters has been that no one single factor can account for the profound divide now separating the main regions of the Sudan, nor for the ferocity of the multiple civil wars which pit different parts of Sudanese society against each other. The final problem in a book attempting to explain the wars in the Sudan is to account for their continuation and for the failure to reach a resolution. Here I will examine ideas of peace and war, not only within the Sudan, but about the Sudan, attempts at peace-making between Sudanese, and the interventions of outsiders.

The tentative success of the 'people-to-people', or grassroots, peace movement inaugurated at the Wunlit Dinka-Nuer conference in 1999 gave hope to many that this, at last, was the way forward which would allow peace to spread 'all over the south'.[2] Insofar as the grassroots peace movement has succeeded, it has done so by building on ideas implicit in what anthropologists have termed the 'moral community'. Broadly speaking, moral communities are a product of a sense of responsibility for others. Godfrey Lienhardt's description of the moral community among the Nilotic societies of the southern Sudan refers specifically to that social community whose relations are marked by obligations of reciprocity among its members, who recognize that they must accept mediation and exchange compensation between themselves in order to overcome disputes and live at peace.[3] Questions concerning peace imply answers about war. When a society defines with whom it can, or must, make peace, it also defines, perhaps only by implication, on whom it can, or must, make war. These answers are themselves mutable, fixed to specific

[1] See Tony Hodges, *Angola from Afro-Stalinism to Petro-Diamond Capitalism* (Oxford/Bloomington IN, 2001).

[2] Julie Flint, 'The spirit of Wunlit', *Christian Aid News*, Summer 2000, pp. 18–19.

[3] Pnina Werbner, *Imagined Diasporas among Manchester Muslims: The Public Performance of Pakistani Transnational Identity Politics* (Oxford/Santa Fe 2002), p. 61; R. G. Lienhardt, 'Getting your own back: themes in Nilotic myth', in J.H.M. Beattie & R.G. Lienhardt (eds), *Studies in Social Anthropology: Essays in Memory of Evans-Pritchard by his Former Oxford Colleagues* (Oxford, 1975). See also D.H. Johnson, *Nuer Prophets* (Oxford, 1994), especially chapters 2 & 9; and D.H. Johnson & D.M. Anderson, 'Revealing Prophets', in D.M. Anderson & D.H. Johnson (eds), *Revealing Prophets: Prophecy in Eastern African History* (London/Athens OH, 1995).

times and circumstances and not embedded in an undecipherable antiquity or the purity of blood lines. To illustrate this I will look at two terms, *cieng* and *Umma*, which can be translated as embodying moral communities, and show the different applications both have had at different times in the nineteenth and twentieth centuries in the Sudan.

Cieng is used as a verb in Dinka and as a noun in Nuer. In Dinka it means to put in order; in Nuer it describes a closeness of relationship and can be applied at different scales of social inclusiveness. It is both elastic and situational, describing not only the most local community to which a person belongs, but the other elements of a wider community that impinge and build upon it. *Cieng* can be applied at different times to the village, the lineage and the tribe; it encapsulates them all.

During the late nineteenth and early twentieth centuries, there was an expanding definition of moral community in certain parts of Nuer and Dinka society, a redefinition which responded to changing social situations, and which was formulated by religious thinkers and leaders. It is no coincidence that these reformulations were most marked along political frontiers, either the Nuer–Dinka frontier within Upper Nile, or the Dinka–Arab frontier between Bahr al-Ghazal, Kordofan and Darfur.

The Nuer society which grew up in the plains east of the White Nile and Bahr al-Jabal systems in the mid-to-late nineteenth century was originally founded on raiding and settlement of land formerly belonging to Anuak, Dinka and other peoples. Occupation was not uniform, and the territory occupied by the concentric circles of the Nuer *cieng* contained individuals and whole communities of the dispossessed owners. There was a progressive expansion of that moral community, between newly settled groups of Nuer and those they dispossessed, by the steady expansion of kinship ties through marriage and adoption. Tensions were frequently reintroduced along the frontiers between the new and old communities when incoming groups of Nuer, uninhibited by local marriages and alliances, began pushing against or raiding the older settlements of Dinka or Anuak in their own turn. Such actions upset existing accommodations and contributed to the internal fracturing of Nuer groups; for war against one Dinka or Anuak group often led to a feud with related neighbouring Nuer. It was within this context of the Nuer-Dinka frontier that the Nuer prophet Ngundeng articulated a social philosophy, drawing on the symbols of divinity and authority of both peoples, which was aimed explicitly at ending feuds between Nuer sections and raids between Nuer and their neighbours. Ngundeng never completely banished either feuding or war, but his pronouncements had the effect of expanding the accepted boundaries of a moral community willing to accept mediation. This contributed to the progressive expansion of the pastoralist common economy of the flood region, which in turn reinforced the acceptance of reciprocal obligations between groups whose relations had once been defined by conflict. Later prophets and generations of Nuer *and* Dinka would refer back to the principles Ngundeng enunciated, especially during the unsettled times of the Sudan's post-independence civil wars.

The twentieth-century Dinka prophet Arianhdit appeared among the Abiem Dinka of northern Bahr al-Ghazal towards the end of the First

World War, at a time when this region bordering on Darfur and Kordofan was still disturbed by the events surrounding the conquest of Darfur by the Anglo-Egyptian government of the Sudan. Not only had slave- and cattle-raiding by Baqqara from Darfur and Kordofan gone largely unchecked by a government whose military resources were committed elsewhere, but the rudimentary administrative system had also failed to cope with the spread of internal Dinka feuds. As Ngundeng had done before him, Arianhdit combined religious symbols and roles to bring spiritual sanctions to bear on feuds, not only between his own people and others, but between more distant Dinka. His influence was such that he attracted supplicants from as far away as the Luo to the south. The peace that he brought to this once turbulent region even won the confidence of Arab traders to the north, who began entering Bahr al-Ghazal through his territory.

It was the fate of both Ngundeng and Arianhdit that their peace-making activities attracted the adverse attention of government, who saw the prophets as competitors to their own authority. The removal or neutralization of prophets was actively pursued as an administrative policy throughout most of the 1920s and was effectively completed by 1930.[4] The suppression of the Nilotic prophets by the Condominium government was followed by the construction of hierarchies of chiefs and chiefs' courts within the system of Native Administration. Religious figures were not removed completely from the daily life of the Nilotes, but some form of separation between religious and secular authorities was imposed. A regulated and supervised law replaced spiritual inspiration in the settling of disputes. A similar process was experienced throughout the South, even though the religious confrontation with government was not as pronounced for many other Southern peoples. In establishing its right to rule, government drew on the legitimacy of 'custom' by cooptation; in return it gave 'custom' official standing by subordinating it to the higher authority of government.

The Arabic *Umma* refers to the Muslim Community, or more precisely, the Community of Believers. In principle it applies to all Muslims, everywhere. In practice within the Muslim world there have often been conflicts over what constitutes 'belief' and who are, therefore, 'believers'. It is true, as many Islamic scholars rightly remind us, that at different times and in different parts of the world there have been Muslim states which have practised a high degree of religious tolerance. But it is also true that there have been schisms within the Muslim world, which have had the effect of narrowing the focus of tolerance.

This was the case during the Mahdiyya, the Sudanese religious movement now frequently described as 'nationalist' or 'proto-nationalist'. During the Mahdiyya there was a contracting definition of the *Umma* in the northern Sudan: not only was there a sharper division between Muslims and non-Muslims, but there appeared divisions among Muslims themselves.

---

[4] Johnson, *Nuer Prophets*, chapters 1, 3, 6. Damazo Dutt Majok, 'Resistance and cooperation in Bahr el-Ghazal 1920 [*sic*] – 1922', M. O. Beshir (ed.) *Southern Sudan: Regionalism & Religion. Selected Essays* (Khartoum, 1984), pp. 111–26.

In one of his earliest proclamations, the Mahdi declared,

> And the Prophet has many times informed me that whoever doubts my Mahdiship is an unbeliever in God and His Apostle, and that whoever is hostile to me is an unbeliever, and whoever fights me is abandoned [of God] in the Two Abodes [i.e. the present world and the world to come], his possessions and children being booty for the Muslims [i.e. the followers of the Mahdi].

In the same letter he went on to declare,

> The information was given that preaching will not purify the Turks; only the sword will purify them, save him to whom God shall grant grace. The Prophet informed me that the Muslim Community (*al-Umma*) shall be guided by me without the difficulty that befell the Prophet and his followers, and that I am created from the light of the core of the Prophet's heart.[5]

Thus it was established that the boundaries of the *Umma* contracted to contain *only* the Ansar – those who acknowledged the mission of the Mahdi – and to exclude others who, nevertheless, also proclaimed themselves to be Muslims. There were further divisions and restrictions on members of that newly refined *Umma*: Muslim marriages between Ansar and non-Ansar were invalidated in a decree issued as early as 1883.[6]

Jihad, which was an obligation for all Ansar, was initially aimed at the 'unbelievers' within the wider Muslim community. In the South, however, there was little demonstration of zeal to convert the true unbelievers. The main concern was the removal of the Egyptian forces in the South (which was not completed until 1888), after which the question of the 'discipline' of the southern Sudanese would be taken in hand. Southerners were almost always referred to in official Mahdist correspondence as *abid* (slaves).[7] Even within the Mahdist forces there was an internal distinction between free Muslim volunteers – the *mujahidin* – and slave riflemen – the *jihadiyya*. In the South, as in many other parts of the country, the Mahdist State represented an internal colonialism which was stratified according to contemporary ideas of race and religion.[8]

Insofar as the Mahdist state represented 'government' (*hakuma*), by the end of the nineteenth century there was no sense in which all peoples of the Sudan had the experience that 'government' was inclusive and overarching, or that the rule of 'government' required or facilitated the resolution of disputes, the mediation of feuds, or created the conditions by which breaches of peace could be restored.

By the beginning of the twentieth century, with the Anglo-Egyptian reconquest of the Sudan, the experience of most peoples in the outlying areas of the Mahdist State, or along the fringes of that state, was that 'government' was a separate, often hostile entity. The history of Condominium rule was the gradual transformation of this perception,

---

[5] Letter dated 28 Sha'ban 1299 AH (15 July 1882 AD), quoted in P. M. Holt, *The Mahdist State in the Sudan 1881–1898*, 2nd ed. (Oxford, 1970), pp. 109–10.
[6] Letter dated 3 Dhu al-Qa'da 1300 AH (5 September 1883 AD), ibid., p. 129.
[7] R.O. Collins, *The Southern Sudan 1883–1898* (New Haven, 1962), pp. 56, 72.
[8] For a description of Mahdist internal colonialism over Muslim peoples in Dar Masalit, for instance, see Lidwien Kapteijns, *Mahdist Faith and Sudanic Tradition: the History of the Masalit Sultanate, 1870–1930* (London, 1985).

where 'government' remained a separate (not an inclusive) entity and never lost its coercive aspect, but where its role included the resolution of internal conflicts and the regulation of external relations. One of the most profound contributions of British administration in the South was the involvement of 'government' in law and local courts. Government's insistence on its authority over law and justice was eventually accepted, so that in some Southern communities today it is often asserted that the aims of the government and the aims of those indigenous religious authorities who were the targets of government strictures were in fact one and the same: to promote peace and well-being. Government courts along the Nuer–Dinka frontier in Upper Nile Province, for instance, gave a sustained (if unintentional) expression to the same principles of inclusion and mediation enunciated by the nineteenth-century prophets; so much so that by the time of the outbreak of the current civil war Nuer spoke of their intermittent hostility to neighbouring Dinka not by the extreme and irreconcilable term of 'war' (*kor*), but as a 'feud' (*ter*). A feud breaks out only between related peoples, and the combination of common spiritual sanctions and accepted procedures for resolution can be applied to prevent such fighting from escalating into war. The practical boundaries of *cieng* had thus been expanded to include peoples formerly at war with each other.

Government's involvement in law was not without its ambiguity, which was particularly evident in cases of murder or homicide. Government insisted on and facilitated the payment of compensation, even between different political communities speaking different languages, thus expanding the boundaries of the moral community. Yet, when government took life, as in punitive campaigns or in judicial executions, it insisted that it owed no compensation; therefore it placed itself outside the circle of reciprocal obligations.

There was also a tension within the broader legal system in which the mutually conflicting spheres of English law, *shar'ia* (Islamic) law, and customary law (as applied in parts of the Muslim North as well as the non-Muslim South) were expected to co-exist. During the Condominium, customary law was always subject to the tests of a higher (codified) law or civilized 'common sense'. After independence, customary law continued to be subject to tests by a judiciary trained in other forms of higher law. The first generation of northern Sudanese administrators in the southern Sudan after independence generally followed this pattern.[9]

With the civil war of the 1960s, civil government retreated as the rural areas of the South were placed under military rule. There was often a conflict between civil and military authorities, in which civilian officials, when they were not entirely coopted by the army, were powerless to intervene in the arrest and execution of chiefs and ordinary citizens by the military administration. Government began to fail to fulfil its own meaning. Many Southerners remember that the most notorious massacres of civilians during the 1960s took place under Umma Party governments, giving a clear indication that the community the Umma represented excluded them, and reinforcing nineteenth-century memories of the

---

[9] See: John Wuol Makec *The Customary Law of the Dinka People of Sudan in Comparison with Aspects of Western & Islamic Law* (London, 1988); H. Bleuchot, *Les Cultures Contre l'Homme? Essai d'Anthropologie Historique du Droit Pénal Soudanais* (Aix, 1994).

Ansar who murdered civilians, cut off persons' hands and abducted slaves and cattle.

In the revival of Muslim sectarian politics in the Sudan after the overthrow of Nimairi in 1985, the Khatmiyya emphasized its innate 'Sudanese-ness', in part as a Muslim opposition to Mahdism. Sadiq al-Mahdi based his revival of the Umma Party on a new *ijtihad*, or consensus, among Muslims as part of a broader international Islamic revival, from which, however, he excluded 'renegades' (i.e. secular Muslims), but from which he did not fully exclude the principle of *jihad*.[10] Sadiq never resolved the contradiction between respecting rights of non-Muslims and privileging the obligations and extra rights of Muslims. Nor did he ever completely lay to rest the fear that his own form of *ijtihad* would exclude some Muslims from the exercise of power or full rights.

The National Islamic Front, who were behind the 1989 coup that brought the current regime to power, made these fears a reality. While politically and doctrinally opposed to the Ansar of the Umma Party, they represent a logical extension of the thinking that also guided Sadiq al-Mahdi. The NIF represents a specific interpretation of the Muslim Community and Muslim law which has embraced the law against apostasy, the suppression of the rival sects such as the Khatmiyya, *jihad* as Holy War, and enforced conversion and circumcision in some of the newly reconquered parts of the southern Sudan.

The use of tribal militias reintroduced tensions and conflicts into areas where some mechanism previously existed to overcome inter-communal disputes: as on the Arab–Dinka frontier between Kordofan and Bahr al-Ghazal, and on the Nuer–Dinka border of Upper Nile. The establishment of SPLA military control in the late 1980s made possible the reassertion of civil order in some areas, most particularly the Arab–Dinka and the Nuer–Dinka frontiers. The split in the SPLA upset that. It is not just that 'war' seems to have replaced 'feud' along the Nuer–Dinka frontier; war is replacing feud between related groups of Nuer. This has happened for two reasons: 1) those who claimed governmental authority ceased to operate as government is expected to, in that they were no longer capable of overseeing the institutions established for the resolution of conflict, and 2) the authorities who replaced government were themselves actively involved in promoting disputes which in earlier times they would have attempted to contain. Political divisions generated from the top were being felt lower down, where communities not constructed along 'primal' lines were forced to divide within themselves. For instance, Dinka and Nuer border communities have sometimes been forced to divide themselves out as *either* Dinka *or* Nuer, but not as a combination of both.

Local people recognized this long before external observers realized it. In 1991, when the fighting between the two factions of the SPLA produced the first wave of refugees out of Kongor County, I met a Twic Dinka chief on the flooded road north of Bor. The previous year he had told me how the local Dinka had been assisting destitute Nuer. I asked him how, given that recent experience, their neighbours could now be

---

[10] H. Bleuchot, 'Islam, droit pénal et politique: sur deux ouvrages de Sadiq al-Mahdi', in H. Bleuchot, C. Delmet, D. Hopwood (eds), *Sudan: History, Identity, Ideology* (Reading, 1991).

attacking him? Could not the chiefs meet together to bring an end to the fighting? This was not a problem to be settled by the chiefs, he told me, it was to be settled by those with the guns, higher up, who started it. Methods of mediation and accommodation which have in the past been used in these areas – either to avoid the breakdown of local peace, or to make and reinforce peace – have been overshadowed and superseded by the patterns of civil war. In short, the persons who organize and direct war have not been subject to the strictures of local public opinion, nor the restraints of the processes of mediation. They can override them whenever they choose. The earth master, spearmaster and man of divinity are no match for the commander of the Kalashnikov.

The process begun at Wunlit has given public opinion a forum in which it can be expressed and brought to bear on local commanders and political leaders. It has been enabled to do this through the assistance of external agencies – the UN, the churches, and foreign human rights organizations – and these organizations in turn have been able to act only because of the strength of local feeling. But the peace built on these foundations can spread only so far. Government-organized raids by the *murahalin* and PDF along the northern Bahr al-Ghazal border and through the railway corridor to Wau repeatedly override and undermine local Baqqara–Dinka truces. The continuing fall-out of the collapse of the government's 'peace from within', with armed factions of Nuer fighting each other, sometimes in alliance with and at the bidding of the government or the SPLA, has meant that peace at the grassroots remains tenuous.

There are in the Sudan today numerous moral communities which the current civil wars are in the process of making exclusive of each other. The moral community of the *Umma* continues to exclude non-Muslims from reciprocal rights and, under the formulations of both the Ansar and the National Islamic Front, restricts the rights of some Muslims (whether secularists or members of other sects or guerrilla armies) by denying them full incorporation into the Muslim community. 'Government', which towards the end of the Condominium period acquired widespread acceptance across the country and enforced mediation within a moral community while remaining outside of it, has abdicated its own moral authority.

The current government's federal system reinforces, and indeed, seems based upon exclusive moral communities. As under Nimairi, the participatory language of decentralization is once again cloaking the fact that weak states are being created whose powers do not circumscribe those of the central government, but rather exist at the pleasure of the central government. As Riek Machar discovered to his cost, the central government refuses to devolve its practical control over economic and security matters. The regions created by Nimairi were based on the old pre-independence provinces. The states created by the current government are based, instead, on the smaller units of the old districts. Native administration is being reintroduced in parts of the North very much on the old Sudanic pattern, with the central government recognizing new tribes, and bringing them and their leaders directly into a political relationship with the state. This is just one step on the road to an ethnic federalism where small-scale communities must operate independently of each other in a political arena still controlled by the central government.

It is not surprising, therefore, that at a time when the powerlessness of so many peoples and regions in the country is most pronounced, the question of self-determination has begun to move to the centre of Sudanese politics, not just as a mechanism for the South to achieve its independence, but as a process whereby peoples take more control for the running of their own affairs.

The NIF government's halt to substantive constitutional discussions in 1989 and its open pursuit of the Islamist agenda revived talk of separation among many southern Sudanese living in the government-held areas. The SPLA was already preparing a new position on self-determination in 1991 when the Nasir declaration finally brought the issue of southern Sudanese independence to the fore, not just for debate among southern Sudanese, but between southern and northern Sudanese. At first the SPLA's response seemed equivocal, in that it proposed a number of alternative plans to self-determination, including confederation within a united Sudan and an association of sovereign states.[11] But talks between the Nasir faction and the NIF government produced equally equivocal results, and the Frankfurt Declaration of January 1992 did not mention either self-determination or secession, using circumlocutions, open to contradictory interpretations, instead (Section **8.1**).

Under pressure from the Nigerian government and OAU observers at Abuja the two SPLA factions formulated a united negotiating position, championing the right to self-determination for all the peoples of the southern Sudan, Abyei, the Nuba Mountains and southern Blue Nile. This was reaffirmed in the meeting between Garang and Riek in Washington DC in October 1993 (Section **7.6.1**). Neither of these joint declarations led to a new collaboration between the factions, but their significance was that they finally put the principle of self-determination – for other regions of the Sudan as well as the South – back into public circulation as a method for resolving the war.[12]

The Abuja talks may have brought the two Southern factions ideologically closer together, but they also brought out into the open the government's firm rejection of the process of self-determination or the option of secession secured by any other means than force. The Southern peoples were to be limited to the right of affirming their constitutional position within a united Sudan, but the Northern majority were to have the right to decide on a state religion for the entire country. The unity of the Sudan, and centrality of the Islamic state, were non-negotiable.[13]

The second round of the Abuja talks ended with the government and the SPLA sharply disagreeing over the issue of religion and the state. The failure of Abuja opened the way for a joint initiative proposed by the

---

[11] See resolution 3.2 of the SPLM/SPLA Torit Resolutions, 1991, in John Garang, *The Call for Democracy in Sudan* (ed. Mansour Khalid) (London/NY, 1992), p. 284.

[12] For summaries of the succession of negotiating positions, see Ann Lesch, *Sudan: Contested National Identities* (Bloomington/Oxford, 1998), pp. 148–209.

[13] For the details of the Abuja negotiations see Steven Wöndu & Ann Lesch, *Battle for Peace in Sudan: An Analysis of the Abuja Conferences 1992–1993* (Lanham MD, 2000), especially chapters 4, 5 & 9.

Sudan's partners in IGADD (Inter-Governmental Agency for Drought and Desertification) – Eritrea, Ethiopia, Kenya, Uganda – all countries bordering the Sudan and affected by the war.[14] A Declaration of Principles (DOP), drafted by Ethiopia, revised by Eritrea, and adopted by the IGAD mediators, proposed the options of self-determination for the South through a referendum, or a secular government for a united country. At the time these principles were proposed (1994) the government was militarily resurgent and refused to discuss either self-determination or the secular state. The IGAD meetings broke up with the Sudan government delegation declaring that it had a mission to Islamize all of Africa. Formal meetings with the Sudan government did not resume until 1997, when the government's military position was more precarious. It then agreed to accept the DOP as one of many bases on which negotiations could take place.

The strong regional support for self-determination, especially from Eritrea and Ethiopia, enabled the SPLA to urge the acceptance of these basic principles by the NDA at their 1995 meeting in Asmara. The exile northern Sudanese parties of the NDA were clearly reluctant to concede self-determination to the South, but in the Asmara Declaration of 1995 they committed themselves to a fixed interim period, following which the southern Sudan would vote on whether to remain united with the rest of the Sudan, under federal or confederal options, or to separate. The issue was far from resolved: the SPLA and the Northern parties did not agree on those areas to be allowed self-determination; other regions currently in rebellion, such as the East, southern Blue Nile and the Nuba Mountains, do not necessarily want to join an independent South; and the nature of a united Sudan in the future still awaited resolution of the question of the Islamic state. But even accepting these uncertainties, the SPLA achieved what it failed to achieve prior to the 1986 elections: an agreement from the Northern parties on the process by which Southern grievances were to be addressed, and possibly solved. It also opened the way for the inclusion of non-Arab Muslim areas in this process, moving a step away from entrenching a North–South divide.

The weakness of the Asmara Declaration, of course, was that it was an agreement between parties who were out of power and could not deliver what they had agreed. It was known that the main Northern parties were unhappy about the prospect of an independent South, and Southerners fully anticipated that they would attempt to back away from the implementation of this referendum.

It was up to Riek to show that he could get something more from the government. The agreements he signed in 1996 and 1997, which constituted the Sudan's 'peace from within', committed the Southern 'secessionists' to a highly centralized form of federation with very limited devolved powers to a combination of Southern states (a reworking of the semi-autonomous regional government structure first introduced by the Addis Ababa agreement). But even this was to be deferred to the indefinite future. As events quickly proved, Khartoum did not intend to devolve any substantial powers to their own creation, the Council of Southern States. When Riek finally left in 2000, he left empty-handed.

---

[14] In 1997 IGAD dropped 'drought' and became the Inter-Governmental Agency for Development, the abbreviation which is used here.

The intrusion of an Egyptian–Libyan (ELI) initiative in 1999 helped not only to halt the IGAD process, but to split the NDA's temporary unity. Both Egypt and Libya have long had ambitions to form a broader Arab unity incorporating their countries and the Sudan in some form of union. Conflicts between the leaders of all three countries have kept this vision as nothing more than a dream. But both Egypt and Libya continue to want to keep the Sudan within the Arab fold, and neither want to see Southern secession. Qadaffi ended his support to the SPLA in 1985, partly on this issue. Egypt is opposed to an independent southern Sudanese state sitting astride what it has always considered its own strategic water reserve.

IGAD began to unravel in 1999: first with the inclusion of Egypt among the club of governments forming the 'Friends of IGAD'; secondly, with the Friends' proposal to link humanitarian relief to a peace agreement between the government and the SPLA. As the government has always tried to restrict relief deliveries to the South, many Southerners saw this as a means by which the SPLA was to be pushed into making an unsatisfactory peace. Then Libya, eager to bring about a reconciliation between the Northern parties and the government, proposed its own peace plan in Tripoli in 1999, seconded by Egypt. At first it had only three provisions: a cease-fire, acceptance of the unity of the Sudan, and an end to hostile propaganda. Implementation of these three points would then lead to negotiations.

The NDA leadership accepted this initiative, and there were moves to incorporate it into the IGAD process, though it was in conflict with the DOP. The SPLA was equivocal, havering between acceptance and rejection. In breaking with Garang and leaving the NDA late in 2000, Sadiq al-Mahdi cited the SPLA's final opposition to the Egyptian–Libyan initiative as clear evidence of the SPLA's lack of commitment to peace. The remaining members of the NDA committed themselves to two different proposals which cancel each other out: the 1995 Asmara Declaration and the 1999 Tripoli Declaration. The opposition was once again divided against itself about its declared goals, and the fracture appeared along the North–South divide.

This is apparently what the Egyptian government had in mind when it linked the Egyptian-Libyan initiative to reconciliation between the northern parties and Khartoum. 'Egypt possesses cards it has not yet used in preventing the separation of southern Sudan', Egypt's ambassador to Khartoum declared in 2000.[15] In 2001 the initiative was further elaborated into nine points, with the preservation of the unity of the Sudan as the first principle, conceding only citizenship rights and decentralization, but with no mention of the central questions of religion and the state, or self-determination for the South, or any other region.

Throughout the West, there were also many professional diplomats, academics and conflict-resolution experts who rejected the 'clash of cultures' theory of international affairs and sought to 'engage with Islam', whether out of political or religious conviction. The specific facts of the war in the Sudan became less important than the Sudan as a symbol of a growing polarity in global politics, replacing the old hostilities of the Cold War. In advocating some form of engagement with the Khartoum regime,

---

[15] 'Delusions of peace', *Africa Confidential* 42/6 (10 August 2001), p. 1.

they tacitly accepted the NIF's presentation of itself as truly representative of Islam and have overlooked or downplayed the degree to which
the NIF regime has used religion as an ideology of repression.[16] The
opening up of the Sudan's oilfields increased the audience receptive to
these generalized arguments.

By 2001 the regional coalition for peace was broken and the prospects
for agreement were bleak. Within the region there were two governments,
Libya and Egypt, resolutely set against self-determination for the South.
Two other governments previously strong supporters of that principle,
Eritrea and Ethiopia, had been to war against each other, and each was
making its own accommodation with the Sudan government. Uganda, still
hostile to Khartoum, was embroiled in a number of other regional conflicts
in Rwanda and the Democratic Republic of the Congo to the extent that
many within the country advocated a general disengagement from such
foreign entanglements. The European countries in the Friends of IGAD
were frustrated with the deadlock in the peace process, but were increasingly interested in doing business with the Sudan over its oil. The United
States had just replaced one administration hostile to the Khartoum
government with a new administration whose policy on the Sudan was
unknown and ambivalent: it had strong links to the oil industry, but it was
also politically sensitive to the holy alliance between the American religious right and African-American anti-slavery activists, who were strongly
represented in Congress and supportive of the South.

The events of September 11 and the war against terrorism gave a new
focus to American efforts in the region, but there are two tracks to the
American approach, which are not necessarily connected: the international assault on Usama bin Ladin's al-Qaida network and terrorism
generally, and the search for areas of negotiation between the
government of the Sudan and the SPLA. The President's special envoy
on the Sudan, former Senator John Danforth, has not been involved in
the former; yet it is over the issue of terrorism that the US has exerted
most pressure on the Sudan.

Contacts between the Sudan government and the CIA and FBI over
Islamist terrorist networks began as early as May 2000, when Khartoum
released some dated information on Usama bin Ladin, but held back
more. Khartoum has always shown itself willing to shop its former
terrorist friends to the West (as it did when handing Carlos 'the Jackal'
over to France), and it appears to have nothing to lose, and much to gain,
by cooperating with the US over information on al-Qaida. Since
September 11 it has suddenly released files it at first claimed not to have.
How much disinformation is mixed with the information is anybody's
guess.[17]

---

[16] John L. Esposito, *The Islamic Threat: Myth or Reality?*, 3rd ed. (Oxford/New York, 1999), pp.
84–92, for a political analysis which largely removes religion from the centre of the Sudan's
civil wars. A faith-based approach is that of Douglas Johnston (no relation), founder of the
International Center for Religion and Diplomacy in Washington DC, who sought to engage
Khartoum's leaders through 'talking about Jesus' and building on Islam's respect for Jesus as a
prophet (Larry Witham, 'Faith seen as path to peace in troubled Sudan', *Washington Times*, 3
May 1999).

[17] 'Sudan/USA: Who's selling who?', *Africa Confidential* 42/20 (12 October 2001), p. 4.

With terrorism the priority in US foreign policy, the US has used the threat of maintaining the Sudan on its list of 'terrorist states' as a means of extracting further intelligence. The threat has not been used to introduce leverage in potential peace talks.[18] Danforth, who initially came to his task declaring that the US had no master plan it wished to impose on both sides, has since tried to link the beginning of the peace process to agreements on humanitarian relief (the issue which helped to sabotage the IGAD process) and has focused on separate arrangements for the Nuba Mountains. He has reassured European nations that the US no longer seeks the overthrow of the Bashir government, and encouraged Egypt's involvement in negotiations. Like so many Americans, including the southern Sudan's political friends, he sees the Sudan's politics in terms of America's own preoccupations with identity politics and minority rights. Possibly, like so many in the West, he was also persuaded by the standard tag attached to news stories on the Sudan that 'the Christian and animist SPLA is fighting for greater autonomy for the South'. By January 2002 he had made up his mind on two significant issues: the Sudan would not become a secular state, and self-determination would not encompass independence for the South. In his final report of 26 April Danforth stated a preference for a self-determination which would merely 'ensure the right of the people of Southern Sudan to live under a government that respects their religion and culture.'[19] Thus was Khartoum's Abuja position casually conceded.

Self-determination could not be dismissed so lightly. Southerners, even within the SPLA, increasingly wanted the South to go it alone, and take their self-determination while they could. Danforth's willingness to separate the Nuba Mountains from other issues in the war added impetus to this movement. But there were still major points of disagreement between the Southern exile leadership and John Garang.

The first was over the options to be voted on in self-determination: Garang wanted them to be defined in advance, before a cease-fire and interim arrangements were put in place; others suggested that the interim arrangements themselves should constitute the alternative to independence at whatever time Southerners were asked to choose between unity and independence. The second was over who would be given the right of self-determination. Garang's public position has been to keep options open for the other regions. His critics insisted that a resolution for southern Sudanese should not be delayed by attempts to accommodate the other marginalized areas.

There were, and are, strong points in favour of Garang's position. For self-determination to work there must be clear, practical options presented; in other words there must be a real choice. Given the scale of the fighting throughout the Sudan, the South jeopardizes any peace it may achieve if it is seen to be abandoning allied groups now fighting

---

[18] As former Ambassador Robert Oakley, Danforth's chief adviser, admitted to me, 'I am not about to lie down in front of the speeding train of the war against terrorism.'

[19] Jon Sawyer, 'Danforth wants assurances cease-fire will be honored', *St. Louis Post-Dispatch*, 13 January 2002, and Jon Sawyer, 'Danforth offers hope for peace', *St. Louis Post-Dispatch*, 14 January 2002. John C. Danforth, 'Report to the President of the United States on the outlook for peace in Sudan', 26 April 2002.

against the current regime, a move which will only entrench the Islamist government in what remains of the northern Sudan. But there was also much common ground between the SPLA and the most ardent advocates of self-determination: they agreed that only when independence for the South is a real choice will the North be forced to choose what it really wants – unity or the Islamic state.

The round of meetings and agreements which spun off from the US peace initiative in early 2002 produced greater clarity. Garang and other spokespersons for the SPLA repeated in private and in public the SPLA's continued preference for a united, restructured, reformed, secular Sudan, *failing which* southern Sudanese independence must be a real alternative. Self-determination is now seen as more than a vote in a referendum; it embraces the structure of government at all levels. Sadiq al-Mahdi, too, in private as well as public, seems to have accepted that Northerners can no longer back away from agreeing to the option of Southern independence, if they are to have a credible chance of persuading Southerners to freely choose to remain part of a united Sudan.

The IGAD talks re-opened in June with the active involvement of US, British and Norwegian 'facilitators'. The US drafted a text restricting self-determination to the formation of an autonomous Southern region. The release of this draft created a furore. Southern Sudanese vigorously lobbied against it; Kenya backed a redraft in line with the DOP; and in Washington a rift opened between the White House and the State Department, with the White House signalling support for self-determination. The Machakos Protocol signed on 20 July 2002 was hailed as a major step towards peace, resolving the issues of self-determination and state and religion. Its provisions were far more ambiguous. It was not a peace agreement, but an agreement on the framework for further discussions about peace. The option of independence for the South was reconfirmed, but the option of a secular state for the whole Sudan was removed: non-Muslims living in the North would still be subject to *shari'a* law. The type of unity to be offered was deferred to later discussions, as were the equally important issues of a cease-fire, human rights and wealth sharing.

The restatement of the principle of self-determination was immediately undermined by conflicting interpretations. Egypt announced its opposition to independence for the South; spokesmen for Khartoum denied that the protocol allowed the partition of the Sudan; US Assistant-secretary of State for Africa, Walter Kansteiner, reiterated the State Department's position that only autonomy, not independence, was on offer; members of the NDA and southern Sudanese civil society groups voiced their concern about being excluded from any future constitutional redefinition of the Sudan. Doubts that the Sudan, Egyptian, US and British governments would really allow a free referendum on the South's future remained.

There are now many opposing ideas of peace for the Sudan: an Islamist idea, based on a belief in the historic inevitability of the conquering, assimilationist power of Islam; a democratic idea espoused by a coalition of undemocratic organizations, such as the SPLA, or former democratic parties who did not themselves practise this ideal when they were in power; and an international consensus seduced by the language of development. The connections any have with indigenous moral communities are either entirely absent, or still only tenuous. But can a positive peace be achieved without establishing a connection between the broader structural principles on which the country is to be constructed, and the moral communities it will contain? Peace can be imposed, as it has been in the past, but such peace has turned out to be only temporary. A bad peace is still not a viable option.

Every internationally-sponsored peace forum has ended at the same place: self-determination as the principle on which the war is to be resolved. The dilution of this principle has come through alternative initiatives outside formal mediation. Khartoum's evasion has received international support, especially from Egypt, Libya and those in the West advocating 'constructive engagement' with Khartoum. These are principally those European countries, including Britain, wishing to benefit from the Sudan's new oil boom, and a US oil lobby that wants not only access to a share in the Sudan's oil industry, but now proposes a national energy strategy of decreasing America's dependence on Middle Eastern oil by increasing its imports from Africa. But given the failure of past efforts of 'constructive engagement' with Khartoum over humanitarian issues, and Khartoum's history of evading the unpalatable conclusions of past negotiations, what precedents are there which realistically suggest that 'constructive engagement' will produce a better result now?

There are comparisons to be made with the Anglo-Egyptian negotiations of 1946–53. The Egyptians made the same arguments the NIF later did: that the right to self-determination is so self-evident, it does not have to be explicitly mentioned in any agreement. The South is now learning the importance of a public definition of the extent of self-determination, and the procedures by which it will be exercised. Riek Machar's willingness to accept ambiguously worded promises proved disastrous, both for him personally, and for the Sudanese generally.

The SPLA, which began the war with a clear idea of past mistakes to be avoided, has achieved some incremental agreements: getting the Northern parties first to admit the right of self-determination for the South; then to agree the explicit options between federation, confederation (not just a vague unity), and independence; and finally to extend that agreement in principle to areas previously unconsidered (Abyei, Nuba Mountains, southern Blue Nile) in order to avoid the fudge of the Addis Ababa Agreement. It is because the SPLA was seen to wobble in its own commitment to this process that it is now in jeopardy, confronted as it is by a growing international consensus against self-determination. But this international consensus is aimed only at an accommodation between two warring parties, not at a comprehensive peace for the whole country. If the existing incremental agreements are built upon, however, then the Sudan has a chance to avoid the repetition of the shambles of independence, when international intervention circumvented the self-determination process, the general populace was denied a final vote on their own future, and a decision on the form of government under which the Sudanese were to live as one people was deferred to a never-realized future.

The Sudan is no less divided in its historiography than in its politics. The very diversity of peoples, languages and sources presents researchers with real difficulties when attempting a comprehensive account of the country's past. To date, those scholars who have attempted to provide general histories of one sort or another have been primarily concerned with central state institutions, ruling elites and the dominant political culture. There has been an apparent reluctance to come to grips with the alternative perspectives that different regions have on a common past. In this respect nationalist and Condominium historiographies, in particular, have failed to give an adequate foundation for understanding the current crisis in the Sudan's political, economic and cultural future.

Histories of the southern Sudan which are part of the prevailing historiographic tradition have generally taken for granted the region's geographical and historical isolation from its immediate neighbours. The South has entered history only with the production of external documentary sources, and the studies based on these sources have focused on the activities of alien governments, administrations and administrators, rather than on the southern Sudanese peoples themselves. Internal history has been left mainly to ethnographers, some of whom have been pioneers in their methods, while others now appear to be very old fashioned in their treatment of 'history'.

I have presented critiques of specific aspects of Sudanese historiography in other essays. First, as an invitation to new research questions for the southern Sudan in 'The future of the southern Sudan's past', *Africa Today* 28/3 (1981), and 'The isolation of the southern Sudan: a re-examination of the evidence', *Heritage: A Journal of Southern Sudanese Cultures* 1/2–3 (Juba, 1982). Then, a challenge to Condominium historians was offered in 'The Sudan under the British', *Journal of African History* 29/3 (1988). Finally, with barely concealed frustration when neither the invitation nor the challenge was taken up, these themes were explored further in '"The Sudan is *sui generis*": past failures and future prospects in Sudanese History', *Sudan Studies* 20 (1997). In *The Southern Sudan* (The Minority Rights Group Report No. 78, 1988) I proposed in brief outline the interpretation of modern Sudanese history on which I have elaborated here. In *Nuer Prophets. A History of Prophecy from the Upper Nile in the Nineteenth and Twentieth Centuries* (Oxford: Clarendon Press, 1994) I attempted to produce the type of detailed, local history I have advocated, focusing on a continuum of regional experience through the pre-colonial, colonial, and post-colonial periods, drawing on both indigenous and external sources, and bringing the historical experience of one area of the southern Sudan to bear on broader aspects of Sudanese history.

There is to date no fully integrated history of the southern Sudan, linking it with other parts of the Nile basin. Yet in recent years there have been a variety of stimulating and innovative studies on various aspects of the Sudanese past, and it is on the foundation of these works that such a reinterpretation is, or could be, built. The discussion of secondary sources that follows is not intended to be a comprehensive bibliography (and can be faulted for its omissions), but is offered to give the reader some idea of where to locate interpretations, debates, and source materials.

Early Sudanese history
Chapter 1 is an all too brief outline of a crucial period in Sudanese history, and an extended commentary is perhaps necessary to acquaint readers with the literature on some of the more contentious issues of that period. The standard history of Arab incursions and Arabization, to which all other subsequent books refer, is Yusuf Fadl Hasan's *The Arabs and the Sudan* (Edinburgh: Edinburgh University Press, 1967 & Khartoum: Khartoum University Press, 1973). An alternative interpretation of the significance of Sudanese Arab genealogies, drawing attention to their fictive character, was put forward by the anthropologist Ian Cunnison in 'Classification by genealogy: a problem of the Baqqara belt', in Yusuf Fadl Hasan (ed.), *Sudan in Africa* (Khartoum: Khartoum University Press, 1971). The historian Jay Spaulding, whose work is always stimulating, often controversial and generates a great deal of heated debate, has taken the study of such genealogies a step further by comparing them with land charters and other indigenous Arabic documents of the eighteenth and nineteenth centuries, producing a rich new social history of the northern Sudan, the results of which have been presented in *The Heroic Age in Sinnar* (East Lansing: African Studies Center, Michigan State University, 1985). Another anthropologist, Wendy James, has applied modern fieldwork experience on the Sudan-Ethiopian border to examine historical ambiguities of power and status in 'The Funj mystique: approaches to a problem of Sudan history', in R.K. Jain (ed.), *Text and Context* (Philadelphia: ISHI, 1977). This theme (among others) has been taken up for Darfur by R.S. O'Fahey in his *State and Society in Dar Fur* (London: C. Hurst, 1980), and 'Fur and Fartit: the history of a frontier', in J. Mack & P. Robertshaw (eds), *Culture History in the Southern Sudan. Archaeology, Linguistics, Ethnohistory* (Nairobi: British Institute for Eastern Africa, 1982). For good measure, readers can examine a similar treatment of terms of status and ethnicity crisscrossing the border in Don Donham's 'Old Abyssinia and the new Ethiopian empire: themes in social history', in Donald Donham & Wendy James (eds), *The Southern Marches of Imperial Ethiopia* (Cambridge: Cambridge University Press, 1986; paperback edition Oxford/Athens OH/Addis Ababa: James Currey/Ohio University Press/Addis Ababa University Press, 2002), a book with a number of valuable chapters on the Sudan–Ethiopian border regions.

Turkiyya
The standard, and still unsurpassed, general history of the Turco-Egyptian conquest and occupation of the Sudan is Richard Hill's *Egypt in the Sudan 1820–1881* (London: Oxford University Press, 1959), to which can be added Afaf Lutfi al-Sayyid Marsot's *Egypt in the Reign of Muhammad 'Ali* (Cambridge: Cambridge University Press, 1984) for an analysis of Muhammad Ali's motives for and methods of conquest. Richard Gray, *A History of the Southern Sudan 1839–1889* (London: Oxford University Press, 1961) is still the only general history of the southern Sudan in the Turco-Egyptian period. Based on external sources, its only access to the internal histories of southern Sudanese peoples is through the ethnographies produced during the colonial period. Gray's analysis of the 'spiral of violence', whereby intrusive commercial interests intervened in, and thereby transformed local warfare, continues to have relevance in the study of the twentieth century and after. Janet Ewald, *Soldiers, Traders and Slaves. State Formation and Economic Transformation in the Greater Nile Valley, 1700–1885* (Madison: University of Wisconsin Press, 1990) brings a new style of interpretation to the history of the Nuba mountains in the eighteenth and nineteenth centuries, showing how, and why, the historical experience of that region differs significantly from that of the South.

History of slavery
The most important issue of the Sudan's nineteenth-century history is the rapid expansion of both slave trading and slave owning during the Turco-Egyptian period. Jay Spaulding's 'Slavery, land tenure and social class in the northern Turkish Sudan', *International Journal of African Historical Studies* 15/1 (1982), has revolutionized our understanding of that expansion. Anders Bjørkelo, *Prelude to the Mahdiyya: Peasants and Traders in the Shendi Region, 1820–1885* (Cambridge: Cambridge University Press, 1989), has built on Spaulding's analysis considerably by looking at the economic impact of the Turkiyya on one part of the riverain Sudan, connecting this to the process of the exploitation of the southern Sudan. R.S. O'Fahey has given a nuanced analysis of slavery and the social legacy of slave raiding in Darfur, in 'Slavery and the slave trade in Dar Fur', *Journal of African History* 14/1 (1973), and 'Fur and Fartit' (both of continuing relevance to events in the twentieth century). Wendy James provides an anthropological perspective on slave-producing areas in 'Perceptions from an African slaving frontier', in L. Archer (ed.), *Slavery and Other Forms of Unfree Labour* (London: Routledge, 1988). My own attempts to delineate military and commercial aspects of slavery in Sudan can be found in D.H. Johnson: 'Sudanese military slavery from the eighteenth to the twentieth Century', in ibid.; 'The structure of a legacy: military slavery in northeast Africa', *Ethnohistory* 36/1 (1989); 'Recruitment and entrapment in private slave armies: the structure of the *zara'ib* in the southern Sudan', in E. Savage (ed.), *The Human Commodity. Perspectives on the Trans-Saharan Slave Trade* (London: Frank Cass, 1992); and 'Muslim military slavery', in Paul Finkelman & Joseph C. Miller (eds), *Encyclopedia of World Slavery*, vol. II, (NY: Macmillan, 1998). The history and practice of slavery in twentieth-century Sudan has now been

brought up to date with Jok Madut Jok, *War and Slavery in Sudan* (Philadelphia: University of Pennsylvania Press, 2001).

The Mahdiyya

The Mahdiyya continues to inspire Sudanese nationalists of different ideologies. P.M. Holt, *The Mahdist State in the Sudan 1881–1898*, 2nd ed. (Oxford: Clarendon Press, 1970) is still the main general account of the Mahdist state, based on internal and external documents. Given the importance of the period there are surprisingly few regional studies of the Mahdiyya. R.O. Collins, *The Southern Sudan 1883–1898* (New Haven: Yale University Press, 1962) is a description of Mahdist incursions in the southern Sudan, based on European and Mahdist sources. Like Gray before him, Collins' only access to southern Sudanese testimony comes through colonial ethnography. L. Kapteijns, *Mahdist Faith and Sudanic Tradition. The History of the Masalit Sultanate, 1870–1930* (London: KPI, 1985) is a model of what can be achieved by combining official Mahdist records with internal sources to write the history of a region which contested Mahdist colonial rule. My own 'Prophecy and Mahdism in the upper Nile: an examination of local experiences of the Mahdiyya in the southern Sudan', *The British Journal of Middle Eastern Studies* 20/1 (1993) attempts to bring some southern Sudanese perceptions of the Mahdiyya into the historical discussion.

The Condominium period

A comprehensive bureaucratic and administrative history of the Condominium period (Chapters 2 & 3) can be found in Martin W. Daly's two-volume study, *Empire on the Nile. The Anglo-Egyptian Sudan, 1898–1934* (Cambridge: Cambridge University Press, 1986), and *Imperial Sudan. The Anglo-Egyptian Condominium, 1934–56* (Cambridge: Cambridge University Press, 1991). R.O. Collins, *Land Beyond the Rivers: The Southern Sudan, 1898–1918* (New Haven: Yale University Press, 1971), and *Shadows in the Grass: Britain in the Southern Sudan, 1918–1956* (New Haven: Yale University Press, 1983) provide an administrative history of British rule in the South. The great value of these studies lies in their description of the evolution of the bureaucratic institutions of the twentieth-century Sudanese state. Both authors focus on the personalities of imperial administration rather than the broader structural patterns of colonial rule. Neither systematically incorporates into their studies Sudanese sources concerning British rule; what they can say about the impact of Condominium rule on Sudanese societies is therefore limited.

The importance of policy, as opposed to personality, is powerfully asserted in L. Passmore Sanderson & N. Sanderson, *Education, Religion & Politics in Southern Sudan 1899–1964* (London: Ithaca Press, 1981). It is the most detailed account of any single aspect of British policy in the Sudan and is illuminating in what it reveals of both the racial attitudes which shaped educational policy, and the limited impact of the Christian churches on the southern Sudanese peoples prior to the first civil war.

Books which do draw significantly on indigenous sources and testimony concerning the Condominium period are: Talal Asad, *The*

Kababish Arabs. Power, Authority and Consent in a Nomadic Tribe (London: C. Hurst, 1970); Francis Deng, *The Man Called Deng Majok: A Biography of Power, Polygyny, and Change* (New Haven: Yale University Press, 1986); Wendy James *'Kwanim Pa: The Making of the Uduk People* (Oxford; Clarendon Press, 1979), and *The Listening Ebony: Moral Knowledge, Religion, and Power among the Uduk of Sudan*, (Oxford: Clarendon Press, 1988); D.H. Johnson, *Nuer Prophets*; and Sharon Hutchinson, *Nuer Dilemmas: Coping with Money, War and the State* (Berkeley: University of California Press, 1996). The anthropological studies, in particular, trace specific social and political changes from the late-colonial period to the present, and provide the foundation for further analyses of the impact of Condominium rule on the Sudanese.

Nationalism
The standard accounts of the Sudanese nationalist movement (Chapter 3) are written from the northern Sudanese perspective. Muddathir Abd al-Rahim, *Imperialism and Nationalism in the Sudan. A Study in Constitutional and Political Development, 1899–1956* (Oxford: Clarendon Press, 1969) presents the orthodox interpretation of a nationalism firmly rooted in Islam and Arabism. Mohamed Omer Beshir, *Revolution and Nationalism in the Sudan* (London: Rex Collings, 1974), is a more secularist view, though both are triumphalist presentations of nationalism. An influential dissenting view was presented by G. N. Sanderson, 'Sudanese nationalism and the independence of the Sudan', in M. Brett (ed.), *Northern Africa: Islam and Modernization* (London: Frank Cass, 1978). A recent generation of scholars, both Sudanese and expatriate, has begun a critical re-examination of the roots and nature of Sudanese nationalism: Hasan Abdin, *Early Sudanese Nationalism, 1919–1925* (Khartoum: Khartoum University Press, 1985); Mahasin Abdel Gadir Hag al Safi (ed.), *The Nationalist Movement in the Sudan* (Khartoum: Institute of African & Asian Studies, University of Khartoum, 1989); and University of Juba, *The Role of Southern Sudanese People in the Building of the Modern Sudan* (Khartoum: Arrow Commercial Printing Press, 1986). Yoshiko Kurita's extended study of Ali Abd al-Latif and the White Flag movement has the most far-reaching implications of all these newer works. In her contribution to Mahasin al-Safi (above), and in her full length Arabic biography, *'Ali 'Abd al-Latif wa Thawra 1924* ('Ali Abd al-Latif and the Revolution of 1924') (Cairo: Sudanese Studies Centre, 1997), she lays bare the racial tensions which split the Sudanese nationalists at the commencement of the movement in the 1920s. Against all of these can be set a critical re-evaluation of the Sudan's nationalists by Mansour Khalid (former minister under Nimairi and one of the few northern Sudanese members of the SPLM) in his *The Government They Deserve. The Role of the Elite in Sudan's Political Evolution* (London: KPI, 1990). He rejects the notion of an essentially Muslim and Arab national identity of the Sudan and criticizes the nationalist movement for its failure to embrace a truly nationalist ideology.

P. Woodward, *Condominium and Sudanese Nationalism* (London: Rex Collings, 1979) was written before the British Foreign Office files on Sudanese independence were fully released, but use of Sir James

Robertson's papers provides the official view of the Sudan administration as a counterpoint to nationalist views. It is, on the whole, a benign view of the nationalist parties. By far the most successful and comprehensive analysis of the social and economic base of northern Sudanese politics is T. Niblock, *Class and Power in Sudan. The Dynamics of Sudanese Politics, 1898–1985* (London: Macmillan, 1987). A selection of official British government documents concerning the independence of the Sudan can be found in the British Documents on the End of Empire Project (BDEEP), series B, vol 5 (two parts), D.H. Johnson (ed.), *Sudan*, (London: The Stationery Office, 1998).

The first civil war
For Sudanese perspectives on the first civil war (Chapter 3), the Report of the Commission of Enquiry, *Southern Sudan Disturbances, August 1955* (Khartoum: McCorquedale, 1956) is still the only general description of the events surrounding the 1955 Equatorial Corps mutiny (though interesting comments concerning the writing of this report can be found in Woodward, *Condominium and Nationalism*, and BDEEP, *Sudan*, both above). The southern Sudanese case was stated by a number of exile politicians, the first being J. Oduho & W. Deng, *The Problem of the Southern Sudan* (London: Oxford University Press for the Institute of Race Relations, 1963); and the most complete being O. Albino, *The Sudan. A Southern Viewpoint* (London: Oxford University Press, 1970). Contemporary northern Sudanese arguments were put forward by the journalist Beshir Mohammed Said, *The Sudan. Crossroads of Africa* (London: Bodley Head, 1965); and by the political scientist Mohamed Omer Beshir in *The Southern Sudan, Background to Conflict* (London: C. Hurst, 1968), and *The Southern Sudan: From Conflict to Peace* (London, 1975), the latter book being more of an account of the author's personal involvement in the peace process, downplaying what is universally acknowledged as the critical role played by the World Council of Churches in securing a negotiated settlement.

Scholarly discussions of various aspects of the war by southern Sudanese academics include: D.A. Wai, *The African-Arab Conflict in the Sudan* (NY: Africana Publishing Co., 1981); E.N. Wakoson, 'The southern Sudan: the political leadership of the Anya-Nya movement', in H. Dickinson (ed.), *Post-Independence Sudan* (Edinburgh: Centre of African Studies, 1980), and 'The origin and development of the Anya-Nya movement, 1955–72', in M.O. Beshir (ed.), *Southern Sudan: Regionalism & Religion* (Khartoum: Graduate College, University of Khartoum, 1984). The results of a colloquium of mainly Sudanese scholars (both northern and southern) examining general aspects of problems of conflict and national integration were published in Sayyid H. Hurreiz and Elfatih A. Abdel Salam (eds), *Ethnicity, Conflict and National Integration in the Sudan* (Khartoum: Institute of African & Asian Studies, University of Khartoum, 1989).

Nimairi
The Nimairi period (Chapters 3–5) is the subject of a number of personal accounts by leading Sudanese of the time. The scholar-diplomat, Francis

M. Deng, produced two optimistic statements during the early years of the Addis Ababa peace: *Dynamics of Identification: A Basis for National Integration in the Sudan* (Khartoum: Khartoum University Press, 1973), and *Africans of Two Worlds: The Dinka in Afro-Arab Sudan* (New Haven: Yale University Press, 1978). A more sombre and pessimistic analysis followed in *War of Visions: Conflict of Identities in the Sudan* (Washington DC: The Brookings Institution, 1995). Equally disillusioned testimony by former members of Nimairi's governments include: Bona Malwal, *People & Power in Sudan: The Struggle for National Stability* (London: Ithaca Press, 1981), and *The Sudan: A Second Challenge to Nationhood* (NY: Thornton Books, 1985); Mansour Khalid, *Nimeiri and the Revolution of Dis-May* (London: KPI, 1985), and *The Government They Deserve*; and Abel Alier, *Southern Sudan: Too Many Agreements Dishonoured* (Exeter: Ithaca Press, 1990). Some critical studies by southern Sudanese scholars can be found in: Mom K.N. Arou & B. Yongo-Bure (eds), *North-South Relations in the Sudan Since the Addis Ababa Agreement* (Khartoum: Institute of African & Asian Studies, University of Khartoum, 1988); E.N. Wakoson, 'The politics of Southern self-government 1972–83', in M.W. Daly & A.A. Sikainga (eds), *Civil War in the Sudan* (London: British Academic Press, 1993); and B. Yongo-Bure, 'The underdevelopment of the southern Sudan since Independence', ibid. Expatriate analyses include: N. Kasfir, 'Southern Sudanese politics since the Addis Ababa Agreement', *African Affairs* 76 (1977); T. Niblock, *Class and Power in Sudan*, and 'Numayri's fall: the economic base', in Abd al-Rahim, Badal, Hardallo & Woodward (eds), *Sudan Since Independence* (Aldershot: Gower, 1986); D.H. Johnson, *The Southern Sudan*, and 'North-South issues', in P. Woodward (ed.), *Sudan After Nimeiri* (London: Routledge, 1991).

French and French-based scholars have also recently begun to analyse modern Sudanese history, especially the post-independence period, and are producing a new perspective largely freed from Anglo-Sudanese preoccupations with the Condominium. Some of their work can be found in the edited collections of M. Lavergne (ed.), *Le Soudan contemporain* (Paris: Karthala, 1989), and H. Bleuchot, C. Delmet & D. Hopwood (eds), *Sudan: History, identity, ideology/Histoire, identités, idéologies* (Reading: Ithaca Press, 1991).

Development issues
The role of development in the Sudan (Chapters 4 & 10) has been the subject of a number of sophisticated studies and analyses. The anthropologist and former Oxfam country representative in the Sudan, Mark Duffield, has produced a number of stimulating and perceptive critiques of the politics of development in the Sudan, two of his most important early published papers being, *Sudan at the Crossroads: From Emergency Preparedness to Social Security*, Institute of Development Studies, University of Sussex (May 1990), and 'Famine, conflict and the internationalization of public welfare', in M. Doornbos, *et al.* (eds), *Beyond the Conflict in the Horn: The Prospects for Peace, Recovery and Development in Ethiopia, Somalia, Eritrea and Sudan* (London: James Currey, 1991). He has expanded on these in his pessimistic analysis of the role of development in

international insecurity, *Global Governance and the New Wars: The Merging of Development and Security* (London/NY: Zed Books, 2001). Another influential analysis of the political economy of famine in the early 1980s is Jay O'Brien, 'Sowing the seeds of famine: the political economy of food deficits in Sudan', in Peter Lawrence (ed.), *World Recession and the Food Crisis in Africa* (London: James Currey, 1986). An important contribution to the understanding of the new phenomenon of Islamic banking is E. Shaaeldin & R. Brown, 'Towards an Understanding of Islamic Banking in the Sudan: The case of the Faisal Islamic bank', in T. Barnett & A. Abdel Karim (eds), *Sudan: State, Capital and Transformation* (London: Croom Helm, 1988). The most comprehensive discussion so far of all aspects of the Jonglei Canal can be found in P. Howell, M. Lock & S. Cobb (eds), *The Jonglei Canal. Impact and Opportunity* (Cambridge: Cambridge University Press, 1988). T. Tvedt, *Angels of Mercy or Development Diplomats? NGOs and Foreign Aid* (Oxford: James Currey, 1998) focuses on pre-war NGO involvement in the southern Sudan as an example of a global shift of international aid and Third World service provision into the hands of NGOs.

Law

Law and Islam (Chapters 4, 6, 9 & 11) are related subjects which received little scholarly attention in general accounts of the Sudan prior to the 1980s. An early sympathetic survey of Islamic law in the Sudan can be found in Carolyn Fluehr-Lobban, *Islamic Law and Society in Sudan* (London: Frank Cass, 1987). A salutary warning about the clash between Islamic and customary law was published by the Dinka jurist, John Wuol Makec, *The Customary Law of the Dinka People of Sudan in Comparison with Aspects of Western & Islamic Laws* (London: Afroworld Publishing, 1988). Arguments in favour of Islamic reform in the Sudan were presented in Abd el-Wahab al-Affendi, *Tourabi's Revolution: Islam and Power in Sudan* (London, 1991). For critical discussions of Islamic law in the Sudan see: J.F. Rycx, 'The Islamisation of law as a political stake in Sudan', in P. Woodward (ed.), *Sudan After Nimeiri*; P.N. Kok, *Governance & Conflict in the Sudan, 1985–1995: Analysis, Evaluation & Documentation* (Hamburg: Deutsches Orient-Institut, 1996) and 'Conflict over laws in the Sudan: "From pluralism to monolithicism"', in Bleuchot, Delmet & Hopwood (eds), *Sudan: History, Identity, Ideology* ; T. Niblock, 'Islamic movements and Sudan's political coherence', ibid; H. Bleuchot, *Les Cultures Contre l'Homme? Essai d'Anthropologie Historique du Droit Pénal Soudanais* (Aix: Presses Universitaires d'Aix Marseille, 1994); R. Marchal, *Eléments d'une sociologie du Front national islamique soudanais'*, Les études du CERI no 5 (Paris, September 1995); R.S. O'Fahey, 'The past in the present? The issue of sharia in the Sudan', in H.B. Hansen & M. Twaddle (eds), *Religion & Politics in East Africa* (London/Athens OH/Nairobi/Kampala: James Currey/Ohio University Press/EAEP/Fountain Publishers, 1995); and Abdel Salam Sidahmed, *Politics and Islam in Contemporary Sudan* (London: Curzon, 1997). Ann Lesch's *Sudan: Contested National Identities* (Bloomington/ Oxford: Indiana University Press/James Currey, 1998) provides excellent, clear summaries of the positions of various parties on Islamic law, the secular state and citizenship rights. Steven

Wöndu & Ann Lesch, *Battle for Peace in Sudan: An Analysis of the Abuja Conferences 1992–1993* (Lanham MD: University Press of America, 2000) analyses the positions taken on these issues by the government and the Southern factions during formal peace talks.

The second civil war
Information regarding current events (Chapters 4–9) inevitably must rely on journalism, the reliability of which varies with the journalist and the journal. *Africa Confidential* has offered a systematic, and usually informed interest in events throughout the Sudan since the 1960s. The *BBC Summary of World Broadcasts*, (Part 4: Middle East, Africa, Latin America) regularly offers transcripts of radio broadcasts from the region, and has been a regular source of broadcasts from the Sudan government and the opposition. The *Indian Ocean Newsletter* includes articles dealing with current events in the Sudan, Ethiopia and Eritrea. Extracts (in English) from the Arabic press, official press releases, and other news sources are regularly published (usually without comment) in the *Horn of Africa Bulletin* (Uppsala) and *Sudan Update* (London & Hebden Bridge). The great difficulty with these news digests is that false or erroneous stories cannot be checked, nor are they always later corrected. Prior to the banning of the free press in the Sudan in 1989 *The Sudan Times* was one of the most widely read Sudanese newspapers and its editor (Bona Malwal) produced the *Sudan Democratic Gazette* from England between 1990 and 2001. Government publications include *Sudanow* (Khartoum) and *Sudan News* (London). Field reports by scholars and relief personnel working in the region often appear in *Disasters*, which thus gives some non-political counter-balance to the political reporting found elsewhere.

The internet now provides vastly increased access to instant, if unverifiable, news, press releases, chat and spin. The most comprehensive website dedicated to the Sudan is Sudan.Net (http//www.Sudan.net), with links to various news services in English, Arabic and French, and to the websites of the government and opposition parties and factions. European organizations closely associated with the government are the London-based Sudan Foundation, run by a former RENAMO lobbyist, and the EU-Sudan Forum, both of which use the internet to post a pro-government response to events. The Sudanese opposition has yet to generate or to fund similar lobby organizations, but various humanitarian agencies and independent activists keep up their own circulation of news and opinions through dedicated email address lists. With politicians constructing personal websites, each new faction posting their own national constitutions on the web, and chat rooms repeating every rumour, 'virtual reality' has taken on a new meaning in Sudanese politics.

A few journalists have recorded fleeting impressions of the war, focusing mainly on the international relief effort and relying on expatriate sources. One book that goes beyond the surface, providing a remarkably intimate portrait of some Sudanese experiences of the war, relying heavily on Sudanese testimony is paradoxically about a foreign relief worker, Deborah Scroggins, *Emma's War: Love, Betrayal & Death in the Sudan* (NY: Pantheon Books, 2002).

There has been far more coverage of insurgents in this war than in the last (Chapters 5–9). Important early statements outlining the SPLM's position can be found in: Sudan People's Liberation Movement, *Manifesto*, 31 July, 1983 and John Garang, *The Call for Democracy in Sudan*, edited and introduced by Mansour Khalid (London: KPI, 1992). The outcome of the SPLM/SPLA's first national convention was published in *A Major Watershed. SPLM/SPLA First National Convention. Resolutions, Appointments and Protocol* (Chukudum, March/April 1994). This can be compared with the SSIM/A manifesto, charter and resolutions produced at the Founding Convention of the South Sudan Independence Movement (Akobo, 26 September to 10 October 1994). An outline of the early development of the SPLA is given in D.H. Johnson & G. Prunier, 'The foundation and expansion of the SPLA', in Daly & Sikainga (eds), *The Civil War in the Sudan*. A disenchanted account of the SPLA-split can be found in Peter Adwok Nyaba, *The Politics of Liberation in South Sudan: An Insider's View*, (Kampala: Fountain Publishers, 1997), and other aspects of the split are briefly outlined in D.H. Johnson, 'The Sudan People's Liberation Army and the problem of factionalism', in C. Clapham (ed.), *African Guerrillas* (Oxford/Bloomington/Kampala: James Currey/Indiana University Press/Fountain Publishers, 1998).

Descriptions of specific regional aspects of the war can be found in Johnson, *Nuer Prophets*; Hutchinson, *Nuer Dilemmas*; and in a valuable collection of papers based on field observations by anthropologists, K. Fukui & J. Markakis (eds), *Ethnicity and Conflict in the Horn of Africa* (London/Athens OH: James Currey/Ohio University Press, 1994). Two of the most useful chapters are Eisei Kurimoto, 'Civil war and regional conflicts: the Pari and their neighbours in south-eastern Sudan', and Wendy James, 'War and "ethnic visibility": the Uduk on the Sudan-Ethiopia border'. Aspects of the conflict in Darfur can be found in G. Prunier, 'Ecologie, structures ethniques et conflits politiques au Dar Fur', Bleuchot, Delmet & Hopwood (eds), *Sudan: History, Identity, Ideology*; and Sharif Harir, '"Arab belt" versus "African belt": ethno-political conflict in Dar Fur and the regional cultural factors', in Sharif Harir & T. Tvedt (eds), *Short-Cut to Decay: the Case of the Sudan* (Uppsala: Nordiska Afrikainistitutet, 1994). The eastern Sudan is not so well studied, but a new Franco-Sudanese collection analyzing issues relevant to the war has been edited by Catherine Miller, *Land, Ethnicity and Political Legitimacy in Eastern Sudan* (Lawrenceville: Red Sea Press, 2002).

After 1992 the main factions of the SPLA intermittently issued their own newsletters and journals from Nairobi: the SPLA's *SPLA/SPLM Update* (weekly) and *NewSudan* (bi-monthly), and the SPLA-United's *Southern Sudan Vision* (monthly). Evans-Pritchard's dictum (learned in Zandeland during the 1920s) that research advances when informants fall out with each other has been demonstrated by the SPLA factions. Their publications are essentially propaganda instruments, but they have also reproduced facsimiles and transcripts of each other's intercepted and captured messages, thus providing some insight into the internal workings of the rival movements which would otherwise have remained hidden. After the demise of *Southern Sudan Vision*, the short-lived,

London-based *Southern Sudan Bulletin* provided a forum for Southerners critical of Garang's leadership. *Nafir. The Newsletter of the Nuba Mountains, Sudan* was dedicated to information specifically about the Nuba Mountains. In its short publication life it departed from the factional newsletters in that, while essentially sympathetic to the SPLA, it corrected erroneous news items and provided a forum for open debate about the future of the Nuba. It has recently been succeeded by *Nuba Vision*, under the same editor.

Human rights
Human rights and the conduct of war (Chapters 5–10) are, again, topics which have received far more coverage during the current war than in the first war. The international interest in human rights issues and abuses in the Sudan came rather belatedly, and can be dated to the publication of Ushari Ahmad Mahmud & Suleyman Ali Baldo, *Al Diein Massacre – Slavery in the Sudan* (Khartoum, 1987). Sudanese observers and commentators have continued since that time, but mainly publishing abroad, for instance in the Sudan Human Rights Organization's *Sudan Human Rights Voice*. Abdullahi A. An-Na'im & Peter N. Kok, *Fundamentalism and Militarism: A Report on the Root Causes of Human Rights Violations in the Sudan*, The Fund for Peace (February, 1991), and Jok Madut Jok, *War and Slavery in Sudan* continue the growing tradition of Sudanese scholarly investigation into fundamental human rights issues.

International agencies have been particularly active in monitoring and reporting on human rights since the 1990s. Their reports have come out with growing frequency, including a number of specific case studies with a wealth of corroborated detail and internal testimony which would have been unobtainable in the 1960s. An updated and expanded Minority Rights Group report (incorporating the 1988 report) was edited by Peter Verney, *Sudan: Conflict and Minorities*, Minority Rights Group International, 95/3 (London, August, 1995). The French Comité de Vigilance pour les Droits de l'Homme et les Libertés au Soudan issues a bimonthly *Vigilance Soudan* in French, but have recently suspended their English language quarterly edition. Amnesty International has followed its mandate of monitoring illegal detention, torture and executions since 1985 with a number of detailed reports. Africa Watch took a broader definition of human rights and entered the field with: *Denying 'The Honor of Living'. Sudan. A Human Rights Disaster* (NY/Washington DC, March 1990), and *Evil Days. 30 Years of War and Famine in Ethiopia* (NY/Washington DC, September 1991). After being reabsorbed into Human Rights Watch its reports have become slightly more legalistic: *Civilian Devastation. Abuses by All Parties in the War in Southern Sudan* (NY/Washington DC, 1994); *Children of Sudan. Slaves, Street Children and Child Soldiers* (NY/Washington DC/London/Brussels, 1995); and *Behind the Red Line: Political Repression in Sudan* (NY/Washington DC/London/Brussels, 1996).

The 'break-away' agency, African Rights defined its differences with Human Rights Watch by continuing a more sceptical line towards international agencies, while pursuing as wide a mandate in the definition of human rights. Since 1994 it has released a series of discussion papers on humanitarianism and civil society in the Sudan, as well as longer, more detailed reports, such as *Sudan's Invisible Citizens. The Policy of Abuse against Displaced People in the North* (London, February 1995) and, the most impressive of all for its close analysis of internal data, *Facing Genocide: the Nuba of Sudan* (London, July 1995). Other publications by Alex de Waal, a founding director of African Rights are: *War in Sudan. An Analysis of Conflict,* Peace in Sudan Group (London, June 1990), and 'Some comments on militias in contemporary Sudan', in Bleuchot, Delmet & Hopwood (eds), *Sudan: History, Identity, Ideology.* Since forming the London-based Justice Africa, Alex de Waal has fostered open discussions of human rights issues. *The Phoenix State: Civil Society and the Future of Sudan,* A.H. Abdel Salam & Alex de Waal (eds) (Lawrenceville NJ/Asmara: Red Sea Press, 2001) records the outcome of a public forum in Kampala of Northern and Southern Sudanese engaged in outlining the future of human rights and civil society in the Sudan.

Oil and the war have attracted increasing attention, especially since the outbreak of fighting in the oilfields (Chapters 8 & 10). Oil as an issue was discussed before these recent developments by the Sudanese scholars R.K. Badal, 'Oil and regional sentiment in the South', in Abd al-Rahim, *et al* (eds), *Sudan Since Independence*; and Peter Nyot Kok, 'Adding fuel to the conflict: oil, war and peace in the Sudan', in Martin Doornbos, *et al* (eds), *Beyond Conflict in the Horn.* The most detailed human rights reports have been: Peter Verney, *Raising the Stakes: Oil and Conflict in Sudan* (Hebden Bridge: Sudan Update, 2000); Amnesty International, *Sudan: The Human Price of Oil* (2000); John Harker, *Human Security in Sudan: The Report of a Canadian Assessment Mission* (Ottawa: Ministry of Foreign Affairs, 2000); Christian Aid, *The Scorched Earth: Oil and War in Sudan* (London: Christian Aid, 2001); Canadian Sudan Inter-Agency Reference Group (SIARG), *Report of an Investigation into Oil Development, Conflict and Displacement in Western Upper Nile, Sudan* (Ottawa, 2002); Human Rights Watch, *Sudan, Oil, and Human Rights Abuses* (NY/Washington, DC, forthcoming), the latter giving a very detailed description of fighting in the oilfields, and the determinedly blinkered actions of the main international oil companies currently involved in the Sudan.

Relief issues
Some of the more analytical (and critical) discussions of relief issues in the Sudan (Chapter 10) can be found in: Duffield, *Sudan at the Crossroads* (1990); Alex de Waal, 'Starving out the South, 1984–9', in Daly & Sikainga (eds), *Civil War in Sudan*; David Keen, *The Benefits of Famine: A Political Economy of Famine and Relief in Southwestern Sudan, 1983–1989* (Princeton: Princeton University Press, 1994); Sharif Harir & Terje Tvedt (eds), *Short-Cut to Decay. The Case of the Sudan* (Uppsala: Nordiska Africainistitutet, 1994); T. Allen (ed.), *In Search of Cool Ground. Displacement & Homecoming in Northeast Africa* (London: James Currey, 1996); Alex de Waal, *Famine Crimes* (Oxford/Bloomington: James Currey/Indiana University Press, 1997); African Rights, *Food and Power in Sudan: A Critique of Humanitarianism* (London: African Rights, 1997);

Human Rights Watch, *Famine in Sudan, 1998: The Human Rights Causes* (NY/Washington DC/London/Brussels, 1999); and Geoff Loane & Tanja Schümer (eds), *The Wider Impact of Humanitarian Assistance: The Case of Sudan and the Implications for European Union Policy* (Baden-Baden: SWP-Conflict Prevention Network, 2000).

The UN relief effort in the Sudan, especially Operation Lifeline Sudan, is the subject of a growing, if variable literature. Larry Minear, *Humanitarianism Under Siege. A Critical Review of Operation Lifeline Sudan* (Trenton NJ: Red Sea Press, 1991) is a UNICEF-commissioned evaluation of the first year of OLS. While acknowledging some important critical questions about the operation, it is, ultimately, evasive in its answers. It was compressed and incorporated in Francis Deng and Larry Minear, *The Challenges of Famine Relief. Emergency Operations in the Sudan* (Washington DC: Brookings Institution, 1992), a book which deals also with the famine of 1983–6 and includes additional material on the split in the SPLA. Neither of these books get beneath the surface of the issues they address and are essentially anecdotal in their presentation of data. J. Millard Burr and Robert O. Collins, *Requiem for the Sudan. War, Drought, & Disaster Relief on the Nile* (Boulder CO: Westview Press, 1995) is a more ambitious attempt to chronicle the civil war, and presents the efforts of expatriate relief agencies in heroic terms. None of these studies surpasses Keen's *Benefits of Famine*. By counterpointing official documents with field-based testimony he calls into question the circumscribed horizons, self-congratulatory reports and doubtful statistics frequently produced by relief agencies, on which, for instance, Burr and Collins rely.

A general review of OLS was commissioned by the UN Department of Humanitarian Affairs only in 1996. The critique presented in Ataul Karim, *et al*, *Operation Lifeline Sudan. A Review* (Geneva: UN Department of Humanitarian Affairs, 1996) is based on internal documentation and extensive interviews. A summary of some of its arguments can be found in Joanna Macrae, Mark Bradbury, Susanne Jaspars, Mark Duffield & Douglas Johnson, 'Conflict, the continuum and chronic emergencies: a critical analysis of the scope for linking relief, rehabilitation and development planning in Sudan', *Disasters* 21/3 (1997). Other independent bodies have issued their own reports about OLS's vicissitudes and failures, notably African Rights, *Food and Power in Sudan*, and Human Rights Watch, *Famine in Sudan, 1998*. The Sudan case has entered into the general critique of international aid and relief operations, most notably by de Waal, *Famine Crimes*, John Prendergast, *Crisis Response: Humanitarian Band-Aids in Sudan and Somalia* (London/Chicago: Pluto Press, 1997), and Duffield, *Global Governance and the New Wars*.

The growing body of 'grey literature' includes periodic situation reports and general assessments which contain valuable information about conditions in specific areas of the southern Sudan affected by the war. For a full list of those consulted see the bibliography of Karim *et al*, *Operation Lifeline Sudan. A Review*. Another, earlier, useful evaluation of an international relief effort was produced by Mark Duffield, Helen

Young, John Ryle & Ian Henderson, *Sudan Emergency Operations Consortium (SEOC): A Review* (Birmingham, February 1995).

Between 1990 and 1993 some descriptive and authoritative reports were produced by United Nations agencies in OLS by field workers with previous experience in the Sudan, one of the most important general overviews being United Nations, Lifeline Sudan, *An Investigation into Production Capability in the Rural Southern Sudan. A Report on Food Sources and Needs* (Nairobi, June 1990), to which I contributed. A revealing picture of local conditions in the southern Sudan can often be found in the reports of some NGOs, such as ACORD, Oxfam-UK/I, or SCF-UK who have tended to keep their staff in the field longer than UN agencies do (security permitting) and who spend more time developing local county profiles. With the departure of reporting personnel who had long experience either in the Sudan or with UN/OLS field operations, there has been a noticeable decline in the quality of information and analysis presented in reports since 1993. With some notable exceptions, later assessments have not built effectively on the foundation of accumulated data produced by earlier field reports. Despite an increased concern with quantifiable statistics, presented in sophisticated computer-generated graphs and charts, recent reports tend to be less reliable in their collection and analysis of data, mainly because data is currently gathered in a succession of 'rapid rural appraisal' visits rather than from long-term observation. Statistics gathered in this fashion are notoriously unreliable and difficult to use, but most who cite them nowadays do so without caution. With numerous agencies presently in the field whose fundraising is linked to numbers of starving fed or slaves redeemed, there is a natural impetus towards inflation. In this respect we have returned to the situation at the turn of the nineteenth and twentieth centuries, where exaggerated estimates of population displacement and decline were entered into the historical record as reliable fact.

Peace negotiations, violations, Darfur, since 2003

Texts of the protocols from the peace negotiations are posted on the IGAD website (www.igad.org/pressroom/sudpress.html). IRIN (UN Office for the Coordination of Humanitarian Affairs) has issued reports on recent fighting in other parts of the Sudan: 'Sudan: fighting escalating in Shilluk kingdom' (19 March 2004); 'Sudan: the neglected east' (24 March 2004); 'Sudan: thousands displaced by militias into Malakal' (14 April 2004) (www.irinnews.org). Government action in Shilluk country in 2004 was reported on by the Civilian Protection Monitoring Team, *Final Report of Investigation No. 36: Fighting in The Shilluk Kingdom and Killing of Civilians*, posted on www.cpmtsudan.org, along with the Sudan government's response. The most detailed reports on Darfur are: Amnesty International, *Sudan: Empty Promises? Human Rights Violations in Government-controlled Areas* (16 July 2003), and *Darfur: Too Many People Killed Over No Reason* (3 February 2004); IRIN, 'Sudan: the escalating crisis in Darfur' (31 December 2003), and 'Sudan: Special report II: Chad and the Darfur conflict' (16 February 2004); International Crisis Group, *Darfur Rising: Sudan's New Crisis* (25 March 2004); Human Rights Watch, *Darfur in Flames: Atrocities in Western Sudan* (2 April 2004). Other useful websites include, Sudan Tribune at www.sudantribune.com, the official Sudan News Agency (Suna) at www.fananews.com/Sudan/larchive.htm, and the SPLM at www.splmtoday.com.

Chronology
of Events

1972

SSU established as the only legal party in the Sudan (*Jan*).
Negotiations between government & SSLM in Addis Ababa (*16–27 Feb*) lead to peace agreement; Addis Ababa Agreement ratified in Khartoum by Nimairi & Lagu (*2 March*) and embodied in the Regional Self-Government Act (*3 March*); Southern Region established under an interim government led by former Minister of Southern Affairs, and leader of the government negotiating team, Abel Alier.
Diplomatic relations with the US resume.
Constituent Assembly elected (*Oct*).

1973

Sudan government and Arab Fund for Economic & Social Development begin a twenty-five-year Basic Programme for Agricultural Development in the Sudan.
Permanent Constitution, incorporating the Addis Ababa Agreement, approved by Nimairi (*8 May*).
First elections to the Southern Regional Assembly (*Oct*); SSU nominates Abel Alier as its official candidate for President of the HEC, forestalling the nomination of other candidates.

1974

Plan for economic & political integration with Egypt signed (*12 Feb*).
Plans for the Jonglei Canal announced; HEC agrees 'not to oppose' them; public demonstrations against the plans in Juba end in shooting of demonstrators, and the arrest or flight of Regional Assemblymen opposed to the canal (*April*).
General election to the People's Assembly in Khartoum (*May*).
Ex-Anyanya battalion in Juba refuse to move into new barracks and beat their commander, Peter Cyrillo.

1975

Mutiny of ex-Anyanya troops in Akobo; mutineers kill Southern commander and flee to Ethiopia; become nucleus of a revived Anyanya, eventually known as Anyanya-2 (*March*).
Attempted coup against Nimairi by Islamist officers in the army (*5 Sept*).

1976

Mutiny of ex-Anyanya in Wau, killing senior ex-Anyanya officers in the army (*Feb*).
Sadiq al-Mahdi's Libyan-backed coup fails after fighting in the streets of Khartoum, in which Southern troops play a prominent role in crushing the coup (*2 July*); defence agreement between Egypt and Sudan (*July*).

1977

Mutiny of ex-Anyanya in Juba, with failed attempt to take airport (*6 Feb*).
National Reconciliation between Nimairi, Sadiq al-Mahdi, Hassan al-Turabi, and other exiled opposition politicians (*July*); Bona Malwal resigns as Minister of Information in central government in protest.
Elections in Southern Region (*Dec–Feb*).

1978

Nimairi requests Alier not to stand for re-election and Lagu is elected President of the HEC (*Feb*).
Elections to People's Assembly (*Feb*), re-emergence of Umma, DUP and Islamic Charter Front (Muslim Brothers) in electoral politics; Hassan al-Turabi becomes Attorney General.
Opening of the first Islamic banks in Khartoum.
Sudan unable to pay external debts; US helps to reschedule debt repayment and further IMF loans.
Nimairi supports Camp David agreement between Egypt & Israel.

1979

Lagu attempts to dismiss the Speaker & Deputy Speaker of the Regional Assembly and replace them with his own candidates; conflict between Lagu and judiciary leads to temporary shutting down of courts throughout the Southern Region.
Fall of Idi Amin in Uganda; return of southern Sudanese formerly working in Uganda.
Sudan agrees to IMF's conditions for loans and cuts public expenditure.
Oil discovery in Upper Nile & southern Kordofan by Chevron confirmed.

1980

Nimairi dissolves Southern Regional Assembly and calls for new elections (*Feb–May*); Alier elected President of the HEC with Nimairi's support (*June*).
Anyanya-2 based in Ethiopia begin hit-and-run attacks inside Upper Nile Province.
National Assembly attempts to redraw the boundaries of the Southern Region, transferring the oilfields to the North (*Nov*).

1981

Five new regions in the North, created by the Regional Government Act, 1980, come into being; other programmes of administrative devolution, are covered in the Local Government Act, 1981. Dispute between the central & regional governments over the siting of the oil refinery.
Disturbances in Darfur: some two million Chadian refugees enter the country following the Libyan invasion of Chad; Darfur protests against the appointment of a non-Darfuri governor lead to the appointment of a Fur, Ibrahim Diraij, as governor.
March Regional Assembly debates and rejects proposals to divide the South.
US government announces $100 million in military & economic aid for Sudan.
Sept Beginning of *kasha* – the rounding up and deportation of 'jobless and vagrants' in Khartoum, the main targets being Southern & Western (Nuba) Sudanese men; justified by government as a means of ridding the Three Towns of an excessive, unproductive population, and seen by most Southerners as racially inspired; *kasha* is carried out periodically over the next few years.
Oct Nimairi dissolves the National & Regional Assemblies (*5 Oct*) and calls for new elections; appoints an interim regional government (led by soldiers) to oversee elections in the South and to conduct a referendum on redivision of the South.

Nov Following the government's introduction of stringent economic measures on the recommendation of the IMF, there are riots in Khartoum; the cabinet and the SSU executive urge Nimairi to resign; he dismisses the cabinet & the executive (*9 Nov*).

A Council for the Unity of the Southern Sudan is formed, drawn from all provinces of the Southern Region, questioning the constitutionality of Nimairi's dismissal of the Regional Assembly and his proposal for the division of the South before the matter has been taken up by the National Assembly.

1982

Street brawling in Juba between rival Divisionist & anti-Divisionist gangs; Equatorian politicians urge local Mundari to take a leading role in fights against Dinka.

Jan The executive committee of the Council for the Unity of the Southern Sudan is arrested on orders of the President (*4 Jan*); anti-Divisionist candidates elected to the National Assembly from the Southern region outnumber pro-Divisionist candidates by 2 to 1.

March Nimairi announces that there will be no referendum in the South and that elections to the Regional Assembly will take place within the context of a united Southern Region; administrative decentralization is to be implemented under the Local Government Act, 1981.

April Elections to the Regional Assembly in the South; pro-Divisionists form the majority in Eastern & Western Equatoria, but pro-Unionists are elected by a substantial majority in the other four provinces.

July Tembura is elected president of the HEC in Juba on a platform of administrative reform and decentralization; appoints Mundari Commissioner of Eastern Equatoria, who bulldozes Dinka squatter camps in Juba and breaks the Dinka control over the Juba meat market, replacing them with Mundari.

Oct Integration Charter between Egypt & Sudan is signed; this meets widespread opposition and some demonstrations in the Southern Region; many members of the HEC in Juba oppose it, but it receives the public support of the president of the HEC, and of Joseph Lagu, now Second Vice-President of the Republic; the charter, which allows Egyptian citizens to purchase land in Sudan, revives fears of Egyptian colonization along the Jonglei canal.

Nov–Dec Khartoum supports an Iraqi recruiting drive in the Southern Sudan to get volunteers to fight against Iran; this meets with little response in the South, despite the high financial incentives offered; the central government announces the recruitment of 500 Southern Sudanese 'volunteers' in Khartoum.

Dec President Nimairi asks the HEC to recommend to him the further division of the South; the HEC cannot agree on the issue and takes no action; students at Rumbek Senior Secondary School demonstrate in front of Nimairi against the Integration Charter and re-division; Nimairi orders the school closed, some students and teachers are arrested; students begin to leave for Ethiopia to join Anyanya-2; some half-dozen prominent pro-Unity Southern politicians are arrested.

Battalion 110 stationed at Aweil, containing large numbers of ex-Anyanya troops, is ordered to Darfur and leaves under pressure.

1983

Jan–Feb Battalion 105 stationed at Bor, composed of some 200 ex-Anyanya troops, is ordered to hand in their arms prior to being transferred to the North; they refuse; 1000 Northern troops are sent to reinforce the Southern Command.

The Regional Congress of the SSU meeting in Juba votes against re-division and for the continued unity of the South.

March Five Dinka leaders from Abyei are arrested for advocating a plebiscite to decide whether the district should join the Southern Region.

Dhol Acuil (Vice President of the HEC) & Matthew Obur (Speaker of the Regional Assembly), are arrested in Khartoum after warning Nimairi at a public meeting against dividing the South (*3 March*).

April–May Presidential referendum to re-elect Nimairi (unopposed) to a third term is carried out; the policies on which he is standing for re-election (including further decentralization) are not publicly discussed in the South; low voter turn out in the South and many parts of the North.

May Defections from the police & army to Anyanya-2 increase.

After the presidential referendum, units of battalion 105 are attacked at Bor & Pibor (*16 May*); those at Bor (under Kerubino Kuanyin Bol) repel the army advance; on *17 May* the battalion units at Bor, Pibor & Pochalla withdraw into the bush and head for Ethiopia.

Nimairi announces that the Southern Region is to be abolished and replaced by 3 smaller regions (*24 May*); two weeks prior to this announcement Bona Malwal, another pro-unity Southern leader, is detained in Khartoum.

June Nimairi's Republican Order 1 dissolves the Southern regional government, repeals specific clauses of the Regional Self-Government Act, 1972, sets up three regional governments in Bahr al-Ghazal, Upper Nile & Equatoria, and announces the appointment of the three regional governors and their cabinets (*5 June*).

Ex-Anyanya in battalion 104 at Ayod under William Nyuon Bany repel an attack from Malakal and escape to Ethiopia (*6 June*); mutinies follow in Waat, Rumbek & Nzara, with desertions reported from Malakal, Fangak, Nasir, Bentiu, Wau, Aweil, Torit & Kapoeta.

July Boma incident: a group of American missionaries are taken hostage by a guerrilla group led by Lukurnyang Lado at Boma; the Sudanese army (with American military assistance) attacks Boma with helicopter gunships and the hostages are rescued.

Formation of the SPLM & SPLA in Ethiopia; issue of manifesto.

Sept National Assembly passes a series of laws based on *shari‘a*; the central government instructs the three southern regional assemblies not to discuss these laws.

Split inside the SPLA between Gai Tut & Garang; Gai Tut and his troops escape into the Sudan when the Ethiopian army and the SPLA attempt to disarm them.

1984

Small scale engagements throughout many parts of Upper Nile & Bahr al-Ghazal; SPLA confines itself to ambushes or overrunning and then withdrawing from police and army outposts.

Tension rises in the Nuba Mts as an envoy from the Misiriyya tours Baqqara areas making preparations for operations against the Nuba; farmers in Jebel Haiban are harassed and murdered resisting encroachments of new commercial land schemes; Yusif Kuwa joins the SPLA.

April Nimairi declares a state of emergency (*29 April*).

May Conflict between SPLA & Anyanya-2 in Upper Nile grows: Samuel Gai Tut is killed by Kerubino's troops; William Abdallah Cuol kills Akwot Atem and takes over command of Anyanya-2; William Abdallah Cuol attacks and kills nearly 3000 SPLA recruits in Fangak on their way to Ethiopia; the governor of Upper Nile, D.K. Matthews, brings the Anyanya-2 over to government; SPLA begins retaliation against Anyanya-2, attacking Lou & Jikany Nuer villages near border.

July Nimairi introduces amendments to Islamicize the constitution; these are supported by the Muslim Brothers, but opposed by more than two-thirds of the National Assembly; Nimairi withdraws the amendments in the face of this opposition.

1985

First SPLA incursions into southern Blue Nile and the Nuba Mts; destruction of Baqqara village at Qardud (eastern Nuba Mts) leads to TMC arming Baqqara *murahalin*, transferring local Nuba officials, and imprisoning Nuba leaders; incidents of arbitrary killings by *murahalin* begin to rise.

SPLA retaliation against Anyanya-2 includes purge of suspected Anyanya-2 sympathizers (mainly Nuer) within SPLA.

Jan Nimairi executes Mahmud Muhammad Taha, leader of the Republican Brothers and opponent of the September Laws, for apostasy (*18 Jan*).

SPLA sends two columns of 1500 troops each into Eastern Equatoria (*Dec 1984 & Jan*): one clashes with the Mundari at Terekeka and is repulsed by the army and Mundari; the other attacks civilians in Torit & Acoli areas and is defeated and chased into Uganda (*Feb*); recruitment of Pari from Jebel Lafon into SPLA begins.

March Nimairi arrests Turabi and more than a hundred Muslim Brothers in an attempt to stem their power (*10 March*); Nimairi begins official visit to the US; *intifada* calling for his overthrow begins in Khartoum (*25 March*).

April Nimairi is overthrown by demonstrations in Khartoum (*6 April*); the SPLA take Boma.

Dec The SPLA occupy Yirol; Chevron suspends its operations in Bentiu.

1986

Murahalin raids in northern Bahr al-Ghazal reach a peak this year.

Anyanya-2 continue attacking SPLA recruits on their way to Ethiopia; 2000 recruits from Rumbek are attacked in Lou Nuer area.

Feb SPLA attack Haluf area in Kordofan, and there is fighting between the SPLA & Fartit in western Bahr al-Ghazal.

March SPLA briefly take Rumbek. Meeting between the SPLM and the National Alliance for Salvation at Koka Dam, Ethiopia (*20–24 March*).

April SPLA take and hold Pochalla. Elections held throughout the country (*1–12 April*), but voting takes place in only 27 of the South's 68 constituencies.

May Mundari at Tali join SPLA; Anyanya-2 attack and briefly take SPLA camp at Bukteng, with assistance of Nuer officers inside SPLA.

National elections completed; Umma party drops its support of the Koka Dam agreement and forms a coalition with the DUP.

July Sadiq & Garang meet in Addis Ababa (*31 July*).

Aug SPLA shoot down civilian airliner over Malakal (*26 Aug*); Sadiq accuses SPLA of terrorism and breaks off contacts; UN Secretary General forbids UN agencies from having any dealings with the SPLA.

Sept Popular discontent and unrest in Darfur.

1987

Feb Libyan troops enter Darfur; leave by agreement with government (*March*).

March–May SPLA take Pibor, Ayod, Jokau; beginning of counter-insurgency in southern Blue Nile and SPLA evacuation of refugees to Ethiopia.

April Garang calls for the resumption of negotiations, meets with Samuel Aru Bol, Deputy Prime Minister and head of SSPA.

May SPLM meets with a DUP MP and delegations from the Nuba Mts & Kordofan in Addis Ababa.

July State of emergency declared (*2 July*). SPLA 'Volcano' battalion, under Yusif Kuwa, enters eastern Nuba Mts, occupies area around Talodi, and begins recruiting local Nuba, sometimes by force; *murahalin* retaliate by attacking Nuba villages.

Aug–Sept The army massacre civilians in Wau and fighting breaks out between army & police.

Meetings between SPLM & USAP delegations in Addis Ababa (*20–25 Aug*) and Nairobi (*19–20 Sept*); joint declaration on the South issued by SPLM, Anyanya-2 & southern political parties (*22 Sept*).

Sept–Oct Arrest of Kerubino Kuanyin for attempting to overthrow Garang (*Sept*) followed by arrest of SPLA officers and civilians in Itang (*Oct*).

Nov Fur–Zaghawa conflict in Darfur escalates, resulting in the convening of a security conference in El Fasher.

Nov–Dec The SPLA take and briefly hold border towns of Kurmuk & Qaissan in Blue Nile Province.

1988

Escalation of inter-group conflict in Darfur, fuelled by access to weapons provided by Chadian factions.

Jan The majority of Anyanya-2 troops join the SPLA; SPLA take Kapoeta (*12 Jan*). USAP drafts Transitional Sudan Charter, declaring Sudan an African & Arab nation, and calling for a resolution of the issue of religion in politics through a national constitutional convention; Umma & DUP sign (*10 Jan*).

March 52,000 farmers are estimated to have been displaced by militias in the Nuba Mts; by the end of the year the SPLA has some 3000 troops in the area and the Umma Party reorganizes the Misiriyya *murahalin* into paramilitary PDF without authorization from the Constituent Assembly.

Arok Thon Arok arrested by SPLA (*8 March*).

April Joseph Oduho arrested by SPLA in Addis Ababa (*8 April*).

Sadiq al-Mahdi forms a new cabinet including the NIF as well as the DUP.

July SPLM & USAP meet to reaffirm commitment to the Koka Dam agreement (*5–7 July*).

Aug First DUP–SPLM meeting in Addis Ababa (*18–20 Aug*).

Sept–Oct Islamic legal code, including the *hadud* punishments of flogging, stoning and amputation, is tabled in the Constituent Assembly (*19 Sept*), and referred to a legislative committee (*4 Oct*) following the walk-out of the Southern opposition.

Oct Second DUP–SPLM meeting results in the signing of an agreement in principle (*15–17 Oct*).

Nov DUP-SPLM talks in Addis Ababa; Muhammad Uthman al-Mirghani & John Garang sign a DUP–SPLM accord (*14 Nov*).

Dec DUP resigns from the government following the refusal of the Council of Ministers to endorse the DUP-SPLM accord (*28 Dec*); Turabi becomes Foreign Minister.

1989

Jan–May SPLA take Nasir, Torit, Nimule, Gemmaiza, Mongalla, Akobo, Bor & Waat; in the Nuba Mts they overrun police posts close to Kadugli, defeating army & militia at Korongo Abdallah (*Jan*); the 'New Kush' battalion enters the region under Yusif Kuwa (*March*) and infiltrates Tuleshi in the western hills (*April*); remnants of Anyanya-2 militia moved to Kadugli.

Feb Memorandum addressed to Sadiq al-Mahdi by senior military leaders demands major changes in the government and its policies towards peace (*20 Feb*).

March Sadiq al-Mahdi announces intention of reviving peace process along the lines of the DUP–SPLM Nov 1988 agreement; NIF resigns from government in protest. Agreement between Sudan government, SPLA & UN on terms of reference for OLS; international relief effort begins with great public fanfare.

April Council of Ministers & Assembly endorse DUP–SPLM accord (*3 April*); government representatives meet SPLM in Addis Ababa.

May SPLA declare a one month ceasefire (*1 May*) and government lifts the state of emergency (*6 May*).

June SPLA & government delegations meet and agree on a ceasefire, lifting of the state of emergency, freezing of the implementation of Islamic laws, and the abrogation of military pacts with Egypt & Libya (*10 June*); Sadiq al-Mahdi initials law embodying suspension of Islamic laws (*29 June*); Council of Ministers set to endorse law (*30 June*) and Assembly to enact legislation (*1 July*). Sadiq al-Mahdi's government overthrown by Brigadier Umar al-Bashir (*30 June*).

July New government suspends constitution, dissolves parliament & political parties, bans newspapers, trade unions & strikes, and renounces the DUP–SPLM agreement.

Aug Meeting in Addis Ababa between SPLM and new government; government rejects provisions of Koka Dam and DUP-SPLM peace initiative and refuses to suspend Islamic laws or convene a national constitutional convention.

Sept Government's own national dialogue conference produces proposals for federal system under Islamic law.
Fighting between SPLA & Ethiopian Anuak around Punyido refugee camp; SPLA kill a number of Anuak civilians, but blame fighting on GPLF.

Oct NDA formed (*21 Oct*)

Oct–Dec Chadian troops fight Chadian rebels inside Darfur; SPLA take Kurmuk, Deim Mansur, Ora, Chali al-Fil & Khor Yabus (where the OLF have a camp) in southern Blue Nile; Sudanese army retake them all by the end of the year; Popular Defence Forces Act decrees the Baqqara & other militias as officially recognized paramilitary forces; Misiriyya *murahalin* massacre Daju & Nuba in the Lagowa area of Southern Kordofan; Sudanese air force bombs Moyo, Uganda; massacre of southern Sudanese agricultural workers in Jabalain.

Dec Carter peace initiative in Nairobi (*1–5 Dec*); neither government nor SPLM delegations compromise on their positions.

1990

Jan The OLF, supported by TPLF & Sudan army, attack and destroy Assosa (*1 Jan*); Sudanese refugees (mainly from Blue Nile) in Tsore refugee camp flee and the camp is destroyed; the refugees spend several months in the wilderness before the majority arrive at Itang.
SPLA take Kajo Kaji, Kaya, Morobo and briefly overrun Yei.

Feb The *Jundi al-Watan al-Wahid* ('Soldiers of the United Homeland') column sets out from Malakal for Juba; fighting around Ayod (which the army burns); the column is diverted to the region between Waat & Duk Fadiat and is ambushed near Mongalla before reaching Juba. Sudanese airforce bombs Moyo, Uganda.

March SPLA & NDA agree to unite their efforts (*4 March*).
Fighting between Fur & Zaghawa in Darfur.
USA ceases all military and economic aid to Sudan.

March–June US Assistant Secretary of State Herman Cohen proposes withdrawal of government forces from the South and a constitutional convention, both of which are rejected by Khartoum.

May–Sept Chadian forces enter Darfur.

Sept Formation of Legitimate Command of the Armed Forces under General Fathi Ahmad Ali, based in Alexandria; Legitimate Command broadcasts over Radio SPLA (*25 Sept*)

Nov–Dec SPLA begins operations in Western Equatoria; SPLA signs agreement with the Legitimate Command; government retakes Melut.

1991

March SPLA take the last government garrisons in Western Equatoria.
First NDA summit, Addis Ababa.

Government adopts Islamic Penal Code with 189 articles (including article on apostasy); Southern regions allowed to exempt themselves from only five articles dealing with *hudud* punishments.

March–April National Founding Conference for the Political System (Khartoum) adopts a National Charter for Political Action which forms the basis for the Islamist state.

May Mengistu falls, the SPLA are forced to leave Ethiopia & Sudanese refugee camps are evacuated (*26–29 May*); Sudanese government monitors reports on UN OLS radio network and bombs locations where returnees are said to be gathered; returnees along the Baro are attacked by Ethiopian Gaajak Nuer militia.

Aug Three Nasir commanders (Riek Machar, Lam Akol, Gordon Kong) announce the overthrow of John Garang (*28 Aug*); Bul Nuer Anyanya-2 under Paulino Matip at Mayom, and the Lou Nuer Anyanya-2 of Yohannis Yoal Both at Doleib Hill, declare for Riek.

Oct–Dec Fighting between the Nasir & Torit factions of SPLA around Kuacdeng, Kongor, Adok, Ler & Bor. A ceasefire agreement between the two factions, signed in Nairobi (*22 Nov*) lasts only five days. Kongor & Bor destroyed by SPLA-Nasir soldiers & Nuer levies before both towns retaken by SPLA-Torit. Virtually entire population of Kongor District is permanently displaced by fighting.

Nov SPLA-Torit forces led by Daud Bolad (ex-NIF member) begin military operations in Darfur.

Dec Temporary truce between SPLA factions.

Government operations in Nuba Mts, where the governor of Kordofan and the head of the local militia declare a *jihad* (*29 Dec*).

1992

Jan Fatwa issued by *ulama* defines civil war as *jihad* against unbelievers and apostates.

SPLA-Torit defeated in Darfur; Daud Bolad is captured and executed.

Government begins expulsions of displaced Southerners from shanty towns surrounding Khartoum.

Meetings are held between Lam Akol of SPLA-Nasir & Ali al-Hajj Muhammad of government in Frankfurt, resulting in a joint statement which refers to a 'special political and constitutional status' for the South, but makes no explicit mention of self-determination or the option of total independence (*25 Jan*).

Feb The first resignations from SPLA-Nasir, as Dengtiel Ayuen Kur & Telar Deng Takpiny (both from Bahr al-Ghazal) denounce the agreement reached between Lam Akol & Ali al-Hajj in Frankfurt as a retreat from the position of self-determination and separation.

Reconciliation talks in Nairobi between SPLA factions fail (*13–17 Feb*).

Government offensive against SPLA-Torit begins.

March–July The Sudan army retake Pochalla (*9 March*), Bor (*4 April*), Yirol (*11 April*), Pibor (*23 April*), Kapoeta (*28 May*), Torit (*13 July*), and outposts along Juba–Torit–Kapoeta road; up to 100,000 persons are displaced by the fighting.

April Religious leaders in Kordofan issue a *fatwa* justifying *jihad* in the Nuba Mts & South Sudan (*24 April*).

May–June Abuja talks: the two SPLA factions merge their delegations under the leadership of William Nyuon Bany and agree on a programme of self-determination for the South, Abyei, the Nuba Mts & southern Blue Nile; this is rejected by the Sudan government.

June Chevron sells its oil interests in Sudan to the Sudanese government (*June 15*).

June–July SPLA-Torit attack Juba; repulsed with heavy losses; government retaliation follows against Southern civilians inside Juba.

Aug Government prepares large mechanized farms in newly cleared areas in the Nuba Mts.

Sept Further split in the SPLA when William Nyuon breaks with Garang (*27 Sept*); fighting within the SPLA as Nyuon and his troops head for Magwi; three international relief workers and one journalist killed in this fighting; prominent detainees, including Kerubino Kuanyin Bol, Arok Thon Arok, Faustino Atem Gualdit, & Joseph Oduho are released by Nyuon and escape to Uganda.

Oct Ex-Anyanya-2, SPLA-Nasir forces & Nuer militia attack Malakal (*19 Oct*), enter the town and are repulsed; there are disagreements within the SPLA-Nasir command on whether to take credit for the attack; Achol Marial Deng is reprimanded for broadcasting news of the attack and resigns (*9 Nov*).

Nov William Nyuon Bany's forces attack Garang's troops at Magwi; some Equatorian commanders & troops defect to Nyuon.

Dec Some 45,000 government reinforcements reported entering the Nuba Mts, beginning of government's Haiban offensive.

Canadian Arakis Energy Corp. forms a partnership with State Petroleum (*7 Dec*).

SPLA repulses government convoy pushing out from Kapoeta to Narus (*23 Dec*); army retaliates by killing 200 Toposa around Kapoeta (*24 Dec*).

1993

As a result of US/UN actions in Somalia, government postpones its 1993 dry-season offensive; government gets continued Iranian & Iraqi military assistance in addition to increased arms shipments from South Africa; friction reported between regular Sudan army & PDF units in South; attempts by convoys to break out of Wau & Kapoeta fail; aerial bombardment of SPLA-Torit positions and civilian centres continue.

Jan William Nyuon is attacked and defeated at Madugi (*8 Jan*); he joins up with the Sudanese army at Mogiri, Eastern Equatoria (*10 Jan*), and visits Juba (*16 Jan*).

March The formation of SPLA-United is announced (*26 March*) when several of Garang's former detainees join the SPLA-Nasir command; a dispute over the separation of the political from the military wing arises between Joseph Oduho & Lam Akol; Oduho is killed when a meeting convened at Panyagor, outside of Kongor, is disrupted by an attack by a unit of Garang's troops (*27 March*).

April–June Fighting between SPLA-United & SPLA continues around Kongor area; Garang's forces attack Yuai, Ayod, & Waat; a 'demilitarization' agreement signed by the two factions (*28 May*) breaks down.

April Nairobi Declaration (*17 April*) affirms NDA's commitment to human rights and religious equality, but does not address the questions of a secular state or self-determination.

May Resignation of seven Equatorian members from SPLA-United (*5 May*), citing disagreements between Oduho and the two SPLA-United commanders, and the faction's contacts with government as reasons.

Abuja 2 talks between government & SPLA; SPLA proposal of two confederal states in the Sudan is rejected by the government; SPLA claim that talks broke down over the questions of religion and the state, and the devolution of powers. Separate talks held between government & SPLA-United in Nairobi produces a joint communiqué agreeing on the future participation of the South in 'constitutional and political institutions at the national level' whether as one or more entities, and an unspecific referendum in the South at an unspecified future date (*23 May*).

Truce negotiated by US Ambassador Petterson concerning cease-fire in 'hunger triangle' area providing for the withdrawal of all troops within a week (*28 May*); the government denounces it (*30 May*); no troops are withdrawn.

June Heavy fighting between SPLA factions in the Kongor, Ayod & Waat areas begins (*16 June*).

June–Aug Government renews offensive, advances on Nimule & Kaya (*25 June*); advance on Nimule is halted (*16 July*); column out of Yei meets severe resistance (*3 Aug*) but retakes Morobo (*8 Aug*); column advancing from Wau to Rumbek gets pinned down between Tonj & the Gel river; aerial bombardment by the Sudan airforce continues throughout most of the rest of the year; 60,000 Southern Sudanese flee to Uganda.

Aug Lam Akol (SPLA-United) reaches an agreement with the governor of Upper Nile State to maintain 'peace and stability' in the area and ensure relief aid (*4 Aug*); government announces a date later in the month for the resumption of talks between it and SPLA-United; Timothy Tot Col leaves SPLA-United, denouncing it for its collaboration with government and its promotion of inter-Nuer fighting, and forms a reconciliation committee with the goal of reuniting the SPLA (*Aug 10*); more fighting between SPLA-United forces under William Nyuon & SPLA at Kongor (*13 Aug*); Nyuon and part of his force take refuge in government garrison at Bor (*18 Aug*); Um Durain, the SPLA's last town in the Nuba Mts, falls to government troops (*25 Aug*); Kerubino Kuanyin Bol is reported to have begun moving SPLA-United troops into the Bentiu area; 42,000 Sudanese refugees, mainly from southern Blue Nile, leave SPLA-United territory and enter Ethiopia.

Sept Government delegation (including the State Minister for Peace Development, the head of state security, and the governor of Upper Nile) is killed when its airplane is shot down and crashes near Rubkona on its way from Malakal to meet with SPLA-United commanders in western Upper Nile (*5 Sept*).

The heads of the Ethiopian, Eritrean, Ugandan & Kenyan governments establish a committee to resolve the civil war in Sudan, in their capacity as members of the Intergovernmental Authority on Drought and Development (IGADD) (*7 Sept*). Bashir accepts regional initiative (*9 Sept*). President Moi of Kenya holds talks individually with Garang (*21 Sept*) and Riek (*30 Sept*).

Oct Bashir announces that the coming year will see the end of the rebellion in the Nuba Mts. Government advance on Nimule from Juba is halted and pushed back (*7–10 Oct*). Government delegation signs an agreement with SPLA-United representative Faustino Atem in Bentiu to 'maintain peace and stability in the Bentiu area' (*11 Oct*).

US Congress hosts a meeting between John Garang & Riek Machar (*21–22 Oct*); the two appear to agree on a number of points concerning self-determination, a cease-fire and reconciliation between the two factions, and opposition to the NIF government; Garang signs the joint declaration, but Riek disputes Garang's signing on behalf of SPLM/A only (rather than 'Mainstream') and publicly refuses to sign until after leaving Washington.

Nov William Nyuon Bany attacks SPLA forces around Ikotos (*1 Nov*); further fighting between SPLA factions around Magwi, the 'triple A' displaced camps & Yom Ciir (north of Bor); a reconciliation meeting scheduled for *15 Nov* in Nairobi is postponed indefinitely.

Government and both factions of the SPLA formally endorse the new IGAD initiative seeking a resolution to the war in South Sudan.

Dec Clash between the Eritrean army & Jihad Eritrea, a group infiltrated from Sudan (*16 Dec*); Eritrean government alleges that 'foreign Muslim extremists' have declared war on Eritrea.

Government begins new offensive in the oilfields, clearing civilian villages from area around Heglig field.

1994

Jan Foreign Ministers from Ethiopia, Eritrea, Uganda & Kenya hold IGAD talks with SPLA factions in Nairobi (*4–6 Jan*); the factions agree to a common agenda for peace talks, calling for self-determination for the South, Nuba Mts and 'other marginalized areas' through a referendum (*6 Jan*).

Sudan government military build-up against the Zaghawa in Darfur; renewed fighting in Nuba Mts; bombing raids by the Sudan airforce are intensified in Western Equatoria and along the Uganda border in preparation for the dry season offensive; South Africa sends military advisers to Khartoum.

Feb Ame displaced people's camp is attacked either by William Nyuon Bany's forces or local Equatorian militias; 41,000 displaced Dinka flee; government opens its offensive on five fronts in Equatoria, displacing some 100,000 civilians; government advance on Mundri repulsed (*12 Feb*); fighting between SPLA & SPLA-United in Eastern Equatoria.

Secret contacts between the French & Sudanese governments reported.

Riek Machar dismisses Lam Akol from the SPLA-United (*12 Feb*); Lam Akol returns to Kodok in government-held part of Upper Nile.

March Khartoum's link with Juma Oris & the Lord's Resistance Army in Uganda revealed.

SPLA-United announces a unilateral cease-fire with SPLA (*17 March*), but fighting continues between William Nyuon Bany & Garang's forces around Jebel Lafon.

Fighting between Lou & Jikany Nuer reaches its height when the Lou attack and destroy Nasir (*29–30 March*).

April Aswa camp evacuated, but government offensives stalled.

SPLA convenes its first National convention at Chukudum (*28 March–11 April*), with delegates from throughout South, the Nuba Mts, Ingessana Hills, and Misiriyya & Rizaiqat Arabs: the principle of self-determination for the South is affirmed, proposals for an independent civil administration are adopted.

May Muhammad Uthman al-Mirghani, leader of the DUP issues a statement denouncing the IGAD talks, reaffirming his support for democracy and 'pluralism', but rejecting self-determination for the South and a secular state for the Sudan (*7 May*). The second round of IGAD peace talks takes place in Nairobi; draft declaration of principles, covering self-determination and a secular democratic state, issued to all parties for further discussion (*17–22 May*).

Arok Thon Arok resigns from SPLA-United, accusing Riek Machar of 'dictatorial tendencies' (*17 May*).

Government reoccupies Warrap & Thiet in Tonj district, Bahr al-Ghazal.

June–July Factional fighting between different Nuer groups within SPLA-United.

June John Luk is arrested in Waat on the orders of Riek Machar; SPLA-United troops under Kerubino Kuanyin Bol & Faustino Atem Gualdit cross into Gogrial from western Upper Nile. Government reoccupies Aswa (*2 June*) and retakes Kajo Kaji (*11 June*), but the advance on Nimule remains stalled.

July Kerubino Kuanyin Bol & Faustino Atem Gualdit occupy Mayen Abun in northern Bahr al-Ghazal (*5–15 July*) with a force of some 2000 SPLA-United soldiers; 1000 civilians are reported killed in fighting between units of the two SPLA factions; Kerubino retreats to Abyei.

The third round of IGAD peace talks is held in Nairobi; government delegation rejects the principle of a secular state and objects to the wording of the self-determination clause of the declaration of principles; SPLA delegations issue a joint statement accepting the declaration of principles and reaffirming their commitment to self-determination for South Sudan and other marginalized areas (*18–29 July*).

Sudanese army attempts to cross the Aswa river and is repulsed.

Police expel 50,000 displaced people from Khartoum.

Aug A number of senior figures in SPLA-United either resign or defect to government. Fighting between SPLA factions continues around Torit & in northern Bahr al-Ghazal. Attacks by the LRA in northern Uganda halt relief convoys to Sudanese refugee camps; NRA begins operations against the LRA.

Sept Lou–Jikany peace conference held at Akobo (*6–15 Sept*), agrees to resolve inter-Nuer dispute (Riek Machar subsequently fails to ensure the implementation of this agreement).

The final round of IGAD talks is convened in Nairobi; consultations between the heads of state and the leaders of both factions of the SPLA (*19 Sept*) reveal an impasse, as Khartoum refuses to concede either the right of self-determination to the South, or discuss the option of a secular state; Bashir announces government intention to liberate all country controlled by the SPLA (*29 Sept*).

SPLA-United holds its first National Convention in Akobo (*26 Sept–16 Oct*), renaming the movement the South Sudan Independence Movement/Army (SSIM/A). Lam Akol denounces the idea of self-determination for areas outside South Sudan (*7 Sept*) and later announces his assumption of chairmanship of SPLA-United.

Oct Fighting continues in the Nuba Mts; government accuses Eritrea of harbouring 3000 insurgents from eastern Sudan.

Internal fighting reported among William Nyuon's troops at Jebel Lafon (*7 Oct*); earlier some 200 Lou Nuer soldiers desert from his command and walk back to Waat.

Government offensive begins (*21 Oct*) with fighting in several locations in Eastern & Western Equatoria; forces of Riek Machar's SSIA attack Akot in Bahr al-Ghazal (*21 Oct*), killing some 100 civilians and looting several thousand head of cattle; the relief camp at Akot is subsequently looted by local SPLA.

Nov Heavy fighting between the SPLA & Kerubino Kuanyin Bol's forces (including Baqqara *murahalin*) in northern Bahr al-Ghazal ends in Kerubino's retreat to government garrison at Gogrial; about 27,000 persons displaced by the fighting.

Dec Eritrea breaks off diplomatic relations with Sudan (*5 Dec*), threatens full-scale conflict unless Sudan ceases interference in Eritrea's internal affairs (*12 Dec*). Uganda announces strengthening of forces on its border because of Khartoum's support for LRA (*5 Dec*).

Kapoeta besieged by SPLA; PDF re-invade northern Bahr al-Ghazal.

Lam Akol, Arok Thon Arok & Peter Sule announce a reformulated command for SPLA-United (*22 Dec*).

Chukudum agreement between the Umma Party & the SPLA (*12 Dec*) accepting the right of self-determination for South Sudan: Umma Party insists that self-determination be confined to the South's current boundaries, while SPLA calls for self-determination for the peoples of the Nuba, Ingessana & Abyei areas as well. Asmara agreement (*27 Dec*) between the SPLA, Umma, DUP & SAF (preparatory to larger meeting of NDA) stresses national unity, but accepts the principle of a referendum in the South.

1995

Jan PDF units continue to burn villages in northern Bahr al-Ghazal & Nuba Mts; government incursions into Uganda, in concert with units of SSIA & LRA; Riek Machar officially dismisses William Nyuon & Kerubino Kuanyin from SSIM/A, accusing them of collusion with Khartoum & the LRA (*24 Jan*).

Feb PDF units reported to have attacked SSIA forces at Daja, on the Ethiopian border (*8 Feb*), and begin advance on Nasir along the Sobat (*10 Feb*); Riek Machar announces an immediate cessation of hostilities against the SPLA (*10 Feb*); Kerubino Kuanyin & William Nyuon announce they have dismissed Riek Machar from SSIM/A.

SPLA inflicts heavy losses on government convoys moving out from Aswa & Parajok; some 400 refugees a day reported crossing into Uganda to escape government offensive and SPLA conscription.

US begins implementation of policy of strengthening the military capability of Sudan's neighbours (especially Uganda & Eritrea) against Islamist incursions.

Mar Government forces reoccupy Nasir (*26 March*); Kerubino Kuanyin, with a force of 200 men, continues raids in northern Bahr al-Ghazal.

April Junior officers of SSIA garrison at Lafon decide to change sides and capture a small government advance force (*31 March*); William Nyuon arrives from government base at Mogiri with his own SPLA-United troops, joins the officers at Lafon, assumes overall command and establishes radio contact with the SPLA (*1 April*); government forces attack Lafon and SSIA forces evacuate, with the assistance of SPLA detachments (*9–10 April*); combined SSIA/SPLA force besieges government troops in Lafon; negotiations between local SSIA & SPLA result in Lafon Declaration (*27 April*) which announces the end of hostilities between the two organizations, the reunification of the movement and the reintegration of forces; this is approved by John Garang & William Nyuon, but Riek Machar (still in Nairobi) holds out for the continued parallel existence of SSIM/A in alliance with the SPLM/A.

Protocol for a Sudanese-Iranian military agreement signed in Khartoum: Iran receives naval facilities in Port Sudan & Suakin in return for training Sudan's secret service and PDF; both countries to collaborate to expand the fundamentalist Islamic network, especially in Africa.

Massacre of civilians near Gulu in northern Uganda by the LRA; Uganda breaks off diplomatic relations with Sudan (*23 April*).

May Yusif Kuwa returns to take command of the SPLA Nuba forces after an absence of two years (*5 May*); SPLA begins new sustained military operations against government forces in the Nuba Mts.

SAF & the Beja Congress in Eritrea agree to the overthrow of the NIF 'by all means' (*6 May*).

June Riek Machar dismisses three members of SSIM/A, including D.K. Matthews & John Luk (*10 June*).

NDA meets in a conference in Asmara chaired by John Garang (*15–23 June*); the conference agrees to the establishment of an interim government upon the overthrow of the NIF and affirms: the South's right to self-determination, choosing between the options of confederation/federation and independence; Abyei's right to choose whether it should join the South; and referenda to ascertain the views of the Nuba Mts & southern Blue Nile on their political future (*23 June*).

SAF & the Beja Congress are admitted to the NDA at the insistence of Eritrea, and against the objections of the Legitimate Command & the DUP.

July Kerubino Kuanyin continues raiding in Gogrial county; a raid from Bahr al-Ghazal into Ganyliel (western Upper Nile) (*30 July*) is attributed to the SPLA, who insist that it was carried out by local people seeking revenge for SSIA's 1994 attack on Akot.

Aug Sudan army retakes Kaya, allegedly with the assistance of Ugandan troops under Juma Oris (*12 Aug*).

William Nyuon & other SSIM/A leaders announce the dismissal of Riek Machar and the reformulation of the movement under William Nyuon as chairman and John Luk as deputy chairman (*14 Aug*).

Sept The new leadership of SSIA/M claims it has asserted its control over Akobo, Waat & Ayod; Riek Machar is accused of seeking a military alliance with Khartoum.

Assassination attempt on Egyptian president Hosni Mubarak during OAU summit in Addis Ababa, Sudanese government implicated in plot.

Oct SPLA launches offensive (*23 Oct*) and retakes Parajok (*25 Oct*), Owingkibul (*26 Oct*), Palotaka (LRA HQ) & Magwi (*27 Oct*).

Nov SPLA retakes Obbo, Panyikwara, Ame, Moli, Pageri, Loa & Kit; Mundari militia reported to have come over to the SPLA.

Delegation of Hawazma Baqqara from Kadugli area in Nuba Mts agree to a non-aggression pact with the SPLA and to reopen markets (*15 Nov*).

Dec Government counter-attack on the south bank of the Kit river fails (*9–16 Dec*); SPLA offensive in the Nuba Mts is in its third month and claims to have taken a number of Government outposts.

1996

Jan SPLA on offensive around Dilling & Kadugli. Aswa retaken by the SPLA (*8 Jan*). William Nyuon killed in ambush near Ayod by forces loyal to Riek Machar (*13 Jan*).
SSIM refused NDA membership.
Feb Government offensives against SPLA on Kit River & at Labone fail (*7–8 Feb*).
March Government dry season offensive in the Nuba Mts east of Kadugli (*21–26 March*). Three Misiriyya *murahalin* & PDF units attack along the Kiir River, coordinated with Nuer militia raids on grazing areas; Rizaiqat raid area north of Aweil & Nyamlell (*29 Feb–29 March*).
SPLA under Malik Agar launch offensive in Blue Nile (*17 March*), retake Khor Yabus & Chali in Blue Nile, & Pochalla in Jonglei (*24 March*). Sudanese army battalion at Yirol surrenders to SPLA.
April Forces of Beja Congress clash with Sudan army near Assiss Hills in eastern Sudan (*4 April*).
Riek Machar & Kerubino Kuanyin Bol sign a Peace Charter with Bashir in Khartoum (*10 April*).
John Luk's SSIM/SSIA merge with SPLA (*27 April*).
May Kerubino moves out of Gogrial on his way to Wau, attacking villages on the way.
Usama bin Ladin leaves the Sudan (*16 May*).
June Umma/NDA delegation tour northern Bahr al-Ghazal, meeting with Dinka & Baqqara to counter government propaganda.
July LRA attack Sudanese refugee camp at Kitgum inside Uganda, slaughtering at least 100 refugees (*12–13 July*).
Sept Major-General Paulino Matip is reported unhappy with the Peace Charter (to which he is not a signatory), and refuses orders to remove his men from the Bentiu oilfields to Ler.
Oct A unified NDA battalion, composed of recruits from SPLA and two other member groups formed in eastern Sudan.
Nov US announces that some $20 million in surplus military equipment will be channeled to Ethiopia, Eritrea & Uganda, 'in their own defense', much of it items suitable for outfitting a guerrilla force. SPLA reported to be receiving help from US Operational Detachment-Alpha Teams (A-Teams) in Uganda.
Khartoum is protecting its oilfield by bringing in 'Arab Afghans' & Executive Outcomes.
Dec Arakis sells 75 percent of its Sudan oil interests to the Greater Nile Petroleum Operating Company (GNPOC), a consortium owned by the Chinese National Petroleum Corp., the Malaysian state Petronas Carigali, and the Sudanese state Sudapet (*6 Dec*).
Sadiq al-Mahdi escapes from Sudan to Eritrea and reconfirms opposition's commitment to achieve peace through a comprehensive constitutional conference (*11 Dec*).
John Garang becomes overall Commander of the NDA forces.
SPLA under Yusif Kuwa in Nuba Mts launches offensive to prevent Sudan army from interrupting harvest. SPLA New Sudan Brigade & NDA in eastern Sudan ambush Sudan army columns, enter Hamesh Koraib near Kassala and shoot down helicopter (*28–9 Dec*).

1997

Jan Ethiopian army & SPLA 13th Division, in a continuation of the Operation Black Fox begun in March capture Kurmuk, Qaissan, Kailik, Deim Mansur, Ora,

Chali al-Fil in southern Blue Nile & Meban in Upper Nile; in same period NDA forces of Umma, DUP, SAF & SPLA capture Yakuru, Abutera & Menza in Blue Nile, 80 km SE of Damazin. NDA claims to be within 40 miles of Damazin, to have captured 15% of Blue Nile State and to have killed more than 1200 soldiers. Government Information Minister al-Tayyib 'Sikha' Muhammad Khair claims that less than 10 soldiers have been killed (*12–16 Jan*). Khartoum accuses Ethiopia & Eritrea of involvement in the loss of Kurmuk & Qaissan and declares a *jihad* against the Sudan's enemies (*17 Jan*).

Iranian-supplied chemical warheads reported sent to Juba, following NDA offensive in eastern Sudan.

March Operation Thunderbolt launched in Central Equatoria; Kaya taken (*9 March*), Bazi (*10 March*), Morobo & Yei (*12 March*), Loka (*13 March*), Lainya (*15 March*), Kagwada (*16 March*), Kulipapa (*17 March*), Kajo-Kaji (*24 March*). SPLA captures heavy equipment plus 1700 POWs; claims 8000 enemy troops were 'put out of action'. SPLA defeat Juma Oris's West Nile Bank Front in the battles at Morobo & Yei; 800 WNBF soldiers killed, 1000 captured and subsequently handed over to the Uganda government. Government counterattack on Juba-Yei road repelled (*26 March*).

Government mechanized column from Melut recaptures Meban & Chali (*15 March*); SPLA retake both towns, capture large quantities of government equipment, and claim to have destroyed 70% of a 2000 man brigade (*19 March*). SSIA battalion of 600 men attack the Agar Dinka at Adol & Payak in Rumbek county, killing 74 Dinka and wounding 60 others; counterattacked by the Agar local militia, losing up to 500 men killed & wounded, and abandoning some 400 personal weapons and 12 heavy artillery pieces (*21 March*). Government forces fail to retake Menza in Blue Nile (*15–24 March*). NDA forces (Tana Brigade of SPLA 13th Division) repulse counterattack by 5 battalions of government troops in the Khor Gana/Yarada & Yakuru area north of Blue Nile river (*24 March*).

NDA capture Red Sea garrison of Karora, an outpost guarding Port Sudan, and then threaten naval base of Aqiq (*26 March*). SAF overrun one of Usama bin Ladin's training camps at Hamesh Koraib, capturing large stores of Iranian military equipment.

SPLA under Yusif Kuwa in Nuba Mts repulse 8 army convoys in the month of March.

April SPLA capture Amadi, Lui, & garrisons at Goja, Boje, Moga, Jambo Junction (*2–3 April*), Mukungu (*9 April*), & Kit (*12 April*).

Lawrence Lual Lual, Secretary for Education in the SPLM/A NEC defects to Khartoum.

Riek Machar, Kerubino Kuanyin, Arok Thon Arok (Bor), Kawac Makuei (Bahr al-Ghazal), Dr Theopholus Chang Loti (Equatoria Defence Force) & Muhammad Harun Kafi (Nuba SPLA) sign peace agreement with government (*21 April*).

SPLA recaptures Wunrok on Lol river from Kerubino's forces (*21 April*). SPLA in Nuba Mts repulse 6 out of 8 army convoys in April. NDA capture all the small garrisons between Tokar & the Red Sea in April.

SPLA capture Rumbek (*30 April*).

May SPLA capture Tonj (*9 May*) & Warrap (*13 May*).

June Sudanese army, with aid of Riek's SSIA, retake Meban. SPLA take Tali (*29 June*).

July New Joint Military Command of the NDA established with John Garang as chairman & Lt.-Gen Abd al-Rahman Said (former deputy chief of staff for operations of Sudanese army) as deputy chairman (*1 July*). SPLA operating in the South & Nuba Mts; SPLA 13th Division under Malik Agar operating on the South Blue Nile Front, and SPLA & SAF operating together on the North Blue Nile Front; SPLA New Sudan Brigade, SAF, the Beja Congress, & forces from the

Umma & DUP active in the Eastern Front along the length of the Sudan/Eritrean border, engaging in small-scale guerrilla operations.

Kerubino's SPLA-Bahr al-Ghazal recapture Litnhom (*3 July*). Government claims that troops assisted by Misiriyya militia were forcing SPLA onto defensive in Bahr al-Ghazal & Nuba Hills. SPLA take Tindilo (120 km NW of Juba) and retake Ayod (*13 July*). Kerubino's forces overrun Akon (*29 July*).

Aug Sudan army announces it has taken Temenbelu from SPLA (*6–7 Aug*).

Riek Machar appointed president of Southern States Coordination Council, which is supposed to rule the South for the next 4 years. The 4-year transition period for South Sudan will begin once a 23-member co-ordination council is appointed (*7 Aug*).

Kerubino Kuanyin, Arok Thon, Nikanora Atem Acek & Faustino Atem reinstated in the Sudanese army under a presidential decree. Kerubino reinstated as a Major-General, the rest as Brigadiers (*23 Aug*).

SPLA claims to have captured Krakaria, Andolo & al-Rujeci villages near Kadugli in Nuba Mts (*26 Aug*).

SPLM/A announce the return of Dhol Acuil, Richard Mulla & Sebit Sendani (*29 Aug*).

Government accepts truce unilaterally declared by SPLA-United (*1 Sept*).

Sept NDA military operations in eastern Sudan bogged down by seasonal rains but claim to be 'edging towards' the objective of cutting Port Sudan off from Khartoum.

'Fashoda Accord': Lam Akol & SPLA-United, under the mediation of Reth Kowongo Dak Padiet at Fashoda, sign an agreement with government, incorporating SPLA-United into the 21 April Khartoum Peace Agreement (*20 Sept*).

Oct Government introduces compulsory conscription for all male students 18–32. No exceptions are to be allowed, and school-leavers who do not sign up for military service will lose the chance to go to university, go abroad or do business.

Dec Lam Akol defeated in election for governor of Upper Nile State by Timothy Tong Tut Lam, a Nuer (*1 Dec*).

Governor of Darfur complains of deteriorating security in his state, blaming it on instability in neighbouring countries and availability of cheap arms (*3 Dec*). Bashir declares a state of emergency in Darfur (*22 Dec*).

1998

Jan Defence Minister Lt-Gen Hassan Abd al-Rahman Ali claims that 1787 SPLA soldiers surrendered to Kerubino at Marial Bai (*2 Jan*). First Vice-President Al-Zubair Muhammad Salih says that those who came over to government from SPLA should be absorbed into the organized forces, 'to widen the circle of peace'. He expects 80,000 defectors in Bahr al-Ghazal.

Soldiers of the Southern Sudan Defence Force, guarding the oil concessions of a Chinese firm near Bentiu, fight each other for 10 days, killing 38, following the election of Taban Deng Gai as Governor of Unity State. Fighting breaks out between his supporters and that of Paul Lilli, the defeated candidate.

SPLA releases over 2000 army POWs held near Yei at request of NDA (*26 Jan*). Some join SPLA, some join armed opposition in eastern Sudan, others remain in Koboko & Arua awaiting repatriation to northern Sudan. SPLA capture some 900 soldiers in Yei and over 1000 more in Tonj, Rumbek & Yirol in 1997, but had trouble feeding them. Most POWs provide cheap and free labour in order to feed themselves (SPLA unable to get NGOs to agree to feed them).

SPLA launch attack on Wau (*29 Jan*), capture army headquarters, the airport, railway station and other locations in the city. Seize Marial Ajith (NW of Wau), Grinti, Zagalona (N of Wau), Zara (to NE), Ariath, and agricultural area east of Wau. Also attack Aweil & Gogrial. All of this done by prior arrangement with Kerubino, who, when it became clear he wanted to rejoin SPLA, was given 2000 men and their families to infiltrate Wau. Government counterattacked on airport in Wau (*31 Jan*).

Feb WFP starts airdrops into Bahr al-Ghazal, from C-130s based in Kenya (*3 Feb*), but government bans flights into Bahr al-Ghazal (*4 Feb*). Laurence Lual Lual elected by SPLA-Bahr al-Ghazal to replace Kerubino (*5 Feb*), and government arrests several officers said to have been accomplices of Kerubino in Wau attack.

Fighting in eastern Sudan as SAF attacks garrisons around Kassala & Qallabat, Sudanese army shells villages inside Eritrea, and government announces closure of Eritrean border (*9 Feb*).

Fighting around Wau reaches stalemate by *10 Feb*, with SPLA holding railway north of town, and within shelling distance of airport. Government in barracks to west of Wau, also holding airport, and using Antonov to bomb towns where civilians dispersed by fighting are located. SPLA bringing up reinforcements from Western Equatoria via Tonj & Rumbek. SPLA claim that when they briefly took Wau they killed nearly 1000 government troops and 500 deserted to SPLA, along with 1800 policemen, prison officers and game wardens. When government retook Wau army and militias butchered hundreds of Dinka residents, 150 students from Wau University were rounded up and disappeared, and 80,000 of the town's residents fled to countryside. SPLA force under Paul Matong Awan manage to enter Aweil, but unable to dislodge army from garrison. Retreat and take Ariath on railway line 60 km to the north.

Plane carrying First Vice-President Al-Zubair Muhammad Salih, Arok Thon Arok and others crashes in Sobat at Nasir (*12 Feb*). Al-Zubair, Arok, Timothy Tutlam (governor of Upper Nile) & 25 others killed, Lam Akol & 14 others injured but survive.

Ali Uthman Muhammad Taha, NIF Foreign Minister, replaces al-Zubair as First Vice-President, ahead of Second Vice-President Major-General George Kongor & President of Southern Coordinating Council Riek Machar (*20 Feb*).

UN aid flights to Akuem, Adet, Ajiep, Pakor, Wau & Aweil in Bahr al-Ghazal resume, following a 3 week ban by government (*26 Feb*).

Bashir dismisses and replaces the state ministers, commissioners and advisers of Buheyrat (Lakes), Eastern Equatoria, Northern Bahr al-Ghazal, Western Bahr al-Ghazal, Warap & Wahda (Unity) states (*27 Feb*).

Riek Machar announces that the peace accord with government was only 'slightly affected' by Kerubino's defection, and that a new joint technical military committee between the army and the factions would establish new camps and control over the militias (*28 Feb*).

March Government bombs Yei hospital (*5 & 7 March*).

Paulino Matip announces his decision to pull out of SSIM, because it is not sincere in resolving internal disputes (*5 March*). Matip's forces, renamed South Sudan Unity Movement/Army (SSUM/A) will continue to support April Peace Agreement.

NDA claims to have taken Gezirat, al-Farza & Karima districts near Ethiopian border in Feb & March (*17 March*).

Famine alert in Bahr al-Ghazal, especially affecting Gorgrial & Twic counties (*18 March*). Government allows relief flights to only 4 locations in SPLA territory. WFP claim 350,000 people in urgent need of food and have no seed for planting.

Arab tribesmen reported to have attacked three Masalit villages (also claim 57 villages burned), killing 23 people and making 3000 families homeless (*26 March*).

April Government allows flights into all parts of Bahr al-Ghazal (*2 April*).

Some 130 student conscripts killed by soldiers or drowned when trying to escape the Ailafun military camp outside Khartoum (*2 April*).

Government claim to be mopping up resistance in Bahr al-Ghazal, inflicting heavy defeats on SPLA, and reopening railway, land routes, and airports at

Aweil & Wau. Fighting is reported in Upper Nile & Eastern Equatoria. SPLA claims to have repulsed attack by two government columns in a battle north of Juba (*4–6 April*).

SPLA & Uganda claim Sudan is organizing a special strike force in the Garamba National Park on Congo/Sudan border, composed of former Zairean army, Sudanese soldiers who fled to Zaire after being defeated by SPLA in 1997, and about 1500 Ugandan rebels. Are being supplied by Antonov airdrops (*9 April*).

Skirmishes reported in Qallabat & Qadarif areas.

Some 100 people die & 45 villages destroyed in fighting in western Darfur. Fighting over water & grazing rights between Rizaiqat & Masalit began in *Jan* and is renewed in *April*. Some 4000 families displaced.

SPLA releases some 400 government soldiers from Yei. A further 800 are still being held (*27 April*).

Misiriyya militia attack Abyei & Twic Dinka areas at end of April but are repulsed by SPLA.

April–May Government dry season offensive in Nuba Mountains takes place carried out by PDF through ambush and raiding villages. Smaller than usual, possibly because more government forces committed to Bahr al-Ghazal & eastern Sudan. Attempt, but fail, to seize airstrip in Kalkada & Kauda, used by Nuba Relief Rehabilitation & Development Society.

May Umma Liberation Army (400 men) finally begin operations in eastern Sudan. Government launches a major offensive to recapture Kurmuk in southern Blue Nile (*2 May*), but SPLA fight back and capture Wadega garrison (*5 May*).

Rizaiqat militia attack villages and cattle camps in Aweil area (*4–14 May*). Rizaiqat militias being used in Darfur against Fur, Zaghawa & Masalit. After Misiriyya militia are repelled by SPLA in late April, they regroup with the Nuer militia and attack same areas along Kiir in Abyei & Twic. SPLA units there run out of ammunition, and the militias are able to overrun the area.

June Rizaiqat & Misiriyya militias attack Bahr al-Ghazal but are twice beaten back by the SPLA in northern Gogrial, who force them to flee back to Abyei. Misiriyya attack northeastern Aweil in late June but are repulsed by SPLA at Warawar. By end of June government invasion of area between Kiir & Lol has failed.

Riek requests Bashir to arrest Matip in Khartoum. Bashir declines. Riek orders his bodyguard to arrest Matip. There is a shootout at Paulino's residence on the outskirts of Khartoum. Bashir reprimands Riek, who replies that as leader of the southern Sudan, any Southerner is under his jurisdiction anywhere in Sudan.

SPLA forces under Malik Agar capture Ulu & Meban; find over 4000 sacks of UN WFP grain in government garrisons at Wadega, Ulu & Meban. Umma Liberation Army & New Sudan Brigade active in Kassala area (*5–11 June*).

Chinese convicts reported being sent to build the oil pipeline in the Bentiu area.

June–July Fighting between Matip's & Riek's forces in Unity State. Matip's & government forces sack Ler, OLS evacuates personnel from town, and thousands of Nuer flee into Twic & Gogrial districts to escape the fighting and famine in western Upper Nile. Riek complains of government support for Matip and accuses Matip of planning to defect to the SPLA.

July Brigadier Abd al-Aziz al-Nur, SAF commander on Ethiopian frontier, dies of malaria and typhoid.

Government & SPLA agree to a 3-month ceasefire in Bahr al-Ghazal.

Aug Government forces bomb Kauda & Limon in Nuba Mts (*3 & 4 Aug*), despite claiming to have declared a unilateral ceasefire on all war fronts. Still denies OLS permission to assess reports of famine in Nuba Mts.

SAF claim to have repelled militia advance in Abu Qadaf area 35 km SE of Roseires (*4 Aug*). NDA forces continue to harass government forces in Kassala & Port Sudan areas. Government counter-offensive fails; government alleges an invasion from Eritrea.

Police intervene in a fight between Riek's & Matip's forces at a wedding in Omdurman (*9 Aug*); Matip's forces attack and take Ler again.

Canadian Talisman oil company announces acquisition of Arakis (*17 Aug*); purchase is completed in *Oct*.

US launches cruise missile against al-Shifa pharmaceutical plant in Khartoum in retaliation for bombings of US embassies in East Africa (*20 Aug*).

Sept 400 people reported killed in factional fighting around Bentiu since late August. Government arranges a cease-fire in August, but Matip declares he will no longer abide by that agreement. Matip begins withdrawing his forces from Ler, but Riek's troops attack at Wankai (*5 Sept*). Matip retakes Wankai and moves on Ler. Another truce between Matip & Riek announced on *30 Sept*.

Uganda People's Defence Forces move troops and equipment to Kidepo & Karenga on Uganda-Sudan border, in response to reports that Kony's rebels are planning to enter the country through Kotido district. Uganda regards attack as imminent.

SPLA launches offensive in Equatoria (*14 Sept*), taking Jabalain, 60 km south of Juba, and Liria on the road to Torit (*16 Sept*). By *21 Sept* are reported to be 35 km from Juba centre, and are shelling Torit. Joseph Kony, leader of LRA, reported to have been wounded when SPLA take Jabalain, Kony's biggest camp. Government accuses Uganda and Eritreans of involvement in fighting near Juba; launches extensive bombing campaign close to Uganda border, hitting 8 civilian targets, including Yei hospital and Lobone displaced persons camp. Announces general mobilization to counter Ugandan–Eritrean aggression: classes in universities suspended, students drafted to be sent to the front.

SAF & SPLA report fighting around Qallabat and near Damazin and Roseires (*11–25 Sept*).

Oct Government reported to have brought 60,000 PDF troops into Eastern Equatoria. Drive SPLA back 26 km towards Nimule. SSDF troops under Elijah Hon & LRA forces retake Liria from SPLA (*9 Oct*).

Lawrence Lual Lual, SPLA-Bahr al-Ghazal group, withdraws from the UDSF coalition in protest against the actions of Riek Machar; announces its forces will cooperate with Paulino Matip (*11 Oct*).

Government & SPLA agree to renew ceasefire in Bahr al-Ghazal; SPLA unilaterally extend it to include the Western Nuer.

Nov Skirmishes in Kassala area continue. Government dry season offensive in Nuba Mts begins early (*11 Nov*); attacking on four fronts with 2000 troops.

Sudan & Eritrea sign a memorandum of understanding to resolve their differences in Qatar (*13 Nov*).

Shoot out in Nairobi (*14–15 Nov*) as Kerubino's guard attack Garang's house.

Government disarms bodyguards of commanders of SSDF, including Riek Machar, in Khartoum (*18–22 Nov*).

SSDF battalion stationed in Upper Nile State defects to the SPLA.

Dec PDF units attack Dinka villages in Aweil West, breaking government's own cease-fire, repulsed by local SPLA (*1–3 Dec*).

Khartoum claims that Ethiopian troops have withdrawn from Kurmuk, leaving it in the hands of the SPLA, marking an improvement in Sudan–Ethiopian relations (*12 Dec*).

Kerubino flies out of Nairobi on small plane to Mankien (*15 Dec*).

SPLA halts government offensive by *23 Dec* and forces government garrison at Koya to evacuate.

Throughout *Dec* refugees from Bentiu continue to come to Twic Dinka country in eastern Gogrial. Some of Matip's troops reported to have appealed to SPLA for help. Kerubino's forces in northern Bahr al-Ghazal complete their reintegration into SPLA.

1999

Jan Bashir dissolves state parliaments with effect *1 Jan* to make way for new elections; the only party registered with organizations throughout the various states is the National Congress (successor to NIF); Riek Machar's United Democratic Salvation Front agrees to register as a political party under the legislation which binds all registered political associations to the unity of the Sudan as a federal state and to acceptance of *shari'a* law.

Government forces begin siege of Ulu, southern Blue Nile (*6 Jan*).

Nuer militia leader Gatwic Gatkuoth in Juba breaks with Riek and forms SSDF-2, following clashes between Gatwic and Riek's men (*20 Dec* & *11 Jan*). Southern militias ordered out of Juba and are redistributed along the east and west banks.

GOS attempt to retake Meban, Yabus & Khor Adar in southern Blue Nile fails (*12 Jan*).

Shoot-out between SPLA and Didinga in Chukudum (*16–17 Jan*).

Fighting breaks out between Baqqara, Zaghawa and Masalit (*19 Jan*). Governor of Northern Darfur state orders army to disarm Masalit. Masalit later claim at least 400 of their people killed by paramilitary Arab horsemen.

Government bombs Kajo Kaji and Yei hospitals, Narus, Lobone, Chukudum, Nimule, and the Sudanese refugee camp of Koboko in Uganda.

Umma Party's armed wing attacks several government targets in eastern Sudan.

Feb Bashir puts own representative in charge of Western Darfur State (*1 Feb*). Government declares situation in Darfur stabilized, after 50–100,000 people take refuge in Geneina, 40,000 flee to Chad, 76 villages are burned and 23 villages completely destroyed.

Government offensive in Nuba Mts, begun before Christmas, succeeds in taking 8 out of 10 SPLA airstrips, but in early *Feb* SPLA regain control of all airstrips and GOS resorts to bombing civilian targets.

Bashir dissolves all southern state parliaments.

Train returning from Wau disembarks mounted PDF between Aweil & Ariath stations, attacking Warawar, Marol, Anyuol, Mariik, Liith, Rumrol, Dheer, Majok, Warlang, Mayen, Kuel, Padaai, Lanayor & Rumdier (*3–6 Feb*). 12 villages burnt, over 400 women & children reported captured before SPLA force PDF to retreat.

Kerubino leads Nuer forces in an attack on 3 fronts in northeastern & eastern Gogrial but is repulsed (*8–12 Feb*).

Arab militia, mounted on horseback, commanded by regular Sudanese army officers, attack airstrip in Akoc, northern Bahr al-Ghazal where relief supplies are being distributed (*26 Feb*). Akoc razed and some 60 persons abducted.

Reconciliation conference organized at Wunlit, on border of Upper Nile, Tonj, Rumbek & Yirol, supported by NSCC and other agencies.

March NDA activity reported along roads from Kassala to Port Sudan.

Ugandan intelligence report that Usama bin Ladin is buying children abducted by the LRA for 1 Kalashnikov per child. Children are sold in Nsitu camp (33 km south of Juba) then taken to Juba and flown to Khartoum where they are taken to Bin Ladin's sunflower and marijuana farms on the Nile north of Khartoum.

Wunlit peace agreement between Dinka of Bahr al-Ghazal and Nuer of western Upper Nile signed (*13 March*).

Raiders attack Akoc a second time, but are ambushed and repulsed by local cattle guard force (*26 March*).

SPLA 13th Division break siege of Ulu (*27 March*), inflicting heavy losses on 5 Sudanese army brigades of 8000 men. SPLA now in artillery range of the Khor Adar oil wells.

April Swedish Lundin oil company begins drilling well at Thar Jiath in Ler County.

SPLA 13th Division captures Samaa West and Adrob in southern Blue Nile (*8 April*).

1st NDA Unified Brigade, supported by commandos from Umma Liberation Army and elements from the New Sudan Brigade, overrun garrison at Dar el Umda Hamid on Khartoum-Port Sudan road (*11 April*), capture Umbireiga near Kassala on Khartoum-Port Sudan road (*15 April*).

EU governments pass a resolution praising the NIF's commitment to democratization at meeting of the UN Commission on Human Rights in Geneva (*21 April*).

May Government attempt to dislodge SPLA from Ethiopian border areas in Kurmuk, Ulu and Meban fail.

Meeting between Turabi and Sadiq al-Mahdi in Geneva (*2 May*).

Presidents of Sudan and Eritrea sign reconciliation accord in Doha, Qatar, following mediation by Libya, agreeing to stop supporting each other's rebel movements (*2 May*). NDA troops capture army garrison at Rasay, NE of Kassala (*5 May*).

Fighting between Tito Biel of SSDF and Matip's forces and government troops in the Bentiu oilfields throughout May, attacking Thar Jiath well site (*2 May*). Tito Biel forced to retreat southwards, seeking refuge with SPLA at Yirol (*11 May*). Youk Teny Youk, state minister and spokesman for the UDSF blames GOS for clash between army and SSDF at Mayen Dit, north of Ler (*11 May*). Government re-establishes control over Adok area. Government launches own offensive against Dinka villages in Ruweng County (*9–23 May*). Aerial bombardment of villages in northern Bahr al-Ghazal continues mid-May; Kerubino's attempt to infiltrate eastern Bahr al-Ghazal with a force of Matip's Nuer troops is repelled (*20 May*). Lundin announces discovery of oil deposits of as much as 300 million barrels of oil at Thar Jiath (*21 May*).

June SSDF troops in Akobo defect to SPLA. Galuak Deng, former minister in NIF regime and Commander of Nasir, retakes Akobo for government a few days later. First privately-owned oil refinery in Sudan is inaugurated (*30 June*).

July Tripoli Declaration (*1 July*), signed by NDA, endorsing Egyptian-Libyan initiative for negotiations on the basis of the unity of the Sudan.

Matip's forces kill 4 Ministers attached to Unity State and loot OLS relief food stored in Mankien, Mayom & Ler. Control of Ler disputed by Matip's & Riek's forces, but most of Riek's forces reported to have redefected to the SPLA. More people are moving into Bahr al-Ghazal to get away from fighting.

Aug IMF reinstates Sudan following partial repayment of loans and beginning of export of oil (*27 Aug*); first shipload of 600,000 barrels of Sudan's oil exported from Port Sudan, earning government $2.2 million (*30 Aug*).

Sept Kerubino killed by Peter Gatdet's troops when they break away from Matip at Mankien (*10 Sept*).

NDA force blow up section of oil pipeline near Atbara (*19 Sept*).

Oct SSDF abandon western Nuer to Matip and retreat to eastern Upper Nile.

Open power struggle between Bashir and Turabi at ruling National Congress annual conference in mid-October.

SPLA opposes amalgamating Egyptian-Libyan initiative with IGAD at NDA meeting in Cairo.

Nov 16 SSDF commanders agree to formally de-link themselves from the government and resume armed struggle under an Upper Nile Provisional Military Command Council in cooperation with other opposition groups (*2–4 Nov*).

EU officially restarts dialogue with Sudan government and resumes aid suspended since 1990 (*10 Nov*).

Fighting between SSDF and government forces at Rubkona and Fangak (*10–12 Nov*).

Turabi introduces proposals for constitutional amendments to restrict powers of President Bashir (*15 Nov*).

Government and Umma sign agreement in Djibouti, promising democracy for Sudan and referendum on autonomy for South at end of four year transitional period (*25 Nov*). This is rejected by SPLA (*29 Nov*), and by the NDA (*2 Dec*).

US Senate passes 'Sudan Peace Act', authorizing direct deliveries of food aid to the SPLA (*19 Nov*); President Clinton signs legislation (*29 Nov*).

Dec Sudan and Uganda renew diplomatic relations (*8 Dec*).

Bashir decrees three-month state of emergency and dissolves parliament, *12 Dec*, preventing scheduled debate for 14 Dec on constitutional amendments limiting his power. Turabi calls for resistance, but the NC agrees to reform its executive branch, and Bashir announces a reshuffle (*31 Dec*).

2000

Jan Bashir announces at 44th anniversary of independence that 'We are on the way which leads to an Islamic State' (*1 Jan*).

SRRA insists that all NGOs working in SPLA-held territory sign a new memorandum of understanding (MOU) with the movement by the end of February (*12 Jan*).

New government announced in Khartoum, with the NC still in full control (*24 Jan*).

20 metres of oil pipeline destroyed by Beja Congress, and pipeline put out of action for a week in January.

Sudan and Eritrea resume diplomatic relations, and return Sudanese embassy building (formerly used as NDA headquarters) to the Sudan government. Eritrea agrees to prevent cross-border operations by NDA.

South Sudan Liberation Movement (SSLM) launched (*31 Jan*) in Waat, under chairmanship of Wal Duany, aimed at bringing about peace and reconciliation within Upper Nile, and working closely with the SPLA. An SPLA spokesman announces they were 'not very enthusiastic' about the new movement.

Riek Machar resigns from government and the leadership of UDSF, but claims to retain command of the SSDF (*31 Jan*).

Feb Elijah Hon in Khartoum elected to take over command of SSDF (*8 Feb*). Peter Gatdet and his entire militia formally rejoin SPLA.

IGAD-sponsored talks between government and SPLM end when Khartoum refuses to give up Islamic law or allow the right of self-determination to be extended to Abyei, Southern Kordofan and southern Blue Nile (*28 Feb*).

March Of 43 NGOs working in South, 32 sign MOU by *1 March*, and only 11 refuse.

Harry Johnston, US Presidential Special Envoy on the Sudan meets with Sudan's Foreign Minister in Khartoum (*4 March*).

Sudan and Ethiopia normalize their relations in agreement to cooperate in political, security and other spheres (*6 March*).

Bashir extends the state of emergency (*13 March*).

Egypt resumes ties at ambassadorial level with Sudan (*14 March*).

Government offensive in Nuba Mts launched with 8 army divisions from Kadugli *15 March*, displacing some 14,000 persons.

Umma Party resigns from NDA over disagreement about rapprochement with government (*16 March*).

Khartoum resumes offensive in Kassala, southern Blue Nile (*16 March*).

PDF & Baqqara militias launch 3 raids into Aweil and Twic counties (*10–22 March*); repulsed in two raids but take 300 captives in third.

EU allocates $11.3 million in humanitarian aid for use in government-held areas only (*23 March*).

NDA captures government garrison at Hamesh Koraib (near Kassala) in March, finding some 40,000 children there, mostly southern Sudanese. SPLA New Sudan Brigade conscripts older boys, but leaves remainder to fend for themselves.

African states vote Sudan to fill vice-presidency of Africa group in the Human Rights Commission.

April Sudanese Red Crescent announces that 160,000 persons have been displaced by fighting in Kassala State.

Government launches offensive in southern Blue Nile (*1 April*) but is held back by SPLA.

SPLA counter-offensive in Nuba Mts begins mid-April.

May Section of oil pipeline in eastern Sudan blown up (*2 May*).

NSCC-sponsored peace conference at Lirlir in Bor County between groups of Dinka, Nuer, Anuak, Murle, Jie and Kichepo (*9–15 May*). Gaawar Nuer prevented from attending by Riek Machar's faction.

Peace meeting between Dinka, Misiriyya and Rizaiqat leaders at Wanyjok, Aweil East, establishing agreements on movement and grazing rights (*28 May*).

Government launches attack on Panaru area north of Bentiu, late May–early June, displacing large numbers of Ruweng Dinka.

Government and allied militia attacks on Masalit border village of Geriko, as well as separate attacks on Fur, Dagu, and Senya settlements. Western Sudanese publish 'The Black Book' in Khartoum, documenting discrimination, marginalization and atrocities at hands of peoples of Central Sudan.

June Government offensive to dislodge SPLA from area near Khor Adar oilfields fails.

SPLA launch offensive along railway line in northern Bahr al-Ghazal. SPLA capture Gogrial town (*24 June*).

Peter Gatdet captures Mankien in late June.

Sudan army spokesman announces that revenues from the Sudan's oil industry are enabling the Sudan to manufacture its own weapons (*30 June*).

Egypt revives Egyptian–Libyan initiative; 'Egypt possesses cards it has not yet used for preventing the separation of southern Sudan', declares Egypt's Ambassador to Khartoum, Muhammad Asim Ibrahim.

July NDA leadership meeting in Cairo accept Egyptian proposal for reconciliation with Khartoum.

Forces loyal to Riek Machar and forces under Peter Gatdet cooperating with the SPLA in fighting Paulino Matip in oilfields; Riek's troops complain that SPLA favour Gatdet over them. Matip retakes Mankien from Gatdet at end of July.

SPLA take town of Meban in northern Upper Nile.

July–Aug SPLA offensive in northern Bahr al-Ghazal succeeds in taking most of the railway line and seizing the Lol River bridge; government retaliates by bombing over 33 civilian targets in northern Bahr al-Ghazal; UN temporarily suspends all humanitarian flights to southern Sudan to protect UN relief personnel (*Aug 11*).

Sept Violent demonstrations, organized by Turabi's Popular National Congress (PNC), reported in El Fasher, Nyala, El Obeid, Umm Ruwaba, Kosti, Sennar, Wad Medani, Qadarif, Kassala, Port Sudan and Atbara.

Second NDA conference convenes in Masawa, Eritrea, endorses proposal for reconciliation talks with Khartoum but does not abandon commitment to overthrow regime. Umma Party finally withdraws completely from NDA. Bashir and al-Mirghani meet in Asmara in presence of Afwerki (*26 Sept*).

Oct Government regains control of railway between Babanusa and Wau and rebuilds bridges over Kiir and Lol; failure of SPLA offensive in northern Bahr al-Ghazal is blamed on the diversion of SPLA troops and equipment to the eastern Sudan.

Bashir publicly reveals existence of Sudan's weapons factory, built with the assistance of Iraq; Turabi claims that the military assistance between Iraq and Sudan was financed by Usama bin Ladin.

Nov Following withdrawal of Eritrean support for NDA forces in eastern Sudan, government launches attack on Hamesh Koraib. NDA forces (mainly SPLA's

New Sudan Brigade) evacuate town, but are attacked and heavily defeated outside of the town. Reports that northern forces of NDA melted away when government attack began, and government mobilized local people to inform army of whereabouts of SPLA.

NDA forces attack Kassala town, (*8–9 Nov*). Heavy fighting inside town. NDA claims to have destroyed and captured military equipment before withdrawing.

Chinese National Petroleum Corporation (CNPC), Gulf Oil of Qatar and a United Arab Emirates company form a consortium with Sudan's state-owned Sudapet for exploitation of Adar oil fields (*12 Nov*).

Sadiq al-Mahdi returns to Khartoum (*23 Nov*).

Dec Government arrests seven members of the NDA for meeting with a US diplomat in Khartoum (*6 Dec*).

SPLA capture Biemnhom garrison on Kiir River, between Gogrial and Bentiu.

General election in Sudan boycotted by major opposition parties, including Turabi's PNC; low turnout reported; Bashir re-elected to a second presidential term.

2001

Jan Government begins dry season offensive in northern Bahr al-Ghazal with destruction of several villages in Aweil West (*12 Jan*) by a force of regular army, PDF units, and Rizaiqat and Misiriyya *murahalin*; Baqqara are being encouraged to settle in depopulated territory.

SPLA loses ground in Nuba Mts. Government takes Ayod in Upper Nile. Aerial bombardments intensified in Equatoria (Yei) and Bahr al-Ghazal (Rumbek); government suspends all relief flights into southern Sudan (*20 Jan*).

Colonel James Gatluak appointed chairman of the Council for the South.

Feb SPLA and Turabi's Popular National Congress Party (PNC) sign a memorandum of understanding in Geneva, agreeing to work jointly for a democratic system, a just peace and a federal government in the Sudan (*Feb 19*); Turabi and close aids are arrested in Khartoum (*21 Feb*).

Forces allied with SPLA attack and burn Nyal (*22 Feb*).

March Sadiq al-Mahdi and Muhammad Uthman al-Mirghani sign an 8-point 'Appeal from Sudan' in Cairo, calling for a relaunch of the Egyptian–Libyan peace initiative and moves towards peace (*1 March*).

May SPLA begin offensive in Western Bahr al-Ghazal.

June SPLA take Raga (*2 June*) and Deim Zubair.

House of Representatives pass Sudan Peace Act, barring foreign firms investing in the Sudan from being listed on NY stock exchange, and allocating assistance to the Sudanese opposition.

July Senate pass less restrictive version of Sudan Peace Act.

Egypt publicizes new 9-point Egyptian-Libyan Initiative [ELI] (*6 July*), calling for an immediate cease-fire, the preservation of Sudanese unity and decentralization, but avoiding mention of the issues of religion and the state, and self-determination agreed in the IGAD DOP.

Sudanese foreign minister Mustafa Uthman Ismail fails to persuade South African Foreign Minister Nkosazana Zuma to permit investment in Sudan.

Aug US State Dept spokesman says the administration opposes the Sudan Peace Act's prohibition of access to capital markets in the US.

SPLA commando force attacks oil installation at Heglig, inflicting minor damage (*5 Aug*); SPLA claim to have attacked and destroyed a battalion-size government convoy at Panaru (*9 Aug*).

Sudanese Vice-President Ali Uthman Muhammad al-Taha announces, 'Whether through the ELI or IGAD, anyone who believes that the government will accept peace that dilutes Islam is deluded.'

Fighting between LRA and Sudanese army reported.

Sept President Bush appoints former Senator John Danforth as special envoy on the Sudan (*6 Sept*).

Nuba Mountain General Union, Sudan National Party and Sudan National Free Party form a Charter for Coalition in Khartoum to achieve unity and co-ordinate position on the future of the Nuba Mts (*9 Sept*).

Talisman stock falls nearly 8 percent following 9/11 terrorist attack.

Sudan government begins co-operating with the CIA and FBI in tracking down al-Qaida members and remaining network in the Sudan, following 9/11 attack.

House of Representatives Republican leaders agree to administration's request to pull Sudan Peace Act (*25 Sept*).

UN Security Council lifts diplomatic sanctions against Sudan (*28 Sept*); US abstains from vote, but maintains own sanctions against Sudan.

South Sudan Democratic Forum founded in London (*29 Sept*).

Taban Deng Gai persuades Peter Paar and Peter Gatdet to stop fighting each other in western Upper Nile.

Oct Sudan government recaptures Raga and Deim Zubeir.

Danforth begins his Sudan mission (*13 Nov*).

Government offensive in oilfields begins.

2002

Jan 'Nairobi Declaration' (*7 Jan*), between Riek Machar and Garang, reuniting Riek's SPDF with the SPLA.

Danforth's second trip to Sudan (*10–16 Jan*); during the journey Danforth is quoted as saying independence for the South was a bad idea, and that the Sudan would not be expected to give up an Islamic state.

Heavy fighting reported between Nhialdiu and Bentiu; Lundin suspends drilling operations in Block 5A, following attacks by SPLA and SPDF forces (*22 Jan*); government convoy sent to reinforce garrison at Pultuni, near Lundin's rigs, ambushed by Gatdet's forces (*25 Jan*).

Ceasefire agreement for Nuba Mts signed between government and Nuba SPLA in Switzerland (*19 Jan*).

EU decides to resume aid to Khartoum, pledging $130 million over five years.

'Abyei Declaration': Misiriyya and Ngok sign a peace agreement (*31 Jan*) after negotiations assisted by the UNDP, the EU and the Netherlands Embassy in Khartoum.

Feb SPLA commander Peter Gatdet and SPDF commander Peter Paar sign merger agreement at Koc; government offensive in oilfields intensifies throughout Feb with shift of troops from Kassala and Nuba Mts fronts; fighting concentrates on Bentiu–Ler road; Nimne bombed (*9 Feb*); Sudanese helicopter gunship attacks UN feeding centre at Bieh (*20 Feb*); US suspends participation in the Sudanese peace process; Sudan government captures Nhialdiu airstrip (*22 Feb*); Sudan government admits attack on Bieh, comparing it to accidental killing of civilians by US forces in Afghanistan (*28 Feb*); bans relief flights to 45 locations in the South.

Tony Blair announces the appointment of former ambassador to Khartoum Alan Goulty as special envoy for the Sudan (*7 Feb*); over 500 persons (mostly Sudanese) petition Blair to remove Goulty because of his perceived bias in favour of the government.

Sudanese airforce bombs Akuem in Bahr al-Ghazal (*10 Feb*).

Amnesty International urges Talisman to press Sudanese government on human rights violations (*23 Feb*); Sudan government and Talisman cited in a class action suit in a US District Court in New York (*25 Feb*); Talisman CEO Jim Buckee sends a letter to Sudanese government condemning military attacks on non-combatants (*26 Feb*).

LRA attack on Agoro market in Kitgum district; Ugandan army crosses border into Sudan in hot pursuit (*23–4 Feb*).

South Sudan Democratic Forum issues 'Political charter for peace', calling for a broad-based alliance of southern Sudanese civilian and political groups to work for the self-determination for the South according to the IGAD DOP, and to support the struggle of other marginalized areas in the Sudan (*25 Feb*).

EU agrees to import sugar from the Sudan (*27 Feb*).

SPLA, the Sudanese National Alliance, and its military wing, the Sudanese Alliance Forces agree to merge (*28 Feb*).

March Ugandan army seals off border where LRA crossed from Sudan (*2 March*); Uganda and Sudan sign agreement allowing Ugandan army to enter the Sudan in pursuit of LRA (*13 March*); Uganda begins operations inside Sudan (*29 March*).

SSLM Nairobi spokesman warns that SPLA is planning to attack and seize SSLM towns of Akobo and Maiwut (*5 March*).

Umma Party and SPLM agree to restore ties (*5 March*).

Talisman profits reported down by 82 percent because of fall in world's oil prices, but it generated a record \$2.5 billion cash flow for 2001, up by \$0.1 billion over 2000 (*6 March*).

Sudan and SPLA sign US-brokered agreement on the protection of civilians (*10 March*); at government insistence the agreement pledges them to 'civilian protection from all types of military operations', rather than a specific pledge to cease aerial bombardment of civilians.

April Sudan army begins major offensive in Bahr al-Ghazal and Upper Nile.

Sudan and Russia begin talks on military-technical co-operation (*23 April*).

Senator Danforth delivers report to President Bush, recommending continued US engagement in Sudanese peace process; proposes oil revenue sharing arrangement between North and South and guarantees for religious freedom, but rejects both Southern independence and a secular state (*26 April*).

May Sudan government rejects oil revenue sharing proposal in the Danforth report (*1 May*). Sudan army retakes Qaissan (*30 May*).

June Intensification of fighting in South; dramatic increase in government's aerial bombardment against both military and civilian targets; SPLA retakes Kapoeta (*9 June*); government retakes Mankien (*20 June*) and Gogrial (*29 June*).

Bush administration Sudan policy criticized in House of Representatives hearing (*5 June*).

Peace talks begin in Nairobi with Sudan government insisting on unity of country (*17 June*); transferred to Machakos (*18 June*); US drafts proposal preserving the country's unity and limiting self-determination to the establishment of an autonomous Southern Region.

Indian cabinet approves state-owned Oil & National Gas Corp. bid for Talisman's share in Sudan's oil (*19 June*).

Lam Akol resigns from government (*26 June*).

Amnesty International reports sharp increase in executions in Darfur (*28 June*).

July Umma Party splits, Mubarak al-Fadil al-Mahdi declares Sadiq al-Mahdi dismissed as party leader and party's willingness to join the government (*11 July*).

SPLA retakes Jabal Lafon (*14 July*).

Assistant-secretary of State for Africa, Walter Kansteiner meets government officials in Khartoum (*2 July*); Bush administration Sudan policy criticized in Senate hearing (*12 July*); premature release of text of US-drafted agreement leads to sustained southern Sudanese protest and disagreement between White House and State Department; Kenya supports re-insertion of self-determination in agreement; Machakos Protocol on the framework for future talks signed by the government and SPLM (*20 July*); government and SSLM sign separate peace charter (*21 July*); Sudanese presidential adviser, Qatbi al-Mahdi, publicly denies that protocol implies partition of the Sudan (*22 July*); Bashir and Garang meet for first time in Kampala and pledge continued support for peace process

(*27 July*); Kansteiner claims that Machakos Protocol 'is just a framework agreement that involves autonomy for the South, not independence for the South' (*29 July*); Christian coalition Sudan lobby in US drops support for capital markets sanctions against Sudan, 'in light of' the Machakos Protocol (*30 July*).

July-Sept Fighting between government and SPLA in western Upper Nile, Jonglei, Eastern Equatoria, Blue Nile and eastern Sudan; government retakes Jabal Lafon; SPLA take Torit (*1 Sept*); government suspends peace talks (*2 Sept*).

Oct Government retakes Torit (*8 Oct*); government and SPLA agree cessation of hostilities in South (*15 Oct*); peace talks resume in Kenya (*16 Oct*); US Sudan Peace Act signed into law (*21 Oct*); Talisman agrees to sell Sudan assets to Indian state oil company (*30 Oct*).

Dec Government begins offensive in western Upper Nile oil fields (*31 Dec*).

2003

Jan Government takes Ler (*27 Jan*).

Feb Government and SPLA agree to ceasefire verification and monitoring team (*4 Feb*); Amnesty International warns of deteriorating situation in Darfur (*21 Feb*); Darfur Liberation Front (DLA) seizes Golo in Northern Darfur (*26 Feb*).

March-Aug DLA renames itself Sudan Liberation Movement/Army (SLM/A) (*14 March*); fighting between government forces and opposition SLM/A and Justice and Equality Movement (JEM) in Darfur escalates with co-ordinated government attacks by air, *Janjawid* Arab militias, and regular army; some 100 villages destroyed and 100,000 persons displaced.

July IGAD draft framework for resolving outstanding issues rejected by government (*12 July*).

Sept Garang and 1st Vice-President Ali Uthman Muhammad Taha begin direct talks in Kenya, reach interim agreement on security arrangements (*25 Sept*).

Oct-Dec Turabi released from house arrest; Lam Akol rejoins SPLM/A (*31 Oct*); fighting in Darfur results in 700,000 internally displaced and 110,000 refugees in Chad; peace talks in Chad collapse; NDA and government sign accord in Jedda supporting peace process.

2004

Jan Government and SPLM reach agreement on wealth-sharing (*7 Jan*); government begins offensive in Shilluk kingdom (*17 Jan*).

Feb Bashir declares law and order restored in Darfur (*9 Feb*); SLM/A and EJM renew offensive; peace talks resume in Naivasha; SLM/A admitted into NDA (*13 Feb*); government suspends contacts with NDA.

March SPLM and Equatoria Defence Force merge (*6 March*); 75,000 persons reported displaced in Shilluk kingdom; government arrests Turabi and announces it has foiled coup attempt (*31 March*).

April Peace talks in Naivasha reach impasse; President Bush reports to US Congress that both parties are negotiating 'in good faith' (*21 April*); African bloc in the UN Human Rights Commission vote down strong criticism of atrocities in Darfur and adopt a compromise resolution (*23 April*); ceasefire agreement reached between government and Darfur rebels in N'djamena (*25 April*).

May Number of Darfur refugees and displaced persons estimated at one million, despite ceasefire; number of persons displaced by militias in Shilluk kingdom estimated at 150,000; final protocols signed between government and SPLM (*26 May*), opening way to a formal peace settlement.

June Sudan government continues aerial bombardment in Darfur, attacks SPLA at Nimne in Western Upper Nile (*1 June*), captures Akobo (*2 June*); Taha and Garang sign Nairobi Declaration, reconfirming their commitment to a strict observance of the cessation of hostilities and producing a comprehensive peace agreement based on the six protocols (*5 June*).

Abbasids 3
Abbud, General 30–2
Abdallahi, Khalifa 6–7, 9
Aborom 98
Abuja 100–2, 104, 112–13, 120,
    174–5, 178
Abyei 44, 82, 100, 114, 151–2,
    154, 174, 180
Acholi people 82, 86
Acuil, Dhol 61
Addis Ababa 84–5, 92, 102;
    Agreement (1972) 39–41,
    43–5, 51, 53, 55–6, 59–64, 71,
    75, 80, 124, 136, 175, 180
Adok 98
Africa, West 137 see also name of
    country
Agar, Malik 137
agriculture 12, 18–19, 43, 49–50,
    80–2, 129–33, 136–9, 145–6,
    151, 153, 155–7, 159
aid see relief
aircraft 147, 153
Akobo 89, 93, 114, 117–18, 121
Akol, Lam 92–9, 112, 119–20,
    126, 150
alcohol 129
Al-Da'ain 82, 156
Alier, Abel 34, 36, 42–3, 45–7,
    51–4, 86, 142
al-Qaida 177
Amadi 70
American Anti-Slavery Group 158
Amin, Idi 36, 43, 52, 60
Amnesty International 163–4
Anglo-Egyptian Treaty (1899) 21
Anglo-Egyptian Treaty (1936) 22

Angola 165, 167
animism xvii–xviii, xx–xxi, 178
Anja, Hamdan Abu 7n
Ansar sect see Islam
anthropology xix
Anuak people 87–8, 93, 118,
    168
Anyanya Armed Forces 31–4, 37,
    41–3, 54–6, 59, 61, 63–5, 91,
    138; Anyanya-2 60, 62, 66,
    68–9, 73, 82–5, 88, 92–4,
    96–8, 112, 117, 127, 147, 151
Anyanya National Organization 33
Anyidi Revolutionary Government
    33
apostasy 128–9, 133, 172
Arab Group International 162
Arab-Israeli War (1967) 30, 36, 57
Arab League 57
Arabic language 1–3, 30, 51, 63,
    169
Arabs and Arabization xxii, 1, 65,
    67, 75, 79, 81, 136, 138,
    140–1, 158, 168, 172, 176;
    entrepreneurs and traders
    133, 169; militias 84, 93, 125,
    152, 154; pastoralists 44, 131,
    137, 151; Rashaida 137
Arakis oil company 162
Arianhdit 168–9
armed forces 40, 45, 51–2, 57, 95,
    99, 115, 120, 123, 170; Anglo-
    Egyptian Condominium 9, 11,
    13, 15; children 97; Ethiopia
    118; local defence units 108;
    Mahdiyya period 10, 170;
    militias 49, 81–8, 93, 114,

122, 124–5, 132–4, 136,
140–1, 145, 147–8, 151–2,
163–4, 172–3; Uganda 36,
100, 113 *see also* mutinies;
slavery – slave soldiers *and
under name of force or area*
arms xxii, 31, 37, 57–8, 60–1,
68–9, 85–6, 88, 100, 116, 118,
120, 137, 139–41, 152
Arok, Arok Thon 66, 92, 113, 119
Asmara 104–5, 138, 175–6
Assosa 94, 136
Atem, Akwot 32–3, 61, 65–6, 68
Atem, Faustino 120
Atlantic Charter 23
atrocities 81, 88, 113 *see also*
massacres
Australia 102
Austria 162
Aweil 61, 69, 82; Rice Scheme
50
Ayod xvii, 68, 89, 97–8, 114–18,
150
Azania Liberation Front 32–3
Azande kingdom xx, 12
Azande people 18
Azhari, Ismail al- 23–5, 27–8

Ba'athism 128
Babangida, Ibrahim 101
Bahr al-Arab *see* Kiir
Bahr al-Ghazal 2, 49, 55, 80, 82,
91, 97, 103, 106–9, 114, 119,
124, 126, 140, 149–59, 168–9,
172–3; Anglo-Egyptian
Condominium 11–12, 15, 18,
28; armed forces 51–2, 60, 62,
69–70, 85, 93, 117, 122, 147,
173; borders 44; clans xx;
displaced persons 148, 156,
159; famines 134, 146; labour
50, 133, 151; Region 55, 80;
SANU 34; slavery 157–8; trade
154
banks and banking 44, 49, 80,
135, 144
Bany, William Nyuon 65–6, 97,
100, 113, 115–16, 119–21
Baqqara people 3, 5, 7, 9, 69,
131–2, 139–40, 157, 163–4,

169, 173; Misiriyya militia 44,
69, 81–2, 83n, 127, 132, 151,
153–4; Rizaiqat militia 81–2,
141, 151, 153
Bashir, Umar al- 83, 99, 103–4,
107–8, 121, 123, 141, 178
Beja Congress 104, 130, 138
Beja peoples 34, 137–8
Bengal 149
Bentiu 45–6, 49, 60–1, 64, 69,
120, 122–4, 162
Beshir, Mohamed Omer 34n
Biafra 31
Bildt, Carl 164
Bilpam 70
Blue Nile 80, 83, 85, 89–91, 95,
104, 122, 127, 132, 135–8,
142, 145, 151, 174–5, 180
Bol, Kerubino Kuanyin 61–2,
65–6, 92, 100, 103, 107,
113–14, 119–23, 125–6, 150,
152, 154
Bolad, Daud 140
Boma 70, 92
Bonga 70
Bor 9, 15, 18, 42, 45, 54, 61–2,
67–8, 84, 89, 98, 114–17
borders 44–5, 49, 60, 62, 64, 121,
123
Boya people 86
Britain xxi, 1, 28, 57, 102, 142,
163, 165, 179, 180; Foreign
Office 24–5 *see also* Sudan –
Anglo-Egyptian
Condominium
Buganda 14
Bush, Vice-President 67

camels 137
Camp David Accord 57, 60
Canada 102, 162–5
Carlos ('the jackal') 177
Carter, Jimmy xv
Catholicism *see* Roman
Catholicism
cattle 11, 16, 44, 48, 60, 82, 88,
114–15, 117, 124, 132, 137,
151–4, 157, 165, 169
Cattle Guards 108
censuses *see* population

Central African Republic 87, 152
Central Intelligence Agency 177
Central State 156
cereals 154 *see also name of crop*
Chad 139–41
Chali 44–5, 135–6
Chevron oil company 45–6, 57, 68, 83n, 127, 162
chiefs 12, 85, 105–6, 131, 133–4, 148, 169, 172–3
children 138, 157–8 *see also* armed forces
China 124, 137, 162–3
Chinese National Petroleum Company 162
Christian Aid 163
Christian Solidarity International 158
Christian Solidarity Worldwide 158
Christianity xx–xxi, 2–3, 14–15, 31, 35, 56, 67, 101–2, 132, 136, 142, 178 *see also* missionaries *and name of sect*
Chukudum 104, 109
civil administration 105–7 *see also* state
civil service 9, 13–15, 18, 23, 25–7, 32, 43, 49, 55, 68
clans xix–xx
Clinton, Bill 102
coffee 154, 165
Cohen, Herman 111
Cold War xxii, 59, 67, 76, 102, 176
colonialism xxi, 6–7, 11, 21n, 28, 57, 63, 105, 170
Communism 56–7, 64, 128
Congo *see* Democratic Republic of the Congo
Constituent Assembly 29, 34
Constitutional Amendment Commission 26
constitutions 27, 29–30, 33–5, 41–2, 55–6, 71–2, 84, 103, 125, 141, 174
Coordinating Council for the Southern States 122–3
corruption 43
cotton 17, 32, 137
Council of Ministers 84, 156
Council of Southern States 175

courts *see* law
courts martial *see* law
culture xxi, 18, 63, 131, 138, 176, 178
Cuol, Gordon Kong 97, 126
Cuol, William Abdallah 61, 65–6, 68–9
custom 169

Dafallah, al-Jizuli 71
Dahab, Suwar al- 67, 70–1, 81
Daly, M. W. xviii
Damazin 135–7
Danaqla people 5
Danforth, John 165–6, 177–8
Darfur 2–3, 44, 49, 82–3, 85, 93, 127, 133, 139–42, 145, 151–3, 156–9, 168–9
Darfur Development Front 130
Dawa al-Islamiyya 136
debt 5, 43, 57, 144, 162
Declaration of Principles 102, 104, 175–6, 178
Democratic Republic of the Congo 19, 31, 87, 152, 177
Democratic Unionist Party 35, 55, 71–3, 79–80, 84, 103–5, 130, 138 see also National Union Party
Deng, Gatluak 96
Deng, William 31–2, 34–5
Derg 59, 93–4, 146
development, socio-economic xxi, 16–19, 52, 57, 63–4, 66, 107, 123–4, 135, 156, 159, 164, 179 *see also* economy and economic factors
diamonds 165
Didinga Hills 109
Didinga people 109
Dimma 88, 89, 149
Dinka language 1, 51, 168
Dinka people 3–4, 43, 97–8, 106, 109, 112, 114–19, 125, 153, 164, 167–9, 171–3; Anglo-Egyptian Condominium 18, 28–9; cattle 108, 151; clans xx; 'Dinka domination' 51–3, 73; displaced persons 133, 150, 152; labour 50, 133, 156–7; Ngok section 104;

pastoralism 44; slavery 82, 157–8; SPLA/M 65–70, 83, 85
displaced persons 155–9, 164
District Commissioners 12
Doleib Hill 94, 96–7
Dongola 9
droughts 44, 49, 82, 137, 139, 157
Duar 99
Duffield, Mark 166
Duk 98
Duk Faiwil 116

economy and economic factors xxii, 39, 53, 75–6, 80–2, 100–1. 130–1, 137, 162, 165; and USA 142; and war 143–7, 149–57, 166; Bor Dinka and Mundari 68; confrontations with Khartoum 43–51; cotton exports 32; economic objectives and planning 40, 42, 133–4, 143; Equatoria 27–8; Nubia 5; women 129 *see also* development, socio-economic
education 14–15, 18, 30, 42, 45, 52, 132
Egypt 1–2, 14, 21–4, 27–8, 47–8, 54, 57, 64, 67, 102, 127, 142, 170, 176–80; Free Officers' coup (1956) 22, 26 see also Sudan – Anglo-Egyptian Condominium; Sudan – Turkiyya period
El Obeid 133
elections 24, 26–7, 30, 34, 42–3, 47, 52, 54, 67, 71–3, 81, 84, 106, 136, 140, 175
élites xxii, 63–4
English language 30
Equatoria 43, 51–5, 70, 73, 82–3, 86–7, 93–7, 109, 112; Anglo-Egyptian Condominium 15, 19, 27–8; early history 12–13; Eastern 50, 91, 99, 103, 108, 113–16, 149, 151; Region 53, 55, 68, 80; Western 19, 27, 50, 85, 100, 160
Equatoria Defence Force 126
Equatorial Corps 18, 27–8

Eritrea 36, 59, 63, 102, 104, 107, 120, 137–8, 141–2, 175, 177
Eritrean Islamic Jihad 137
Eritrean People's Liberation Front 87, 138, 147, 162
Ethiopia 2, 37, 45, 65, 67, 82, 90, 99, 102, 120–1, 135–8, 140, 145–9, 151–2, 175; alliance with Soviet Union 57–8; armed forces 42, 59–60, 62, 65–6, 69–70, 84–5, 87–8, 93–6, 118, 132–3; displaced persons 89; Koka Dam meeting (1986) 71; Marxism 63; Provisional Government 88; Wallega Province 87; war with Eritrea 107, 142, 177
Ethiopian People's Revolutionary Democratic Front 94, 96
ethnicity xix, 174
ethnography xviii
Europe 177–9 *see also name of country*
European Union 107, 142
Evans-Pritchard, E. E. 116
exports 16, 32, 43, 46, 80, 130, 145, 151, 154, 162, 165–6

families 158
famines 6, 80, 82, 107–8, 134, 136, 139, 144, 146, 148–9, 151, 154–5
Fangak 61, 116–17
Fartit people 18, 82–3, 85
Faruq, King 22
Fashoda 4, 9, 120
Federal Bureau of Investigation 177
Federal Party 30
federation 27, 29–30, 39–40, 68, 73, 79, 96, 112, 121–3, 173–5, 180
Fellman, Michael xxiii
feuds 168–72
finance 42, 44, 50, 53, 73, 80, 99, 120, 144, 158–9, 162, 165
fishing 117–18
floods 68, 115, 148
food 86, 89, 95–6, 115–17, 139, 145, 148–57, 159–60

France 142, 177
Frankfurt Agreement (1992) 112, 124, 174
Front Line States 85
Fungyido 88, 89, 95
Fur people 139–40

Gai, Taban Deng 96, 99, 123
Gambela 45, 87–9, 94, 118
Gambela People's Liberation Front 87–8, 94
Gâmk people 135
Garang, John xix, 61–2, 64–5, 70–1, 81, 86–7, 92–101, 103–4, 106–10, 113–22, 134, 138, 142, 178–9; and Bona Malwal 109; and Mengistu 88, 91, 93, 96; and Muhammad Uthman al-Mirghani 84; and Riek Machar 110, 126, 174; and Sadiq al-Mahdi 72, 85, 148, 176; and William Nyuon Bany 113, 121, 125; overthrow 97, 120; split with Anyanya-2 66
Garang, Joseph 36
Garang, Mading de 59
genealogies 3
General Union of the Nuba Mountains 130
Germany 142
Gezira Scheme 17
Gogrial 100, 109, 114, 154
gold 4, 114, 137, 165
government *see* state
Graduates' Congress 23–5
grain *see* cereals
Grand Qadi 13
Great Britain *see* Britain
Greater Nile Petroleum Company 162–3
Gulf Petroleum Corporation 162
Gulf States 67, 81, 85, 135–6 *see also name of country*

Habré, Hissene 140
Haile Selassie 57, 59
Hamas 102, 137
handicrafts 154
Hanlon, Joseph xxi

Harker Report 164
health services 148
Herodotus 2
High Executive Council 40, 42–3, 47, 51–5, 61, 125
historiography xviii
Hizbullah 137
Hofrat al-Nahas 44
Holt, P. M. xvii
human rights xvi, 49, 60, 79, 81–2, 97–8, 104, 107, 119, 125, 163–4
Human Rights Watch 163

identity xxii, 24, 30, 63, 118, 178
Igga, James Wani 87
Ilemi Triangle 166
income 157, 165–6
Independent Bahr al-Ghazal Group 126
Independent Bor Group 126
Independent Group from the Nuba Mountains *see* Sudan People's Liberation Army/ Movement
India 14
infrastructure 50, 53, 57, 105, 147
Ingessana Hills 135–6
Ingessana people 135–6
Integration Charter (1982) 54, 64
Intergovernmental Authority on Development 76, 100–2, 104, 134, 141–2, 160, 175–6, 178
Intergovernmental Authority on Drought and Desertification *see* Intergovernmental Authority on Development
International Center for Religion and Diplomacy 177n
International Committee for the Red Cross 149
International Monetary Fund 43, 144, 162
International Petroleum Company 162
investment 44, 49, 80, 134–5, 162–3
Iran xv, 54, 60, 79, 102
Iraq 54, 73, 85, 102, 144
irrigation *see* water

Islam xvi, xviii-xxii, 1, 45, 63, 67, 75–6, 108, 127–33, 135–42, 169–75, 177, 179; and Arabism 140–1; and Christianity xx–xxi, 14–15, 132; Anglo-Egyptian Condominium 13–15, 17, 171; Ansar sect 7, 9, 21, 24, 81–2, 128–30, 140, 170, 172–3; Ansar-Sunna sect 129; Community of Believers 169–70, 172–3; Darfur 139; Dinka 158; finance 43–4, 80, 135, 144; Islamic state 3, 29–30, 34–5, 49, 54–5, 71, 79–80, 84, 101, 103, 111–12, 128, 138, 175; Khatmiyya sect 9, 24, 26, 79, 81, 128–30, 137, 172; law 3, 12–14, 43–4, 56–8, 71–2, 79–80, 84, 111, 122, 128–9, 172; Mahdiyya period 6–7; NGOs 159; Nile Valley before 1820 2–4; revolution 100, 102; Turkiyya period 4–6 *see also name of sect or organization*
Islamic Charter Front 35
Islamic Consultative Council 123
Israel 30, 36–7, 57, 60
Italy 102
Itang 65, 70, 82, 88, 89, 92, 95–6, 149
ivory 5, 16

Ja'aliyyin people 5, 9
Jabal Lafon *see* Lafon
Jaden, Aggrey 31–3
Jikany people 117–18
Joint Defence Treaty 64
Jokau 84, 121
Jonglei 45, 60–1, 68, 82–3, 91, 93, 99, 115, 117, 120, 123, 125, 149–52; Canal 47–9, 64, 66, 97
journalism and journalists xvi, 148
Juba 47, 63, 68, 85–7, 94–5, 98–100, 103, 107, 113–15, 122, 130, 145; Conference (1947) 25, 32, 34; Conference (1954) 27

Judaism 56
Juk, Kuol Manyang 93
Jur people 18
Kafia Kingi 44
Kajo-Kaji 85–6
Kampala 33, 126
Kansteiner, Walter 179
Kapoeta 68, 84, 86, 114
Kassala 9, 127, 137–8
Kaya 85
Kenana Sugar Refinery 49
Kenya 46, 60, 101, 109, 120, 146, 152, 161, 166, 175
Khalid, Abd al-Aziz 138
Khalid, Mansour 40, 94
Khartoum 3, 10, 63, 82, 95, 103, 126, 145, 148–50, 152–3, 155–6, 162; and Nasir 99; coup attempt (1976) 55–6; demonstrations (1985) 70; meeting between Bush and Nimairi (1984) 67; mutiny (1924) 23; Round Table Conference (1965) 32–3
Khatmiyya sect *see* Islam
Khor Adar 137
Kiir 44, 82
kings xix, 3, 7
kinship 117, 149, 153, 168
Kirkpatrick, Jeane 67
Koka Dam meeting (1986) 71–3, 80, 84
Kongor 66, 97–8, 100, 114–17, 119, 150, 172
Konye, Ismail 68
Kordofan 82, 89, 125, 127, 131, 149, 151–4, 162–3, 168–9, 172; agriculture 137, 145; droughts 44, 49; labour 156, 158–9; slavery 157–8; SPLA/M 69, 83, 85, 93, 132
Kosti 95–6
Kurmuk 44, 84–5, 122, 136–7, 141
Kush 2
Kuwa, Yusif 132, 134–5

labour 16, 49–50, 80–1, 132–3, 136–7, 143, 145–6, 151–9, 166
Ladin, Usama bin 102, 137, 141, 177

Lafon 113, 116, 121
Lagu, Joseph 32–3, 37, 39, 42–3, 47, 52–3, 62, 65, 67
Lake Nasser 137
Lakes 60, 68, 89, 114, 152–3
land 5, 13, 16, 49–50, 82, 130–5, 138, 140, 145, 156, 160, 168
languages 1, 131 *see also under name*
Latif, Ali Abd al– 23
law 3, 11–14, 22, 43–4, 56–8, 128–30, 156, 159–60, 162, 172; courts 12, 49, 105–6, 129, 132–3, 148, 169, 171; courts martial 92; September Laws 71–2, 79; *shari'a* 12–13, 56, 79–80, 84, 111, 122, 129, 171, 179
Legislative Assembly 25–6
Legislative Council 25
Legitimate Command of Armed Forces 103–4
Ler 98–9, 122, 124
Liberal Party 26–7
Libya 55, 57–8, 59–60, 67, 81, 139–41, 176–7, 180
licensing 17, 163
Liech State 123
Lienhardt, Godfrey 167
literacy 3
livestock 139–40 *see also name of animal*
Lloyd, Selwyn 24
local defence units *see* armed forces
Lohure, Saturnino 30–2
Longarim people 86
Lonrho 46, 85, 99, 120
Lord's Resistance Army 100, 113
Lotuko people 82
Lundin oil company 162–4
Luo people 169

Machakos Protocol 179
Machar, Riek 93–100, 106, 109–10, 112–13, 116–26, 150, 173–6, 180
Madi people 86
Mahdi *see* Muhammad Ahmad
Mahdi family 35

Mahdi, Sadiq al– 34–5, 46, 51, 55–6, 59–60, 72, 79–85, 108, 128, 130, 136, 138, 140–2, 148, 172, 176, 179
Mahdi, Sayyid Abd al-Rahman al– 16–17, 21, 23–4, 26, 35
Mahdiyya period *see* Sudan
Maiwut 125
Majier, Martin 91
Malakal 28, 61, 89, 95–6, 113, 115–16, 118, 147
Malawi 31
Malaysia 162–3
Malek 15, 18
Malwal, Bona 46–7, 53, 109, 142
Mankien 150
manufactures 165–6
Maridi 86
markets 16, 49, 87, 139, 151–2, 154, 159 *see also* trade
marriage 13, 168, 170
Marxism 63–4
Masalit people 141
massacres 34, 130, 171 *see also* atrocities
Matip, Paulino 69, 114, 122–6, 154
Matthews, D. K. 68
Mayardit, Salva Kiir 66
Mayen, Gordon Muortat 32–3
Mayom 85, 96–8, 123
Mboro, Clement 32, 34, 36
McCune, Emma 115, 125n
meat supply trade 68, 151
Meban 45; people 97
Mechanized Farming Corporation 132, 136
medical services *see* health services
Melut 94
Mengistu, Haile Mariam 59, 64, 67, 76, 87–9, 91–6, 102, 136–8, 149, 162
migration 49–50, 132, 137, 139–40, 153 *see also* refugees
militias *see* armed forces *and under name*
millet 49
minerals and mining 40, 123–4, 136 *see also* gold

Mirghani family 9
Mirghani, Muhammad Uthman al-
    84, 105
Mirghani, Sayyid Ali al- 23–4
missionaries 14–15, 28, 30, 35, 44,
    135
Mombasa 46
moral communities 167–8, 173,
    180
mosques 133
Mubarak, Hosni 102
Muhammad (Prophet) 3
Muhammad Ahmad 6–7, 9, 170
Muhammad Ali 4
Muhammad, Ali al-Hajj 99, 112
Multi-Donor Technical Mission 89
Mundari people 68, 82–3, 86, 127,
    151
Mundri 70, 86
Murahalin militia 82, 84–5, 132,
    151, 173
murder 171
Murle people 68–9, 82–3, 93, 114,
    151
Mursi people 88
Musaddiq, Muhammad xvi
Museveni, Yoweri 86, 102
Muslim Brothers *see* National
    Islamic Front
Muslims *see* Islam
mutinies 21, 23, 27–9, 31, 42,
    61–2, 68
Muwafaq 157

Nairobi 99, 101, 120, 125, 148–9
Najib, Mohammed 22
Namibia 85, 91n, 95
Nasir 45, 61, 69, 84–5, 89–90;
    faction see Sudan People's
    Liberation Army/Movement
Nasir, Gamal Abdel 22
National Alliance for National
    Salvation 70–1
National Assembly 43, 47, 54,
    56–7, 81, 111, 123, 148
National Congress 107 *see also*
    National Islamic Front
National Convention 106, 108, 119
National Democratic Alliance
    102–5, 107–8, 110, 121–2,
    135, 137–8, 140–2, 175–6

National Development Foundation
    144, 159
National Executive Council 106,
    109
National Islamic Front 35, 87,
    102, 104, 112, 121, 128–31,
    133, 141, 173–4, 177, 180;
    and Beja peoples 138; and
    Islamic banks 49, 80; and
    Islamic law 79; and Nimairi
    43, 46, 55–6; coup (1989)
    84–5, 101, 140, 144, 172;
    elections (1986) 72–3; ghost
    houses 130; Koka Dam
    meeting (1986) 71, 80;
    Kurmuk 136; National
    Reconciliation 46, 56 *see also*
    National Congress
National Union Party 24, 26–8 *see
    also* Democratic Unionist
    Party
nationalism xxii, 6, 21–5, 28–9,
    31, 128, 131, 169
Native Administration 12–13, 15,
    18, 105, 130–3, 139, 169
Netherlands 163
New Fangak 85, 94, 96–7
New Kush Division see Sudan
    People's Liberation Army/
    Movement
New Sudan Brigade see Sudan
    People's Liberation Army/
    Movement
New Sudan Council of Churches
    125
Ngundeng 168–9
Nigeria 101, 174
Nile Provisional Government 33
Nile, River 2, 97
Nile Waters Agreement (1959) 47
Nilotic peoples 43, 51–2, 54, 68,
    85, 134, 167, 169 *see also
    under name*
Nimairi, Jaafar Mohammed 7,
    42–3, 47, 51–8, 62–4, 68–72,
    76, 79, 81, 139–40, 172–3;
    and Addis Ababa Agreement
    (1972) 39, 41, 45, 53, 55–6, 60;
    and agriculture 130, 145; and
    Eritrea 59; and oil industry
    45–6; and USA 57–8, 62,

66–7; coup (1969) 34–5; executes Mahmud Muhammad Taha 129; purges Communists 36; returns from exile 141

Nimule 100

non-governmental organizations 50, 105, 107, 136, 142, 144, 147–8, 150, 155, 159–62 *see also under name*

Northern Sector *see* Operation Lifeline Sudan

Norway 102

Nuba Mountains xvii, 49, 130, 145, 165, 180; and SPLA/M 82–3, 91, 107, 122, 126, 138, 147, 174–5, 180; agriculture 80; Arabization 158; displaced persons 156; holy war 131–5; relief 151, 155, 178; slavery 11

Nuba peoples 34, 104, 131–5, 138, 142, 157

Nubia 2, 5, 7

Nubian languages 2

Nubians 4, 137

Nuer language 168

Nuer people 60, 68, 73, 93–4, 98, 154, 164, 168; Anglo-Egyptian Condominium 18, 28–9; animism xvii; Anyanya-2 69, 97, 127, 151; civil war 111–26; clans xx; Ethiopia 87–8; feuds 171–2; labour 50; Nasir 85; SPLA/M 49, 65–6, 96, 106, 109, 113–19, 121, 125, 127, 163, 173; Wunlit Conference (1999) 167

Nyang, Wut 113

Nyangatom people 88

Nzara 28

oaths 6

Obote, Milton 36, 60

Oduho, Joseph 31–2, 85–6, 91, 113, 119

oil industry xvi, xxii, 43–9, 61, 64, 75, 107, 111, 122–4, 126, 137–8, 142, 162–5, 177, 180; Chevron 45–6, 57, 68, 83n, 127, 162

Omdurman 23, 139, 151–2; Battle (1898) 9

OMV (Sudan) Exploration GmbH 162

Operation Lifeline Sudan 89, 95, 107, 133, 142, 145, 147, 152–5; foundation (1989) 93, 148; Northern and Southern sectors 146, 148–51, 156, 159–62

Organization of African Unity 31, 54, 71, 101, 174

Oromo Islamic Jihad 137

Oromo Liberation Front 87–8, 94, 136

Oromo Relief Association 136

Pakok 89

Panyagor 115–16, 119

pastoralism 11–13, 15, 18, 51, 68, 82, 117–18, 134, 139–40, 145, 159, 168; Arab 44, 131, 137, 151

Patriotic Resistance Movement of South Sudan 126

Peace and Development Foundation *see* National Development Foundation

Peace Charter 121–2, 154

'peace from within' strategy 49, 121–6, 133, 141, 150, 154, 163, 173, 175

peace villages 145, 155–6

People's Progressive Party 73

Petronus Carigali Overseas Sdn Bhd 162

Petterson, Donald 116, 120

Pibor 61, 68, 89, 91, 114; River 89, 95

Pochalla 61, 89

police 9, 18, 68, 109, 148

Political-Military High Command *see* Sudan People's Liberation Army/Movement

politics and political factors xix, xxii, 26, 29–31, 53, 55, 83, 91, 104, 122, 126, 139, 141, 173–4, 178; agriculture 146; and development 145, 166; and Islam 3, 35, 76, 79–80, 102,

108, 112, 127–30, 172; and relief 143, 147, 150, 166; Anglo-Egyptian Condominium 9, 17–18, 24; Beja peoples 138; developments (1969–71) 36–7; Dinka 51; Egypt 22; electoral (regional governments) 42–3; Fur people 140; Garang 66, 134, 148; international 57, 60, 142, 177; Juba Conference (1954) 27; legalization of political parties (1964) 32; Nasir faction 113, 115, 118; National Congress 107; Nimairi 63; Nuba peoples 131–2, 135; Nuer xx, 115; Sadiq al-Mahdi 81; SPLA/M 70–3, 94, 109, 113, 115, 150; Turkiyya period 75; Uduk people 136

Popular Defence Forces 83, 100, 108, 114, 125, 129, 138, 140, 145, 151–4, 173

population 51

Port Sudan 46, 64, 137, 162

privatization 43–4, 80

prophets 168–9, 171

Protestantism 14, 44

Punyido 149

Qaddafi, Muammar al- 57, 70, 176

Qaissan 84, 122, 137

Qallabat 127, 138

Qardud 132

Qatar 162–3

racism 52, 65, 71, 75

Radio Juba 56

Radio SPLA 64–5, 92

Raga 108

raids 145, 148, 151–4, 168–9, 173 *see also* slavery

railways 153–4

rainfall *see* water

Rashaida Arabs 137

Reagan, Ronald 67, 146

Red Cross *see* International Committee for the Red Cross

Red Sea 127, 137

referendums 29, 41, 44, 47, 54, 112, 122, 136, 142, 175, 179

refugees 28, 32, 52, 82, 86–90, 94–5, 100, 115, 125, 136–7, 141, 145–50, 152, 172 *see also* displaced persons

Regional Assemblies 40, 43, 47–8, 51, 54–6, 64

regionalization 53–5, 57, 64, 68, 86, 130, 139, 173

Rejaf 9

relief xxii, 44, 89, 134, 139, 178–9; and Islam 136, 157, 159; and oil industry 163–4; and politics 143–62, 166; Dinka 114–15; hunger triangle 116; Ler 124; SPLA/M 100, 107–8, 176; SRRA 87, 106; UN 96, 117, 135, 147–9, 156, 160; USA 43, 57, 90 *see also* Operation Lifeline Sudan *and name of agency*

Relief and Rehabilitation Commission 159

Relief Association of South Sudan 161

religion xvii–xix, 34–5, 75, 103–4, 141, 169, 174, 178 *see also name of religion or sect*

reporting *see* journalism and journalists

Republican Brothers 129

resource targeting 151–9

Revolutionary Council 36

rice 50

rituals *see* spirit rites

Rizaiqat militia *see* Baqqara people

roads 48, 50

Roman Catholicism 14, 28

Roseires 137

Round Table Conference (1965) 32–4

Rowland, Tiny 46, 85, 99, 120

Rufa'a people 3, 5

Rumbek 70, 125

Russia 137, 163 *see also* Soviet Union

Rwanda 177

Salih, Al-Zubair Muhammad 121
Saudi Arabia 79, 85, 144
schools *see* education
Sennar 2–3
September Laws *see* law
sesame 137
Shaiqiyya people 5
sharecroppers 157
shari'a see law
Shilluk 94; kingdom xx, 4, 12;
    people 50, 96–7
Short, Clare 154
Sierra Leone 165
Simbas 31
Six-Day War *see* Arab-Israeli War
    (1967)
slavery xxi, 11, 17, 24, 76, 82,
    102, 108n, 142, 155, 157–9,
    169–70, 177; slave soldiers
    2–6, 9
Sobat 89, 113, 116; River 89–90,
    95, 97, 117, 120, 150
socialism 57, 63
Socialist Republican Party 24
society and social factors 75 *see
    also* kinship; moral
    communities
Somalia 100, 166
sorghum 49, 124
South Africa 31
South Sudan Defence Force
    122–3, 125–6
South Sudan Freedom Front 126
South Sudan Independence
    Army/Movement 119, 121–2,
    125–6, 152, 154, 161
South Sudan Liberation
    Movement 125
South Sudan United Army 126
South West Africa People's
    Organization 95
Southern Front 32–4, 36, 51, 53
Southern Sector *see* Operation
    Lifeline Sudan
Southern Sudan Liberation
    Front/Movement 33, 37, 39–40
Southern Sudan Political
    Association 72–3
Southern Sudan Provisional
    Government 32–3

Soviet Union 57, 63 *see also*
    Russia
Spearmasters xx
spirit rites 138
squatters 156
state xvii, xxi, 2–7, 11, 31, 40, 44,
    102, 104–5, 146–7, 155–7,
    159–60, 172–8, 180; and
    development 44; and NGOs
    50–1, 162; and oil industry
    162–5; and prophets 169;
    Anglo-Egyptian
    Condominium 34, 171;
    Islamic 29, 35, 55–6, 71, 75,
    79–80, 84 101, 103, 111–12,
    128–30, 170, 174–5, 179 *see
    also* civil administration
State Security Organization 64
statistics 143n
students 30–1, 129
Suakin 9
Sudan – Anglo-Egyptian
    Condominium xx, 7, 9–19,
    21–2, 34, 51, 75, 127–8, 131,
    135, 169–71, 173, 180 *see
    also* Britain; Egypt; Civil
    Transactions Act (1990) 130;
    civil war (first) 21, 29–33, 60,
    62, 68, 75–6, 91, 171; civil
    war (second) 55, 59–73, 75–6,
    81–4; Criminal Bill (1988)128;
    Closed District Ordinance 12,
    17; independence (1956) 15,
    18, 21–37, 57, 75, 128, 171;
    Law of Criminal Trespass
    (1974) 130; Mahdiyya period
    3, 6–7, 10, 16, 127–8, 139,
    169–70; Ministry of Energy
    and Mining 163; Ministry of
    Housing 156; Ministry of
    Planning 133; North-South
    divide 4–5; Penal Code (1991)
    128; Popular Defence Forces
    Act (1989) 140; Power of
    Nomad Sheikhs Ordinance
    12; Public Order Act (1991)
    129; Regional Self-
    Government Act (1972) 41;
    Relief Act (1992) 160;
    Southern Policy 11–15;

Southern Region and Southern Regional Government 29, 39–58, 60–2, 64, 73, 80–1, 105, 111, 114–15, 132–3, 136, 146, 175; Turkiyya period 4–7, 10, 12, 75, 139, 145; Unregistered Land Act (1970) 130, 135 *see also name of province, eg* Equatoria
Sudan African Congress 73
Sudan African Nationalist Union 31–5, 51, 53
Sudan African People's Congress 73
Sudan Democratic Gazette 109, 142
Sudan Federal Democratic Alliance 140
Sudan Interior Mission 44
Sudan People's Federal Party 73
Sudan People's Liberation Army/ Movement 48, 55, 76, 81–90, 127, 132–8, 140–2, 145–8, 150–4, 161–3, 165–6, 172–80; advances (1989–90) 85; and Cold War 59; and Mengistu 88–9; Bahr al-Ghazal group 154; Equatoria 85–7; finance 46; foundation 61–73; Independent Group from the Nuba Mountains 126; Manifesto 63, 66, 125; Nasir faction 94–101, 106, 109, 111–18, 120–1, 140, 150, 174; New Kush Division 132; New Sudan Brigade 138; Nuer 49, 163; Political–Military High Command 91–3, 106; split 90, 91–110, 111–26, 150, 163; Torit faction 98–9, 101, 113–15, 120, 150
Sudan People's Revolutionary Party 60
Sudan Political Service 21n
Sudan Relief and Rehabilitation Association 87, 96, 106, 161–2
Sudanese Allied Forces 104, 137–8
Sudanese Socialist Union 63

Sudapet 162
Suez Canal 22
Sufism 3, 13
sugar 49
Supreme Court 42
Surur, Eliaba 33
Sweden 162, 164

Tafeng, Emilio 32–3
Taha, Mahmud Muhammad 129
Tali 86
Talisman Energy Inc. 162, 164–5
Tanzania 31
taxation 5, 40, 46, 50, 55, 80, 83, 148, 152
Tayyib, Umar al- 54
Tembura, James Joseph 54, 67, 73
Terekeka 86
terrorism 107, 142, 162, 177–8
Three Towns 130, 156
Tigrayan People's Liberation Front 59n, 136, 147, 162
timber industry 136, 154, 165
Time xvii
Tonj 70, 125
Toposa people 68, 82–3, 85–6, 88, 114, 127, 151
Torit 21, 28, 84, 108–9; faction *see* Sudan People's Liberation Army/Movement
torture 130
Total oil company 45
trade 2–3, 5, 16–17, 109, 124, 140, 152, 154, 157, (165) *see also* markets
Trafigura Beheer BV 163
Transition Zone 145, 155, 157
Transitional Military Council 67, 70–1, 82
trespass 132
tribes and tribalism xviii-xx, 13, 15, 51–3, 65, 67–9, 81–3, 114–15, 125, 139–41, 148, 151, 173; *see also* armed forces – militias
Tripoli 176
Tsore 136
Turabi, Hassan al- 46, 48, 54, 56, 79–80, 99, 104, 107–8, 111, 123, 128, 141

Turkey 21 *see also* Sudan –
Turkiyya period
Turkiyya period *see* Sudan
Tut, Samuel Gai 61, 65–6, 68

Uduk people 45, 136
Uganda 13, 19, 43, 60, 86, 100,
102, 113, 120, 175, 177; army
36; refugees 28, 32, 52, 87,
146, 152; trade 109, 154, 165
Ulang 118
Umma Party 24, 26, 30, 34–5,
43–4, 46, 55, 71–3, 79–80, 82,
84, 103–4, 130, 138, 140–2,
171–2
Ummayids 3
United Democratic Salvation
Front 122, 125, 141
United Kingdom *see* Britain
United Nations 22, 90, 93, 95–6,
115–17, 144–8, 150, 155, 157,
159–61, 164; Department of
Humanitarian Affairs 160
United Nations Commission on
Human Rights 163
United Nations Development
Programme 133, 135, 156, 159
United Nations High Commission
for Refugees 146
United Nations International
Children and Education Fund
148–9, 155–6, 161
United States 64, 102, 103n, 111,
120, 140; and Iran xvi; and
oil industry 162–5, 177, 180;
and terrorism 107, 142, 162,
177–8; Civil War xxiii;
missionaries 44, 135;
National Security Council
146; relief and assistance 43,
53, 57–8, 60, 62, 66–7, 81,
90, 95–6, 144, 158, 166;
Somalia 100; State
Department 179
United Sudan African Parties 84,
86, 148
Unity State 123, 125

Upper Nile 28, 52, 73, 91, 95,
123–5, 168, 172; Anglo-
Egyptian Condominium
11–12, 17–18, 135; armed
forces 60–1, 82–3, 85, 93–4,
99–100, 106, 114, 117, 132,
151; cattle 154; Chali 44;
courts of law 171;
development 49; Dinka 119;
labour 50, 156; oil industry
45–6, 68, 137, 162; peace
villages 145; Region 55, 80;
relief 89, 149; SPLA/M 70
USAID 30, 43

Waat 66, 68–9, 89, 97, 114–18,
125
Wanji, Barry 33
Washington DC 101, 120, 174
water xxii, 47–8, 50, 75
Wau 107–8, 123, 145, 153–6,
173
weapons *see* arms
welfare 159
White Nile Brewery 50
women 129, 138, 157–8
World Food Programme 89, 146,
149–50, 155–6
World Vision 136
World War I 9, 11, 15–16, 21,
168–9
World War II 17, 21–2, 35
Wunlit Conference (1999) 125,
167, 173

Yabus 135–6
Yambio 27
Yei 85–7, 108–9
Yei River District 18
Yirol 70, 125
Yuai 116–17, 150

Zaghawa people 139–40
Zaïre *see* Democratic Republic of
the Congo
Zande Scheme 19
Zimbabwe 120